D1234477

Hiking Kentucky

A Guide to 80 of Kentucky's Greatest Hiking Adventures

Third Edition

Michael H. Brown
Revised by Carrie L. Stambaugh

FALCONGUIDES

GUILFORD, CONNECTICUT
HELENA, MONTANA

FALCONGUIDES®

An imprint of Rowman & Littlefield
Falcon and FalconGuides are registered trademarks and Make Adventure Your Story is a trademark of Rowman & Littlefield.

Distributed by NATIONAL BOOK NETWORK

Copyright © 2002, 2007, 2016 Rowman & Littlefield

Interior photos: Carrie Stambaugh unless otherwise credited

Excerpt from *Kentucky Is My Land* reprinted with permission from the Jesse Stuart Foundation.
Maps: Moore Creative Designs © Rowman & Littlefield

All rights reserved. No part of this book may be reproduced in any form or by any electronic or mechanical means, including information storage and retrieval systems, without written permission from the publisher, except by a reviewer who may quote passages in a review.

British Library Cataloguing-in-Publication Information available

The Library of Congress has cataloged a previous edition as follows:
Brown, Michael H. (Michael Hunt), 1942-
 Hiking Kentucky : a guide to Kentucky's greatest hiking adventures / Michael W. Brown. — 2nd ed.
 p. cm.—(A Falcon guide)
 Summary: "From old country roads to dense forest paths, Kentucky boasts more than 1,500 miles of marked and maintained trails. Local hiker Michael Brown describes eighty of the best hikes throughout the state from 1-mile nature hikes to multiday backpacks in this revision of the guidebook."—Provided by publisher.
 Includes bibliographical references and index.
 ISBN-13: 978-0-7627-3650-8
 ISBN-10: 0-7627-3650-X
 1. Hiking—Kentucky—Guidebooks. 2. Kentucky—Guidebooks. I. Title.
 GV199.42.K4B76 2007
 796.5109769—dc22   2006024509

ISBN 978-1-4930-1256-5 (paperback)
ISBN 978-1-4930-1451-4 (e-book)

∞™ The paper used in this publication meets the minimum requirements of American National Standard for Information Sciences—Permanence of Paper for Printed Library Materials, ANSI/NISO Z39.48-1992.

The authors and Rowman & Littlefield assume no liability for accidents happening to, or injuries sustained by, readers who engage in the activities described in this book.

Contents

Overview

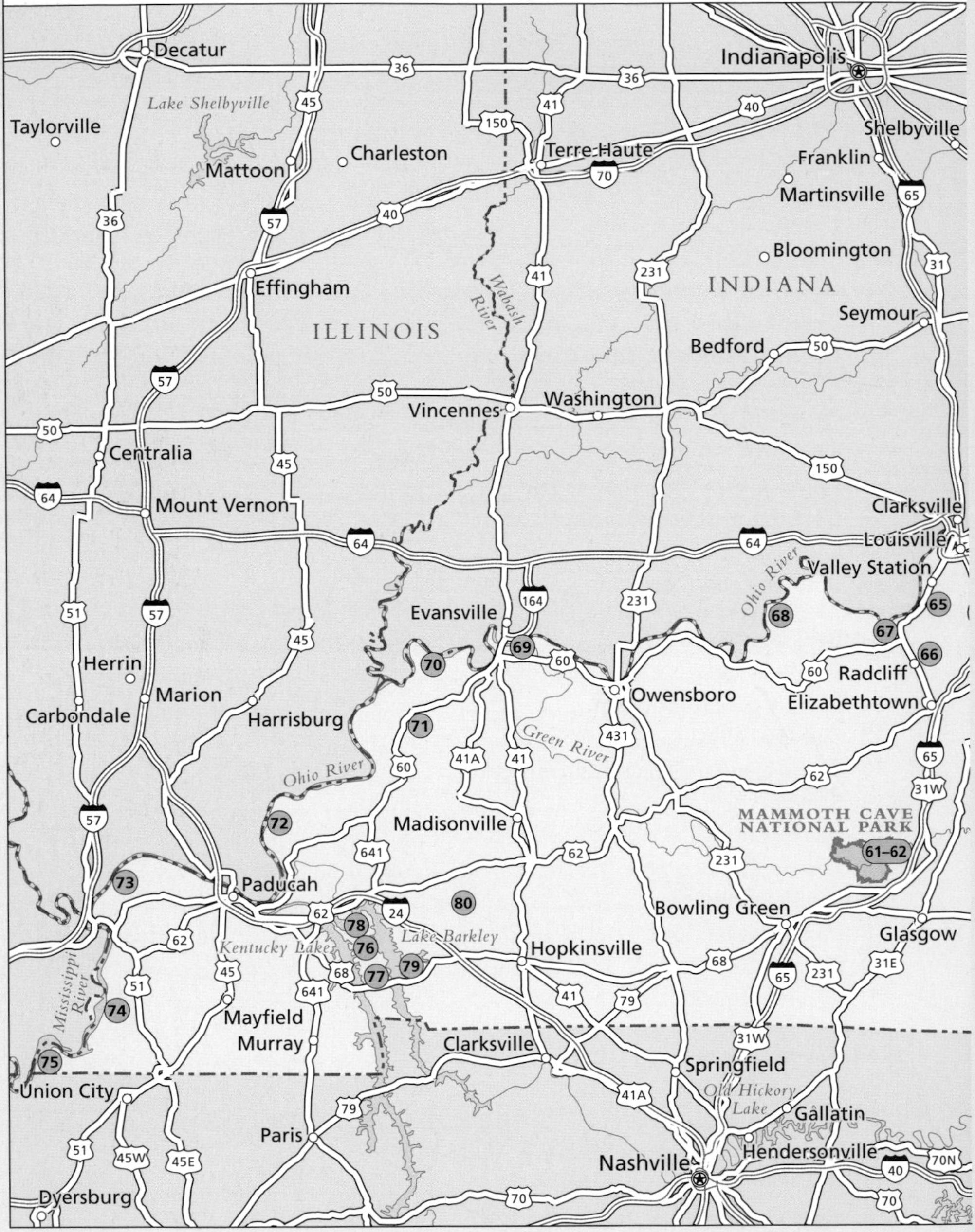
Decatur
Indianapolis
Lake Shelbyville
Taylorville
Charleston
Terre Haute
Shelbyville
Franklin
Mattoon
Martinsville
Bloomington
Effingham
INDIANA
ILLINOIS
Wabash River
Seymour
Bedford
Washington
Vincennes
Centralia
Mount Vernon
Clarksville
Louisville
Valley Station
Ohio River
Evansville
Herrin
Radcliff
Marion
Owensboro
Elizabethtown
Carbondale
Harrisburg
Green River
Ohio River
Madisonville
MAMMOTH CAVE NATIONAL PARK
Paducah
Bowling Green
Lake Barkley
Kentucky Lake
Hopkinsville
Glasgow
Mississippi River
Mayfield
Murray
Clarksville
Springfield
Union City
Old Hickory Lake
Gallatin
Paris
Hendersonville
Nashville
Dyersburg
61–62
65
66
67
68
69
70
71
72
73
74
75
76
77
78
79
80

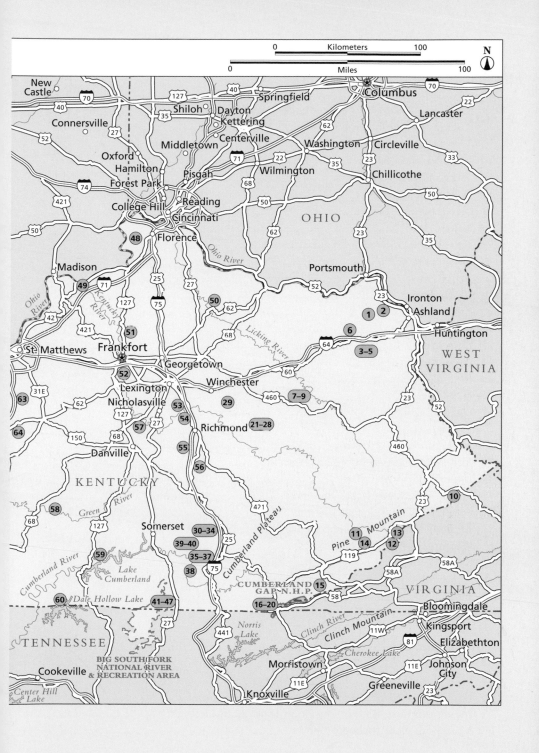

HELP US KEEP THIS GUIDE UP TO DATE

Every effort has been made by the authors and editors to make this guide as accurate and useful as possible. However, many things can change after a guide is published—trails are rerouted, regulations change, techniques evolve, facilities come under new management, and so on.

We welcome your comments concerning your experiences with this guide and how you feel it could be improved and kept up to date. While we may not be able to respond to all comments and suggestions, we'll take them to heart, and we'll also make certain to share them with the author. Please send your comments and suggestions to the following address:

FalconGuides
Reader Response/Editorial Department
246 Goose Lane ·
Guilford, CT 06437

Or you may e-mail us at:

editorial@falcon.com
Thanks for your input, and happy trails!

Acknowledgments

This collection of hikes would not be possible without the incalculable amount of help I received from the individuals who manage and protect Kentucky's diverse landscapes. I consulted dozens of rangers, administrators, receptionists, and information officers along with volunteers and other hikers while writing this book, and all were eager and excited to help. These men and women deserve not only my heartfelt thanks, but also the gratitude of past and future generations of Kentuckians and visitors. In my experience, the state boasts some of the most accessible and well-maintained hiking areas in the country. It is because of these individuals that Kentucky is a paradise for outdoor recreation. My continuing thanks, too, to the men and women of Kentucky, both paid and volunteer, who work tirelessly to maintain and build the state's network of trails.

I also want to thank my husband, Carl Stambaugh, and my parents, Randy and Debbie Kirschner, for being my patient, dedicated hiking partners as I put this book together. Mom and Dad, I will always be grateful to you for instilling in me a love and respect for the outdoors. And to Carl, my love and best friend, thank you for always encouraging me to chase my dreams, even when they involve ticks.

—Carrie Stambaugh, 2016

Introduction

Kentucky is neither southern, northern, eastern, or western,
It is the core of America.
If these United States can be called a body,
Kentucky can be called its heart.

—Jesse Stuart, *Kentucky Is My Land*

My predecessor in writing this book used this Kentucky-centric verse to open his introduction, and I have kept it because it has so much truth and I'm very fond of its author. Kentucky is a widely varied land that fits no convenient classification, whether geographic, political, or otherwise. Stretching from the jagged Appalachians to the flat Mississippi River valley, from industrial plants on the Ohio River to magnolia trees in the Old Confederacy, Kentucky belongs to no one section of the country but is, rather, an intriguing mix of northern, southern, and midwestern. It's also a mix of rural and urban. Of mountains and plains. It is an irony of history but an understandable one that Kentucky was the birthplace of both Abraham Lincoln and Jefferson Davis, the opposing leaders in the great conflict between two views of America.

Today, Kentuckians living on the state's western edge can drive to St. Louis or Memphis in less than half the time it takes them to visit their fellow Kentuckians in Ashland. Southern Kentuckians who can get to Nashville in less than an hour need more than three to get to the northern Kentucky suburbs of Cincinnati. The purpose of this book is to help hikers and would-be hikers explore this diverse collection of mountains and hollows, ridges and bottomlands, rolling fields and thick forests known as the Bluegrass State.

From the Big Sandy in the east to the Mississippi, from the Ohio in the north to the Tennessee line, Kentucky encompasses 40,395 square miles of land and water. Within these borders are:

- Two national parks, two major federal recreation areas, the Daniel Boone National Forest stretching almost the width of the state, and more than a dozen large US Army Corps of Engineers reservoirs with significant amounts of adjacent land;
- More than 160 state parks, forests, wildlife areas, and nature preserves;
- Scores of additional parcels owned by private groups and local governments and open to public use.

This book is a guide to some of the most scenic of these areas and to eighty specific hikes within them. Kentucky is said to have more than 2,000 miles of maintained, marked trails. I certainly haven't been on all of them, but these eighty trails offer a range of experiences and scenery from overnight backpacks in Kentucky's remote eastern mountains to strolls along the Mississippi River in its farthest western corner.

These hikes cover all regions of Kentucky and, I hope, offer enough variety to satisfy people of all ages, experience, and stamina. They range in length from short loops of less than 2 miles to overnight backpacking trips, the longest of which remains the 31.2-mile excursion through Land Between The Lakes National Recreation Area. I, like Michael Brown, who authored the previous two editions of this guidebook, hope that the hike descriptions in this book will be useful and inspiring to both residents and first-time visitors to Kentucky. The state is full of beautiful landscapes, most of which are free and can easily be accessed from every corner of the commonwealth.

The massive earthen works were built by Confederate soldiers along the heavily fortified bluffs (hike 74).

Kentucky Briefly

The Land

The eastern edge of Kentucky is covered with sharp ridges and narrow valleys, while the western edge of the state is low and level. The vast middle is a moderate mix. Kentucky's highest point is 4,145-foot Black Mountain in Harlan County in the southeast corner near Virginia. The low point—257 feet—is in the state's southwest corner on the Mississippi River across from Missouri.

For the hiker, the upshot is that the eastern part of the state, especially the southeast, involves steeper climbs and more of them; as you go west, the terrain generally becomes less demanding. This book includes several western Kentucky hikes along the Mississippi and Ohio Rivers that are literally flat. On the other hand, if you like to hike to high overlooks with dramatic vistas, the eastern third of the state is your best bet.

Eastern Kentucky is on the edge of the long Appalachian mountain system that extends from the Canadian province of Quebec all the way into Alabama. The eastern Kentucky surface is Pennsylvanian-era rock formed 325 million to 290 million years ago and composed of shale, sandstone, conglomerates, and coal. The coal deposits in this and a smaller Pennsylvanian outcrop in western Kentucky make the state a leading coal producer—once first in the nation, now number three, behind Wyoming and West Virginia. One of the constants of Kentucky history has been the struggle, particularly amid the steep slopes of Appalachia, between those who want to reap the financial rewards of this resource and those more interested in protecting the land and streams overlying it. Though muted by federal reclamation requirements enacted in the late 1970s, it is a struggle that continues today. Coal production has fallen steadily since the 1990s, reaching its lowest levels since the 1960s in 2014. It continues to be threatened as domestic natural gas production grows and coal-fired power plant closures increase due to more stringent environmental regulations.

The western edge of the plateau across eastern Kentucky (called the Appalachian or Cumberland Plateau) is lined with a wall of rock known as the Pottsville Escarpment. This escarpment includes hard sandstones able to withstand nature's weathering process better than the surrounding materials. The result is an uneven erosion process that has produced some of the state's most noteworthy physical attributes: the arches and rock houses of the Red River Gorge and other areas along the western side of eastern Kentucky.

In north-central Kentucky, ringed by a series of steep but small hills called the Knobs, is the Bluegrass region. The underlying rock is the oldest in the state (440 million to 510 million years) and contains limestones that naturally fertilize the soil, making this a rich agricultural area that serves as the center of the state's thoroughbred horse industry. Bluegrass, which thrives here and accounts for the state's nickname, is green but has buds that give a field of it a bluish tint. The rolling area immediately around Lexington is known as the Inner Bluegrass; the sharper-ridged, outlying counties as the Outer Bluegrass.

South-central Kentucky and the area south of the western coalfields are covered by a younger rock (from the Mississippian age, 360 million to 325 million years ago) that is rich in soluble limestones and conducive to erosion by underground water flow. Mammoth Cave, the largest known cave system in the world, is a product of this process. Named for the pennyroyal, a mint-family plant that grows in the region, this part of the state is called the Pennyroyal or Pennyrile, and also the Mississippian Plateau.

The southwestern tip of the state is named the Jackson Purchase, because Andrew Jackson of neighboring Tennessee helped negotiate its acquisition from the Chickasaw Indians. It is at the end of the coastal plain that extends north from the Gulf of Mexico and consists of relatively young, easily eroded sediment. This part of Kentucky is flat and full of marshy areas called sloughs, many of them with beautiful bald cypress trees.

The Ohio River flows 664 miles along the northern border, and the state is intersected by several major west-flowing rivers that empty into the Ohio: most significantly, from east to west, the Licking, Kentucky, Green, Cumberland, and Tennessee Rivers. Altogether, Kentucky has 1,100 miles of commercially navigable waterways and claims to be second only to Alaska in total water mileage.

Water travel was an important impetus for Kentucky commerce and development; Louisville, the state's biggest city, started as an Ohio River port. But the flip side has meant a state long plagued by flooding. Flood control was a major reason (along with hydropower and navigation) behind the construction of the extensive system of reservoirs that now runs through the state. Together with federally funded floodwalls for endangered cities, these man-made lakes have curtailed the flooding threat, though not eliminated it. The lakes are also a main source of recreation.

Almost half the state is covered by forest, mainly hardwoods. The predominant species include white and red oak, walnut, yellow poplar, beech, sugar maple, white ash, and hickory. Kentucky is among the top five states producing hardwood lumber, and over the years it has been heavily logged—all of it at least once. But while there are no truly virgin forests, there are several patches of old-growth trees (the Lilley Cornett Woods hike takes you through one of them) and many beautiful wooded spots with tall trees, leafy rhododendrons, ferns, and wildflowers. In springtime, for a rundown of what wildflowers are blooming where, telephone the state Department of Tourism at (800) 225-8747. The official state tree is the tulip, sometimes called the tulip poplar—though it's actually a magnolia, not a poplar. Goldenrod is the state flower.

For more information about the geology and regions of Kentucky, see the Kentucky Geological Survey website: www.uky.edu/KGS.

History

In 1902, in the midst of a bitter, partisan political and legal battle, Kentucky lawyer, politician, and poet James H. Mulligan penned a poem ending:

> *The mountains tower proudest,*
> *Thunder peals the loudest,*
> *The landscape is the grandest,*
> *And politics the damnedest,*
> *In Kentucky.*

The context for Mulligan's often quoted doggerel was the turmoil that gripped Kentucky following the assassination of William Goebel, a candidate for governor in the hotly disputed election of 1899.

If it weren't for the poem's lighthearted nature, those lines would also be an apt description of the state's turbulent Civil War chapter. Kentucky was a slave state but badly split over the question of secession. As a result, it remained in the Union but declared itself neutral in the hostilities. In their readable *A New History of Kentucky*, historians Lowell H. Harrison and James C. Klotter explain how this attempt to stay above the fray failed to protect the state or its families from division and tragedy. They cite estimates that 90,000 to 100,000 Kentuckians fought for the Union, 25,000 to 40,000 for the Confederacy. Nearly one out of every five men who went off to the war did not return.

There were a number of battles on Kentucky soil, but the government in Frankfort, the capital, kept the state in the Union throughout the war. That, however, did not stop Southern sympathizers from setting up their own state government in Bowling Green and securing Kentucky's admission to the Confederacy. Thus, along with neighboring Missouri, Kentucky was on both sides. That's why the flag of the eleven-state Confederacy had thirteen stars.

Several of the eighty hikes in this guide involve the state's Civil War history. Others visit sites linked to the earliest Kentuckians. The first people believed to have inhabited what is now Kentucky arrived about 12,000 years ago, probably in search of game. Over the centuries these hunting groups became less nomadic. By the time Europeans arrived in the New World, the early Kentuckians we call Indians were building large settlements and growing corn and beans.

Even before whites moved into the state, the Native American population was in decline, in part because they had no immunity against European diseases that made their way inland from East Coast settlements. White men began entering Kentucky, then a part of Virginia, in the late 1700s. First came hunters, the best known of whom was Daniel Boone, and then settlers seeking land. Their entry was through Cumberland Gap, a mountain notch that is now a national park with some of the best hiking in the state. In 1792 Kentucky was admitted to the Union as the fifteenth state.

Those who have followed Daniel Boone into Kentucky's pantheon of famous residents (in addition to Lincoln and Davis) include:

- Nineteenth-century statesman Henry Clay
- President Zachary Taylor
- Naturalist John James Audubon
- Supreme Court justices Louis Brandeis and John Marshall Harlan
- Vice President Alben Barkley
- Author Robert Penn Warren
- Boxer Muhammad Ali
- Singer Rosemary Clooney and her nephew, actor George Clooney

The People

Kentucky today has a population just shy of 4.4 million, ranking it twenty-sixth in the nation. In many respects the state retains the flavor of its frontier origins. With about 44 percent of residents living outside urban areas, it's one of the most rural states in the country. Notwithstanding the handsome horse-breeding estates that line the shaded lanes of the Bluegrass, small farms are mainly what you find across the countryside. The state has some 75,000 farms—the fourth-highest number in the country—but they average only 154 acres, and the majority sell less than $10,000 in produce a year. Between 2007 and 2012, Kentucky lost nearly 950,000 acres of farmland to development. Corn and soybeans have replaced tobacco as Kentucky's largest cash crops, but poultry and beef cattle are also important commodities. Tobacco remains, however, with Kentucky ranked No. 1 in the country for the number of farmers producing it.

The central part of the state is a major producer of bourbon, in part because the limestone bedrock provides good water for the distilling process. Thoroughbred horses bred and raised on Lexington-area farms are a multimillion-dollar business, and the Kentucky Derby, run at Louisville's Churchill Downs the first Saturday in May, is the nation's premier horse race. Despite the importance of farms and farm products, the health care industry is the largest employer of Kentuckians, followed by manufacturing and retail.

Louisville, the state's largest urban area, has just over 726,000 residents counting those living in surrounding Jefferson County. Lexington and Fayette County, which also have a consolidated government, are second in population with about 295,000.

Kentucky is not an affluent state: It frequently ranks in the bottom five of states when it comes to the percentage of residents living in poverty and per capita personal income. In 2015 close to 19 percent of its residents were on food stamps. One economic fact hikers should be aware of is that a large amount of marijuana is grown—illegally—in the state, much of it in eastern Kentucky, including in the Daniel Boone National Forest. To protect their crops from theft, growers have been known to booby-trap their marijuana fields with everything from explosives to fishhooks. While none of the routes in this book should entail danger of this kind, eastern Kentucky rangers and park administrators advise hikers to stay on sanctioned trails and be careful not to wander into untrod territory.

A more benign fact of Kentucky life is that the state has two time zones. While the division is not a straight line, basically the eastern half, including Louisville, is on eastern standard time, and the western half is on central.

Weather

Kentucky experiences all four seasons, and during the dog days of summer, you should think long and hard about taking a long, hard hike. In August the average high is 87°F, but humidity rates can be upwards of 90 to 100 percent. Caution is also in order for the dead of winter. January, the coldest month, has an average low of 23°F, but the thermometer can easily drop below that. Although snowstorms are not an everyday occurrence, you can expect one or two a winter. Annual snowfall ranges from 40 inches in the southeastern mountains to 5 to 10 inches in the southwest.

That said, the Kentucky climate is generally temperate. The average annual mean temperature ranges from 60°F at the state's western end to 53°F at the eastern end. One certainty about Kentucky weather is that it's unpredictable and in recent years has been much wetter than normal. A fairly safe statement is that spring, especially early spring, and fall are the most pleasant hiking periods.

However, tornadoes cause significant destruction—and fatalities—in Kentucky, and although they can and do strike any time of year, they are most frequent in spring. In April 1974 a storm packing twenty-eight twisters killed seventy-six Kentuckians, thirty-one in the Ohio River town of Brandenburg. The state's weather-warning system has improved since then, but Kentucky still ranks high in tornado victims. If you are stranded in a tornado without secure shelter nearby, experts say the best course is to lie flat in a ditch or culvert—assuming that flash flooding or lightning is not a threat. If you are in a car and a tornado approaches, the experts advise getting out. Twisters can easily fling an automobile.

Flash flooding is another potential danger, especially on the slopes of eastern Kentucky, where a heavy rain can send what is normally a lazy stream suddenly raging out of its narrow banks. Be careful camping in low-lying areas, and if you come to a swollen stream, don't be afraid to turn around and go back the way you came. When done correctly and carefully, fording a big stream can be safe. But you must know your limits and the limits of your hiking party, especially children.

The first defense against bad weather, of course, is to check the forecast before setting out. Once on your way, watch cloud formations closely so you aren't caught in an exposed setting. In a lightning storm, which is the most common weather threat in Kentucky, you don't want to be on a ridgetop, under a large solitary tree, in the open, or near standing water. Also take these other precautions:

- Lightning can travel ahead of a storm, so take cover before the storm hits.

- Don't try to make it back to your vehicle; it's not worth the risk. Instead, seek shelter in a low-lying area, ideally in a stand of small, uniformly sized trees.
- Avoid anything that attracts lightning, such as metal tent poles, graphite fishing rods, or metal pack frames.
- Crouch with both feet firmly on the ground. If you have a sleeping bag or a pack without a metal frame, put your feet on it for extra insulation.
- Don't walk or huddle together with your hiking partners. Instead, stay 50 feet apart so that if one person is hit, others can give first aid.
- If you are in a tent, stay in your sleeping bag with your feet on your pad.

Wildlife

You don't have to worry about grizzlies, mountain lions, or other four-footed predators in Kentucky. In fact, the biggest threat to a hiker in Kentucky is him- or herself. (Hikers place themselves at risk when they are unprepared for weather changes, underestimate the trail or overestimate their hiking abilities, go off trail, hike alone, or fail to stick to their hiking plan.) The state does have a growing population of black bears, mainly in the far eastern part. After being eliminated in the 1800s by hunting and habitat destruction, they began moving in from neighboring Virginia, West Virginia, and Tennessee when replanted oak forests matured. Sightings are most frequent in the eastern part of the state, especially along Pine Mountain and particularly around Kingdom Come State Park (hike 14), but there has been a rise in the number of human-bear interactions and a handful of attacks in recent years. Most conflicts involve the intentional feeding or access to human-related food sources. It is illegal to feed bears in Kentucky.

The large wild animal you are most likely to encounter is the elk. A program to reestablish elk in the state is proving successful; currently there are believed to be several thousand, all in the southeastern corner. White-tailed deer, of course, are plentiful, and a small, nonaggressive member of the cat family, the bobcat, lives throughout the state. Beavers, foxes, muskrats, opossums, raccoons, woodchucks, coyotes, and wild hogs are also in residence. The state bird is the Kentucky cardinal.

One of the most exciting creatures you are apt to see is the wild turkey, the largest game bird in North America; an adult male can approach 30 pounds. Kentucky's wild turkey population had been all but eliminated a few decades ago. Restoration efforts, however, have now brought it back to well over 225,000, and it's not at all uncommon for one of the birds to blast out of its wooded hiding spot as you traipse by.

There are poisonous snakes in Kentucky—primarily the timber rattlesnake and the copperhead, found in most parts of the state, and the water moccasin, found in the west only. There are occasional snakebite reports but no fatalities in recent years.

Snakes strike humans only in self-defense, or when startled or afraid. The solution is to avoid scaring them. Look where you place your feet, especially in tall grass, and don't reach under or over rocks or logs without looking first. If you do encounter a snake, slowly back away and give it a chance to slither off—an opportunity it will invariably take. Don't throw rocks and sticks at it. If bitten, try not to panic. Running or otherwise speeding up your circulation increases the speed with which the venom travels through your bloodstream. Keep the bite site lower than your heart to decrease the venom spread, and seek medical attention.

Unlike poisonous snakes, ticks are common in Kentucky—and a real pest for the hiker. I encountered several nests of seed ticks—ticks in the nymph and larval stages of life—on a number of my hikes during the summer. Even after removing the ticks using sticky tape, tweezers, and at one point a laminated bank card, I spent weeks scratching at their bites on my ankles. My husband required a steroid shot to overcome his nasty bout with them.

In addition to being a nuisance, ticks can cause serious health problems. Lyme disease, a flu-like sickness whose symptoms include nausea, fever, fatigue, and muscle and joint aches, is spread by the bite of infected deer ticks. Most ticks are not infected, and Kentucky reports few cases of the disease. However, if a red inflammation develops at the site of a tick bite, it should be checked by a doctor; it may signal infection. Another disease, Rocky Mountain spotted fever, is spread by infected American dog ticks; each year the disease strikes about 800 people across the country, though mainly in the southeastern states.

To prevent tick bites and the possibility of disease, follow this advice from officials at Land Between The Lakes, where ticks are out in force much of the year:

- Wear long pants and tuck the legs into your socks or boots, or tape your pant legs closed.
- Spray your clothes with a tick repellent.
- Periodically check your clothes and body for ticks, and remove any you find with tweezers or fingers, taking care not to crush the body of an attached tick.

Hunting Seasons

While animals are not much of a danger in Kentucky, the same cannot be said of the humans trying to kill the animals. Hunting is a major activity in the state, and it's a good bet that no matter what time of year you take a hike, there is some kind of officially sanctioned hunting season under way. The wild hog season is literally year-round. It's widely agreed, however, that two seasons are by far the most dangerous for hikers—or anyone else in the woods. First is Kentucky's modern-gun season, which generally runs for ten days in mid-November. Additional days from late October to December for special hunts are likely. Second is the spring wild turkey season, which starts in early April and lasts three weeks. There is also a short fall turkey season around the first of December. To learn the exact dates for a particular year, call the state Department of Fish and Wildlife Resources at (800) 858-1549.

From Bullock Overlook the Cumberland mountains rolling away to the northeast (hike 14).

I prefer to stay out of the woods during deer season. If you do go hiking then, be sure to wear hunter orange clothing. Also, be aware that in Kentucky hunting is allowed on a wide variety of public lands, including in the Daniel Boone National Forest and in the two national recreation areas—Big South Fork and Land Between The Lakes. And don't be misled by the term *wildlife management area*; most of the close to eighty state-administered parcels with that name allow some kind of hunting.

How to Use This Guide

Type of Hike

The eighty hikes outlined in this book are divided into the following categories:

- Day hike: Best for short excursions due to the shortness of the trail, lack of water, or unsuitable camping opportunities.
- Backpack: Best for backpacking one or more nights, although many can also be completed as a day hike.
- Lollipop: A loop at the end of an out-and-back trail.
- Loop: Start and finish at the same spot with little or no retracing of steps. Sometimes the definition of a loop is stretched to include more creative shapes, like a figure eight or lollipop.
- Out-and-back: Travel the same route going and returning.
- Shuttle: A point-to-point trip that requires two vehicles (one at each end of the trail), or a prearranged pickup, or some other strategy for getting back to your car. One possibility is to arrange for a second party to start at the other end of the trail; the two of you trade car keys when you meet up in the middle, and at the end of the hike, you drive each other's vehicle to a rendezvous point.

Distance

I carried a handheld GPS unit as I hiked, and most of the mileage figures in this book are based on the readings from this instrument, distance figures shown on hiking maps and trail signs, the previous edition of this book, and conversations with local rangers and others familiar with that particular area.

While I have done my best to make the distances in this book accurate, measuring trails is an inexact science however it's done. You should be sufficiently skeptical of distance figures. Trails are dynamic creatures, continually rerouted, added to, and closed down. Years can pass before the signs catch up.

Also keep in mind that distance is often less important than difficulty. A steep 2-mile climb on rocky tread can take longer than a 4-mile stroll through a gentle river valley. For planning, it may be helpful to know that most hikers average 2 miles an hour.

Difficulty Ratings

Difficulty ratings are inherently flawed: What's easy for you might be hard for me. Indeed, as I grow older (if not old), I find my own measurement system is changing: What was once easy is now not nearly so. Still, the ratings are a useful approximation of a hike's challenge. In this book the ratings are based primarily on the difficulty of the terrain, and to a lesser extent on the hike's length. The general guidelines for the ratings are:

- Easy: Suitable for any hiker, young or old. Expect no serious elevation gain, trail hazards, or navigation problems.
- Moderate: Suitable for hikers who have some experience and an average fitness level. Includes some elevation change and possibly places where the trail is faint.
- Strenuous: Suitable only for experienced hikers with above-average fitness. Includes hazardous trail sections, navigation problems, or serious elevation change.

Best Seasons

As noted earlier, hiking can be miserable at the height of a Kentucky summer. That's a given, and so this guide is generally geared to other considerations, such as water availability and scenic conditions.

Permits and Fees

When applicable, the hike descriptions alert you to any permit that must be secured or fee that must be paid before using a trail. In Kentucky, requirements of this nature are the exception.

Maps

The maps in this book serve as a general guide only. Except for the most elementary day hike, don't hit the trail without a better, more detailed map. For each hike the book tells you what maps are available and gives you a telephone number to call. The detailed US Geological Survey quads (1:24,000 scale) listed for each hike can be ordered through sports stores or directly from the USGS at:

USGS Map Sales
Box 25286, Federal Center, Building 810
Denver, CO 80225
(888) ASK-USGS
www.usgs.gov

Trail Safety and Ethics

Make It a Safe Trip

The Boy Scouts of America have been guided for decades by what is the single best piece of safety advice: Be prepared! For starters, this means carrying survival and first-aid gear, proper clothing, a compass, and a topographic map—and knowing how to use them. Cell phone service is now abundant in most areas of Kentucky, including remote ridgetops.

The second-best piece of safety advice is to tell somebody where you're going and when you plan to return. Pilots must file flight plans before every trip, and anybody venturing into a blank spot on the map should do the same. File your "flight plan" with a friend or relative before taking off.

Third in importance is physical conditioning. Being fit makes wilderness travel not only more fun, but also safer. Here are a few more tips:

- Check the weather forecast. Be careful not to get caught at high altitude by a bad storm or along a stream in a flash flood. Watch cloud formations closely so you don't get stranded on a ridgeline during a lightning storm. Avoid traveling during prolonged periods of cold weather.

- Avoid traveling alone in the wilderness; keep your party together and stay on the trail where possible. The latter is particularly important in some parts of eastern Kentucky, where the illegal cultivation of marijuana has become a business. None of the hikes in this book should involve danger of this kind, but remember that hidden fields of marijuana are sometimes protected by dangerous booby traps.

- Don't exhaust yourself or other members of your party by traveling too far or too fast. Let the slowest person set the pace.

- Study basic survival and first aid before leaving home.

- Before you leave for the trailhead, find out as much as you can about the route, especially the potential hazards.

- Don't wait until you're confused to look at your maps. Follow them as you go along so you have a continual fix on your location.

- If you get lost, don't panic. Sit down, have a snack, and relax for a few minutes while you carefully check your topo map and take a compass reading. Confidently plan your next move. It's often smart to retrace your steps until you find familiar ground, even if you think it might lengthen your trip. Lots of people get temporarily lost in the wilderness and survive—usually by calmly and rationally dealing with the situation.

- Stay clear of all wild animals.

- Take a first-aid kit that includes, at a minimum, a sewing needle, aspirin, antibacterial ointment, antiseptic swabs, butterfly bandages, adhesive tape, adhesive strips, gauze pads, two triangular bandages, codeine tablets, two inflatable splints, Moleskin or Second Skin for blisters, 3-inch gauze, CPR shield, rubber gloves, and lightweight first-aid instructions.
- Take a survival kit that includes, at a minimum, a compass, whistle, matches in a waterproof container, cigarette lighter, candle, signal mirror, flashlight, fire starter, aluminum foil, water purification tablets, space blanket, and flare.

Hypothermia: The Silent Killer

Be aware of hypothermia—a condition in which the body's internal temperature drops below normal. It can lead to mental and physical collapse and death.

Hypothermia is caused by exposure to cold and is aggravated by wetness, wind, and exhaustion. The moment you begin to lose heat faster than your body produces it, you're suffering from exposure. Your body starts involuntary exercise, such as shivering, to stay warm, and it makes involuntary adjustments to preserve normal temperature in vital organs, restricting blood flow in the extremities. Both responses drain your energy reserves. The only way to stop this drain is to reduce the degree of exposure. In full-blown hypothermia, as energy reserves are exhausted, cold blood reaches the brain, depriving you of good judgment and reasoning power. You won't be aware that this is happening. You lose control of your hands. Your internal temperature slides downward. Without treatment this slide leads to stupor, collapse, and death.

To defend against hypothermia, stay dry. When clothes get wet, they lose about 90 percent of their insulating value. Wool loses relatively less heat; cotton, down, and some synthetics lose more. Choose rain clothes that cover the head, neck, body, and legs and provide good protection against wind-driven rain. Most hypothermia cases develop in air temperatures between 30 and 50°F, but hypothermia can develop in warmer temperatures.

If your party is exposed to wind, cold, and wet, watch yourself and others for uncontrollable fits of shivering; vague, slow, slurred speech; memory lapses; incoherence; immobile, fumbling hands; frequent stumbling or a lurching gait; drowsiness; apparent exhaustion; and inability to get up after a rest. When a member of your party has hypothermia, he may deny any problem. Believe the symptoms, not the victim. Even mild symptoms demand the following treatment:

- Get the victim out of the wind and rain.
- Strip off all wet clothes.
- If the victim is only mildly impaired, give him or her warm drinks. Then get the victim in warm clothes and a warm sleeping bag. Place well-wrapped water bottles filled with heated water close to the victim.

- If the victim is badly impaired, attempt to keep him awake. Put the victim in a sleeping bag with another person—both naked. If you have a double bag, put two warm people in with the victim.

Leave No Trace

Going into a wild area is like visiting a famous museum. You obviously do not want to leave your mark on an art treasure in the museum. If everybody going through the museum left one little mark, the artwork would be quickly destroyed—and of what value is a big building full of trashed art? The same goes for pristine wildlands. If we all leave just one little mark on the landscape, the backcountry will soon be spoiled.

A wilderness can accommodate human use as long as everybody behaves. But a few thoughtless or uninformed visitors can ruin it for everybody who follows. All backcountry users have a responsibility to follow the established Leave No Trace principles.

These days wild places are becoming rare, and the number of users is mushrooming. To cope with the unending waves of people who want a perfect backcountry experience, a new code of ethics is growing. Wilderness visitors today are encouraged to enjoy the wild, but make no changes to it. The seven basic principles as established by the Leave No Trace Center for Outdoor Ethics are:

- Plan ahead and prepare.
- Travel and camp on durable surfaces.
- Dispose of waste properly.
- Leave what you find.
- Minimize campfire impacts.
- Respect wildlife.
- Be considerate of other visitors.

© Leave No Trace Center for Outdoor Ethics: www.LNT.org

Most of us know better than to litter—in or out of the backcountry. Be sure you leave nothing, no matter how small, along the trail or at your campsite. Pack out everything—including orange peels, flip tops, cigarette butts, and gum wrappers. Also, pick up any trash that others leave behind.

Follow the main trail. Avoid cutting switchbacks and walking on vegetation beside the trail. Don't pick up "souvenirs" such as rocks, antlers, or wildflowers. The next person wants to see them, too, and collecting such souvenirs violates many regulations.

Avoid making loud noises on the trail or in camp. Be courteous—remember, sound travels easily in the backcountry, especially across water.

Carry a lightweight trowel to bury human waste 6 to 8 inches deep at least 200 feet from any water source. Pack out used toilet paper.

Go without a campfire. Carry a stove for cooking and a flashlight, candle lantern, or headlamp for light. For emergencies, learn how to build a no-trace fire.

Camp in obviously used sites when they are available. Otherwise, camp and cook on durable surfaces such as bedrock, sand, gravel bars, or bare ground.

Put your ear to the ground and listen carefully. Thousands of people coming behind you are thanking you for your courtesy and good sense.

Backcountry Essentials

- Where required, get a permit.
- Camp only in appropriate places (see Leave No Trace above).
- Stay on trails (where possible) and don't create shortcuts.
- Dispose of human waste in a cat hole at least 200 feet from all water sources and campsites. Dispose of bathing and dishwater well away from water sources.
- Use camp stoves rather than cooking fires whenever possible.
- Carry out all trash. If you can pack it in, you can pack it out.
- Limit your group size to ten or less.
- Suspend food out of reach of animals.
- Do not feed or in any way disturb the wildlife. Do not leave behind food scraps.
- Do not operate any mechanized vehicle in official wilderness areas.
- Do not destroy, deface, disturb, or remove from its natural setting any plant, rock, animal, or archaeological resource.
- Please read Leave No Trace (above) for more details on minimizing impact on the wilderness.

Trail Finder

Trail #	Trail Name	Best Back-packing	Water-falls	For Geology Lovers	For Small Children	Great Views	For Lake Lovers	For Nature Lovers	For History Lovers
Northeastern Kentucky									
1	Greenbo Lake	•					•	•	•
2	Jesse Stuart Nature Preserve							•	
3	Lick Falls		•				•		
4	Grayson Lake Wildlife Management Area					•	•	•	
5	The Little Sandy				•				
6	Carter Caves State Resort Park	•		•				•	
7	Carrington Rock Overlook					•		•	
8	Cave Run Lake					•	•		
9	Leatherwood Creek							•	
Southeastern Kentucky									
10	Breaks I-Park					•			
11	Lilley Cornett Woods				•				
12	Bad Branch	•		•		•		•	•
13	Pine Mountain Trail Highland Section	•				•		•	•
14	Raven Rock			•		•			•
15	Martins Fork Lake						•	•	

Trail #	Trail Name	Best Back-packing	Water-falls	For Geology Lovers	For Small Children	Great Views	For Lake Lovers	For Nature Lovers	For History Lovers
16	Gibson Gap					•		•	•
17	Hensley Settlement	•							•
18	Pinnacle Overlook					•			
19	Cumberland Gap				•	•			•
20	Chained Rock				•	•			•
Red River Gorge									
21	Koomer Ridge	•		•					
22	Gray's Arch	•		•				•	
23	Courthouse Rock and Double Arch	•		•		•			
24	Tower Rock			•	•				
25	Swift Camp Creek	•		•					
26	Rock Bridge		•	•	•				
27	Natural Bridge and Hood Branch			•		•			
28	Natural Bridge Park Perimeter			•		•		•	
29	Pilot Knob					•		•	
Lower Rockcastle									
30	Laurel River Lake						•		
31	Cane Creek							•	

#	Name								
32	Rockcastle River					•		•	
33	Rockcastle Narrows and Bee Rock			•		•		•	
34	Rockcastle–Cumberland Confluence			•		•		•	
Cumberland Falls Area									
35	Dog Slaughter Falls	•	•						
36	Eagle Falls	•	•			•			
37	Blue Bend	•						•	
38	Natural Arch			•		•		•	
39	Three Forks of Beaver Creek	•	•		•	•		•	
40	Bowman Ridge					•			
Big South Fork									
41	Yahoo Falls	•	•			•			
42	Blue Heron					•			•
43	Big Spring Falls	•	•			•			
44	Buffalo Arch	•		•					
45	Gobblers Arch	•		•					
46	Lick Creek		•	•					
47	Laurel Creek			•					
Central Kentucky—North									
48	Middle Creek: Two Loops					•		•	•
49	General Butler State Park					•		•	•

Trail #	Trail Name	Best Back-packing	Water-falls	For Geology Lovers	For Small Children	Great Views	For Lake Lovers	For Nature Lovers	For History Lovers
50	Quiet Trails State Nature Preserve							•	
51	Kleber Wildlife Management Area							•	
52	Clyde E. Buckley Wildlife Sanctuary and Life Adventure Center				•			•	
53	Raven Run Nature Sanctuary		•	•	•	•			•
54	Kentucky River Palisades			•	•	•			•
55	Central Kentucky Wildlife Management Area							•	
56	Berea Forest			•		•			•
57	Shaker Village of Pleasant Hill				•	•			•
Central Kentucky—South									
58	Green River Lake						•		
59	Lake Cumberland				•		•		
60	Dale Hollow Lake						•		
61	Mammoth Cave Big Hollow Loop Trails	•						•	
62	Mammoth Cave Turnhole Bend	•			•			•	
Louisville Area									
63	Bernheim Forest							•	

#	Site	1	2	3	4	5	6	7	8
64	Vernon–Douglas State Nature Preserve		•						
65	Jefferson Memorial Forest		•		•				
66	Fort Knox	•	•					•	
67	Otter Creek		•		•				
68	Yellowbank Wildlife Management Area		•						

Western Kentucky

#	Site	1	2	3	4	5	6	7	8
69	John James Audubon State Park		•	•					
70	Sloughs Wildlife Management Area		•						
71	Higginson-Henry Wildlife Management Area		•						
72	Mantle Rock	•					•		
73	Ballard Wildlife Management Area		•						
74	Columbus-Belmont State Park	•			•	•			
75	Reelfoot National Wildlife Refuge		•	•		•			
76	Honker Lake			•					
77	North/South Trail		•	•					•
78	Canal Loop			•					
79	Lake Barkley State Resort Park			•					
80	Pennyrile Forest			•					•

Map Legend

Municipal

- 65 Interstate Highway
- 231 US Highway
- 700 State Road
- 569 Local/Forest Road
- ==== Gravel Road
- ——+——+—— Railroad
- ——·—— State Boundary

Trails

- —————— Featured Trail
- —————— Trail

Water Features

- Body of Water
- Marsh
- River/Creek
- Waterfall
- Spring

Land Management

- National Park/Forest
- National Wilderness/Recreation Area
- State Park/Forest, County Park
- Wildlife Management Area

Symbols

- ⏝ Bridge
- Boat Launch
- ■ Building/Point of Interest
- ⛌ Campground
- ∩ Cave
- † Cemetery
- Gate
- Lodging
- P Parking
- Picnic Area
- ▲ Primitive Campsite
- Ranger Station/Park Office
- Restaurant
- Restroom
- Scenic View/Overlook
- Tower
- ○ Town
- ① Trailhead
- ? Visitor/Information Center

Northeastern Kentucky

Mention eastern Kentucky and people tend to think of the Appalachian Mountains, coal mining, and isolated hollows. In northeastern Kentucky the land is more rolling than mountainous, farming is the big activity, and not much is isolated at all. Indeed, lacking a rugged terrain, northeastern Kentucky has traditionally not gotten much attention from hikers. With a number of man-made lakes in the region, boating has been the main source of recreation, not walking. But that is changing. In recent years there have been efforts to increase the hiking possibilities, and a number of nice walks can be found in the area. Happily, they are located near I-64, the region's main drag running west from the industrial area around Ashland at the West Virginia border.

Just keep in mind that for the most part, these hikes run through quiet wooded bottomlands and up and down small foothills or alongside man-made lakes.

Migrating swans during a stop over on Greenbo Lake (hike 1).

1 Greenbo Lake

This pleasant trail follows a wooded ridge, meanders along a small stream, and ends on the shore of a fishing lake. Day hikers will find a number of good lunch spots, and there is a backwoods shelter if you want to make this into a leisurely overnight journey.

Start: Lodge at Greenbo Lake State Resort Park

Distance: 8.7-mile lollipop

Hiking time: About 4 hours

Difficulty: Moderate

Best seasons: Any

Other trail users: Mountain bikers and, in some spots, equestrians

Canine compatibility: Leashed dogs permitted

Land status: State park

Nearest town: Greenup

Fees and permits: Free permit, available at park lodge, required for use of overnight shelter, the only place backcountry camping is permitted in the park

Maps: Greenbo Lake State Resort Park trail guide; USGS Oldtown and Argillite

Trail contact: Greenbo Lake State Resort Park, (606) 473-7324

Parking and trailhead facilities: Restaurant and overnight accommodations, water, and restrooms are available in the lodge; a campground is nearby. There are lots of parking spaces.

Finding the trailhead: Greenbo Lake State Resort Park is about 22 miles west of Ashland. From exit 172 off I-64, take KY 1 north for 14.5 miles and turn left (west) onto KY 1711. In 2.7 miles, turn right at the sign to the state park lodge, which you reach in 0.8 mile. Park and walk to the signboard at the eastern end of the parking lot. GPS: N38 28.875' / W82 52.324'

The Hike

The park lodge is named for Jesse Stuart (1906–1984), a Kentucky poet laureate who lived a few miles away. Not so well known outside the area is Michael Tygart, an early Kentucky frontiersman. A contemporary of Daniel Boone and Simon Kenton, a creek, state forest, and the trail that you will take on this hike are named in his honor.

At 3,000 acres Greenbo is one of the largest parks in the state system. The name is a combination of the *Green* in Greenup County and the *Bo* in adjoining Boyd County, where Ashland is located. In the late 1940s, residents of both counties initiated the damming of three small streams to create 225-acre Greenbo Lake. The lake is a favorite of anglers, but swimming is prohibited. However, the park has opened the state's first scuba-diving refuge in 10 acres near the lodge.

From the lodge parking lot, Michael Tygart Trail heads north on an old roadbed. It is marked throughout with bright yellow blazes. At mile 0.2 Fern Valley Nature Trail forks off to the right. Just after that Tygart Trail branches off to your left and follows the lakeshore westward via a narrow path.

A lone heron stands watch at Greenbo Lake, which is stunning in every season.

After curving south the trail winds north and west. At mile 0.8 it hits the park road leading down to the campground and boat dock. Cross the road and proceed west up the hill to the Buffalo Furnace Cemetery, which has graves dating back to the 1800s. In the early nineteenth century, this part of Kentucky was a major iron producer, and the 36-foot-high Buffalo Furnace was an important part of the industry. At one time it employed 150 people. The output was transported to the Ohio River for shipment by barge. In 1850 Greenup County had nineteen iron furnaces; the last one ceased operations in 1891. The remains of the Buffalo Furnace are just south of the trail but not visible. West of the cemetery, the trail passes the old pits where the ore was dug.

From the cemetery the trail climbs to a ridgetop and merges with an old roadbed. At 1.8 miles you come to Blackberry Shelter, a three-sided wooden structure left over from the old Tygart Trail. It can sleep six comfortably, and is in good condition with benches and a table. There is no source of water. Backcountry camping is prohibited everywhere in the park except at this shelter.

From the shelter the trail heads northwest on the ridgetop paralleling the park's western boundary. After crossing a power-line clearing, the trail runs alongside an old road. After crossing a second power-line clearing at mile 2.8, it comes out on Bays Ridge Road.

Take a right onto Bays Ridge Road, passing a horse barn on your left and several houses and a parking lot on the right for users of two horse trails that run eastward

Greenbo Lake

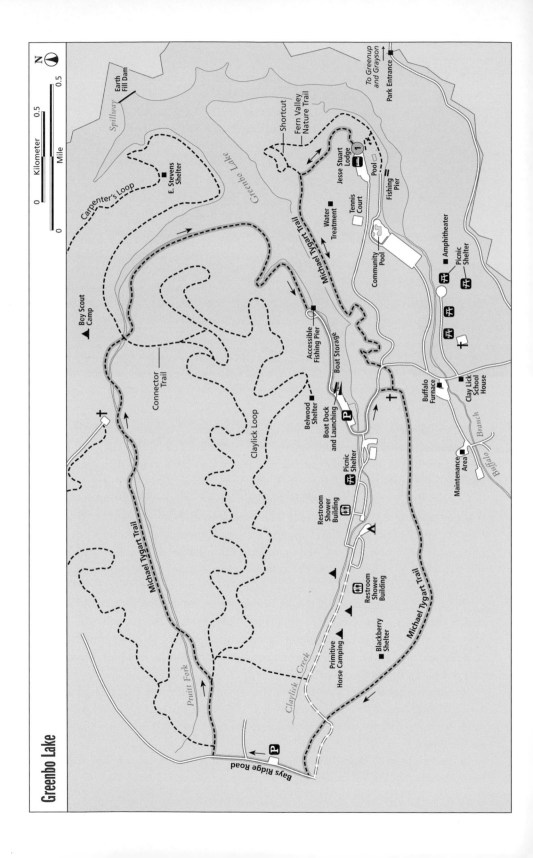

N

Kilometer
0   0.5

Mile
0   0.5

Spillway

Earth Fill Dam

Carpenter's Loop

E. Stevens Shelter

Greenbo Lake

Boy Scout Camp

Connector Trail

Claylick Loop

Michael Tygart Trail

Pruitt Fork

Belwood Shelter

Accessible Fishing Pier

Boat Storage

Boat Dock and Launching

Picnic Shelter

Restroom Shower Building

Blackberry Shelter

Primitive Horse Camping

Restroom Shower Building

Claylick Creek

Michael Tygart Trail

Bays Ridge Road

Shortcut

Fern Valley Nature Trail

Jesse Stuart Lodge

Pool

Fishing Pier

Water Treatment

Tennis Court

Community Pool

Amphitheater

Picnic Shelter

Buffalo Furnace

Clay Lick School House

Maintenance Area

Buffalo Branch

Park Entrance

To Greenup and Grayson

into the park's interior. Past the parking lot is a gravel service road that goes east to the park campground. The paved road then turns to gravel and signs mark the boundary of the state forest on your left. Watch for yellow blazes on telephone poles.

At mile 3.2 Tygart Trail leaves Bays Ridge Road, splitting right into the woods and descending eastward to a trickle of water named Pruitt Fork, one of the three streams that feed Greenbo Lake.

Where the Tygart Trail leaves the road is the trailheads for Carpenter's Run Trail and Claylick Loop Trail. Carpenter's runs along the park's northern boundary line before meeting back up with the Tygart Trail farther east, providing horseback riders with a 10-mile loop. The Carpenter's Run Trail is blazed in red. Because the Tygart Trail is part of this loop, be on the lookout for horses over the next 2.5 miles.

Just before reaching Pruitt Fork, Claylick Loop Trail splits off to the right. This 7-mile loop, like Carpenter's Run Trail, is open to hikers and mountain bikers as well as equestrians. With the addition of the two horse trails, the park's trail system totals 25 miles. Claylick is blazed in blue. There is a small collection of benches at this junction.

The Pruitt Fork ravine is the most pleasant part of the hike. The remnants of several old homesteads are visible, and the bottomlands retain some of the openness they once had as farm fields. You will also pass the entrance to the Boy Scouts of America Troop 202 camp. From the trail a nice fire circle is visible, just underneath the wooden gateway.

After crossing the creek numerous times, you reach a spot where the stream empties into a thin lake arm. The trail curves south, and at mile 5.8, just after the arm meets the main body of the lake, you pass a small cove. There is a fire pit, some benches, and tables for fish cleaning in the shade of this small cove.

From the cove to the fishing pier at mile 6.0, there are a number of other delightful places to stop by the water. Don't expect a sandy beach, but you will find rocks to sit on and shade from trees growing along the shore.

From the fishing pier, the trail follows a park road along the lake to the marina parking lot and a bridge crossing Claylick Creek. There are no yellow blazes, but follow the road carefully uphill for 0.5 mile, passing the entrance to the camping area.

At the bottom of the cemetery hill, take a left into the woods and retrace your steps 0.8 mile on the Tygart Trail east to the lodge parking lot.

Key Points

1.8   Overnight shelter.

3.4   Pruitt Fork.

5.8   Shaded lakeside spot.

2 Jesse Stuart State Nature Preserve

A lovely, tree-lined ridgetop and an old barn and cabin in a wildflower-laden meadow are the highlights of this loop hike in rural northeastern Kentucky.

Start: Parking lot of Jesse Stuart State Nature Preserve
Distance: 3-mile loop
Hiking time: About 2 hours
Difficulty: Easy
Best seasons: Any
Other trail users: None
Canine compatibility: No dogs allowed
Land status: State nature preserve

Nearest town: Greenup
Fees and permits: None
Maps: Kentucky State Nature Preserves Commission trail map of Jesse Stuart preserve; USGS Greenup
Trail contact: Kentucky State Nature Preserves Commission, (502) 573-2886
Parking and trailhead facilities: There's room for 7 cars, but no facilities.

Finding the trailhead: From Greenup, take KY 1 south for 1.8 miles, turn right onto W-Hollow Road, and after 1.6 miles park in the nature preserve's gravel lot on your right. The trail starts at the lot. GPS: N38 32.850' / W82 50.515'

The Hike

This 733-acre state nature preserve in W-Hollow was once the home of Jesse Stuart (1906–1984), a prolific novelist, poet, and short-story writer whose works focused on eastern Kentucky hill life. W-Hollow figured prominently in both his fiction and real life. If you want to get a feel for Stuart's writings, try *Head o' W-Hollow*, a collection of short stories, or *The Thread That Runs So True*, about his experience as a teacher.

But even if you have never read a word written by the former Kentucky poet laureate, you should enjoy this pleasant loop across ravines and ridges in the preserve's western half. The walk includes a long stretch on an old tree-lined dirt road that winds along the top of a ridge. It offers views of Greenup and the Ohio River to the north and the Little Sandy River valley to the west when the leaves are off the trees.

This little preserve is a real gem. It has three loops of varying lengths, with this hike the longest and taken in a counterclockwise direction. All three hiking loops start and end at the parking area. As with all Kentucky nature preserves, the trails are for hikers only.

From your car, go through the gate and turn right onto the narrow path, passing under a large oak tree and past a little area of wildflowers. On my visit in August, the cardinal flowers were in bloom. The trail goes east at first but quickly turns north as it descends a set of switchbacks on the way to a small, wet-weather stream. Crossing it on a small footbridge, you climb northeast through hardwoods blazed with red paint, and at mile 0.3 cross a grass clearing above a buried liquefied petroleum gas (LPG) pipeline.

Uncle Op's cabin and old barn stand among a field of wildflowers on the Seaton Ridge Loop Trail.

You then drop partway down a ravine, named Shingle Mill Hollow, and walk northwest along its side. At mile 0.6, after turning right and descending, you cross the bottom of the ravine and immediately on the other side come to a fork. Shingle Mill Hollow Trail, the shortest of the three loops, goes left; you bear right (north) onto Seaton Ridge Loop Trail, the longest.

Climbing northeast up the ridge side, you come to another fork at 0.7 mile where Coon Den Hollow Trail, the third loop, branches off to your left; continue straight. After dipping briefly into a drainage, you climb steeply up a hill and, at the top, head northwest along the level ridgetop.

After following a small ravine downhill, cross the stream at the bottom of Stuart Lane Hollow and, on the other side, climb up to an old dirt road at 1.2 miles. (This is a lovely 0.4-mile hike when it is open and cleared, but downed trees have currently closed this spur.)

Continue to follow the main Seaton Ridge Loop Trail, which goes south and then southwest on the dirt road. The road hugs the right side of the ridge, allowing you to see a good distance to the west.

After the road curves south, you come into an open grass field, where the trail is marked by stakes in the ground. At mile 2.0 you pass an old white-clapboard cottage

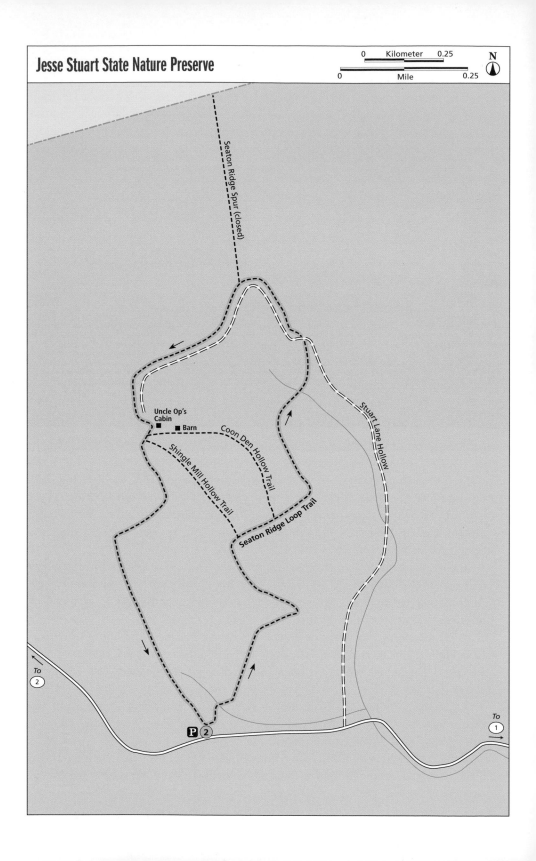

Jesse Stuart State Nature Preserve

and a beautiful old barn in a hilltop meadow. A mowed path through wildflowers connects the two. This is a lovely spot for lunch.

Just past the structures on the edge of the woods, the preserve's two shorter loop trails rejoin Seaton Ridge Loop Trail, which goes straight down the same mowed grassy pipeline strip that you crossed earlier. In another 0.2 mile the trail leaves the pipeline clearing, angling right on a roadbed along the edge of the ridge. At mile 3.0, after an easy descent, the old road ends at the parking area.

Key Points

0.6 Right at fork onto Seaton Ridge Loop Trail.

0.7 Straight at intersection with Coon Den Hollow Trail.

1.2 Straight at junction of Seaton Ridge Loop Trail and a dirt spur trail. Continue the counter-clockwise loop.

2.0 Uncle Op's cabin and old barn.

2.2 Straight at junction with shorter loop trails.

3 Lick Falls

This wooded walk takes you to a scenic overlook where a small stream tumbles down a high cliff into Grayson Lake. In dry spells the falls may be a mere trickle, but even so, it's a beautiful spot.

Start: Near amphitheater and campground office of Grayson Lake State Park
Distance: 2.7-mile lollipop
Hiking time: 2 hours or less
Difficulty: Easy
Best seasons: Any
Other trail users: Mountain bikers
Canine compatibility: Leashed dogs permitted
Land status: State park
Nearest town: Grayson

Fees and permits: None
Maps: Grayson Lake State Park map; USGS Bruin
Trail contact: Grayson Lake State Park, (606) 474-9727
Parking and trailhead facilities: Restrooms, water, and a campground are available in the park. There's room for about 10 cars in the lot and plenty of additional parking space nearby.

Finding the trailhead: From exit 172 off I-64, take KY 7 south through the town of Grayson. After 11 miles, turn right onto the road for the Grayson Lake State Park camping area. Follow the signs for the park campground, and in a mile you come to a parking area on the left, near a covered pavilion. Just beyond the parking area, in the middle of the road, is the campground office. Park in the lot by the pavilion and walk across the road and over the small grassy rise until you see the amphitheater in front of you. Just to the left of the amphitheater in a clump of pine trees is a trailhead regulations sign and the start of a path marked by painted yellow and blue blazes. Follow the path downhill a short distance until you come to a fork, which is the start of the Lick Falls Trail, the loop route for this hike. GPS (at trailhead sign): N38 12.082' / W83 01.764'

The Hike

In the 1960s the US Army Corps of Engineers dammed the Little Sandy River and created a long, skinny, 1,500-acre reservoir named Grayson Lake. As with most Corps reservoirs, flood control was the main purpose. Unlike many, however, this one has some beautiful stretches of shoreline. Instead of mudflats, rock cliffs rise out of the water at a 90-degree angle, some reaching 200 feet in height. This hike follows a Grayson Lake State Park trail that takes you along one of these palisades to an overlook where Lick Branch tumbles over a cliff into the lake. At least, that's what it's supposed to do. The actual condition of the falls depends on whether there has been enough rain to keep the little stream flowing. Even if there's no water, it's a great place for a picnic, reading, or just daydreaming.

A fork marks the very beginning and end of the Lick Falls Trail loop. The right-hand prong heads downhill and is blazed in solid yellow; the left-hand prong has both

Steep sandstone cliffs line Grayson Lake.

yellow and blue blazes and goes south. You can go either way, of course, but I suggest following the yellow and blue blazes to the left.

If you go to the left, you quickly come to another fork. Here the blue-blazed Beech Hemlock Trail branches off to the left, ending in 0.8 mile at the park campground. The Lick Falls Trail, which you follow, is marked by solid yellow blazes from here on. It turns right and descends to Bowling Branch just before the stream flows into the lake. After crossing the brook on a bridge, you walk southwest through a hardwood forest between the golf course above and on your right, and the lake on your left. Paralleling the lakeshore, the trail winds around another inlet where a second small creek, Buckeye Branch, empties into the lake. This is a particularly pretty spot, full of ferns and rocks. You then turn south, continuing to follow the lake but staying high above the water. Watch small children here; a fall could be deadly.

After descending through a thicket of mountain laurel, you come to the overlook at mile 1.3. Lick Falls—which has a robust flow after rains—is to your right. The cove

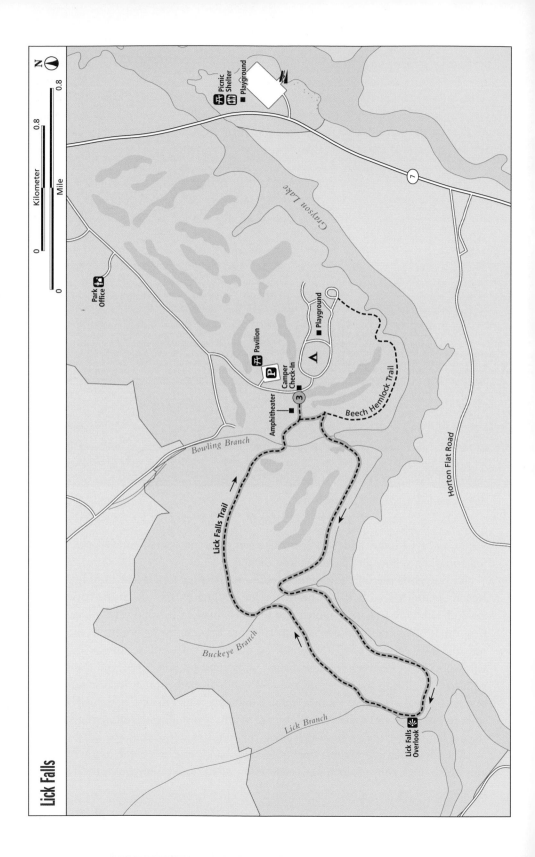

Lick Falls

below is a favorite anchoring spot for boaters, so you may be looking down on the tops of several watercraft as well as the dark green lake water. At the overlook the trail curves east and immediately comes to Lick Branch just before it plunges over the cliff into the lake. From here the trail goes northeast along the stream bank and comes out on an old road. At this point the creek goes north, but you continue northeast on the old road and climb.

At mile 1.6 the trail leaves the road and climbs on a path through the woods up to a point about 50 yards from the top of the ridge. The trail then descends eastward and, after rejoining the old road, recrosses Buckeye Branch at mile 2.2. After several more ups and downs, the trail makes a right turn off the road and follows a path up a small ridge. After crossing a concrete golf cart track, the trail descends to Bowling Branch and then climbs the hill to the start of the loop.

Key Points

1.3 Lick Falls overlook.

4 Grayson Lake Wildlife Management Area

Secluded woods on the ridgetops above Grayson Lake offer plenty of day-hiking opportunities in this corner of the state. This hike uses a network of paths called the Api-Su-Ahts Trail developed by area Boy Scouts in cooperation with the state government and the US Army Corps of Engineers.

Start: Small parking area just off KY 1496 near Grayson Lake dam
Distance: 7.8-mile loop
Hiking time: About 5 hours
Difficulty: Moderate
Best seasons: Any, but avoid on hot summer days
Other trail users: Mountain bikers and equestrians allowed on some portions; hunters present in season
Canine compatibility: Dogs permitted; must be leashed Mar 1 through third Sat of Aug to protect ground-nesting wildlife
Land status: State wildlife management area
Nearest town: Grayson
Fees and permits: None

Maps: Api-Su-Ahts Trail guide; USGS Willard and Bruin
Trail contacts: US Army Corps of Engineers office at Grayson Lake, (606) 474-5107; Grayson Lake Wildlife Management Area office, (606) 474-8535
Special considerations: Overnight camping is not allowed. This is a wildlife management area and open to hunting according to the state seasons. Hikers using this trail system are urged to wear an article of blaze orange. The area is closed to hikers on the first weekend of Nov for an annual youth deer hunt.
Parking and trailhead facilities: There's space for 6 to 10 cars, but no facilities.

Finding the trailhead: At exit 172 off I-64, take KY 7 south through the town of Grayson. After 7 miles, turn left onto KY 1496 just west of the Grayson Lake dam. (If you drive over the dam on KY 7, you missed the turn.) In 1.8 miles, turn right off KY 1496 onto a paved road marked with signs for both the Api-Su-Ahts Trail and Camp Robert C. Webb, a conservation camp for young people. In 0.2 mile, stop at the parking area on the left side of the road at the end of the lake's eastern arm. GPS: N38 13.982' / W82 58.199'

The Hike

Api-Su-Ahts, which is said to be Pawnee Indian for "morning star" or "early riser," is the name of a collection of hiking trails on the southeast side of Grayson Lake's main trunk. The trails were originally developed in the 1970s by the Boy Scouts, but Mother Nature reclaimed them. In the late 1990s Grayson businessman Tim Wilson, volunteering his time and considerable energies, led an effort to reestablish the paths with cooperation from the Kentucky Department of Fish and Wildlife Resources and the Army Corps of Engineers. The area, encompassing almost 15,000 acres, is owned by the Corps and leased to the state for wildlife management. It's full of deer, raccoons, and wild turkeys, and while busy KY 7 and a popular lake marina are nearby, you feel you're in the backwoods.

Using old roadbeds and newer gravel roads in addition to trails, the Api-Su-Ahts system consists of four connected walking loops totaling 26 miles. This hike is Loop #2, the longest of the four and rated the most difficult. Don't let that stop you. There are a number of ups and downs but for the most part they are gentle, and much of the walk is level—both along Grayson Lake and on the ridgetops. Be aware, however, that some stretches are in the open sun. On a summer day this could be a hot one, although there are spots along the lake to take a swim.

A white blaze above the guardrail at the end of the parking area marks the start of the hike on an old, grass-covered road heading south along Deer Creek. The track is named, appropriately enough, Deer Creek Trail. In several spots along the way, I had trouble finding my way through thick vegetation. These stretches were brief, and I got assurances that the Corps and the state are committed to keeping the trail well maintained in coming years. However, if high grass makes the trail difficult to see early on, just keep the creek close by on your right and you'll be fine.

At mile 0.2, disregard the gravel road crossing the creek and continue straight ahead. In the early morning of a late-spring day, when I made the hike, this was an especially pleasing area, with deer romping in a creek-side field and wild turkeys blasting into the air. At mile 0.5 the trail crosses the creek and soon passes a trail splitting off to the east. This is a cutoff that creates Loop #1. Continuing south on the old road, you climb slightly and at 1.2 miles a sign instructs you to make a right-hand turn off the road onto a path going west. You shortly enter a field and continue west, sticking close to the trees lining the left side of the field. This is one of the areas subject to overgrowth, so watch closely. At a white blaze at mile 1.4, turn right and cross a small streambed, leaving the field and entering a forest of mixed hardwoods and pines.

The trail then climbs west and northwest, making use of old roadbeds, and at mile 1.7 reaches its high point before falling to the shore of Grayson Lake at 2.5 miles. You come down close to the lake at an inlet where the water is muddy and altogether uninviting. Keep going; the trail parallels the lakeshore and soon turns into a definite forest road. At this point the lake is more substantial and better for swimming. The "beach" is mud but it's a hard mud, and there's almost an immediate drop-off, eliminating the need for much wading. The water is about 20 yards below you; the bank is fairly steep, but the scramble down isn't difficult.

The forest road follows the shore south to the spot where Greenbrier Branch empties into the lake and, after crossing a feeder stream, develops into a full-fledged gravel road. Here you begin to climb. After curving to the east, the road dead-ends at mile 4.4 at another gravel road, this one running along the ridge. Take this road—which is a continuation of Deer Creek Trail, which you initially walked from the parking area—to your left (north). (As the sign at the junction explains, if you go right instead of left, you will soon reach the start of Loop #3.) The Api-Su-Ahts map and USGS Willard quad both show a lookout tower near the beginning of the third

Waterfalls are abundant at Grayson Lake, especially in wet weather.

loop. However, this old fire tower—about 0.4 mile southwest of the road junction—is in poor condition and off-limits to climbers.

The road climbs north, and in just less than 0.5 mile, an old dirt road splits off to your right. Take this road, heading northeast on top of the ridge. A canopy of trees

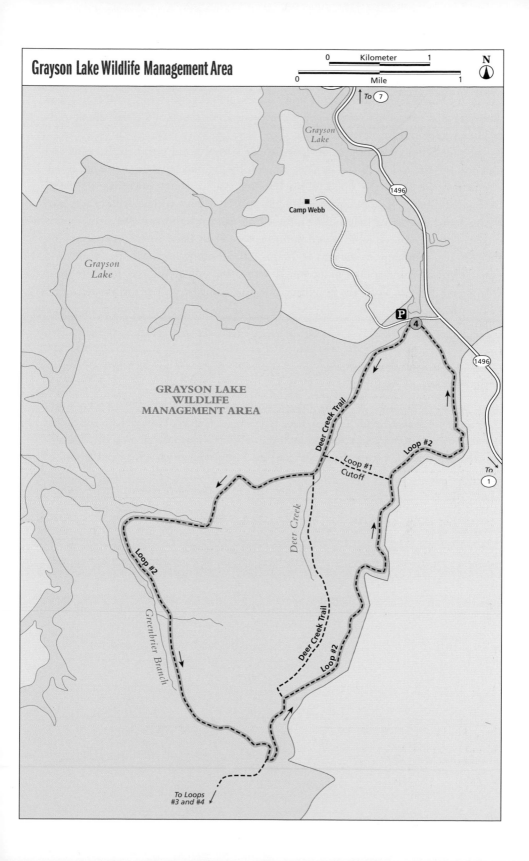

Grayson Lake Wildlife Management Area

Grayson Lake

Grayson Lake

To 7

1496

Camp Webb

1496

GRAYSON LAKE
WILDLIFE
MANAGEMENT AREA

Deer Creek Trail

Loop #1
Cutoff

Loop #2

To 1

Deer Creek

Loop #2

Greenbrier Branch

Deer Creek Trail

Loop #2

To Loops
#3 and #4

makes this a pleasing walk but also blocks any views. Soon you see wildlife management area signs along the trail; you are now following the wildlife area's eastern boundary line as it meanders north along the ridgeline, gently rising and falling and alternating between old roadbeds and narrow paths. For much of the way, the boundary line is reinforced by a fence.

At mile 5.5 a clearing provides the first of several good views to the east. The cliff you see due east in the far distance was left by a surface coal mine that locals say operated in the late 1970s. A federal law regulating strip mining now makes it illegal to leave behind this kind of uncovered "high wall." But what you see is an example of the widespread scarring that mining inflicted on eastern Kentucky over many years.

At mile 6.3 you come to a sign pointing to a right-hand turn and announcing that you're 1.5 miles from the end of the hike. Continuing northeast, you climb and pass a dilapidated one-room cabin covered with metal siding. After several more short climbs and descents along the boundary line, the trail descends to the southern end of the parking area.

Key Points

2.5 Beginning of lakeshore section.

5.5 First ridgetop views.

Options: You can extend the hike 6 miles by adding Loop #3; just go south instead of north at the road junction near Greenbrier Branch. However, be aware that backcountry camping is not permitted in the wildlife management area. You can also shorten this hike by taking the cutoff trail for Loop #1, which has a total length of 2.9 miles.

5 The Little Sandy

This easy hike is a good one for little children. It follows the Little Sandy River for a short distance and then climbs to an overlook of the Grayson Lake area.

Start: Base of Grayson Lake dam
Distance: 3.5-mile loop
Hiking time: 2 hours or less
Difficulty: Easy
Best seasons: Fall or spring, before leaves block overlook view
Other trail users: None
Canine compatibility: Leashed dogs permitted
Land status: US Army Corps of Engineers dam site

Nearest town: Grayson
Fees and permits: None
Maps: Army Corps of Engineers map of below-dam area available at office at Grayson Lake; USGS Grayson
Trail contact: Army Corps of Engineers Grayson Lake office, (606) 474-5107
Parking and trailhead facilities: Restrooms, water, a picnic pavilion, and plenty of parking spaces are available.

Finding the trailhead: At exit 172 off I-64, drive south on KY 7 for 7.5 miles. Immediately after crossing the earth-filled dam that makes Grayson Lake, turn right onto the road descending to the below-dam recreation area. This turnoff is 0.6 mile west of the KY 1496 turnoff to the Grayson Lake Wildlife Management Area. The Army Corps of Engineers office, which has information about the lake and surrounding area, is 0.1 mile farther west on the other side of KY 7. Take the below-dam road for 0.5 mile and park in the lot by the restrooms. The trailhead is across the small field behind the restroom building. GPS: N38 15.258' / W82 59.467'

The Hike

On the road below the 120-foot-high dam holding back 20-mile-long Grayson Lake, a sign warns "Blast of horn means fast rise of water." Chances are catastrophe will not strike during this brief hike, which starts off following the scenic Little Sandy River as it flows out of the dam on its way to the Ohio River and then climbs easily to an overlook of Grayson Lake.

Near the dam outflow, wooden steps lead down to an earth-and-gravel path going first west and then north along the river. This is the Army Corps of Engineers' Grayson Lake Nature Trail, a highly developed (benches for resting are sprinkled along the way) loop that you take for the hike's first 1.5 miles. The robustness of the river and the attractiveness of its banks depend on how much rain has fallen recently and at what level the Corps is keeping the lake. But whatever the conditions, the weathered rock outcroppings and ledges that line the far side of the river are interesting.

At mile 0.4 a short spur trail leads straight ahead to a large sycamore tree shown by core drilling to be 200 years old, according to the Corps. The main nature trail turns right, ascends steps, and at the top turns north again to continue following the river from a higher elevation. After passing through a grove of pines, the trail curves

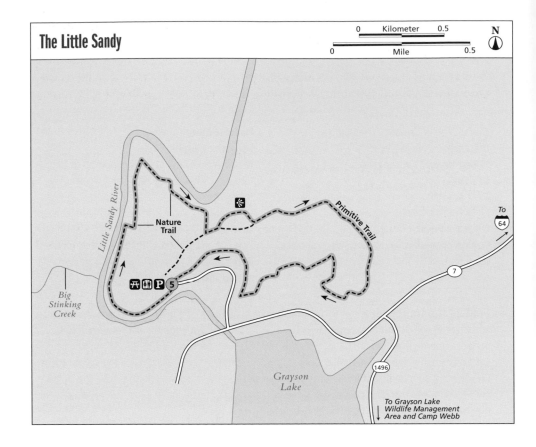

The Little Sandy

Kilometer
0   0.5

Mile
0   0.5

N

Little Sandy River

Nature Trail

Primitive Trail

To 64

7

Big Stinking Creek

5

Grayson Lake

1496

To Grayson Lake Wildlife Management Area and Camp Webb

east and offers a fine view of a pretty farm field across the river. You also pass a short side trail to a blind for viewing wildlife, which in this area includes deer, beavers, wild turkeys, blue herons, and Canada geese.

At mile 1.5, after a brief climb, the Nature Trail comes to the beginning of the Corps' 2-mile Primitive Trail. From here the Nature Trail loops another 0.25 mile back to the parking lot; turn left (east) onto the Primitive Trail. A sign warns of long, steep inclines ahead, but that's an overstatement; even small children should have no trouble. Immediately after turning left onto the Primitive Trail, take another left onto a side trail that leads to a scenic overlook of the lake; a sign marks the turn. If the trees are full, you may not see much from the overlook. The side trail reconnects with the Primitive Trail, so you don't have to backtrack.

After rejoining the Primitive Trail, cross a power-line clearing that is likely to be filled with wildflowers. The trail then heads southeast through a pleasant forest and turns west, staying at a fairly constant elevation near the top of a ridge. After a hairpin turn right (north), you get a westward view of the lake and marina even when the leaves are out.

From here you descend to a ravine bottom and cross two small streambeds, then a creek, and finally the old river channel. A mowed path leads up a hill to a mulch-covered trail through a field sprinkled with demonstrations of methods for promoting wildlife. The Corps says these are tips that people can use to attract wildlife to their own yards. The trail ends at the road leading down from KY 7; follow it back to your car.

Key Points

0.4   Short spur trail to 200-year-old sycamore.

1.5   Start of Primitive Trail.

1.6   Lake overlook.

Option: This would be a good hike to combine in a day with another short, easy stroll—the Lick Falls hike. The turnoff for Lick Falls is about 4 miles south on KY 7.

6 Carter Caves State Resort Park

This backcountry walk up and down ridges takes you to two arches and a fishing lake. There is a backcountry camping area more than halfway through the loop if you want to make this an overnight trip.

Start: Welcome center at Carter Caves State Resort Park
Distance: 8.3-mile loop
Hiking time: About 6 hours
Difficulty: Moderate
Best seasons: Spring and fall
Other trail users: None
Canine compatibility: Leashed dogs permitted
Land status: State park
Nearest town: Olive Hill
Fees and permits: Free permit, available at park welcome center, required for use of trailside camping area, the only place backcountry camping is permitted in the park
Maps: Park map and visitor guide; USGS Tygarts Valley, Wesleyville, Olive Hill, and Grahn

Trail contact: Carter Caves State Resort Park, (606) 286-4411 or (800) 325-0059
Special considerations: A short segment of the hike crosses the spillway of a man-made park lake. Although usually dry, the spillway can become flooded in wet weather. Even when the water recedes, the trail at that spot can be difficult to follow.
Parking and trailhead facilities: Water, restrooms, and information are available at the welcome center; there's also plenty of parking both there and in a lot across the road. A lodge with a restaurant and overnight accommodations is nearby in the park, as is a campground.

Finding the trailhead: At exit 161 off I-64, go east on US 60 for 1.4 miles and turn left (north) onto KY 182. In 2.7 miles, turn left onto the state park road, and after 1 mile park at the welcome center on your right. The trail begins at the stone steps just northeast of the welcome center. GPS: N38 22.642' / W83 07.315'

The Hike

The caves beneath Kentucky's Carter County have been drawing visitors for a long, long time. Early settlers extracted raw materials from them, and for decades their exploration has been a source of recreation. Cave tours were being conducted long before the state park was established in the 1940s. Within the park there are twenty charted caves, four of them open for guided tours during the summer and two year-round. Although the underground sights are the main attraction, the 1,900-acre park also offers 30 miles of hiking trails. One of the longest—and the one you follow on this hike—is the 4Cs (for Carter Caves Cross Country) Trail, which winds through the wooded backcountry of the park and a small section of adjacent Tygarts State Forest.

The 4Cs Trail has one steep stretch—the climb away from Smoky Valley Lake—but otherwise the numerous ups and downs are relatively painless as you range from creek bottomlands to ridgetops. The trail makes use of old roadbeds as well as narrow

Fern Bridge is one of three sandstone bridges visible along the 4Cs Trail.

paths, and features interesting limestone and sandstone formations. In all probability you will also see a good number of deer. The mainly hardwood forest includes oak, hickory, and maple. The one thing you won't see, at least not when the foliage is out, is a panoramic view; there are no good lookout points on this hike. Backcountry camping is not allowed in the park except at a designated site located a little more than halfway through the hike.

After climbing the stone steps northeast of the welcome center, turn left at the 4Cs Trail sign; another trail, the shorter Horn Hollow Trail, goes straight. Walking north, you quickly come to the head of a ravine and turn west onto a narrow, leafy path passing several nice rock outcroppings. The trail is marked with orange blazes, but be especially careful as you wind down to a broad but probably dry streambed at mile 0.6. An old country road following the streambed to your right could fool you into going the wrong way. The trail jogs left, crosses the streambed, and climbs southwest before turning northwest. After crossing over a ridgetop, it then descends into another bottomland, follows a mowed path west through a clearing, and returns to the woods. At mile 1.5, after widening from a path into an old road, the trail reaches another ridgetop; a few paces later it crosses a gravel road coming from the park's

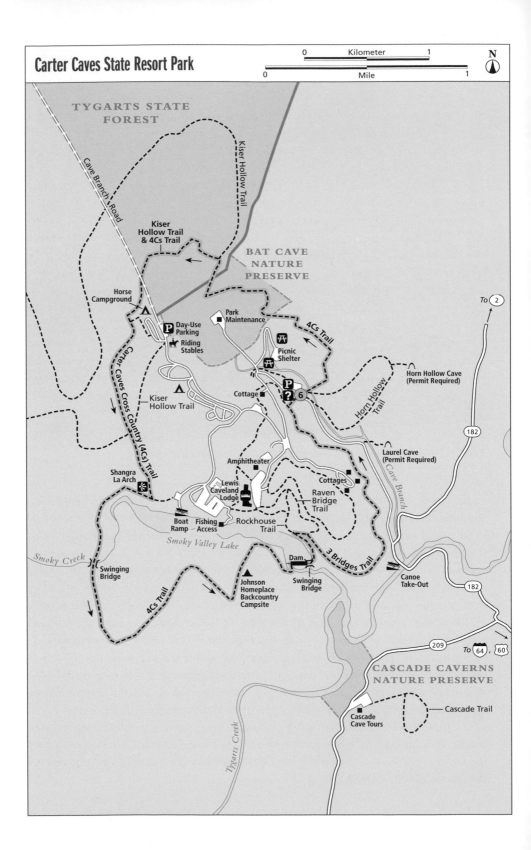

riding stables. Immediately afterward, you pass the abandoned Simon Kenton Trail, an old 9-mile-long route that was partially on private land and is no longer maintained. Kenton, by the way, was a Kentucky frontiersman of the Daniel Boone era.

Heading southeast on the 4Cs Trail, you make another descent and ascent, and at mile 2.5 pass under the Shangra La Arch—a limestone structure that park personnel say was formed by the erosion of what was once a cave. Steep steps take you down to the arch entrance, and most people are able to walk through it standing up. If you're anywhere near 6 feet tall, though, watch your head! The arch is surrounded by scenic rock cliffs and makes a good rest spot.

Almost immediately beyond the arch, you come to a point just above Smoky Valley Lake, a 40-acre man-made fishing reservoir shaped like a snake. Here you turn right (a left would take you a short distance to the boat ramp) and begin circling the lake's western tail. It's doubtful this water will tempt you, but just in case, swimming is prohibited. After paralleling the base of a tall cliff, you cross a streambed that may or may not have water in it, then a second with a healthier flow toward the lake; this is Smoky Creek.

At mile 3.2, immediately after the crossing, you begin a steep climb southward on a broad, very rocky track. Almost at the top of the hill, the Collings Passage Trail joins the 4Cs for about 0.25 mile. After the trail levels off, you come to a fork; here you turn left and walk north on a dirt road. (The Collings Passage Trail, a multiuse trail that connects the Olive Hill Trail to the Kiser Hollow Trail, continues straight at this point.) The road descends and, at mile 3.9, hits another fork; this time you take a path to your right.

After crossing a meadow and another streambed, you come to what a sign identifies as the Johnson Homeplace campsite. A family by the name of Johnson is said to have had a house here once, but nothing is standing now—except a large rock overhang that could provide shelter. There is plenty of tent space and supposedly an unmarked spring that flows heaviest during wet weather; during the heat of summer, it may dry up.

From the campsite you descend and, at mile 4.7, arrive below the dam at what was once the natural creek bed and is now one of two spillways. If you have trouble finding your way here, as rainy-weather flooding routinely sends torrents of water and assorted flotsam down through the ravine, wiping out trail markings, simply cross the creek bed and head north toward the dam, climbing to the top of the earthen embankment.

At the east end of the dam, a wooden suspension bridge carries you over the second spillway, which is now the lake's main outflow. At the other end, take the wooden steps up, and then go west, following the lake's shoreline. After another set of steps, you meet the 3 Bridges Trail, which you take to the right. (A left turn would lead to the park lodge.) From here on, the 3 Bridges Trail and the 4Cs Trail are the same; the trees are marked with red and orange blazes. (The 3 Bridges Trail makes a loop through the park's interior, passing three arches: Smoky Bridge near the lodge, Raven Bridge, and Fern Bridge.)

Climbing eastward, you soon come to a junction on the left with the Raven Bridge Trail, which also leads back to the lodge. Raven Bridge itself is just a short distance down Raven Bridge Trail. To stay on the 3 Bridges/4Cs Trail, turn right and go east, then north, and finally west as you circle the ridge at a constant elevation. An intriguing cliff of pockmarked rock festooned with small trees and mountain laurel lines the left side of the trail, and at mile 5.9 you pass under Fern Bridge. This impressive sandstone arch is 90 feet high and 120 feet long.

From the arch, stone and wooden-block steps take you a bit higher; at the top, turn right and continue a level walk west. (There is also a trail to your left at the top of the steps; disregard it.) Continuing west on the 3 Bridges/4Cs Trail, at mile 6.6 you come to a side trail on your right that drops quickly down the hillside to the welcome center. You come out on the park road across from the center at Saltpetre Cave, where early nineteenth-century miners are believed to have extracted the salty, white mineral for use in making gunpowder.

Key Points

2.5 Shangra La Arch.

4.3 Johnson Homeplace backcountry campsite.

4.7 Dam and spillway.

5.9 Fern Bridge Arch.

BLUEGRASS AND COUNTRY MUSIC

Bluegrass music is synonymous with Kentucky, due in part to Bill Monroe, the "Father of Bluegrass," hailing from the small community of Rosine, in western Kentucky.

From the beginning of spring through the fall, outdoor bluegrass music festivals are commonplace throughout the state, from Williamsburg to Owensboro. Visit bluegrassfestival guide.com for a partial listing of events and venues.

Although Kentucky is best known for the form of folk music named after its famous blue-hued vegetation, the nation's most extensive collection of country music stars hail from along US 23, known as the Country Music Highway. Stretching from South Portsmouth along the Ohio River in northeast Kentucky to Letcher County along the state's southeast border with Virginia, more than a dozen country music artists were born along or near the roadway.

From venues such as the Paramount Performing Arts Center in Ashland, to the Country Music Highway Museum in Paintsville, to the Mountain Arts Center in Prestonsburg, to the Renfro Valley Entertainment Center in Mount Vernon, the hills of Kentucky are filled with opportunities to see great live music.

7 Carrington Rock Overlook

A stone arch and ridgetop overlook are the chief features of this easy walk in the Daniel Boone National Forest. The overlook makes a great spot for lunch.

Start: Iron Furnace picnic area near Clear Creek Lake
Distance: 7-mile out-and-back
Hiking time: About 5 hours
Difficulty: Easy
Best seasons: Any
Other trail users: First mile open to equestrians; mountain bikers
Canine compatibility: Dogs permitted
Land status: National forest
Nearest town: Morehead

Fees and permits: None
Maps: Cumberland Ranger District trail sheet for Section 10 of Sheltowee Trace National Recreation Trail; USGS Salt Lick
Trail contact: Morehead office, Cumberland Ranger District, Daniel Boone National Forest, (606) 784-6428
Parking and trailhead facilities: Ample parking, restrooms, a water faucet, and picnic tables are available. A national forest campground is 0.2 mile south off FR 129.

Finding the trailhead: From exit 133 off I-64, take KY 801 south for about 3 miles to US 60 at the town of Farmers. Turn right (west) onto US 60, drive 4 miles to the town of Salt Lick, and turn left (south) onto KY 211. Take this road 3.7 miles and turn left (east) onto FR 129. In 2.5 miles, just after passing a sign for the boat ramp on man-made Clear Creek Lake, turn right into the Iron Furnace picnic area, the starting point for the hike. GPS: N38 02.969' / W83 35.336'

The Hike

Two centuries ago this part of Kentucky was a major producer of iron. Like the old Buffalo community near what is now Greenbo Lake, the Clear Creek area played a role in that early industry. The 40-foot-tall furnace built on the banks of Clear Creek in 1839 operated off and on until 1875, turning out tons of pig iron for use in the manufacture of railroad wheels. It also consumed acres and acres of the surrounding forest to make fires hot enough to melt the iron ore. Today the remains of this tall stone tower stand as a reminder of Kentucky's long-ago iron business. The spot also marks the beginning of this leisurely ridgetop walk to a cliff overlooking a large rock formation called Carrington Rock.

After examining the furnace and explanatory plaques north of the parking lot, walk west on the footbridge across Clear Creek and turn left (south) onto the path paralleling the creek. This is the Sheltowee Trace National Recreation Trail, which you will take all the way to the Carrington Rock Overlook. The Sheltowee is a north–south route of approximately 320 miles through the Daniel Boone National Forest. *Sheltowee*, which means "big turtle," is said to be the name that the Shawnee gave to Daniel Boone. Thus, the trail is blazed with white diamonds bearing the outline of a turtle. On maps, in addition to its name, the trail is identified by the number 100. This

A yellow lady's slipper (Cypripedium calceolus) *along the Sheltowee Trace.*

section of the Sheltowee begins 0.4 mile north on FR 129 (Clear Creek Road) at the boat ramp turnoff; the mileage signs you see on the hike are to that point, not to the picnic area. If you want to enjoy the creek before the hike, there are several nice wading spots off the Sheltowee just north of the footbridge over Clear Creek.

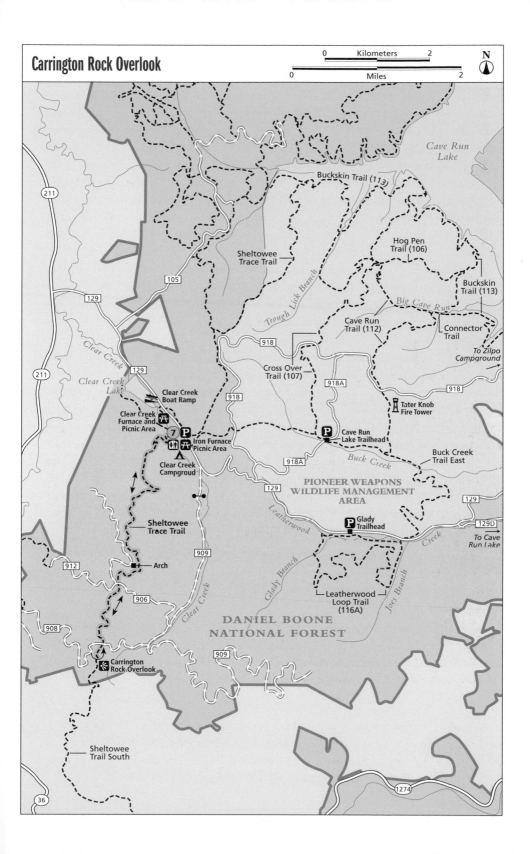

Carrington Rock Overlook

Kilometers
0   2

Miles
0   2

N

Cave Run Lake

211

Buckskin Trail (113)

Hog Pen Trail (106)

Sheltowee Trace Trail

105

Buckskin Trail (113)

129

Trough Lick Branch

Big Cave Run

Cave Run Trail (112)

Connector Trail

To Zilpo Campground

211

Clear Creek

918

Cross Over Trail (107)

918A

918

129

Clear Creek Lake

Clear Creek Boat Ramp

Tater Knob Fire Tower

Clear Creek Furnace and Picnic Area

7

P

Iron Furnace Picnic Area

Clear Creek Campgroud

P

Cave Run Lake Trailhead

Buck Creek Trail East

Buck Creek

918A

PIONEER WEAPONS WILDLIFE MANAGEMENT AREA

129

129

Sheltowee Trace Trail

Leatherwood

P

Glady Trailhead

129D

To Cave Run Lake

909

912

Arch

906

Clear Creek

Glady Branch

Joes Branch

Leatherwood Loop Trail (116A)

908

DANIEL BOONE NATIONAL FOREST

909

Carrington Rock Overlook

Sheltowee Trail South

36

1274

Shortly after you turn left onto the Sheltowee, the trail begins a series of switchbacks that take you west away from the creek and up the side of the ridge. This is the only serious climb of the hike. At mile 0.5 you reach the top of the ridge and head south on generally level ground. Depending on the season and foliage conditions, there are a few limited views east and west to outlying ridges. Through the trees to the north, you catch glimpses of Clear Creek Lake.

After crossing an old roadbed, the trail passes several rock outcroppings and climbs gently. (From this point forward, the trail is only open to hikers. Equestrians must continue straight on the old roadbed.) At mile 2.2—just after the trail begins a descent—you come to a medium-size sandstone arch with ferns and small trees growing out of it. The USDA Forest Service map shows the unnamed arch to the left of the trail, but it's actually on your right and easily missed because it's slightly above the trail.

From the arch the trail descends and, after 0.25 mile, comes to unpaved FR 906 in Glady Hollow. (FR 906 goes east to FR 909, which connects with FR 129 just south of the picnic area.) After crossing FR 906, the trail proceeds south along the ridge spine, climbs over a rock formation, and descends gently to FR 908 3.25 miles from the trailhead. (FR 908 also connects with FR 909.)

The trail crosses the road going southeast and rises to the head of a shady, fern-filled ravine. It then curves left (east) and uses several switchbacks to make a steep but short climb up the ravine wall. At mile 3.5, after making your way around the face of a rock outcropping—a place to keep your eye on small children—you come out on top of a cliff with a grand view to the west. In the distance is a large rock formation with a cave-like hole that makes a shelter. On the right side of the formation is Carrington Rock, which was supposedly used as a lookout point first by Indians and later by soldiers during the Civil War. Today the rock is on private property. The panorama makes this a great lunch spot. It's also where you turn around and begin retracing your steps to your car. Just beyond this point, the Sheltowee leaves the national forest and enters private land on its way to KY 1274 about 5 miles to the south.

Key Points

2.2   Natural arch.

3.5   Overlook.

Option: Instead of retracing your steps, you can take FR 908 and FR 909 back to the picnic area parking lot; the distance is about the same. The two gravel roads are used by national forest vehicles but otherwise are closed to motorized traffic.

8 Cave Run Lake

The shoreline of Cave Run Lake, with spots for wading or swimming if you don't mind a rocky beach, is the highlight of this hike. A fire tower along the trail, once offering hikers a 360-degree view, is now closed due to an arson fire that severely damaged the cab of the tower in 2008.

Start: Roadside parking area on gravel FR 918A

Distance: 10.5-mile loop

Hiking time: About 6 hours

Difficulty: Moderate

Best seasons: Any

Other trail users: Mountain bikers; first 0.8 mile on Buck Creek Trail open to mountain bikers, equestrians, and hikers

Canine compatibility: Dogs permitted

Land status: National forest

Nearest town: Morehead

Fees and permits: None

Maps: Cumberland Ranger District trail pamphlet for Pioneer Weapons Wildlife Management Area; USGS Salt Lick

Trail contact: Morehead office, Cumberland Ranger District, Daniel Boone National Forest, (606) 784-6428

Special considerations: This is a hunting area set aside exclusively for "pioneer" weapons, including flintlock and percussion cap rifles, bows, and crossbows. Avoid deer and turkey seasons.

Parking and trailhead facilities: This is not an official USDA Forest Service trailhead, and there are no facilities. Roadside parking, however, is permitted, and there is room for about 10 cars.

Finding the trailhead: From exit 133 off I-64, take KY 801 south for about 3 miles to US 60 at the town of Farmers. Turn right (west) onto US 60, drive 4 miles to the town of Salt Lick, and turn left (south) onto KY 211. Take this road 3.7 miles and turn left (east) onto FR 129. In 2.5 miles, just after passing a sign for the boat ramp on man-made Clear Creek Lake, pass the Iron Furnace picnic area on your right. Continue for 1.5 miles and turn left (north) onto FR 918, called the Zilpo Scenic Byway. After 0.3 mile, turn right (east) onto gravel FR 918A, and in 1.2 miles pull into a graveled area designated for parking on the north side of the road. The trailhead is across the road at the gated dirt road and is marked Trail 118. GPS: N38 02.833' / W83 33.510'

The Hike

Years ago the farmers in this region tilled the bottomlands of the Licking River while lumbermen harvested trees on the higher ground. Today wood production for furniture and veneers remains a major industry, making the Morehead area Kentucky's biggest hardwood producer. The bottomlands, however, are another story. They are now submerged under 8,300-acre Cave Run Lake, the largest body of water in Kentucky east of I-75. Built by the US Army Corps of Engineers in 1974 by damming the Licking River, the reservoir is principally for flood control. But as you'll see if you visit in spring or summer, it's well used by boaters and anglers.

Sunlight sparkles on the crystal waters of Cave Run Lake.

While the recreational focus is on the water, the adjoining area south of the lake's main stem offers plenty of walking opportunities. This hike uses a number of trails to make a long loop through the hills and hollows near the lake and along a section of the shore itself. It's all within the special 7,610-acre pioneer weapons zone set aside by the Forest Service and state Department of Fish and Wildlife Resources for hunters who do not use modern breech-loading firearms. Despite the name, hikers are also welcome—but as in any national forest, make sure to check the local hunting schedule first. It's advisable to avoid the deer and wild turkey seasons.

The hike's first leg is on Buck Creek Trail (118), a tree-lined forest track along the creek of the same name. From FR 918A, follow the trail east for 0.8 mile to Tater Knob Trail (104), which you take to your left (north). Tater Knob Trail climbs 0.8 mile to the parking lot for the Tater Knob fire tower at 1.6 miles. Just across the lot are steps leading up to the tower, the last one remaining in the Daniel Boone National Forest. The Civilian Conservation Corps built the 35-foot-high structure in 1934; lookouts used to live full-time in the 14-by-14-foot cabin at the top. Spotter aircraft eventually made towers of this type unnecessary, and this one was removed from service in the mid-1970s. Instead of being torn down, it was preserved and opened to the public until an arson fire damaged it in 2008. Tim Eling, Cumberland district ranger with the Daniel Boone National Forest, said officials hope to restore the tower in the coming years and reopen it to the public. At 1,388 feet above sea level, Tater Knob is the highest point in this part of Kentucky, and when the tower is open, visitors can enjoy a 360-degree view of the Cave Run Lake area, which on a clear day can extend 30 to 40 miles.

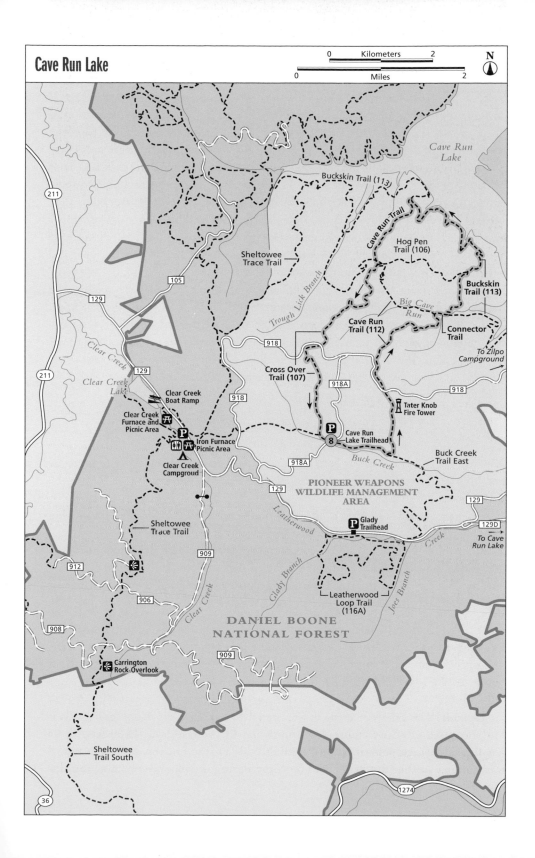

From the tower base, retrace your steps across the parking lot, and just south of it, go right (northwest) onto Cave Run Trail (112), marked initially by white and later by blue diamonds. The trail shadows the fire tower access road to FR 918, which it crosses and parallels north to gated FR 1058 at mile 2.3. Go around the gate, cross FR 1058, and continue following Cave Run Trail as it heads north away from the road and along a ridgetop. After providing a good view of the lake off to your right, the trail begins a series of switchbacks downward and, at mile 3.3, reaches a pleasant bottomland with several streams. Here Cave Run Trail heads northwest; take a short connector trail (108) east for 0.2 mile to Buckskin Trail (113). Take Buckskin Trail, marked by yellow diamonds, to the left (north), first making your way on stones across Big Cave Run and then climbing. After you pass the eastern terminus of Hog Pen Trail (106) on your left, Buckskin Trail enters a small field. Cross the field and begin descending east, then north toward the lake.

At mile 4.7 you arrive just above the lakeshore, which at this spot is likely to be muddy and uninviting. However, after jogging south to get around an inlet, Buckskin Trail comes to a stretch of shore firm enough to make a good stop for resting and swimming, although the rocks may be a bit hard on tender feet. The trail continues northwest along the lake and, after two more jogs to avoid inlets, connects at mile 6.6 with the north end of Cave Run Trail (112). Leave Buckskin Trail and take Cave Run Trail left (south) up an easy incline.

After reaching the top of a ridge, the trail crosses Hog Pen Trail (106) and immediately beyond, at mile 7.6, comes to an unmarked gravel road. The road, FR 1225, does double duty as Cross Over Trail (107), and you take it right (south) for 1.5 miles to paved FR 918. FR 1225 is level but not shaded, and in summer it's certain to be hot. Shortly before FR 918, you can take a path through the woods that cuts off the last bit of road walking.

Once you're at FR 918, go right (west) on the pavement for about 100 yards and look for a sign across the road marking the continuation of Cross Over Trail to the south. From here on, Cross Over Trail is an easy, pleasant path descending through the woods, most of it along a lovely little stream named Boardinghouse Branch. After crossing and recrossing the creek numerous times, you come into a field. At the far end is a path, which you take to the left (east). You are now back on Buck Creek Trail (118), and in several minutes arrive at FR 918A and your car.

Key Points

1.6 Fire tower. (Currently closed due to arson.)

4.7 Lakeshore.

Options: The hike can easily be shortened by taking Cave Run Trail (112) or Hog Pen Trail (106) west instead of continuing to the lakeshore. The hike can be lengthened by continuing west on Buckskin Trail (113) to Sheltowee Trace National Recreation Trail. See the Forest Service map covering the pioneer weapons area.

9 Leatherwood Creek

This pleasant, level walk in the woods mainly follows narrow roadbeds used by loggers.

Start: Glady Trailhead parking area on FR 129
Distance: 4.3-mile loop
Hiking time: About 2.5 hours
Difficulty: Easy
Best seasons: Any
Other trail users: Mountain bikers and equestrians
Canine compatibility: Dogs permitted
Land status: National forest
Nearest town: Morehead

Fees and permits: None
Maps: Cumberland Ranger District trail sheet for Leatherwood Loop Trail (116A); USGS Salt Lick
Trail contact: Morehead office, Cumberland Ranger District, Daniel Boone National Forest, (606) 784-6428
Parking and trailhead facilities: There's plenty of parking space and authorized no-fee primitive campsites.

Finding the trailhead: From exit 133 off I-64, take KY 801 south for about 3 miles to US 60 at the town of Farmers. Turn right (west) onto US 60, drive 4 miles to the town of Salt Lick, and turn left (south) onto KY 211. Take this road 3.7 miles and turn left (east) onto FR 129. In 2.5 miles, just after passing a sign for the boat ramp on man-made Clear Creek Lake, pass the Iron Furnace picnic area and continue for 3 miles to the sign for Glady Trailhead, the starting point of this hike. The sign is on the left side of the road, the gravel parking area on the right. GPS: N38 01.810' / W83 33.232'

The Hike

Some hikes reward you with a scenic overlook or an interesting landmark. This one, near Cave Run Lake and south of the pioneer weapons area, is just a pleasant walk in quiet woods. Instead of dramatic scenery, it offers solitude and an opportunity for reflection. Try it in the late afternoon when the sun's strength and your own energy level are winding down.

The entire hike is on Leatherwood Loop Trail (116A), a 4.3-mile loop that largely follows narrow old roadbeds left behind by loggers. The trail name comes from Leatherwood Creek, which parallels FR 129 and is just south of the parking area. After leaving your car, walk a few steps north across the gravel parking lot toward FR 129. Just before the road, you come to the trail, which is marked by white plastic diamond shapes on the trees. Take a right and walk east through the camping area. At mile 0.2, using rocks or a log, cross shallow Leatherwood Creek and angle southeast away from the road.

At mile 0.7 the path ends at a dirt-and-grass road running south from FR 129. Turn right onto this track. Just to the east you see little Joes Branch on its way to join Leatherwood Creek. This is pretty bottomland with an open forest of pines and hardwoods. The old road rises gradually, and at mile 1.1 you make a distinct right-hand

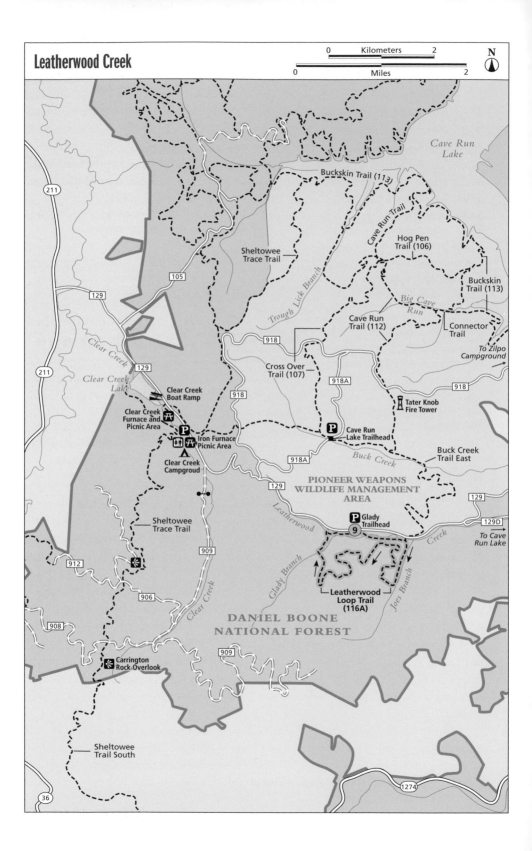

Leatherwood Creek

Kilometers 0 2
Miles 0 2

N

Cave Run Lake

Buckskin Trail (113)

Cave Run Trail

Hog Pen Trail (106)

Sheltowee Trace Trail

Buckskin Trail (113)

211

105

Trough Lick Branch

Big Cave Run

Cave Run Trail (112)

Connector Trail

129

To Zilpo Campground

Clear Creek

918

211

Clear Creek Lake

129

Cross Over Trail (107)

918A

918

Clear Creek Boat Ramp

918

Tater Knob Fire Tower

Clear Creek Furnace and Picnic Area

P

Iron Furnace Picnic Area

P Cave Run Lake Trailhead

Buck Creek Trail East

Clear Creek Campgroud

Buck Creek

918A

PIONEER WEAPONS WILDLIFE MANAGEMENT AREA

129

129

Sheltowee Trace Trail

Leatherwood

P Glady Trailhead

129

129D

909

9

To Cave Run Lake

912

Glady Branch

Joes Branch

Creek

906

Clear Creek

Leatherwood Loop Trail (116A)

DANIEL BOONE NATIONAL FOREST

908

Carrington Rock Overlook

909

Sheltowee Trail South

1274

36

turn west away from Joes Branch to climb steeply but briefly up the ridge side to a level area. Here the trail joins another old roadbed and begins a series of northbound and southbound legs as it takes you west along the ridge side above Leatherwood Creek. There are some ups and downs, but for the most part the trail follows a constant contour. The trail stays below the ridgetop so there are no views, but you'll see plenty of ferns and wildflowers.

Along the way you'll pass a pond built by the Forest Service for wildlife. As the trail heads west, it makes a number of hairpin turns around rock outcroppings. Where it uses cleared ground instead of old roads, the pathway can be faint. But as long as you keep your eye out for the diamond tree markers, you should have no trouble staying on track.

At mile 3.3 the trail starts to descend past several large rock formations into Dark Cave Hollow for the final leg north. This is another pleasant bottom area with inviting rest spots. After crossing and recrossing a feeder stream, you cross Glady Branch and take a right onto a dirt road that winds down into a meadow. At mile 4.0 the road (FR 914) crosses Leatherwood Creek and just beyond dead-ends at FR 129. Cross the creek on pilings, turn right (east), and follow the path back to the parking area.

Key Points

0.7 Joes Branch.

3.4 Dark Cave Hollow.

Southeastern Kentucky

W hen you think of Appalachia, you are thinking of southeastern Kentucky. This is the Kentucky of mountains, coal mining, Loretta Lynn, the Hatfield-McCoy feud, and, yes, poverty. It is the Kentucky that for decades has been alternately pitied and romanticized by the rest of the nation. When presidents and would-be presidents want to talk about helping the pockets of rural America left behind by progress and prosperity, they continue to come to the hollows of southeastern Kentucky. Photos of ramshackle houses inhabited by gap-toothed adults and poorly clad children are a staple of these whirlwind tours—and of the news media's attention.

As with most stereotypes, this one was based on some fact. For generations residents of this remote corner of the state were dependent on the coal industry's boom-and-bust cycle and the benevolence of government aid programs. With a good rain and only a few hours' warning, Mother Nature regularly sent families fleeing their creek-side communities. The steep grades and narrow ravines made modern highway travel only a dream.

But all of this is now changing, as any visitor today quickly realizes. Indeed, in recent years the old Appalachia has become increasingly hard to find. The decline of the state's coal industry is forcing economic diversification. Dams, flood walls, and modern highways—made possible largely through special federal funding secured by influential members of Congress from Kentucky and other Appalachian states—have mitigated Mother Nature's capriciousness. What has not changed is the area's striking geography. For the hiker the mountains of southeastern Kentucky offer the most dramatic scenic rewards to be found in any part of the state.

10 Breaks I-Park

Breathtaking views into the 1,000-foot-deep gorge known as the Breaks is the key reward of this hike. You also walk along the fast-moving stream that made the gorge eons ago.

Start: Towers Tunnel Overlook parking area in Breaks I-Park
Distance: 4.4-mile loop
Hiking time: About 3 hours
Difficulty: Moderate
Best seasons: Any
Other trail users: None
Canine compatibility: Leashed dogs permitted
Land status: Joint Virginia-Kentucky park
Nearest towns: Elkhorn City, KY; Haysi, VA
Fees and permits: None
Maps: Breaks I-Park trail map; USGS Elkhorn City

Trail contact: Breaks I-Park, (276) 865-4413
Parking and trailhead facilities: There's space for 20 cars. You'll find picnic tables at the trailhead, and there are restaurant and restroom facilities at the lodge complex 0.4 mile east on the park road. The visitor center, which has trail information and nature displays, is in a separate building across the road from the lodge complex. The park gates remain open all year, but many of the facilities—including the lodge, visitor center, and campground—are closed from mid-Dec through Mar.

Finding the trailhead: From Elkhorn City (which is about 23 miles southeast of Pikeville), take KY 80 east for 4 miles to the Virginia line and continue on the same road, now VA 80, for another 3 miles to the main Breaks I-Park entrance on your right. The park is in both states, but the developed portion is in Virginia. Take the main park road (VA 702, also called Commission Circle) past the park restaurant, lodge, and conference buildings and turn left into the Towers Tunnel Overlook parking area 1 mile from VA 80. The trailhead is at the far end of the lot, away from the road. (Don't be confused; there is a Towers Overlook 0.3 mile from the park entrance.) GPS: N38 17.189' / W82 18.216'

The Hike

Pine Mountain, one of Kentucky's most prominent land features, is a steep ridge running for 125 miles along the southeastern corner of the state. For generations it and the parallel ridge known as Cumberland Mountain formed a barrier that helped isolate the region. One of the few passes through Pine Mountain is a 5-mile-long gorge made by the Russell Fork of the Big Sandy River. This 1,000-foot-deep cut across the north end is named the Breaks—because it's a break in the ridge.

In the early 1900s the Clinchfield Railroad took advantage of nature's handiwork by constructing a rail line through the Breaks, on the western side just above the stream. This engineering marvel, which includes two tunnels within the gorge, is still in use today as part of the CSX system. Indeed, any hike in the Breaks is certain to be accompanied by the plaintive whistle of locomotives pulling long lines of coal-filled cars.

The view of the Breaks from the Stateline Overlook is especially stunning at sunset.

Beyond its interest as a transportation link, the gorge is impressive for its rugged scenery. "The Grand Canyon of the South" is the promotional tag used in the Breaks I-Park brochure. Park personnel call it the largest canyon east of the Mississippi. The Kentucky-Virginia border runs along Pine Mountain, and in 1954 the two states created the jointly operated park to showcase this unique area. The 4,600-acre park is well maintained and has paved roads, a small water park, a 12-acre fishing lake, a 122-site campground open March through October, and about 10 miles of relatively short hiking trails.

This hike combines several park trails to make a loop that includes both vistas from the top of the gorge and a visit to Russell Fork at the bottom. The stream has a number of rapids and is popular for rafting. This loop route is entirely in Virginia.

From the Towers Tunnel Overlook parking area, take yellow-blazed Towers Tunnel Trail south, passing first a path on your left that leads to a picnic shelter and then the beginning of Prospectors Trail on your right. At mile 0.2 you reach the overlook and get a good view south across the Breaks. Just below, you can see the train tracks and, farther to your left, the opening of Towers Tunnel, one of the two railroad tunnels in the gorge. The Towers is a 600-foot-tall hunk of sandstone that juts out from Pine Mountain into Russell Fork. The rock was too hard for the water to cut through and so the railroad, accomplishing what the stream could not, dug a 921-foot-long tunnel to avoid the obstruction.

From the overlook, retrace your steps to Prospectors Trail at 0.3 mile. The trail descends gently as it parallels the rim of the gorge above. Be especially careful if it has been raining: This mud path can be slippery. There are a few switchbacks, but much of the orange-blazed Prospectors Trail is level. At mile 1.1 the Prospectors Trail intersects the River Trail, a narrower path that winds down toward Russell Fork. Turn left onto the blue-blazed River Trail and shortly come to a large rock on your right that makes an unofficial overlook and a good rest stop. There is no fence, however, so be careful with children. As you get nearer to the stream, the trail becomes steeper and more difficult. Make sure to follow the blue squares painted on trees; there are several unmarked paths off River Trail.

Just above Russell Fork, River Trail turns right, and an unmarked path on your left drops steeply down the bank to the water's edge. This side trail is short (less than 0.1 mile) but difficult; at one point you have to climb over rocks. Nevertheless, several large rocks reaching out into the rapids offer an attractive lunch spot.

Returning to River Trail, head north on level ground, paralleling Russell Fork through a hardwood forest full of mountain laurel and ferns. At mile 2.0, after skirting the base of a tall cliff, you pass another side trail to the water, this one an easy 20 feet in length and worth taking. The stream here is churning through another set of rapids, and there are rocks along the shoreline from which to watch the action.

At mile 2.1 the River Trail ends just above the spot where Grassy Creek empties into Russell Fork. Here you turn right onto yellow-blazed Grassy Creek Trail and follow the creek upstream. The trail climbs, makes a sharp right turn to the southeast, and levels off before meeting Laurel Branch Trail at mile 2.4. Take the red-blazed Laurel Branch Trail right (south) and begin a steady climb back up the gorge wall; this is the most strenuous part of the hike.

At mile 3.0, shortly beyond the other end of Prospectors Trail, turn right onto Geological Trail and take this short, easy path up to the Stateline Overlook parking lot at the top of the gorge; you gain the final bit of elevation on wooden steps. Geological Trail and a companion path named Ridge Trail are self-guided nature trails; a pamphlet explaining plants, rock formations, and other features along these two paths is sold at the visitor center.

From the parking lot, a paved path leads out to the Stateline Overlook at mile 3.4. The overlook is so named because you are looking northwest into both states. Just below you is the 1,523-foot-long Stateline Tunnel, the second of the two railroad tunnels; the large window you see in the rock marks the tunnel's midway point.

From Stateline Overlook, follow the green-blazed Overlook Trail as it heads south along the edge of the gorge rim and past a number of rocky lookout points with excellent views. Watch small children; it's straight down. You are also walking at times along the park road (VA 702). After passing a large outcropping called Pinnacle Rock (fenced off and decorated with No Climbing signs), you reach the parking area for Clinchfield Overlook at mile 4.1; the walk out to the overlook itself is 0.1 mile one-way. At 1,920 feet this overlook is the park's highest observation point, though the view is of what you have already seen. Continuing south along the road, you reach your car at mile 4.4.

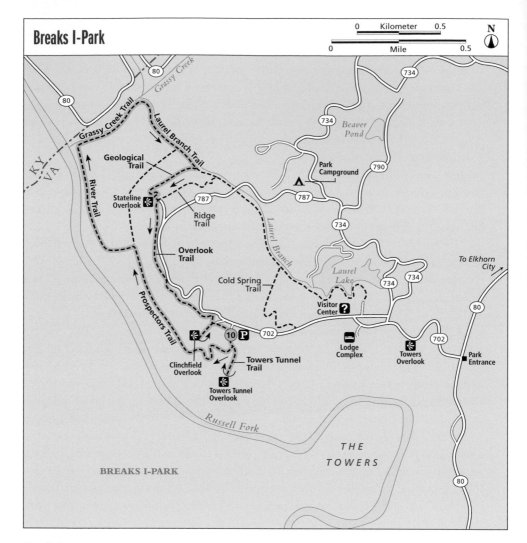

Key Points

- **0.2** Towers Tunnel Overlook.
- **0.3** Prospectors Trail.
- **1.1** River Trail.
- **2.1** Grassy Creek Trail.
- **2.4** Laurel Branch Trail.
- **3.0** Geological Trail.
- **3.4** Stateline Overlook and Overlook Trail.
- **4.2** Clinchfield Overlook.

Options: For a short walk in the park, take Cold Spring Trail to Laurel Branch Trail, a distance of 0.5 mile. You can then either turn right for Laurel Lake or turn left and take Ridge Trail up to the Stateline Overlook.

11 Lilley Cornett Woods

Accompanied by a guide, tour a stand of hardwood trees said to be the largest remaining old-growth forest in eastern Kentucky.

Start: Lilley Cornett Woods visitor center (actual hike starts at log cabin)
Distance: 2.4-mile loop
Hiking time: About 2 hours
Difficulty: Moderate
Best seasons: Apr through Oct
Other trail users: None
Canine compatibility: No dogs allowed
Land status: State-owned forest
Nearest towns: Whitesburg, Hazard
Fees and permits: An escort, provided free of charge, is mandatory.
Maps: USGS Tilford and Roxana
Trail contact: Lilley Cornett Woods, (606) 633-5828

Special considerations: Access to this state-owned forest is by guided tour only. Guided tours are not regularly scheduled, but are available on a first-come, first-served basis from 8:30 a.m. to 5 p.m. daily Apr through Oct. Although reservations are not required, visitors are encouraged to call ahead to make them. Tours are conducted by appointment only Nov through Mar.
Parking and trailhead facilities: There's space for numerous cars; restrooms, water, and nature displays are found in the visitor center. There are no camping facilities.

Finding the trailhead: From Whitesburg, the Letcher County seat, take KY 15 northwest for 8 miles and turn left (west) onto KY 7. Take KY 7 for 13 miles and turn left (south) onto KY 1103. In 7.5 miles, turn left at the sign for Lilley Cornett Woods and park in front of the visitor center. A guide will lead you by car from the visitor center to the trailhead. (The distance from Hazard is about the same. From Hazard, take KY 15 south to KY 7. Turn right onto KY 7 and take it to KY 1103.) GPS: N37 05.213' / W82 59.609'

The Hike

As is apparent to anyone who has done much hiking in Kentucky, the state has been heavily logged. This hike gives you a chance to step back in time and experience the forest as it was in pioneer days. Lilley Cornett Woods contains the largest parcel of old-growth forest in eastern Kentucky, with trees as old as 400 to 500 years. At the visitor center, a display dramatizes this point with a section of an ancient white oak. The tree's annual rings are labeled with important contemporary events—the ring made in 1685, for example, coincided with the birth of composer J. S. Bach.

Lilley Cornett was a local man who began acquiring land along the Line Fork shortly after World War I. Over the years he refused to sell the trees on his property for timber, and after his death his children sought a buyer who would continue to protect them. In 1969, with funding help from the Nature Conservancy and the US Department of the Interior, the state bought the 554 acres of mixed mesophytic

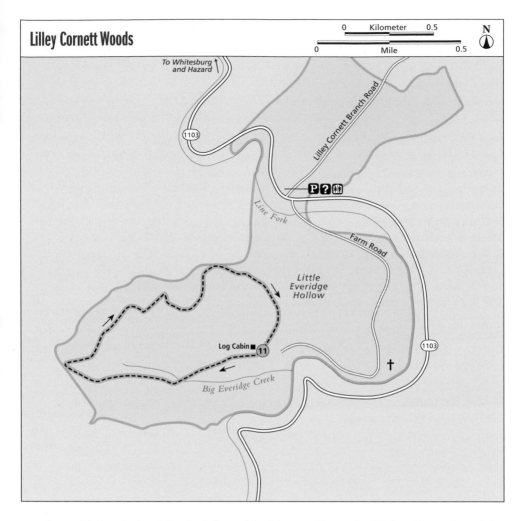

forest. Today the land is administered by Eastern Kentucky University and used for forest research. About half of the acreage, including the portion visited in this hike, has never been logged and contains trees of varying ages and types, including hickories, white oaks, and beeches. It also has more than 500 kinds of flowering plants; there are an estimated 700 pairs of breeding birds here, including red-shouldered hawks and barred owls.

The term for what you see is old-growth forest, not virgin forest. The latter refers to woods that are unaffected by human activities of all kinds, not just logging. As is true across Appalachia, the bottomlands here were cultivated, and cows and pigs used to graze in the forest—activities that no doubt influenced the woods' growth. But while not technically pristine, Lilley Cornett Woods comes close enough. The forest is a registered national landmark and natural area of the Society of American Foresters.

After signing in at the visitor center, you are assigned a guide. You have a choice between a shorter hike, estimated at 2 hours, described here and a longer, 4-hour hike. Visitors are encouraged to call ahead. The trails are not blazed, and there are no signs or mileage markers.

The longer hike goes up Big Everidge Hollow, parallels the ridgetop, and comes down Little Everidge Hollow. The start is across KY 1103 at an old log cabin near Line Fork—a drive of a little more than a mile from the visitor center on an unpaved farm road. Your guide may go with you in your car. The road is gated to keep out unescorted visitors. The purpose of the security is to prevent fire, vandalism, wild-flower digging, and camping. Instruments used in research, such as stream-flow mea-suring devices, are left in the woods.

From the log cabin, you walk west on a mowed path, cross Big Everidge Creek at mile 0.3, and climb, though not steeply, to a rock outcropping just below the ridgetop at mile 0.9. There are a few limited views across KY 1103 but no real vistas. The focus of this hike is trees, and along the way my guide pointed out a number of old ones, which were estimated to be about 400 years old.

The hike parallels the ridgetop eastward along the boundary with a privately owned parcel. After starting down Little Everidge Hollow at mile 1.7, there is a series of switchbacks and the trail passes through hemlocks before coming back out at the log cabin at mile 2.4.

Key Points

0.9   Head of Big Everidge Hollow.

1.7   Head of Little Everidge Hollow.

12 Bad Branch

The bare-rock crest of Pine Mountain provides spectacular vistas to the north. You also visit a 60-foot waterfall on this walk through a little-known preserve on the state's southeastern edge.

Start: Parking area for Bad Branch State Nature Preserve
Distance: 7.2-mile lollipop
Hiking time: About 5 hours
Difficulty: Moderate
Best seasons: Any
Other trail users: None
Canine compatibility: No dogs allowed
Land status: State nature preserve
Nearest town: Whitesburg

Fees and permits: None
Maps: Kentucky State Nature Preserves Commission trail map for Bad Branch State Nature Preserve; USGS Whitesburg
Trail contact: Kentucky State Nature Preserves Commission, (502) 573-2886
Parking and trailhead facilities: There's space for about 15 cars, but no facilities. The lot is on a busy road; leave valuables at home.

Finding the trailhead: From Whitesburg at the intersection of US 119 and KY 15, take US 119 south over Pine Mountain. In 7.2 miles, turn left (east) onto KY 932 (Flat Gap Road). After 1.7 miles, turn into the gravel parking area on the left side of the road. The trailhead is at the edge of the parking area. GPS: N37 04.058' / W82 46.309'

The Hike

The 2,639-acre Bad Branch State Nature Preserve is one of the prettiest hiking spots in eastern Kentucky, just outside the Whitesburg area. Bad Branch, a designated Kentucky Wild River, is a clear stream flowing down the south side of Pine Mountain. It empties into the Poor Fork of the Cumberland River just below the parking area. On this hike you follow Bad Branch upstream part of the way as you climb Pine Mountain to a sandstone cliff known as High Rock. From this big slab of rock on top of the mountain, you have excellent views north of Whitesburg and the valley cut by the North Fork of the Kentucky River. On the way up you pass a short side path to a lovely spot where Bad Branch takes a 60-foot plunge over a cliff. The surrounding forest, last logged in the 1940s, is full of wildflowers, ferns, and rhododendrons. Don't miss this hike.

This is a lollipop-shaped route—a loop at the end of a straight out-and-back trail. From the trailhead, walk northeast on an old road and immediately come to a roofed bulletin board with a map and a history of the preserve. Continuing north, cross Bad Branch, cut through a grove of old-growth hemlocks that escaped the loggers, and recross the stream, putting it once again on your right. Paralleling the stream, you begin to climb and, at mile 0.7, come to a path on your right that leads to the base

Bad Branch tumbles 60 feet down the side of Pine Mountain to form the falls.

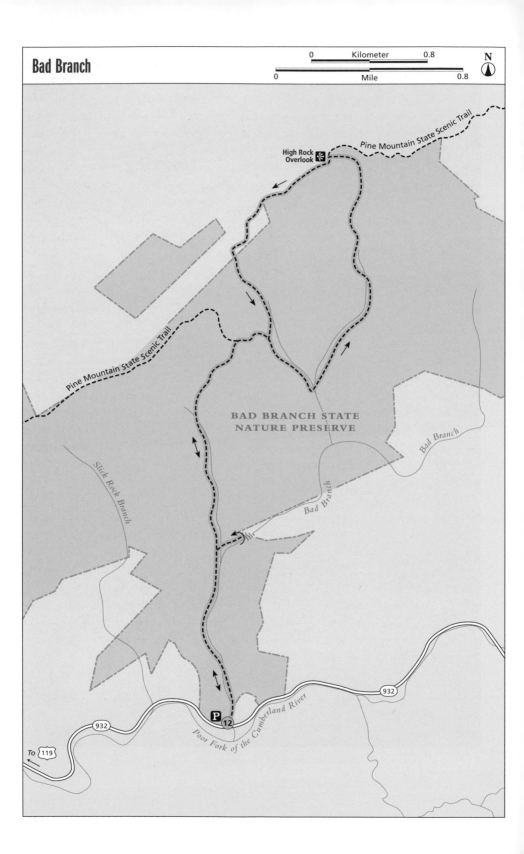

Bad Branch

0   Kilometer   0.8

0   Mile   0.8

N

High Rock
Overlook

Pine Mountain State Scenic Trail

Pine Mountain State Scenic Trail

BAD BRANCH STATE
NATURE PRESERVE

Slick Rock Branch

Bad Branch

Bad Branch

932

932

P 12

Poor Fork of the Cumberland River

To 119

of the falls. This side trail, which is marked by a sign, goes down to a ravine and then climbs steeply through rocks before dropping to the base of the falls at mile 0.9. The cascading water makes a refreshing shower, and there are large rocks for lounging. The trail does not go up to the top of the falls, and you should be extra careful to stay on the trail—for your own safety and to protect the rare plants growing near the falls.

After retracing your steps to the main trail, continue climbing to the north. The trail, which is now blazed with orange squares, becomes narrower as you proceed up the hollow through an increasingly thick forest of hardwoods and young hemlocks. At several points you pass into what is literally a tunnel through thick rhododendrons.

At mile 2.2 you reach a high point and begin descending to the start of the loop portion at mile 2.6. Shortly before the beginning of the loop, the trail turns abruptly from east to north and is an easy spot to get turned around. This turn is at GPS N37 05.508' / W82 46.250'. On the way down to the beginning of the loop, you will go over a small rock outcropping and curve around a large boulder. Just below the boulder, the trail dead-ends into an old logging road; this is the start of the loop, and from here the trail is easily followed.

The shortest route to the top of Pine Mountain is left on the old road; it's only 0.6 mile to the cliff overlook. But I suggest going right so you take the longer portion when you are fresher. After turning right (southeast), you follow the road for only a short distance before the trail veers off right into the woods. At mile 3.0, after crossing two arms of Bad Branch in rapid succession, turn left onto a pleasant old roadbed and go northeast, with the stream on your left. At mile 3.5 the road forks to the right and the trail turns left to cross the stream. It shortly joins with another old road heading north up the hollow. After narrowing again, the trail traverses open woods and climbs steeply to reach the cliff known as High Rock atop Pine Mountain at mile 4.2.

From here you have a panorama to the north that includes Whitesburg and the palisades made by the North Fork of the Kentucky River. For a picture of southeastern Kentucky's rough geography, this one can't be beat. Needless to say, it's a dangerous spot. Use caution.

From the overlook the trail ducks briefly into the woods and comes out again on the cliff. Walking over flat slabs of stone, follow the cliff edge southwest 0.2 mile before turning farther south and descending steeply to an old roadbed. Turn left onto the roadbed and continue descending to the south, but more gently. At mile 5.0 you are back at the beginning of the loop, where you turn right and retrace your steps down the hollow to your car.

Key Points

- **0.7** Side trail to falls.
- **0.9** Falls.
- **2.6** Beginning of loop.
- **4.2** Top of Pine Mountain.

13 Pine Mountain Trail Highland Section

This strenuous hike along the sawtooth ridge of Pine Mountain offers sweeping 360-degree views of the Cumberland Highlands.

Start: Parking behind gas station along US 23 at Pound Gap, VA

Distance: 14.7-mile shuttle

Hiking time: About 12 hours; overnight

Difficulty: Strenuous

Best season: Any

Other trail users: None

Canine compatibility: Mixed. Leashed dogs allowed on portions of trail in Jefferson National Forest; dogs not allowed on portions of trail on Nature Conservancy and Kentucky State Nature Preserve lands

Land status: National forest, state nature preserve, Nature Conservancy

Nearest town: Jenkins (north), Whitesburg (south)

Fees and permits: None

Maps: Maps available for download at pinemountaintrail.org/maps. Be sure to download Highland Section packet, which includes topographic maps, trail elevation profiles, and other information.

Trail contact: Pine Mountain State Scenic Trail Conference, pinemountaintrail.org

Special considerations: The weather can be unpredictable on Pine Mountain. The sandstone formations can become slick in rain and ice, so use caution when traversing exposed areas of the trail. Pay attention to your footing in cliff areas. Bears are plentiful on Pine Mountain. Cooking should not be done in camping areas, and food should be properly stored and hung at night.

Parking and trailhead facilities: The gas stations allow use of their facilities, which include restrooms and a small picnic shelter. Make sure to advise an employee if you plan to leave your car overnight. There is room for about a dozen cars in the area behind the gas stations. Parking is also allowed in a grassy field. Be careful to remove all valuables from your car or place them out of sight. GPS: N37 09.224' / W82 37.918'

Finding the trailhead: To leave the shuttle car, from Pikeville, follow US 23/119 south for 30 miles. From the right-hand lane, merge onto US 119N/US 119S toward Whitesburg / Harlan, continuing on US 119 south. In 10.5 miles turn left to continue on US 119 south. In 1.7 miles take a slight right turn onto US 119 south. In 3.4 miles, at the top of the mountain, turn right into a gravel parking lot at Little Shepherd Trail. Trailhead is located directly across the highway.

To get to the starting trailhead, from Pikeville, follow US 23/119 south for 31 miles. At Pound Gap, the border of Virginia and Kentucky, there is a gas station; park behind it. The trail begins at the southwest corner of the parking lot. GPS: N37 07.627' / W82 81.032'

The Hike

This hike is the most scenic in the book in terms of the panoramic vistas it affords hikers. The Highland Section of the Pine Mountain State Scenic Trail (PMT) is very reminiscent of the Appalachian Trail, in that it traverses the ridgeline and requires a bit of rock scrambling—at one point it involves the aid of three metal handholds on a rock face.

Pine Mountain's forests are one of the last unfragmented stretches in the western Appalachians, and the mountain is also home to a number of rare highland bogs. The completed Highland Section of the planned 42-mile PMT offers commanding views into Virginia and Kentucky, from the highest elevations on Pine Mountain. The trail is also rich in history. Native Americans traversed the top of Pine Mountain centuries before white settlers came to America. Later the mountain played an important role in the settlement of Kentucky and was the site of several Civil War skirmishes.

The Highland Section covers Pine Mountain between US 23 and US 119, two of only six roads that cross the mountain. This hike begins at the trail's intersection of US 23, on the southwest side of the road behind a gas station. The trail's signature bright green reflective blazes are visible on a post from the parking lot, as is a kiosk just at the edge of the woods behind the businesses. This is the boundary of the Jefferson National Forest. You are in Virginia. The trail stays on the Virginia side of the mountain for its first 7.7 miles.

The single-track dirt trail immediately passes the kiosk with a map and trail information before passing through a wooden gate that is meant to keep four-wheelers off the trail. The Red Fox Trail splits off here after 0.1 mile.

The trail immediately begins its 500-foot climb out of Pound Gap, which was at 2,367 feet. By the time you reach Windy Gap, 0.7 mile later, you've climbed to 2,798 feet. Here the trail goes from single track out onto a graveled Forest Service road; take a left, following the trail south for less than 0.1 mile before it turns right and goes back into the woods. Immediately you come to a power-line clearing that gives you the first views of the surrounding misty-topped mountains.

The trail then descends gradually all the way to the Jack Sautter Campsite, which you reach at mile 1.3. The site has four marked tent sites with pads, a permanent fire ring, and a bear pole. A short 0.2-mile side trail here leads you to a highland bog. The bog is one of the biggest on the mountain and is home to a variety of wildflowers, including cardinal flowers, arrow arum, cinnamon ferns, and sweet william.

Climbing out of the campsite, you reach the Twin Cliffs Overlook at mile 2.2 before descending and then climbing again over the next 1.8 miles to an unnamed peak at mile 3.0 that is just over 3,000 feet high. The trail passes through an area here that was heavily damaged in a forest fire. Evidence is abundant, from the charred trunks of trees to the sparse vegetation that is just starting to come back on the forest floor. This section of the trail is heavily wooded with poplars, hickories, oaks, sugar maples, and a variety of other hardwoods.

This section of the trail uses the old Fincastle Trail, which was the original horse trail route from Kentucky into Virginia. It was the second road that Kentucky ever levied a tax to build, according to Pine Mountain Trail Conference president Shad Barker, who is also one of the trail's founders. It was along this stretch of the road, too, that the Mullins Massacre occurred in 1892. Dr. Marshall Benton Taylor, dubbed the Red Fox of the Mountain by author John Fox Jr., and two hired accomplices ambushed the Mullins family, killing four of its members. The shooting stemmed from a feud between Taylor, who was once a lawman, and Ira Mullins, the family patriarch and a well-known moonshiner. Taylor was later hanged for the crime.

At mile 4.3 you reach Indian Grave Gap at 2,595 feet. Here a small semicircle of stones in a low mound mark the grave, which was long ago looted. After a brief but steep 0.5-mile climb—the hardest on the trail—you reach the Indian Grave Campsite at mile 4.8. Tent sites and a water source, marked with blue blazes, are here.

The trail continues climbing, passing Bob Simon's Cave and Hogg Rock before dropping into Bear Track Gap, at 2,865 feet at mile 5.7. Bob Simon was a moonshiner who was caught distilling the illegal spirit inside the large rock house here by Letcher County sheriff Maynard Hogg. From here the trail continues to climb, occasionally dropping into a small gap. After Bear Track Gap, the trail follows an old roadbed then passes over a gas line, which will reappear shortly on your right along the side of the trail, where it will continue for about 0.1 mile.

Be aware of trail markers along this stretch. You will not walk more than 0.1 mile without seeing the hallmark bright green reflective blazes. There are some short sections here—a few dozen feet—that are marked with pink plastic tape, as they can easily become overgrown. At mile 6.3 the trail becomes steeper and follows a rocky drain. At mile 6.6 it quickly turns right and heads into the woods. The intersection is marked with two bright green blazes.

The trail then begins to descend down to the Adena Spring Shelter, which you reach at mile 6.9. The Adena Spring Shelter sleeps twelve and is a two-story, three-sided shelter. A moldering toilet is located here, along with a covered picnic table, fire ring, and bear pole. There are two reliable water sources a short distance away. The first is a small spring at the base of a rock house 0.1 mile farther along the trail, while the second is a stream located another 0.1 mile beyond. In dry weather you may have to travel a distance down the stream to find moving water. A filter is recommended.

After leaving the water source, the trail climbs steadily until you reach the State Line Knob at mile 7.7. The knob is at an elevation of 3,206 feet. From here to the intersection with US 119, the trail is in Kentucky and views on both sides of the ridgeline are of Letcher County.

Over the next several miles, the trail gains and loses small amounts of elevation as you traverses the most scenic ridgeline area of the Highland Section. At mile 8.3 you reach Cohen Gap, where you will see blue blazes marking the boundary of the Nature Conservancy. Be sure to pay attention to the green blazes marking the PMT. Hikers have become confused in this area.

At mile 8.4 you reach Mayking Knob, the highest elevation of Pine Mountain and, sadly, the site of a WIFX Radio Letcher County broadcasting tower and a number of outbuildings. Just at the edge of the outbuildings, the trail descends steeply down a rocky ledge, which requires the use of three metal handholds bored into the rock, at the bottom in Lost John Gap.

The Pine Mountain Trail traverses the steep upper slopes of the mountain.

After less than 0.1 mile, you come to an old tower that has been lashed to the side of the mountain. The tower now serves as a ladder that allows you to descend over the east side of the ridge here to a small campsite at the base of a rock house, Jump Rock Camp. I stayed here on a previous trip with some campers and found the site to be a lovely place for an evening. There are ample campsites along a Forest Service road, which descends for 1.5 miles to the small hamlet of Mayking.

Continuing on the PMT, you reach Slip & Slide Rock at mile 8.9. The large sandstone rock slab is so named because it rests at approximately a 45-degree angle and is covered in lichens, which are slick even when not damp. Pay attention to your footing on this section. If you are brave, climb to the top of the rock for your first sweeping vistas north and west into Letcher County.

The trail then ducks back into the woods for about 0.1 mile before reemerging along another steep angled rock. Again the 360-degree views from here are magnificent. Be careful, though, as the rock is slippery and the sandstone cliff edge of Pine Mountain drops steeply for hundreds of feet below you to the northwest.

At mile 9.2 you reach the Swindall Campsite and Box Rock. The site, tucked into the cliff line, has room for one large or two small tents. The PMT heads back into the woods for 0.3 mile before continuing to follow the ridgeline. A wide access road joins the trail here, but be careful not to follow it down the mountain. After 0.2 mile the PMT takes a hard left turn onto a single-track path, and in another 0.2 mile comes back out onto the ridgeline, where there are again sweeping views.

The trail here is thick with low serviceberry bushes, which were weighted down with fruit on my visit in July. There was evidence along the trail that the area's ample population of black bears were also enjoying the tasty berries. The High Rock Trail joins the PMT in this area, appearing seemingly out of nowhere. Together the trails gradually descend and reach Mar's Rock at mile 10.5. This is another area where the trail traverses rocks, and careful footing is required.

After 0.1 mile the trail heads back into the woods, then comes back out to the rocky cliff line at mile 10.7 at High Rock. Again the views north across the Cumberlands are sweeping from the cliff line here. The community of Whitesburg is visible in the distance, and the community of Mayking is directly below you. On a clear day the communications tower on top of Black Mountain is visible to the south.

The trail follows the ridgeline another 0.3 mile before it begins its descent to meet Bad Branch. At mile 11.4 there is another junction with the High Rock Trail. (The Bad Branch hike, described elsewhere in this book, is a shorter, loop trail that takes hikers to the ridgeline of Pine Mountain and its spectacular views of the Cumberland Highlands.) The High Rock Trail forks and continues to follow Bad Branch downhill to the southeast before turning back northward and rejoining the PMT on the ridgeline near Mar's Rock. The other fork and the PMT make a right turn and continue heading southwest, immediately climbing away from Bad Branch. At mile 11.6 the High Rock Trail turns away to the south and continues 1.9 miles past Bad Branch Falls to the parking lot along KY 932.

A sign at this junction indicates US 119 is 3.2 miles away on the Pine Mountain Trail. From here the trail climbs and then descends, then climbs again to reach the Lemon Squeezer at mile 12.4. Here the trail passes through a narrow gap between two large parallel sandstone boulders, the space between them not wide enough to pass through wearing a backpack.

Another climb brings you to the Blueberry Cliffs at mile 13.2. The trail then descends sharply over the next 0.3 mile, passing over exposed sandstone before climbing 0.2 mile and then descending again over the next 0.2 mile to reach Eagle Arch at mile 13.9.

At mile 14.0 you reach a set of stairs and a sign-in box. The trail then descends down a wide track for the next 0.3 mile. At mile 14.3 you reach the Flamingo Shelter. Identical to the Adena Shelter in design, it sleeps twelve. There is no toilet here. The trail then makes a slight descent, curving northward before turning southwest, and gradually climbs to reach US 119 at mile 14.7.

Key Points

1.3 Jack Sautter Campsite.

4.8 Indian Grave Campsite.

Pine Mountain Trail Highland Section

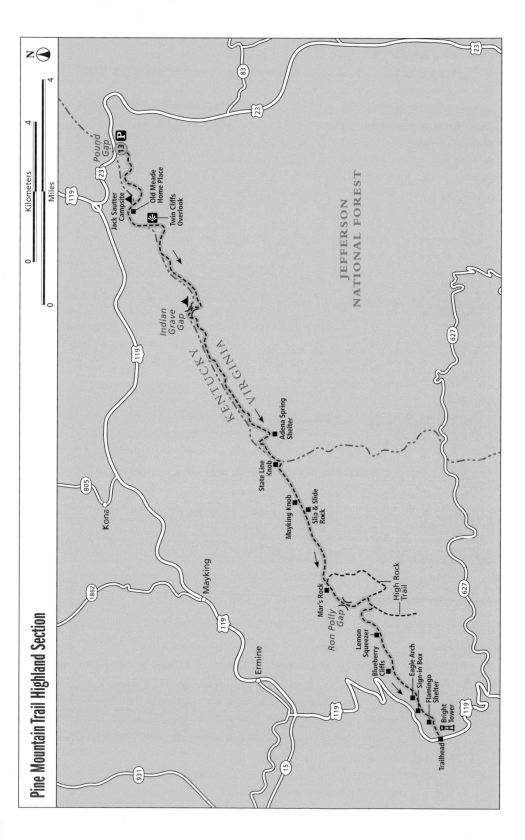

N

Kilometers
0   4

Miles
0   4

Pound Gap

Jack Sautter Campsite

Old Meade Home Place

Twin Cliffs Overlook

Indian Grave Gap

KENTUCKY

VIRGINIA

Adena Spring Shelter

State Line Knob

Mayking Knob

Slip & Slide Rock

Kona

Mayking

Ermine

Mar's Rock

Ron Polly Gap

High Rock Trail

Lemon Squeezer

Blueberry Cliffs

Eagle Arch

Sign-in Box

Flamingo Shelter

Bright Tower

Trailhead

JEFFERSON NATIONAL FOREST

6.9   Adena Spring Shelter.

7.7   State Line Knob.

8.5   Mayking Knob.

8.9   Slip & Slide Rock.

9.2   Box Rock and Swindall Campsite (room for one large or two small tents).

10.5   Mar's Rock.

10.7   High Rock.

12.4   Lemon Squeezer.

13.9   Eagle Arch.

14.3   Flamingo Shelter.

Options: For a longer trip, hike an adjoining section of the Pine Mountain Trail. The Birch Knob Section of the PMT begins at Breaks I-Park. This 26-mile section travels along a network of old logging roads and single-track trail. At its midpoint is Birch Knob, the site of an overnight shelter. The section ends at Pound Gap on US 23 along the Virginia-Kentucky border. Or continue south from the Highland Section to Kingdom Come Park, where the trail runs 14 miles along the paved yet seldom-traveled Little Shepherd Trail (LST) to the Black Bear Shelter in the park. The LST continues another 24 miles, without designated camping or shelters, to US 421 at the Cumberland Gap.

SIDE TRIP: PINE MOUNTAIN AND LITERATURE

While in the area, stop by the June Tolliver Playhouse in the historic district of Big Stone Gap, Virginia. The outdoor amphitheater seats approximately 400 people and is known for its production of *The Trail of the Lonesome Pine*. The longest continually running outdoor drama in the country—it began in 1964—and the official outdoor drama of Virginia, the story was made famous in the early 1900s by novelist John Fox Jr., a Big Stone Gap resident who was born in Kentucky.

It tells the love story of the theater's namesake, June Tolliver, described as a "lovely mountain girl," and geologist Jack Hale from the East. The musical drama depicts the discovery of coal and iron ore in the mountains and the effect it had on the mountain people's way of life.

Performances run from late June through late August on Thursday, Friday, and Saturday nights. Visit trailofthelonesomepine.com for more information, or contact the center at (276) 523-1235.

14 Raven Rock

A climb to the top of a large sandstone rock on Pine Mountain offers great views across the ridgetops to the southeast.

Start: Parking lot near Kingdom Come State Park visitor center
Distance: 2.3-mile loop
Hiking time: About 1.5 hours
Difficulty: Easy
Best seasons: Any
Other trail users: Short section of hike is on a lightly traveled mountain road open to motorists and mountain bikers
Canine compatibility: Leashed dogs permitted
Land status: State park

Nearest town: Cumberland
Fees and permits: None
Maps: Kingdom Come State Park trail guide; USGS Benham
Trail contact: Kingdom Come State Park, (606) 589-2479
Parking and trailhead facilities: There's a large parking area adjacent to the visitor center, restrooms, a telephone, and a miniature golf course. The park picnic area, where camping is allowed, is nearby.

Finding the trailhead: From Whitesburg on US 119, take the first Cumberland exit and drive toward Cumberland a short distance to Park Road on the right. Take Park Road up Pine Mountain for 1.3 miles and turn left at the sign for the lake and hiking trails. The trailhead is next to the lake at the end of the parking lot. (From Harlan on US 119, take KY 160 into the center of Cumberland, then Kingdom Come Drive 0.5 mile to Park Road on your left.) GPS: N36 59.364' / W82 59.104'

The Hike

Raven Rock is a 290-foot-tall hunk of sandstone that sticks up out of Kingdom Come State Park near the top of Pine Mountain. From the rock's sloping top, there is an excellent view across the ridges to the southwest. This hike then takes you up to the crest of Pine Mountain and several good overlooks to the north. Also, keep a lookout for black bears. Kentucky has a growing number of the critters, and in recent years sightings have become more frequent on Pine Mountain, particularly in Kingdom Come State Park.

The 1,238-acre park, which bills itself as Kentucky's highest, is undeveloped as state parks go; there is no lodge, marina, or even a campground (primitive camping is allowed in the picnic area). But it is a park, and this is no walk in the wilderness. It is, rather, a relaxing stroll over a series of short, easy trails with rewarding panoramas along the way—perfect for families with small children or an evening outing. The park's name comes from the title of a novel popular in the early 1900s, *The Little Shepherd of Kingdom Come*. The author, John Fox Jr. (1863–1919), was a Kentuckian, and the book deals with Kentucky mountain life and the Civil War.

More than a dozen short trails weave in and around Raven Rock. This hike cobbles together several to make a loop that hits most of the high spots (figuratively and

The Little Shepherd Trail is a spectacular scenic drive to add to a day hike in the region.

literally). Kingdom Come experienced two forest fires in 2014 and 2015, and parts of the park have been affected. On the route described here, you will notice some evidence of charring and fire breaks in vegetation that firefighters installed to stop the flames. Park manager Rick Fuller says those fire breaks should soon be revegetated.

From the edge of the parking lot next to the small lake, take gravel Lake Trail to the east end of the lake, turn left onto the gravel road, and go west a short distance along the lake's north edge. At mile 0.1 turn right onto a stone path going uphill to a sign for Laurel Trail.

On Laurel Trail climb gently north to a fork at mile 0.3. Here Pine Trail goes right to a playground; go left on Powerline Trail. After wiggling northward in an easy ascent through thin woods, you come out at mile 0.5 on a rock slab next to a utility pole and under a power line—hence the trail name. This is a section of Raven Rock but not the top. Nonetheless, you get a great view into the valley south of Pine Mountain. On the early morning that I visited, a low white cloud blanketed the valley bottom, making a beautiful sight.

From here follow Raven Rock Trail east across the slab and duck into a wooded area of pines and mountain laurel. After descending slightly you pass Possum Trail on the left, cross two small bridges, and come to a wall of rock. This is Raven Rock just below its highest point, and when I was there the stone was marred with painted graffiti—a constant problem, according to park personnel.

Go east along the rock, climb a set of wooden steps, and follow a sign directing you right to a scenic viewpoint, which you reach at mile 0.8. This is the top of Raven Rock. Be careful and keep a close eye on young children. The rock tilts at a 45-degree angle toward the south, and the north side is a straight drop-off. On a far ridge to the southwest, you can see a "high wall" of exposed rock left by a strip mine, a method of extracting coal that has left lasting scars across Appalachia. Federal law now requires mine operators to cover all high walls, but many sites mined before the law's 1977 passage have not been reclaimed. To the southeast is 4,145-foot Black Mountain, the state's tallest.

Back at the sign, continue east 0.1 mile to a fork, unmarked when I was there. Take the left prong, which is Saltress Trail, and climb gently over a rise and then down to a paved road. This is Little Shepherd Trail (KY 1679), a rough, scenic route along the crest of Pine Mountain from Whitesburg to Harlan. It's lightly traveled but open to vehicles and mountain bikers. On your right a road forks right off Little Shepherd Trail and goes downhill through the picnic area, past the lake, and to the park entrance.

Turn left (west) onto Little Shepherd Trail and ascend to a short side path at mile 1.1. The path leads to the 12 O'Clock Overlook and an unlimited view north across the Cumberland Plateau. Immediately below the overlook, you see KY 160 paralleling the mountain.

Continuing west on Little Shepherd Trail, you quickly come to the Halcomb Overlook, where the view is spoiled by a utility wire, and then at mile 1.3 to the Bullock Overlook, the last observation point of the hike. Just before the Bullock Overlook, a road forks left to the park office; disregard it. At mile 1.5 turn left off Little

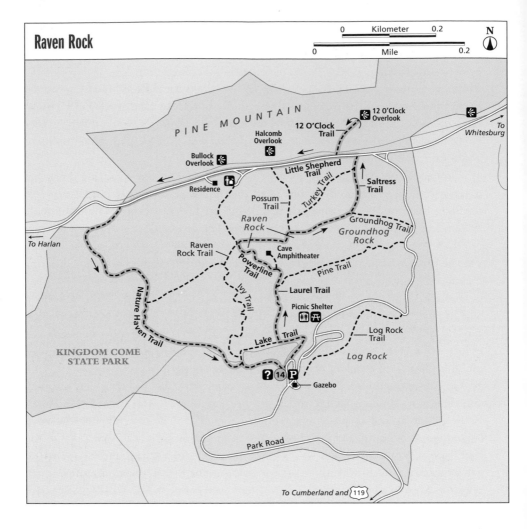

Raven Rock

0 Kilometer 0.2
0 Mile 0.2

N

PINE MOUNTAIN

12 O'Clock Overlook
12 O'Clock Trail
Halcomb Overlook
Bullock Overlook
Little Shepherd Trail
Residence
Possum Trail
Turkey Trail
Saltress Trail
Raven Rock
Groundhog Trail
Groundhog Rock
To Harlan
Raven Rock Trail
Cave Amphitheater
Powerline Trail
Pine Trail
Nature Haven Trail
Ivy Trail
Laurel Trail
Picnic Shelter
Log Rock Trail
Lake Trail
Log Rock
KINGDOM COME STATE PARK
14
Gazebo
Park Road
To Cumberland and 119
To Whitesburg

Shepherd Trail onto Nature Haven Trail, a path that curves southward as it descends through the forest to meet the lake's outflow at mile 2.1.

Follow this drainage up to the west end of the lake and parallel the southern shore to your car at mile 2.3.

Key Points

0.1 Laurel Trail.

0.8 Top of Raven Rock.

1.1 Side path to 12 O'Clock Overlook.

1.2 Halcomb Overlook.

1.3 Bullock Overlook.

1.5 Nature Haven Trail.

2.1 Lake outflow.

15 Martins Fork Lake

This hike on dirt roads alternates between bottomlands and ridgetops as it meanders around one side of a flood-control reservoir. Don't expect dramatic vistas; this is just a simple walk in the woods—and a pleasant one if not attempted on a hot, humid summer day.

Start: Parking lot at Martins Fork Lake dam
Distance: 4.6-mile point-to-point day hike or overnighter. If you don't have a shuttle, it's an additional 2-mile road walk back to your car.
Hiking time: About 4 hours
Difficulty: Moderate
Best seasons: Spring and fall
Other trail users: Mountain bikers, horses, and hunters during fall
Canine compatibility: Dogs permitted
Land status: US Army Corps of Engineers reservoir
Nearest town: Harlan
Fees and permits: None

Maps: Martins Fork Lake Facilities Guide from the Army Corps of Engineers; USGS Harlan and Rose Hill (VA/KY)
Trail contact: Martins Fork Lake office, Army Corps of Engineers, (606) 573-7655
Special considerations: Backcountry camping is permitted, but there is no potable water on the trail. This is also a popular hunting area, especially during the deer and turkey seasons (state dates observed).
Parking and trailhead facilities: There's space for a dozen cars, but no facilities at the trailhead. You will find restrooms, a playground, a beach, picnic tables, and the local Army Corps of Engineers office 1.4 miles south on KY 987.

Finding the trailhead: To park the shuttle car, from the junction of US 119 and US 421 at Harlan, take US 421 south for 10.5 miles and turn right onto KY 987 in the town of Cawood. Drive 6.5 miles southwest on KY 987 and park along the shoulder of the road at the trailhead. GPS: N36 73.083' / W83 26.846'

To return to the trailhead at the dam, retrace your route 1.9 miles along KY 987 and turn left into the Martins Fork Dam parking area. GPS: N36 45.069' / W83 15.356'

The Hike

Eastern Kentucky towns on the Cumberland River long had to endure the constant threat of devastating floods, and Harlan faced a triple danger: Martins Fork and Clover Fork come together in the middle of the city and immediately flow into Poor Fork to form the Cumberland. As part of a series of flood-control measures along the river, the US Army Corps of Engineers dammed Martins Fork in the 1970s to create a reservoir at the base of Cumberland Mountain. The lake ranges in size from 274 to 578 acres, depending on the season and rainfall, and with the surrounding land the Corps project totals 1,324 acres.

Using a series of dirt roads, this hike takes you around the lake's western shore, crossing three major tributaries along the way: Crane Creek, Broad Branch, and

Rosebay rhododendron is common throughout eastern Kentucky.

Harris Creek. As a result, the hike is a series of climbs from the bottomland up the ridge side and back down again. The climbs for the most part are modest in length and grade and seldom reach the ridgetop itself. Consequently, there are no scenic vistas of the countryside; much of the time you don't even see the lake itself. This is a simple walk in the woods, most of it quiet and pleasing. However, over the years the Martins Fork area has been host to lots of coal mining, and a small section of this hike takes you across an old strip mine, its scars still visible in some areas.

Because the bottomlands along the creeks are especially hot and buggy in summer, you'd be wise to avoid that time of year. There are two designated primitive campsites along the trail, but they have no facilities of any kind—and precious little flat space for tents. Backcountry camping is not restricted to the designated sites. The local Corps office likes to know in advance of visitors' camping plans, but a permit is not required. At the end of the trail, instead of retracing your steps, it's quicker to walk back to your car on KY 987—a distance of 2 miles. Be careful on the bridges, which have no shoulders.

The entire hike is on Cumberland Shadow Trail, marked CST on signposts. From the parking lot, walk toward the dam and turn right (east) at the end of the lot just before crossing the concrete drainage culvert. At the turn, which is easily missed, there's a rubber-covered cable to help you pull yourself up the sharp incline. A second such contraption is just beyond the spot where the trail turns north and climbs toward an old dirt road. Go left on this road and continue up for a brief period. Above the dam, but below the ridgetop, the road levels off and follows a stable contour

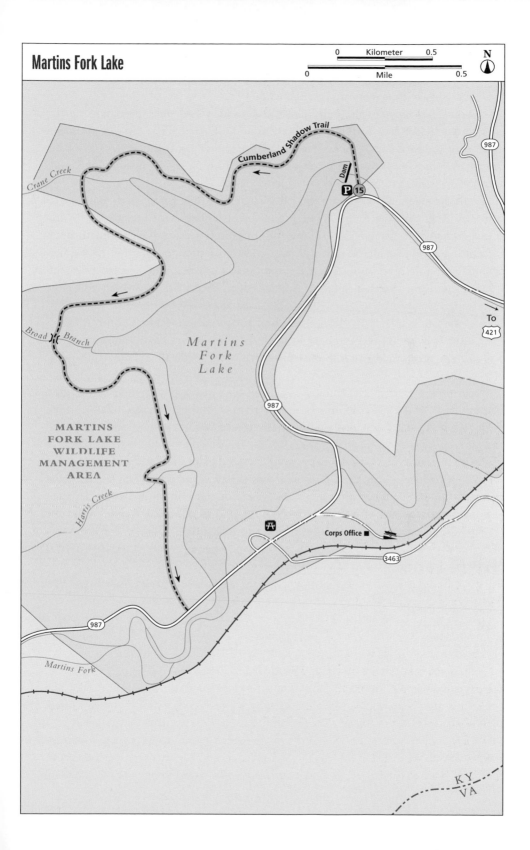

Martins Fork Lake

0   Kilometer   0.5

0   Mile   0.5

N

Crane Creek

Cumberland Shadow Trail

Dam

P 15

987

987

To 421

Martins Fork Lake

Broad Branch

MARTINS FORK LAKE WILDLIFE MANAGEMENT AREA

Harris Creek

987

Corps Office ■

3463

987

Martins Fork

KY VA

through young trees. Disregard the side road off to your left at mile 0.5; it dead-ends into a power-line crossing. Climb briefly again before descending southward to a small cemetery with graves dating to the early 1900s.

Beyond the cemetery the trail follows the Crane Creek inlet upstream (northwest). After descending to the creek bottomland, the trail forks. Go left around a metal gate and turn right onto a gravel road; a signpost marks the turn. This road is unattractive, but you leave it in less than 0.1 mile, turning left to cross Crane Creek at mile 1.6. Again, a signpost marks the turn.

From the creek take a path up the ridge to another dirt road, which you take to your left. After ducking under another gate—which the Corps uses to try to discourage off-road vehicles—climb along the inlet back toward the lake's main stem. Reaching a level shoulder at mile 1.9, you come to a sign pointing left to the first primitive campsite. The roadbed here is winding, leaf-covered, and especially pleasant. It turns southwest and then south as it descends to Broad Branch, which you cross on a bridge at mile 2.6.

On the other side of the bridge, the trail follows a mowed area south through the brush, turns right onto another old road, and then left to begin the ridge climb. You initially go south, then make a hairpin turn to the northeast and descend toward Harris Creek.

Nearing the creek, travel through a cleared area marked as a wildlife food plot. You are now on the old strip mine site. At a signpost the road makes a hairpin turn to the left (east) and descends. At mile 4.0 the road forks and you go right across the creek.

From the creek you climb steeply, going first south and then east, and pass a turn-off to a cleared area above the lake with a good view of the water. This would make a pleasant spot for an overnight camp. From here you descend south along a drainage and at mile 4.6 come to a gate and KY 987. The Corps office is 0.6 mile to the left on the highway; your car is 2 miles north on the road.

Key Points

1.6 Crane Creek.

2.6 Broad Branch.

4.0 Harris Creek.

16 Gibson Gap

Impressive views of the surrounding mountains in Kentucky, Tennessee, and Virginia are the highlight of this walk in Cumberland Gap National Historical Park. Much of the hike is on the ridgeline atop Cumberland Mountain. On the way up and down, there are a number of stream crossings that make pleasant lunch spots.

Start: Wilderness Road Campground on Virginia side of Cumberland Gap National Historical Park

Distance: 9.7-mile loop

Hiking time: About 6 hours

Difficulty: Moderate to strenuous

Best seasons: Any

Other trail users: Equestrians

Canine compatibility: Leashed dogs permitted

Land status: National park

Nearest town: Middlesboro

Fees and permits: Free permit, available at park visitor center, required for backcountry camping at designated sites on ridgetop

Maps: Cumberland Gap National Historical Park trail maps; USGS Middlesboro South, Wheeler (TN/VA), and Varilla (KY/VA). Park maps are free; the visitor center also has commercial trail maps for sale.

Trail contact: Cumberland Gap National Historical Park, (606) 248-2817

Special considerations: The large rock along this hike known as Skylight Cave is currently closed to visitors due to white-nose syndrome, a disorder that has killed millions of bats in the US; the fungus that causes the disease could be spread by humans who venture into different caves. Bring plenty of water; there are no safe sources of drinking water on this hike. Backcountry camping is allowed at designated spots along the ridgetop, but you need a free permit from the park visitor center on US 25E just south of Middlesboro.

Parking and trailhead facilities: There are several designated parking spaces near the campground office; the campground has water, restrooms, and 160 overnight sites, many with 50-, 30-, or 20-amp electrical hookups.

Finding the trailhead: From Middlesboro, take US 25E south through the Cumberland Gap Tunnel, and at the far end exit onto US 58. Follow US 58 east into Virginia and turn left onto the road into the national park's Wilderness Road Campground. Pass the turnoff to the picnic area and park near the campground office, just before the road forks to make a loop through the campsites. The sign for the start of Gibson Gap Trail is a short walk south on the road that forms the left-hand fork. GPS: N36 36.192' / W83 37.799'

The Hike

Cumberland Gap is nature's gate through the Appalachians. It was first used by Native people and later, thanks largely to Daniel Boone, by white settlers. In 1775 Boone and a crew of thirty axmen blazed a trail through the gap that became known as the Wilderness Road. For years it was a thoroughfare not only for pioneers headed west, but also for western farmers and hunters transporting their produce east.

The woods are almost abandoned at Cumberland Gap during fall, when leaves all but hide Station Creek along the Gibson Gap Trail.

There is a trail that takes you through Cumberland Gap, which is about 5 miles west of this hike. Gibson Gap Trail is a longer, more difficult hike that gives you a good feel for the terrain that confronted Boone and all who followed him into this isolated region. The walk to Gibson Gap involves a climb up to the ridgetop, but the idyllic streamside spots and the views of the surrounding mountains in Kentucky, Virginia, and Tennessee are well worth the effort.

From the Gibson Gap Trailhead at the campground, head southeast. At mile 0.1 turn left and walk north on a gravel and dirt park road coming from US 58. Disregard the side path, which leads to an old corral. Soon the trail jogs right and makes the first of what are several crossings of Station Creek. Especially in spring, this delightful stream provides a number of fine lunch spots on the way up the ridge. At mile 0.7 you come to a sign marking the entrance to the park's backcountry. Here the trail leaves the creek temporarily and makes a steep but short climb before beginning a series of gentle ups and downs through rhododendron shrubs and hardwoods.

The trail has mileage markers, and just after mile 2.0, if the season is right, you will see jonquils blooming, a hint that there must have been a gardener around at some point. Sure enough, if you look closely, not far from the trail you find the crumbled remains of a building. After mile 3.0 the grade steepens and you get your first glimpses of the green Virginia valley to the south, although summer views are restricted by foliage. The trail switchbacks northward and then makes a long sweep west. After passing a large rock outcropping, you descend through a canopy of rhododendrons to a streambed, turn north, and begin the final climb to the ridgetop. At mile 4.8 you have arrived at Gibson Gap. The park has designated the gap a backcountry campsite; there is a fire pit and a nearby but unreliable water source. Use Leave No Trace principles. This is also where Gibson Gap Trail intersects with 19-mile-long Ridge Trail.

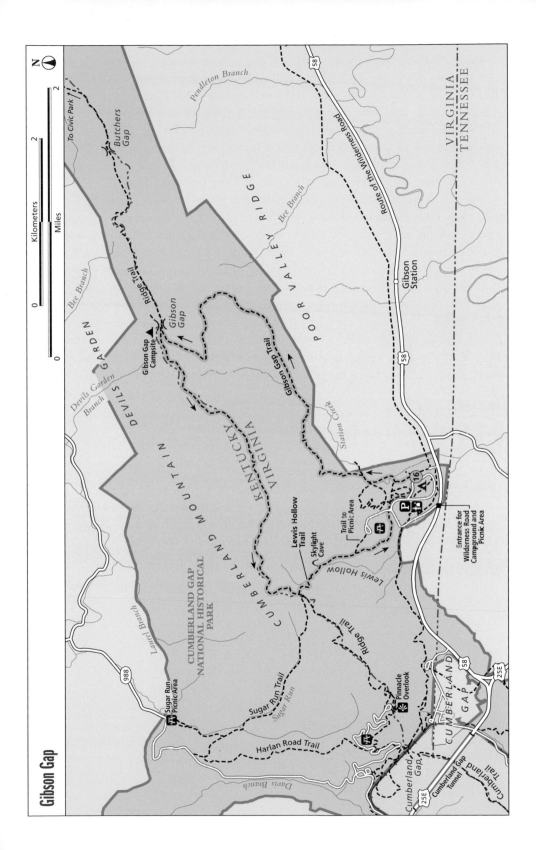

Gibson Gap

N

Ridge Trail, the longest in the park and almost wide enough to serve as a road, starts 14 miles to the east at Civic Park and ends 5 miles to the west at the Pinnacle Overlook near Cumberland Gap. At Gibson Gap take a left onto Ridge Trail and begin a generally level walk west. The ridgetop is the boundary between Kentucky and Virginia, and the trail repeatedly weaves across it, permitting good views into both states as well as a third, Tennessee, which meets the other two just west of Cumberland Gap. There is a particularly spectacular overlook to the southwest just before Ridge Trail descends to a junction with Lewis Hollow Trail at mile 8.1.

Turn left onto Lewis Hollow Trail and descend southeast along a branch of Station Creek. There is not always water here. Station Creek is a "sinking creek," meaning due to karst topography, water often disappears. At mile 8.6 the trail crosses the stream, and just to the left is a large overhanging rock christened Skylight Cave because ceiling openings allow in some daylight. Skylight Cave is currently closed to visitors because of white-nose syndrome. Park rangers say the rock formations you see on the Virginia side of the ridge are generally limestone, and on the Kentucky side sandstone.

For most of the hike's final 1.1 miles, you are coasting downhill. After passing a side trail to a picnic area and crossing a road to the same picnic area, the trail ends at the campground road near the office and just north of the Gibson Gap Trailhead.

Key Points

0.7 Entrance into park's backcountry.
4.8 Gibson Gap.
8.1 Lewis Hollow Trail.
8.6 Skylight Cave.

Option: To lengthen your hike, continue east on Ridge Trail to the Pinnacle Overlook. The round-trip from the Lewis Hollow Trail junction to the overlook will add 3.4 miles to the Gibson Gap loop. See the Pinnacle Overlook hike.

17 Hensley Settlement

An abandoned Appalachian settlement on the top of Brush Mountain is the destination for this steep climb up a narrow gravel road that follows Shillalah Creek partway and passes several attractive limestone formations. Explore the settlement and the rough wooden houses and farm structures that were once home for a hardy bunch of mountain people. In addition to offering an education about a life long past, the settlement is a lovely spot, covered with farm fields and rustic fencing. The grounds and buildings are part of the Cumberland Gap National Historical Park and are well maintained for visitors.

Start: Intersection of KY 217 and gated gravel road, 10 miles east of Cumberland Gap National Historical Park visitor center

Distance: 10.7-mile out-and-back

Hiking time: About 7 hours

Difficulty: Strenuous

Best seasons: Any

Other trail users: Mountain bikers, equestrians, and an occasional van, from May through Oct, taking tourists up to the settlement

Canine compatibility: Leashed dogs permitted

Land status: National park

Nearest town: Middlesboro

Fees and permits: Free permit, available at park visitor center, required for backcountry camping at designated sites on ridgetop

Maps: Cumberland Gap National Historical Park trail maps, including a useful map of Hensley Settlement that identifies individual buildings; USGS Varilla (KY/VA). Park maps are free at the visitor center, which also has commercial trail maps for sale.

Trail contact: Cumberland Gap National Historical Park, (606) 248 2817

Special considerations: The park service runs a van service May through Oct that takes tourists from the visitor center up to the Hensley Settlement and back down, so while the road is usually gated shut, it is possible you will encounter a vehicle. Reservations for the shuttle can be made in advance by telephoning the park (606-248-2817). Overnight camping is not allowed on Shillalah Creek Road or in the settlement. However, there are several authorized backcountry campsites just beyond (east) of the settlement. See options.

Parking and trailhead facilities: There is no formal parking area at the Shillalah Creek Road entrance, only room for 1 or 2 cars on the side of the gravel road just before the gate. Don't block the gate. Also, the shoulder of KY 217 on the far (or north) side has space for about 5 vehicles. This is a narrow highway; you must park completely off the pavement.

Finding the trailhead: From Middlesboro, go south on US 25E less than a mile and take the exit for the Cumberland Gap National Historical Park visitor center, which is just before the Cumberland Gap Tunnel entrance. Instead of entering the visitor center parking lot, continue on the exit road eastward (away from Middlesboro). This is Pinnacle Road, which eventually winds its way up to the Pinnacle Overlook, but don't go that far. At 1.2 miles from the visitor center, turn right onto winding KY 988. Continue past the park's Sugar Run Area (the start of the Pinnacle Overlook hike) and, at 5.2 miles from the visitor center, turn right (east) onto KY 217. Take KY 217 exactly 5 miles to a gravel road with a gate across it on your right. This is Shillalah Creek Road, the hike's starting point. (The gravel road may be hard to spot from KY 217, and so here are two landmarks to watch

The Hike

Cumberland Gap is associated with Daniel Boone, but a latter-day, lesser-known pioneer named Sherman Hensley also left his mark on the long, steep mountain ridge that separates the southwestern tip of Virginia from eastern Kentucky. In 1903 Hensley moved his family to the top of Brush Mountain and started a self-sufficient farming community that lasted until the early 1950s. Today the buildings and fences that remain provide a glimpse into the hard, isolated life of Appalachia before the arrival of electricity and paved roads. The forty-four-page book *The Hensley Settlement* by William E. Cox, the park's former chief of interpretation, provides background on this little village and its lifestyle. The book is sold at the visitor center, which has a good collection of other materials on the area's history and environment.

Hensley Settlement is on the Kentucky side of the ridge, but the best way to get there formerly was on the Virginia side using Chadwell Gap Trail. That was the route the Hensley clan took when venturing down into the modern world for goods they could not grow or make themselves. However, the trail's bottomland section was on private property, and several years ago the landowners closed the trailhead to the public, but it has since been reopened and has a new trailhead, according to Carol Borneman, supervisory park ranger.

Now the most direct way up to Hensley Settlement is from the Kentucky side via Shillalah Creek Road. Although a road, it's narrow and quiet enough that it could almost be a trail—a steep trail, that is. The first half of the 4.6-mile hike to the settlement is a constant climb up what is called Brush Mountain—a ridge on the north side of Cumberland Mountain. Your leg muscles will definitely get a workout, but at least you won't get lost. There are no intersecting roads or trails to lead you astray. Just follow the road all the way.

The road is controlled by the park service and open to hikers, but the park boundary is 2.5 miles up the ridge. Some of the roadside land is in the state's Shillalah Creek Wildlife Management Area. There are also privately owned parcels, as evidenced by the No Hunting signs you see periodically along the road.

The initial stretch, heading southwest and then south through young hardwoods, makes several hairpin curves as it follows the path of Shillalah Creek. The road generally remains a good distance above the stream, but at the first hairpin, 0.9 mile from the start, the road meets the creek at a beautiful little waterfall. A short path leads to a streamside spot that's a good lunch stop.

The higher you go, the more robust and interesting the forest. There are no real lookout points along the way, but depending on the season and tree conditions, there

From 1903 to 1951, Hensley Settlement was a close-knit community of four family farms.
PAM GIBSON

are a few good views west across the Kentucky ridges. You are also likely to spot wild turkeys and deer, and certain to see a number of large limestone formations.

After one particularly steep climb, you pass a private vacation home on your left and almost immediately see park boundary signs on your right. From here on, the trail follows the park boundary line in a generally northeast direction to Hensley Settlement. The worst of the climb is now behind you, but that doesn't mean there are no more steep grades. At 3.5 miles a short stretch of the road—a section called Dynamite Hill—is covered with rough concrete to give the vans better traction.

At mile 4.6 you come to a wide open space on the right and a chain across the road. This is where the van drops off its riders. There is a permanent waterless toilet and also a hitching post; equestrians aren't allowed to take their steeds into the settlement. On the other side of the chain, the road turns left and skirts the northern perimeter of the settlement. You, however, want to go straight on the grassy path, which takes you through the settlement.

A round-trip stroll from this point to the far end of the settlement is about 1.5 miles, although the exact distance depends on how many of the nooks and crannies

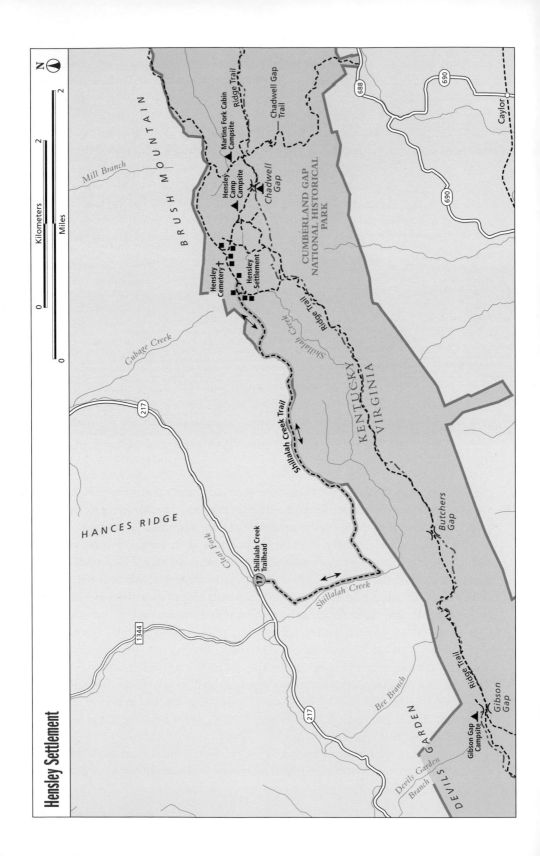

Hensley Settlement

N

Kilometers
0   2

Miles
0   2

MILL Branch

B R U S H   M O U N T A I N

Martins Fork Cabin
Ridge Trail

Chadwell Gap
Trail

Hensley
Camp
Campsite

Chadwell
Gap

Hensley
Cemetery

Hensley
Settlement

CUMBERLAND GAP
NATIONAL HISTORICAL
PARK

Cubage Creek

Shillalah Creek

Ridge Trail

KENTUCKY
VIRGINIA

Shillalah Creek Trail

HANCES RIDGE

Clear Fork

217

Shillalah Creek
Trailhead

17

Shillalah Creek

Butchers
Gap

1344

217

Bee Branch

Gibson Gap
Campsite

Gibson
Gap

D E V I L S   G A R D E N

Devils Garden
Branch

Ridge Trail

688

690

690

Caylor

you explore. Near the last group of buildings—the Bert Hensley farm—there is a water spigot. Another one is located near the Park Hensley house. Both water spigots are seasonal. The old farmhouses and school were refurbished starting in the 1960s. From May through October, volunteers may live in one or two of the houses.

As you walk through the settlement, admire the hand-hewn log construction of the buildings and the beauty of the flat farm fields. But for a reminder of just how tough life here could be, make sure to stop at the cemetery. Sherman Hensley lived to the age of 97 (he died after he left the mountain), but a number of headstones mark the resting places of young children. "A little time on earth he spent / till god for him the angels sent" reads the inscription above the remains of a 14-month-old.

From the settlement retrace your steps to the gravel road and back down the mountain.

Key Points

0.9 Small waterfall and nice lunch spot.

2.5 Park boundary and end of hardest part of the climb.

4.6 Entrance to Hensley Settlement.

5.35 Far end of the settlement.

Options: This hike can easily be made into a one-night or extended backpacking trip. There are two designated backcountry campsites less than a mile from the eastern end of Hensley Settlement. Follow the path leading southeast from the settlement's eastern end, and you quickly come to the 19-mile-long Ridge Trail. Turn left onto the Ridge Trail and almost immediately reach the first of two campsites (Hensley Camp) and soon thereafter the second (Chadwell Gap). If you continue east another 0.2 mile, you come to a side path that goes north to a rustic log cabin (Martins Fork Cabin) that hikers can reserve for a fee. (As with the free camping permits, it is advisable to make arrangements ahead of time through the main park telephone number.)

The Ridge Trail runs along the spine of Cumberland Mountain 19 miles from the Civic Park Trailhead at the east end to Pinnacle Overlook above Cumberland Gap at the west end. From Hensley Settlement the Civic Park Trailhead is about 8 miles and Pinnacle Overlook about 11 miles. Cumberland Mountain marks the Kentucky-Virginia border and offers magnificent views into both states.

18 Pinnacle Overlook

This climb along a beautiful mountain stream to the top of Cumberland Mountain ends at a stunning overlook above Cumberland Gap.

Start: Sugar Run Picnic Area in Cumberland Gap National Historical Park
Distance: 7.8-mile out-and-back
Hiking time: About 5 hours
Difficulty: Moderate
Best seasons: Any
Other trail users: Equestrians
Canine compatibility: Leashed dogs permitted
Land status: National park
Nearest town: Middlesboro
Fees and permits: Free permit, available at park visitor center, required for backcountry camping at designated sites on ridgetop

Maps: Cumberland Gap National Historical Park trail maps; USGS Middlesboro North and Middlesboro South (KY/VA/TN). Park maps are free at the visitor center, which also has commercial trail maps for sale.
Trail contact: Cumberland Gap National Historical Park, (606) 248-2817
Parking and trailhead facilities: You'll find spaces for about 50 cars, along with restrooms, water, and picnic tables.

Finding the trailhead: From Middlesboro, go south on US 25E and take the exit for the Cumberland Gap National Historical Park visitor center, which is just before the Cumberland Gap Tunnel. Instead of entering the visitor center parking lot, drive east (away from Middlesboro) on the exit road. This is Pinnacle Road, which winds its way up to the Pinnacle Overlook, but don't go that far. At 1.2 miles from the visitor center, turn right onto winding KY 988, and after 2.8 miles turn right at the sign for the park's Sugar Run Picnic Area. The trailhead is just beyond the southwest end of the parking lot near the restroom building. GPS: N36 38.189' / W83 40.138'

The Hike

Sugar Run is a small, picturesque stream running down the Kentucky side of Cumberland Mountain. In spring the hollow is full of wildflowers. This hike follows Sugar Run upstream and then takes Ridge Trail southwest along the mountain's crest to the Pinnacle Overlook. From this 2,440-foot observation point, you look down on Cumberland Gap and across the mountains of three states: Kentucky, Virginia, and Tennessee. On clear days you can see all the way to North Carolina. The Pinnacle is the park's single most dramatic feature.

Sugar Run Trail provides an easier, more gradual ascent of Cumberland Mountain than you get on the Hensley Settlement hike. It's also one of the prettiest walks you will find anywhere in Kentucky. The trail isn't hard to follow, but there are few markings along the way. From the southwest end of the parking lot, take the paved walkway a short distance to a fork. You can go either way, because the two prongs soon meet. But on busy spring days, the left path is likely to be less crowded. Turning

Fog forms along the ridgeline at the Cumberland Gap. PAM GIBSON

left, follow a dirt path and rise slightly, the creek on your right. At mile 0.1 you come to a bridge, which you disregard; the bridge carries the right-hand prong of the trail.

Continuing with the creek on your right, go a short distance to a second bridge; this one you do cross, and almost immediately come to a third bridge, which you also cross, putting the creek again on your right. Moss-covered rocks, pine trees, and rich stands of rhododendrons make this a lovely stretch. At mile 0.3 the trail crosses the stream again. Now, with Sugar Run on your left, you begin to move away from the creek and to climb.

At mile 0.5 you come to a junction with another leg of Sugar Run Trail, this one starting at a pull-off on KY 988 nearer the visitor center. The road itself is a short distance to your right; turn left to continue southeast up the mountain.

The trail is now an old roadbed, broad and easy to follow. After crossing a feeder stream on a bridge, you begin to climb steadily. The creek is below and out of sight, though you can hear it gurgle. After a series of level sections, the trail again meets the stream and cuts along a rock outcropping. At mile 1.5 cross Sugar Run twice in rapid succession; afterward the stream dwindles to a trickle before disappearing altogether. At mile 2.0 you emerge from the hollow into more open, level terrain with hardwoods. This signals your approach to the ridgetop.

At mile 2.2 Sugar Run Trail ends and you turn right onto Ridge Trail. When I was there, the junction was marked by a sign for the Pinnacle but not one identifying Ridge Trail. If you miss the turn—as I managed to do—you will go only a few

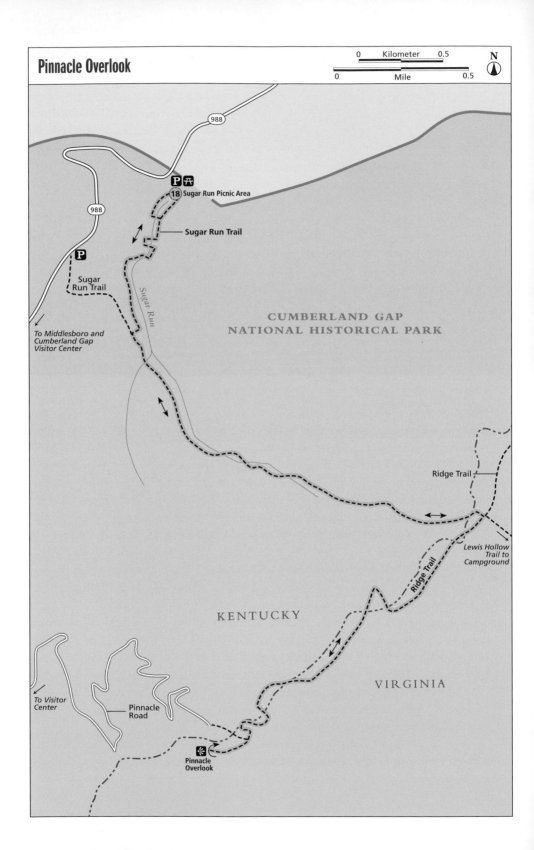

Pinnacle Overlook

0 Kilometer 0.5

0 Mile 0.5

N

988

P ⛺
18 Sugar Run Picnic Area

Sugar Run Trail

988

P
Sugar
Run Trail

Sugar Run

To Middlesboro and
Cumberland Gap
Visitor Center

CUMBERLAND GAP
NATIONAL HISTORICAL PARK

Ridge Trail

Lewis Hollow
Trail to
Campground

Ridge Trail

KENTUCKY

VIRGINIA

To Visitor
Center

Pinnacle
Road

Pinnacle
Overlook

yards before running into the turnoff for Lewis Hollow Trail, which leads to the park campground (see Gibson Gap hike).

From the junction Ridge Trail climbs gently and then more steeply to the southwest as you weave along the Kentucky-Virginia line. This is another old roadbed and easily followed. After a steep climb to the north, you reach a level spot on the Kentucky side with limited views. Curve back to the Virginia side and, at mile 3.1, arrive at an outcropping with excellent views southeast into Virginia and Tennessee. From this unnamed lookout, descend to a Ridge Trail registration box for hikers going the other way, and then climb again.

Disregard the old road on your right and continue south. At mile 3.7, immediately after the dirt path turns into a paved walkway, you come to a fork. The right prong descends to the parking lot at the end of Pinnacle Road; turn left for the Pinnacle. Just beyond the fork are the earthworks of one of the old forts built around Cumberland Gap during the Civil War. Control of this key transportation route was an objective of both the North and South. But while virtually impregnable—the American Gibraltar, a Union general called the gap—the forts were also difficult to resupply. As the sign explains, it was easier for the war to just go around them. First the Confederates held and abandoned the gap, then the Union did the same. Each side held the gap twice.

The paved path reaches the walled Pinnacle lookout at mile 3.9. Directly below is the little Tennessee town of Cumberland Gap. Farther southwest you see the twin highway approaches to the Cumberland Gap Tunnel disappear into the mountain. The tunnel opened in 1996, eliminating the need for a difficult and dangerous stretch of US 25E up the mountain and through the gap. You can see the gap itself; just beyond is Tri-State Peak, where Kentucky, Virginia, and Tennessee meet. (To actually stand there, see the Cumberland Gap hike.) The body of water farther in the distance is Fern Lake, and north of that is the city of Middlesboro. The Pinnacle is also a good spot for seeing hawks.

From the Pinnacle Overlook, retrace your steps to the Sugar Run Picnic Area parking lot.

Key Points

0.5 Junction with other leg of trail.
2.2 Ridge Trail.
3.9 Pinnacle Overlook.

19 Cumberland Gap

You literally follow in Daniel Boone's footsteps on this hike. In 2001 and 2002 the park service restored Cumberland Gap to its original contour and invited visitors to get a taste of the pioneer experience. This walk—a good one for children—takes you through the gap and up to a ridgetop where the states of Kentucky, Tennessee, and Virginia meet.

Start: Daniel Boone parking area in Cumberland Gap National Historical Park
Distance: 4.7-mile lollipop
Hiking time: About 3 hours
Difficulty: Easy
Best seasons: Any
Other trail users: None
Canine compatibility: Leashed dogs permitted
Land status: National park
Nearest town: Cumberland Gap, TN
Fees and permits: None
Maps: Cumberland Gap National Historical Park visitor map of Wilderness Road Area; USGS Middlesboro South (KY/VA/TN). Park maps are free at the visitor center, which also has commercial trail maps for sale.
Trail contact: Cumberland Gap National Historical Park, (606) 248-2817
Parking and trailhead facilities: In addition to restrooms and some 50 parking spaces, the trailhead has signs and exhibits explaining the role that Cumberland Gap played in the nation's westward expansion in the late 1700s and early 1800s. It also has a booth where park service personnel sell tickets for tours of nearby Gap Cave. The town of Cumberland Gap has several restaurants and shops, and the turnoff for the national park campground is 1.4 miles farther east on US 58.

Finding the trailhead: The trailhead is in Virginia on the other side of the Cumberland Gap Tunnel. Take US 25E through the tunnel and immediately exit onto US 58. At 0.4 mile from the US 25E/US 58 intersection, turn left onto the road marked "Historic Area," and in another 0.6 mile turn right into the Daniel Boone parking area. (The road off US 58—North Cumberland Drive—ends 0.5 mile past the parking area in the little Tennessee town of Cumberland Gap.) GPS: N36 36.109' / W83 39.603'

The Hike

Cumberland Gap was an important eighteenth-century doorway through the Appalachian Mountains for settlers on their way westward. In the twentieth century the gap continued as a major transportation route, but one covered in asphalt. For decades US 25E, a key north–south highway, ran smack through this storied mountain notch. Finally, prodded by the region's lawmakers to restore the gap to its historic condition, Congress put up millions of dollars to replace the road with twin 4,600-foot-long highway tunnels through Cumberland Mountain. The tunnels opened in 1996, and in 2001 the park service began removing the pavement and bulldozing the gap back to what research showed was its original contour.

A trail sign reminds hikers to leave only their footsteps behind.

It will be decades before the landscape approximates what confronted Daniel Boone. For one thing, much of the hiking route area is treeless, although the park service has planted some 30,000 saplings in the restoration area. Nevertheless, the park service trail following the old Wilderness Road and a number of interpretive signs along the way give visitors an idea of what it all used to be like.

To be historically correct, of course, you will start in Virginia on the east side of the gap and walk westward. The hike begins beneath a bridge-like pavilion that includes metal statues of pioneers, Indians, and livestock as well as the piped-in sound of footsteps, a crying baby, and neighing horses. A few feet beyond the pavilion, the gravel path splits. To the right is the Boone Trail, which goes to the park campground, about 2 miles to the east. Turn left onto the Wilderness Road Trail, which skirts the parking lot and proceeds westerly, staying just north of the Tennessee border.

At 0.3 mile pass a side trail on the right that leads 0.2 mile to Gap Cave. (For the time schedule and cost of the cave tour, call the main park number, 606-248-2817. Children under age 5 are not permitted.) Continuing west on Wilderness Road Trail, you cross a small stream and at mile 0.6 pass a side trail that descends 0.3 mile to the

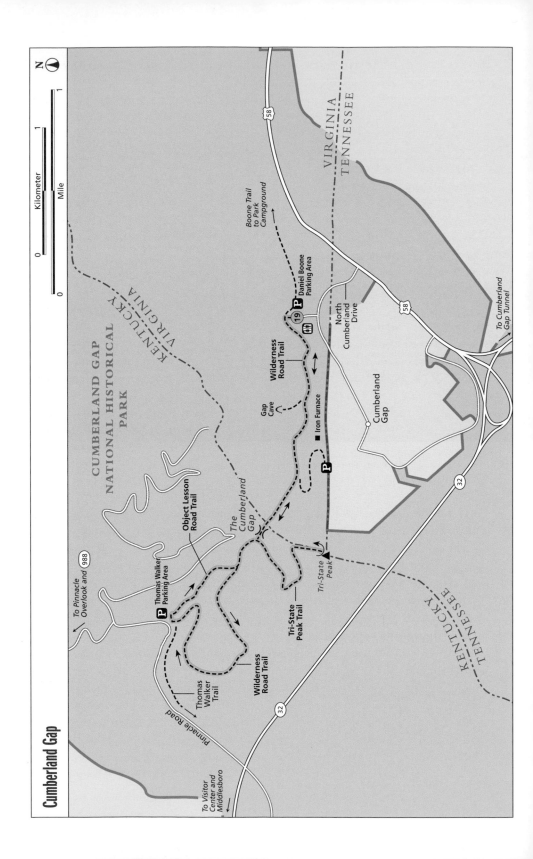

Cumberland Gap

N

Kilometer
0   1

Mile
0   1

CUMBERLAND GAP NATIONAL HISTORICAL PARK

KENTUCKY
VIRGINIA

VIRGINIA
TENNESSEE

KENTUCKY
TENNESSEE

To Pinnacle Overlook and 988

To Visitor Center and Middlesboro

Pinnacle Road

32

Thomas Walker Parking Area

Thomas Walker Trail

Wilderness Road Trail

Object Lesson Road Trail

The Cumberland Gap

Tri-State Peak Trail

Tri-State Peak

Iron Furnace

Gap Cave

Wilderness Road Trail

19

Daniel Boone Parking Area

Boone Trail to Park Campground

North Cumberland Drive

Cumberland Gap

58

58

32

To Cumberland Gap Tunnel

remains of a furnace that produced iron in the nineteenth century. The furnace is on the edge of the town of Cumberland Gap, which you see below.

Remaining on the Wilderness Road Trail, climb a steep but short grade, and at mile 0.9 arrive at the gap, marked by a small wooden sign. A few feet to the left you will find a more elaborate stone monument erected in 1915 to commemorate Daniel Boone's 1769 route from North Carolina to Kentucky.

Beyond the Boone monument a side trail leads 0.6 mile to a point on the Cumberland Mountain ridge where the boundaries of Tennessee, Virginia, and Kentucky meet. Called Tri-State Peak, the spot is marked by a small pavilion with a plaque for each of the states. If your foot is big enough, you can stand literally in the three states at once. Although this side trip to Tri-State Peak is not mandatory, I have included the 1.2-mile out-and-back distance in the 4.7-mile total for this hike. The woods along the Tri-State Peak Trail are more substantial than what you see below the gap, and the walking is pleasant. On the way up you pass the site of a Civil War fortification named Fort Foote. There is little remaining of the fort itself, but from the bluff you get a good view of the Pinnacle (see Pinnacle Overlook hike).

After returning to the gap, continue west on the Wilderness Road Trail and in 0.2 mile come to a fork that begins the loop portion of the hike (mile 2.3). To the right is the Object Lesson Road Trail, the return route. Bear left, staying on the Wilderness Road Trail for another 0.9 mile as it meanders around a hill, crosses a ravine, and dead-ends onto the Thomas Walker Trail a few steps away from Pinnacle Road and the Thomas Walker parking area at mile 3.2. This last section of the Wilderness Road Trail includes a short segment of the original trail—identified by a sign—left untouched by the highway's construction. This section also includes a small stream crossing that would make a delightful place for a lunch break.

Thomas Walker, a physician and surveyor, preceded Boone through the gap by seventeen years. Walker was the first frontiersman of European descent to provide written documentation of the gap. The trail that bears his name runs 1.1 miles from the parking area to the main park visitor center. Don't take this trail; instead, take the Object Lesson Road Trail, which goes from the parking area back to the beginning of the loop, a distance of 0.4 mile. This gravel trail follows the path of a road built in 1907.

Once at the end of the loop at 3.6 miles, retrace your steps through the gap and back to the Daniel Boone parking area.

Key Points

- **0.9** Cumberland Gap.
- **1.5** Tri-State Peak.
- **2.3** Beginning of loop portion of hike.
- **3.2** Thomas Walker parking area.
- **3.6** End of loop.

20 Chained Rock

Follow a lovely wooded trail past a natural arch to an unusual lookout near the top of Pine Mountain.

Start: Parking lot for Laurel Cove lower shelter in Pine Mountain State Resort Park
Distance: 3.8-mile out-and-back
Hiking time: About 3 hours
Difficulty: Moderate
Best seasons: Any
Other trail users: None
Canine compatibility: Leashed dogs permitted
Land status: State park
Nearest town: Pineville
Fees and permits: None

Maps: Pine Mountain State Resort Park Visitor's Guide; USGS Pineville and Middlesboro North
Trail contact: Pine Mountain State Resort Park, (800) 325-1712 or (606) 337-3066
Parking and trailhead facilities: You'll find space for about 50 cars, as well as portable toilets, water, and a picnic pavilion. The park lodge, with overnight and restaurant facilities, is about 6 miles away. The park has no overnight camping facilities.

Finding the trailhead: From the intersection of US 25E and US 119 south of Pineville, take US 25E south for 0.3 mile and turn right onto the park road to Laurel Cove Amphitheater and Chained Rock Overlook. Continue for 0.7 mile; at the top of a hairpin curve, turn right onto the road marked "Laurel Cove Lower Shelter." This road dead-ends into a parking lot in 0.1 mile. Laurel Cove Trail starts just beyond the parking lot near the large pavilion. GPS: N36 44.622' / W83 42.331'

The Hike

At the edge of a rock cliff face on Pine Mountain above the town of Pineville, a huge rock appears to perch precariously. For years local lore had it that only a chain tethering the rock to the mountainside kept the little town below from being flattened. There was, of course, nothing to the story. There was no chain, and the rock wasn't about to go anywhere. According to park officials, the rock is actually connected to the cliff but, due to erosion and weathering, appears to be separated.

In 1933, however, apparently inspired by an out-of-state couple passing through Pineville who were completely taken in by the story, the local Kiwanis Club formed a committee to turn fiction into fact. In an act of truly superhuman proportions, citizens with help from the federal Civilian Conservation Corps hauled a big chain up the mountain by mule and anchored the chain to the rock on one end and the cliff face on the other. It was a master stroke of community promotion, gaining Pineville attention in hundreds of newspapers across the country.

Today this 101-foot-long, 1½-ton chain is still in place, and Chained Rock makes an amusing destination for a hike up Pine Mountain. Kids will love it. The outcropping makes a great lookout, too, with views south to Cumberland Mountain, east along Pine Mountain Ridge, and north down into Pineville.

Pine Mountain was Kentucky's first state park and is certainly one of its prettiest. This hike follows delightful Laurel Cove Trail most of the way to Chained Rock. It is well-used and easy to follow, and is billed as the park's longest and hardest trail. Still, while the hike's inbound leg is mostly uphill, the grades are not severe.

From the Laurel Cove Trailhead near the pavilion, you ascend initially northeast and then northwest, and after a short level stretch reach a small unnamed sandstone arch at mile 0.6. This graceful structure is a toy version of those found so plentifully in Kentucky's Red River Gorge. Beyond the arch, drop down briefly to an intermittent streambed. Then climb some more as you cross and

Chained Rock is held in place above the town of Pineville by a 101-foot-long chain. WADE FRANKLIN

recross the streambed. At mile 0.8 a short side trail leads to a rock slab with limited views south; the rock makes a nice resting spot.

After continuing up through beautiful stands of rhododendrons, descend on stairs beside a rock outcropping and then climb again, curving northeast as you leave the hollow and emerge into more open woods. Immediately beyond the top of a ridge shoulder, the trail descends north, passes a large rock overhang, and dead-ends into Chained Rock Trail at mile 1.75. Turn right and descend on stone steps and rocks to Chained Rock at mile 1.9. (A left turn on Chained Rock Trail would take you to a parking lot at the end of the park's scenic ridgetop road. The parking lot is about 0.5 mile from Chained Rock.)

The good views are from the top of the huge outcropping to which the rock is "attached." There is no set route up the outcropping, and you should watch children carefully. As for the chain, it's made of 1⅜-inch steel, and each link weighs 4½ pounds, according to park information.

When you've had enough of the vistas, retrace your steps down to the parking lot.

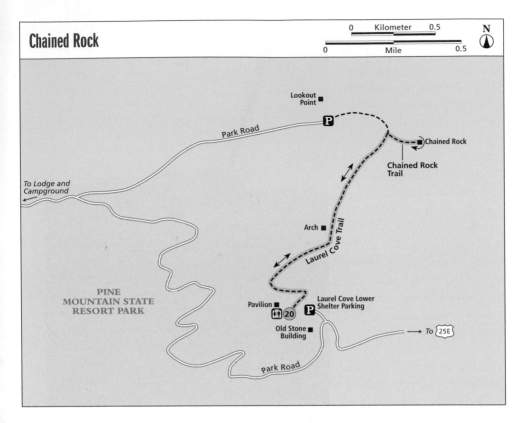

Key Points

0.6 Arch.

1.75 Chained Rock Trail.

1.9 Chained Rock.

Options: The park has a number of other trails, all of them short. A favorite is Hemlock Garden Trail, a loop that starts and ends at the lodge. Including a spur to Inspiration Point, a small bluff at the head of a hollow, this trail is about a mile in length. It winds through old-growth hemlocks as well as interesting rock formations that should intrigue children. Despite its brevity, the scenery makes this hike worthwhile. To reach the lodge, return to US 25E, go south for 0.4 mile, and turn right onto KY 190. In 1.6 miles KY 190 goes left; bear right, following the signs for the lodge.

Red River Gorge

The Red River Gorge is Kentucky's most popular hiking area. The 27,000 acres in the federally designated Red River Gorge Geological Area and adjacent Clifty Wilderness offer nearly 70 miles of trails ranging from short hops of less than a mile to backpacking possibilities of several days. Only foot traffic is allowed—no mountain bikes, horses, or motorized vehicles. Carved out of the Cumberland Plateau eons ago, the gorge serves up a mix of massive cliffs with panoramic views, narrow ravines with peaceful streamside picnic spots, and intriguing rock arches in all sizes. Christmas ferns, rhododendrons, mountain laurel, and a wide variety of wildflowers cover the area. From families with small children to experienced trekkers, there's something here for every kind of hiker. The tall cliffs also attract lots of rock climbers.

That, of course, means trail traffic can be heavy, especially on summer weekends, a good time to avoid. But otherwise each season has advantages—even winter, when water falling over the cliffs freezes into columns of ice. The gorge is in eastern Kentucky about an hour's drive from Lexington and is easily reached on the Bert T. Combs Mountain Parkway, named for a former governor. For a preview of the rugged terrain, you can drive a scenic 35-mile loop through the area using KY 15, KY 77, and KY 715. Part of the drive is along the Red River, which supposedly once had a red tint, hence the name. The loop also takes you through the Nada Tunnel, a one-lane, 900-foot-long cut made in the early 1900s to accommodate a logging railroad.

On KY 715 east of its junction with KY 77, the Gladie Visitor Center houses interpretive exhibits on the natural and human history of the gorge area. The facility, open daily from 9 a.m. to 5:30 p.m. March though November, also has hiking and camping information. Nearby, a reconstructed log cabin dating to the 1800s gives a further glimpse into how settlers here lived. The book *Kentucky's Land of the Arches*, by Robert H. Ruchhoft, outlines the geological and human history of the gorge, including a detailed explanation of how the area's sandstone arches and shallow caves, known as rock houses or rock shelters, were formed. Essentially, they are the result of uneven erosion. The hard sandstone that tops the area was able to withstand the weathering process, while the soft underlying layers were eaten away.

The gorge is part of the Daniel Boone National Forest. The USDA Forest Service has a fifty-four-site fee campground at Koomer Ridge off KY 15 and allows backcountry camping except within 300 feet of a road or developed trail or within 100 feet of the base of any cliff or the back of any rock shelter. This last restriction is to protect the gorge's archaeological sites; as long as 10,000 years ago, Native Americans were living in the rock shelters and cliffs. (For popular Gray's Arch, the no-camping prohibition is 600 feet.)

Fees are charged for overnight users. Vehicles parked in the gorge area between 10 p.m. and 6 a.m. must have a pass hanging on the rearview mirror. Passes are sold at Forest Service offices as well as at stores in the gorge area and Lexington. For a list of outlets, visit www.fs.usda.gov/main/dbnf/passes-permits. You can buy passes covering one night, three nights, or a year. Proper food storage is also required while camping due to the increasing number of black bears. Visitors must store food in a hard-shelled vehicle/camper, hang a bag 10 feet off the ground and 4 feet from the main part of the tree, or place food in a bear-resistant container.

For more information, contact the Gladie Visitor Center at (606) 663-8100 or visit www.fs.usda.gov/main/dbnf/home.

Two notes of caution: The gorge cliffs claim lives all too frequently. Hikers, especially those with small children, should be alert to the danger of falling. No public consumption of alcohol is allowed in Kentucky, and local officials have been cracking down on this, in part, to minimize the perception of the Red River Gorge as a party place, and more importantly to save lives. Too many people have fallen off cliffs, and alcohol is often involved.

Also, while this is a popular recreation area, it is open to hunting during regular state seasons. Be extra careful and wear bright orange during the modern-gun season for deer, usually in November.

The Angel Windows (hike 25).

21 Koomer Ridge

This walk along forested ridges in the Red River Gorge takes you to a small rock arch and a scenic stream.

Start: Koomer Ridge Campground
Distance: 7.7-mile double loop
Hiking time: About 5 hours
Difficulty: Moderate
Best seasons: Any
Other trail users: None
Canine compatibility: Dogs permitted
Land status: National forest
Nearest town: Slade
Fees and permits: Vehicle pass required for overnight parking. Passes are sold at USDA

Forest Service offices and area stores; visit www.fs.usda.gov/main/dbnf/passes-permits for a list of outlets.
Maps: Forest Service map of Red River Gorge; USGS Slade
Trail contact: Gladie Visitor Center, Cumberland Ranger District, Daniel Boone National Forest, (606) 663-8100
Parking and trailhead facilities: There are restrooms and lots of parking space. Water is available mid-Apr through Oct.

Finding the trailhead: From exit 33 off the Bert T. Combs Mountain Parkway, go north for 0.1 mile on KY 11 and turn right onto KY 15, which leapfrogs the parkway several times as both head east toward Campton. After 5 miles, turn left into Koomer Ridge Campground. Bear left at the first fork and immediately take another left onto a road that dead-ends in a few yards at a parking lot for trail users. Park here. Walk back out to the campground road, turn left (north), and walk about 0.2 mile to the tent area. The hike starts past the restrooms at the edge of the forest by the trail signs. GPS: N33 47.063' / W83 38.169'

The Hike

Logging, aided by the construction of rail lines, came to this remote gorge with a vengeance in the late 1800s, and by the 1920s much of the area had been stripped bare. The effects are apparent today in the relatively small size of the trees, especially up on the accessible ridges. Indeed, in some sections lumbering continued into the 1960s—before the gorge got special protection as a geological area.

But humanity's past excesses are not able to dull the beauty of the stark cliffs, intriguing rock arches, and lush ravines—or coves, as they are called here—that cover the area. This hike along ridgetops and a creek bank, using several different trails, is a good sampler of what the Red River Gorge has to offer. One highlight is the stretch along Chimney Top Creek, a lively stream lined with delightful wading pools.

Like most trails in the gorge, these are blazed with a white diamond. Because of trail changes over the years and a tradition of rounding up fractional mileage, distances on trail signs in the gorge are often inaccurate. Those you see on this hike are no exception.

The Red River Gorge is famous for its striking sandstone cliff lines, rock houses, and arches.

Two trails leave the tent area: Koomer Ridge Trail (220), heading north, and Hidden Arch Trail (208). Take the latter, which goes west and north before swinging east to join Koomer Ridge Trail about 0.5 mile north of the campground. The reason to take Hidden Arch Trail is that it's beautiful. The trail follows a narrow, pretty ridgetop through hardwood trees, mountain laurel, and rhododendrons to an overlook with views to the north—the best you get on this hike when the foliage is out. Watch small kids; the drop-off is steep. At 0.8 mile the trail descends on wooden steps to a large outcropping of pockmarked rocks and little Hidden Arch, which would be just that if not for the people who built this trail. More stairs take you under the cliff wall before the trail climbs through rhododendrons to meet Koomer Ridge Trail at 1.0 mile.

Take Koomer Ridge Trail left (north) for a quick, flat walk to meet the southeastern end of Buck Trail (226) at mile 1.8. Later in the hike you will take Buck Trail, but for now continue right on Koomer Ridge Trail as it winds northeast and descends, gently at first and then more steeply, to the western bank of Chimney Top Creek. This creek flows north to the Red River, and Koomer Ridge Trail follows it briefly before dead-ending into Rough Trail (221) at mile 3.0.

Rough Trail, the longest in the gorge, runs generally east to west from KY 715 to KY 77. Take it to your left and continue following the creek north for 0.2 mile before crossing to the eastern bank at mile 3.3. The crossing point is marked by a white diamond on a tree but is easily missed; you can't go too far past it, however, because the path on the western bank soon ends. There is no bridge, and, depending on the

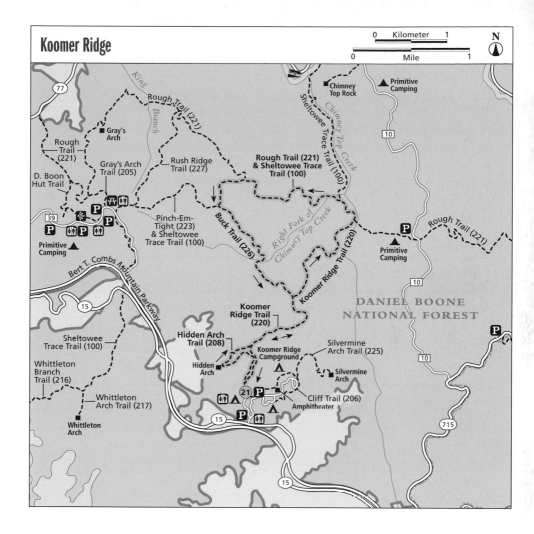

Koomer Ridge

Chimney Top Rock

Primitive Camping

77

King Branch

Rough Trail (221)

Gray's Arch

Rough Trail (221)

Gray's Arch Trail (205)

Rush Ridge Trail (227)

D. Boon Hut Trail

39

Primitive Camping

Pinch-Em-Tight (223) & Sheltowee Trace Trail (100)

Bert T. Combs Mountain Parkway

15

Sheltowee Trace Trail (100)

Whittleton Branch Trail (216)

Whittleton Arch Trail (217)

Whittleton Arch

Buck Trail (226)

Rough Trail (221) & Sheltowee Trace Trail (100)

Sheltowee Trace Trail (100)

Chimney Top Creek

10

Rough Trail (221)

Primitive Camping

Right Fork of Chimney Top Creek

Koomer Ridge Trail (220)

10

DANIEL BOONE NATIONAL FOREST

Koomer Ridge Trail (220)

Hidden Arch Trail (208)

Hidden Arch

Koomer Ridge Campground

21

Silvermine Arch Trail (225)

Silvermine Arch

Cliff Trail (206)

Amphitheater

15

P

10

715

15

creek's level, wading may be necessary. Look downstream about 15 yards for a line of rocks to get you across dry-footed.

Rough Trail continues to parallel the creek and, in 0.1 mile, joins with Sheltowee Trace National Recreation Trail (100), a north–south walking route of approximately 319 miles through the Daniel Boone National Forest. Take a left onto the combined Rough/Sheltowee Trace Trail and cross back over the creek, again wading or using a makeshift bridge of stones and logs. The combined trail climbs northwest above the creek and then west up the ridge side and through an area of about 100 acres that burned in 1999. Rangers believe a campfire got out of control.

After following a constant contour around the head of a ridge, you come to a large bald rock that makes a nice resting spot. Go directly across the rock and pick up the trail again, heading north and then west before the Rough/Sheltowee Trace Trail splits at mile 4.5.

The Rough Trail goes northwest, while the Sheltowee joins with Pinch-Em-Tight Trail (223) and heads west along the ridge toward the Gray's Arch picnic area on Tunnel Ridge Road 1.6 miles away. Take the combined Sheltowee Trace/Pinch-Em-Tight Trail, but go only 0.4 mile to the start of Buck Trail (226). Turn left onto Buck Trail, going southeast and descending to the Right Fork of Chimney Top Creek at mile 5.8. Bear right along the creek before making several easy crossings and climbing through rhododendrons away from the stream and up the ridge.

At mile 6.4 Buck Trail dead-ends into Koomer Ridge Trail, and you are now back at the start of the top loop portion of the hike. Turn right onto Koomer Ridge Trail and walk 1.3 miles south, staying on Koomer Ridge where it intersects the trail to Hidden Arch, to the tent area.

Key Points

0.8 Hidden Arch.

3.3 Chimney Top Creek.

5.8 Right Fork of Chimney Top Creek.

Option: To enlarge the loop to include Gray's Arch, one of the gorge's most popular attractions, continue northwest on Rough Trail (221) to the arch and then head south to near the Gray's Arch picnic area. From there you can take Pinch-Em-Tight Trail (223) east to Buck Trail (226). This will add about 4 miles to your trip. For details see the Gray's Arch hike.

22 Gray's Arch

A 50-foot-high natural arch and a small, shady creek with inviting wading pools highlight this Red River Gorge hike. This trail underwent major renovations in 2014 and is now a much clearer, nicer trail to hike.

Start: Gray's Arch picnic area
Distance: 3.5-mile loop
Hiking time: About 2 hours
Difficulty: Moderate
Best seasons: Any
Other trail users: None
Canine compatibility: Dogs permitted
Land status: National forest
Nearest town: Slade
Fees and permits: Vehicle pass required for overnight parking. Passes are sold at USDA Forest Service offices and area stores; see www .fs.usda.gov/main/dbnf/passes-permits for a list of outlets.

Maps: Forest Service map of Red River Gorge; USGS Slade
Trail contact: Gladie Visitor Center, Cumberland Ranger District, Daniel Boone National Forest, (606) 663-8100
Special considerations: While backcountry camping is generally allowed in the Daniel Boone National Forest, it is not permitted within 600 feet of the arch.
Parking and trailhead facilities: You'll find picnic tables, restrooms, and parking for at least a dozen cars, but no water.

Finding the trailhead: From exit 33 off the Bert T. Combs Mountain Parkway, go north for 0.1 mile on KY 11 and turn right onto KY 15, heading east toward Campton. After 3.5 miles, turn left onto gravel Tunnel Ridge Road (FR 39) and drive north 1 mile to the Gray's Arch picnic area on your right. GPS: N37 48.481' / W83 39.456'

The Hike

Natural arches are formed over thousands of years as water and wind eat away layers of soft rock and leave harder strata behind. The Red River Gorge offers one of the largest collections of sandstone arches in the country. Altogether there are reportedly more than a hundred in the area; without a doubt Gray's Arch is among the most spectacular. It rises 50 feet, spans 80 feet, and appears even bigger because you approach it from the bottom of a ravine, the formation towering over you.

The rest of the scene is equally impressive. Surrounding cliffs drip with water except on the driest of summer days, and thick ferns and rhododendrons carpet the forest floor. This is a perfect spot for a leisurely lunch—or just daydreaming—provided you avoid a busy summer weekend. Gray's Arch is one of the most popular destinations in the gorge. Beyond the arch, however, the number of hikers is certain to thin out, and a delightful little stream named King Branch offers beautiful, quiet spots.

From the picnic area parking lot, take Gray's Arch Trail (205) to the north. Notice the memorial plaque to Jim Graf, a young man killed in a fall from the top of Gray's

Gray's Arch is among the most striking sandstone arches in Kentucky.

Arch in 1986. The gorge is full of signs warning hikers of the danger of falling. This hike, however, is safe even for small children—as long as you stay off the top of the arch. Rappelling, a popular activity in the gorge, is prohibited from the arch.

The name of this trail is a misnomer because it doesn't go to the arch. After jogging west, Gray's Arch Trail dead-ends at 0.2 mile into Rough Trail (221), which actually gets you to the arch. Blazed with white diamonds, Rough Trail is the main hiking route across the gorge area. Take it to your right, walking north, and check out the magnolia trees with huge elephant-ear-like leaves.

Continue north on Rough Trail as it slopes gently downhill. Just after you see Gray's Arch off to your right, the trail descends on a series of steep wooden stairs into a ravine. Here, at mile 1.0, Rough Trail turns left, but you follow a sign pointing straight ahead to the arch. This short side trail takes you up to the base of the arch, which is covered with soft orange-brown sand—proof that the erosion process continues.

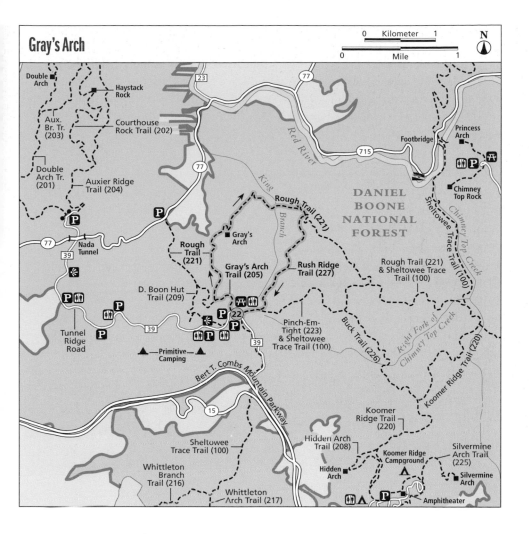

Gray's Arch

0 Kilometer 1

0 Mile 1

N

Double Arch

Haystack Rock

Aux. Br. Tr. (203)

Courthouse Rock Trail (202)

Double Arch Tr. (201)

Auxier Ridge Trail (204)

Red River

Footbridge

Princess Arch

Chimney Top Rock

Rough Trail (221)

King Branch

DANIEL BOONE NATIONAL FOREST

Sheltowee Trace Trail (100)

Chimney Top Creek

Nada Tunnel

Gray's Arch

Rough Trail (221)

Gray's Arch Trail (205)

Rush Ridge Trail (227)

Rough Trail (221) & Sheltowee Trace Trail (100)

D. Boon Hut Trail (209)

Tunnel Ridge Road

Pinch-Em-Tight (223) & Sheltowee Trace Trail (100)

Buck Trail (226)

Right Fork of Chimney Top Creek

Koomer Ridge Trail (220)

Primitive Camping

Bert T. Combs Mountain Parkway

Koomer Ridge Trail (220)

Sheltowee Trace Trail (100)

Hidden Arch Trail (208)

Koomer Ridge Campground

Silvermine Arch Trail (225)

Whittleton Branch Trail (216)

Hidden Arch

Silvermine Arch

Whittleton Arch Trail (217)

Amphitheater

When it's time to move on, return to Rough Trail and continue downhill to the north. At 1.4 miles, after passing a large rock outcropping, you come to King Branch, which is on its way to the Red River. Walking upstream and eastward, cross the creek three times. There are no bridges, but a modest jump should get you over with dry feet unless it has been raining and the water level is up. If you want to get wet, the shaded creek bank offers a number of good wading spots. The gorge was logged into the 1960s, and the trees along the ridges near the roads are young, their trunks no thicker than your waist. Down in this little valley, however, the growth is older, taller, and more pleasing.

At mile 1.5 the trail leaves the creek side and veers up the side of the ridge. This is the only strenuous leg of the hike. Part of the climb is almost straight up; a series of wooden-block steps helps considerably. At mile 2.0, just after reaching the ridgetop, Rough Trail connects with Rush Ridge Trail (227), which you take to the south. The signs at this intersection can be confusing. When I was last there, Rush Ridge Trail was not identified at all. Just be sure to bear right after you reach the ridgetop.

After 1 mile of level walking, Rush Ridge Trail ends at Pinch-Em-Tight Trail (223), which here is combined with Sheltowee Trace National Recreation Trail (100). Take a right onto the combined Pinch-Em-Tight/Sheltowee Trace Trail and walk west 0.2 mile to Tunnel Ridge Road (FR 39). Turn right onto the road; in 0.1 mile you are back at your car.

Key Points

- **1.0** Gray's Arch.
- **1.4** King Branch.
- **2.0** Ridgetop and Rush Ridge Trail junction.

Options: If you want a longer loop, don't take Rush Ridge Trail at the ridgetop. Instead, continue southeast on Rough Trail until it hits Pinch-Em-Tight Trail and take it back to Tunnel Ridge Road. This increases the hike's total distance to just more than 4 miles. Also, from the Gray's Arch picnic area, D. Boon Hut Trail (209) leads for 0.7 mile to the remains of an old saltpeter mine and shelter where a board with the carved letters "D Boon" was discovered. That prompted speculation, never substantiated, that Daniel Boone himself once may have been in residence.

23 Courthouse Rock and Double Arch

A commanding ridgetop view of the Red River Gorge and an unusual rock arch are the chief rewards of this hike.

Start: Auxier Ridge Trailhead parking area at end of Tunnel Ridge Road
Distance: 6.2-mile loop
Hiking time: About 4 hours
Difficulty: Moderate
Best seasons: Any
Other trail users: None
Canine compatibility: Dogs permitted
Land status: National forest
Nearest town: Slade
Fees and permits: Vehicle pass required for overnight parking. Passes are sold at USDA Forest Service offices and area stores; see www.fs.usda.gov/main/r8/passes-permits/recreation for a list of outlets.
Maps: Forest Service map of Red River Gorge; USGS Slade
Trail contact: Gladie Visitor Center, Cumberland Ranger District, Daniel Boone National Forest, (606) 663-8100
Special considerations: Several steep stairways and a high, narrow ridgetop present a potential danger for unattended children.
Parking and trailhead facilities: There are toilet facilities and space for numerous cars.

Finding the trailhead: From exit 33 off the Bert T. Combs Mountain Parkway, go north for 0.1 mile on KY 11 and turn right onto KY 15, heading east toward Campton. After 3.5 miles, turn left onto gravel Tunnel Ridge Road (FR 39). Continue for 3 miles, past the Gray's Arch picnic area, and just before the gate across the road turn right into the parking area for the Auxier Ridge Trailhead. GPS: N37 49.169' / W83 40.877'

The Hike

Courthouse Rock, a boulder the size of an office building, is one of the landmarks of the gorge area. Another is Double Arch, which has a large opening topped by a small one and is positioned prominently on a ridgetop. This hike connects these two works of nature and also includes unobstructed views of the gorge area from a narrow ridge that you cross on the way to Courthouse Rock.

From the parking lot, take Auxier Ridge Trail (204) north. You enter an area of over 1,600 acres that burned in 2010. Some areas along Auxier Ridge burned very hot, and you will still see some tree mortality. The wildfire was started by an escaped campfire on a windy night. The path soon turns left and descends gently through a tunnel of rhododendrons to a ridge that you follow with little elevation change to a junction with Courthouse Rock Trail (202) at mile 0.9. Despite the name of this second trail, continue north on Auxier Ridge Trail. You can get to Courthouse Rock both ways, but this is by far the more scenic.

After the junction, keep your eye out for a bend in the trail to your right (east); it's easy to miss and to continue, instead, straight on a well-worn path that ends at a spot

Unique rock formations like these are commonplace in the Red River Gorge Geological Area.

used by overnight campers. At about mile 1.5 you reach the first of what are progressively better panoramas. The tall white cliff to the east is flat-topped Ravens Rock, where two hang gliders were killed in the 1970s in a gliding tournament. Farther along, several short paths lead left to the edge of a cliff and fine views westward. The trail then tightens into a narrow bridge of rock from which you have unsurpassed views of the Red River valley. Be careful: On both sides it's a straight drop-off.

The trail then climbs over a small rock outcropping, sidesteps another, and comes to a long stairway of metal steps followed by a second made of wood, both very steep and long. At the bottom on the left, at mile 2.1, is the other end of Courthouse Rock Trail (202), and directly in front of you is Courthouse Rock itself. With a little difficulty, you can climb partway up the rock on both its east and west sides. But beware of trying to get all the way up. Veteran ranger Don Fig says that the Forest Service, on more than one occasion, has had to rescue people who were able to scramble to

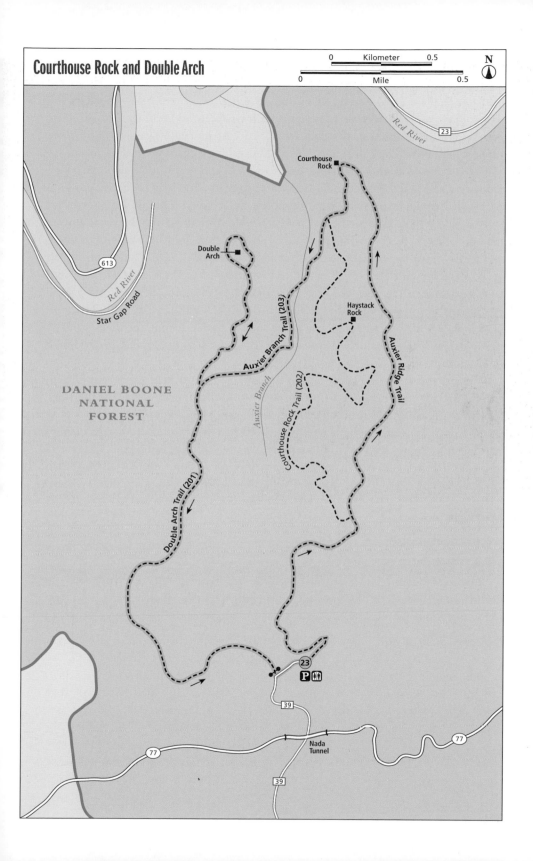

Courthouse Rock and Double Arch

Kilometer
0   0.5

Mile
0   0.5

N

Red River
23

Courthouse
Rock

Double
Arch

613

Red River

Haystack
Rock

Auxier Branch Trail (203)

Star Gap Road

Auxier Branch

Courthouse Rock Trail (202)

Auxier Ridge Trail

DANIEL BOONE
NATIONAL
FOREST

Double Arch Trail (201)

23

P

39

77

Nada
Tunnel

77

39

the top but then couldn't get down. Unless you have climbing experience and equipment, don't try it, he advises.

After exploring the rock, take Courthouse Rock Trail south below the cliffs you just walked across. In 0.3 mile you come to a fork: Courthouse Rock Trail goes left, but you go right onto Auxier Branch Trail (203). The trail takes you down to Auxier Branch, a beautiful creek in a small hollow. This is an excellent place for a rest.

After briefly following the creek upstream, you cross it on rocks and climb first southwest and then west. At mile 3.1 the trail dead-ends into Double Arch Trail (201); a left would take you back to the parking area, but go right, walking north and level along the base of the cliff that holds Double Arch. After curving west around the end of the cliff, the trail stops at the bottom of steps up to the arch (3.8 miles). At the top of the steps is another great view, this one of the ridge that you crossed to get to Courthouse Rock. It's also another long drop-off, so be careful. Double Arch is so named because a thin line of rock separates the bottom opening from a small eye-shaped slit on top. In *Kentucky's Land of the Arches*, author Robert H. Ruchhoft says the lower arch measures 30 feet across and 11 feet in height, the upper arch 25 feet and 1.5 feet. It's the only sizable arch in the area with two openings, according to Ruchhoft.

From the arch, retrace your steps to the Auxier Branch Trail junction and then continue south on Double Arch Trail. In short order the trail climbs up to the ridge and then follows an old roadbed back to the parking area. At one time this was an extension of Tunnel Ridge Road but was closed to vehicles around 2000. Just before you reach the open section of Tunnel Ridge Road and the gate, look for a short 500-yard trail that connects directly to the parking area where you started. You reach your car at mile 6.2.

Key Points

2.1 Courthouse Rock.

3.8 Double Arch.

Option: You can avoid the final roadside segment by retracing your steps to Courthouse Rock Trail (202) and taking it right to Auxier Ridge Trail (204), then following Auxier Ridge Trail to your car. This increases the hike's total length to about 8 miles.

24 Tower Rock

This short walk to a tall rock on the edge of the Clifty Wilderness is perfect for families with small children. Do keep in mind you are entering a federally designated wilderness, which is managed to be more primitive than other areas. Wilderness is also managed to provide solitude, and the maximum group size is ten.

Start: North side of KY 715 near Gladie Visitor Center

Distance: 1-mile lollipop

Hiking time: About 1 hour

Difficulty: Easy

Best seasons: Any

Other trail users: None

Canine compatibility: Dogs permitted

Land status: National forest

Nearest town: Slade

Fees and permits: Vehicle pass required for overnight parking. Passes are sold at USDA Forest Service offices and area stores; see www.fs.usda.gov/main/r8/passes-permits/recreation for a list of outlets.

Maps: Forest Service map of Red River Gorge; USGS Pomeroyton

Trail contact: Gladie Visitor Center, Cumberland Ranger District, Daniel Boone National Forest, (606) 663-8100

Parking and trailhead facilities: There's space for 2 or 3 cars. No facilities are available at the trailhead, but the Gladie center has restrooms, a gift shop, information, and exhibits on turn-of-the-twentieth-century life in the gorge.

Finding the trailhead: From exit 33 off the Bert T. Combs Mountain Parkway, go north for 0.1 mile on KY 11 and turn left onto combined KY 11 and KY 15, heading west toward Stanton. After 1.5 miles, turn right onto KY 77. In 4.3 miles, after passing through the one-lane Nada Tunnel and crossing the Red River, turn right onto KY 715. In 3.2 miles, cross a stone bridge over Gladie Creek, pass the turnoff for the Gladie Visitor Center, and continue east on KY 715 for 1 mile. The Tower Rock Trailhead sign is on the left (north) side of the road, and on the right is a narrow shoulder for parking. Be careful; the shoulder is indeed narrow, and below lies the Red River. GPS: N37 49.643' / W83 35.937'

The Hike

The Red River Gorge includes a number of short trails to popular landmarks: Sky Bridge Trail (214), Princess Arch Trail (233), and Angel Windows Trail (218) are all less than a mile long. Tower Rock Trail (229) is another of these short hops, but it's one easily overlooked. Because of this, and also because the trail is doable by small children and yet has a destination that rewards hikers of all ages, I have included it.

Tower Rock is just that: a huge hunk of sandstone conglomerate towering 90 feet straight up—a height that makes this a popular stop with the climbing community. You are likely to see some climbers in action during your visit.

From the trailhead sign on KY 715, Tower Rock Trail climbs north through a pleasant forest of pines and rhododendrons before turning south to a large split rock,

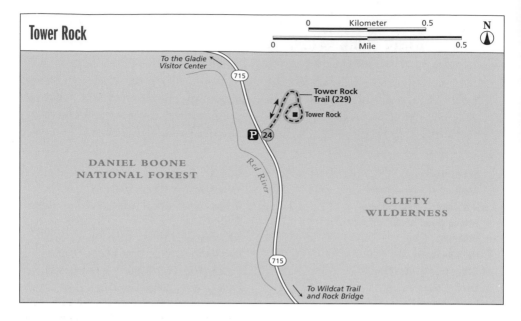

Tower Rock

0 Kilometer 0.5
0 Mile 0.5

N

To the Gladie
Visitor Center

715

Tower Rock
Trail (229)

Tower Rock

P 24

DANIEL BOONE
NATIONAL FOREST

Red River

CLIFTY
WILDERNESS

715

To Wildcat Trail
and Rock Bridge

which you walk through at mile 0.3. Just beyond is Tower Rock, as impressive in size as a European cathedral. In his book *Kentucky's Land of the Arches*, historian Robert H. Ruchhoft explains that the rock is sandstone that has resisted the weathering process while the ridge it was once part of has eroded away. A loop trail, marked by white diamonds, circles the rock. At the south end there is a low ledge, and it's possible to scramble up a few feet. But otherwise—unless you are an experienced climber—Tower Rock is impregnable. The loop ends in 0.2 mile back where it started, and you retrace your steps down to the road.

Key Points

0.4 Tower Rock.

A true American bug, this wheel bug with its characteristic armor is an important predator of invasive insect species.

25 Swift Camp Creek

This peaceful circular walk in the Clifty Wilderness takes you to a sizable creek perfect for cooling off on a hot day. Keep in mind that you are entering a federally designated wilderness. These areas are managed to be more primitive than other areas, in order to provide solitude. The maximum group size is ten in this area for hiking and camping.

Start: Wildcat Trail parking area on KY 715
Distance: 5.75-mile lollipop
Hiking time: About 3.5 hours
Difficulty: Moderate
Best seasons: Summer
Other trail users: None
Canine compatibility: Dogs permitted
Land status: National forest
Nearest town: Campton
Fees and permits: Vehicle pass required for overnight parking. Passes are sold at USDA Forest Service offices and area stores; see

www.fs.usda.gov/main/r8/passes-permits/ recreation for a list of outlets.
Maps: Forest Service map of Red River Gorge; USGS Pomeroyton
Trail contact: Gladie Visitor Center, Cumberland Ranger District, Daniel Boone National Forest, (606) 663-8100
Special considerations: To make a loop, the hike's last 1.3-mile leg is on a paved but lightly used road.
Parking and trailhead facilities: There's off-road parking space for numerous cars, but no facilities.

Finding the trailhead: From exit 40 off the Bert T. Combs Mountain Parkway, take combined KY 15 and KY 715 northeast for 1 mile, where the two routes split. Follow KY 715 to your right and drive 3 miles north to the Wildcat Trail parking lot on your left. GPS: N37 47.443' / W83 35.794'

The Hike

The 12,600-acre Clifty Wilderness, one of two designated wildernesses in Kentucky, was heavily logged before it received protected status in 1985. The old roads and paths used by loggers and homesteaders are still visible, so you won't experience the remoteness found in large wilderness tracts in the western United States. Nevertheless, for a quiet walk in the woods, the Clifty area can't be beat. The cliffs and rock outcroppings are intriguing, and Swift Camp Creek, once used by lumbermen to float logs down to the Red River, makes an excellent picnic spot, especially on a hot summer day.

Wildcat Trail (228), which you take east to the creek, starts just across KY 715 from the parking area. The road marks the western boundary of the wilderness area. Although it initially heads south, at mile 0.1 the trail makes a sharp but poorly marked turn to your left (east). Numerous old paths in this area can be confusing; look for the Wildcat Trail blaze, a white diamond.

Creation Falls along Swift Camp Creek makes an excellent spot for wading.

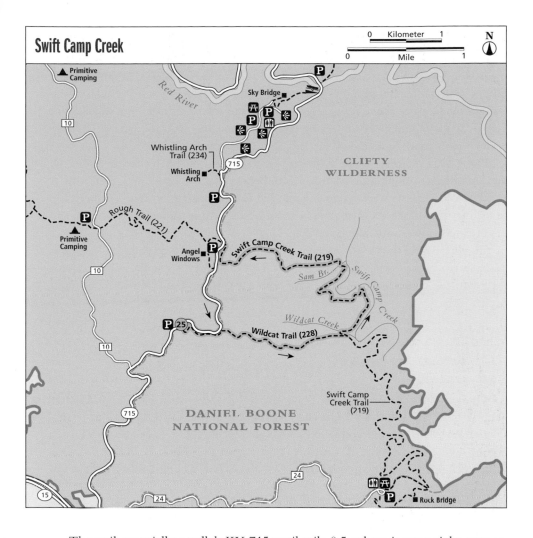

Swift Camp Creek

The trail essentially parallels KY 715 until mile 0.5, where it turns right onto an old dirt road. (A left here would take you to the original Wildcat Trailhead on KY 715. The trailhead was moved several years ago because of insufficient parking space.) Walking east on the old road, you come quickly to a fork and bear left; the right prong goes up a hill to a private cemetery. The road narrows to a path and after a level stretch begins descending, gently at first and then more steeply. The rhododendrons and ferns are thick, and moss-covered rocks along the trail gradually grow into cliffs pocked with cave-like shelters.

At mile 1.7 Wildcat Trail dead-ends into Swift Camp Creek Trail (219), which you take to the left. Swift Camp Creek Trail runs a total of about 7 miles—from Rock Bridge at the southeast corner of the Clifty Wilderness north and then west to KY 715. Combined with Rough Trail (221), it permits a backpacking trip across much of the gorge area, which is described in options below.

Heading north along Swift Camp Creek as it makes its way toward the Red River, cross Wildcat Creek and several smaller streams that are likely to be nothing more than a trickle in summer. Swift Camp Creek remains below at an unreachable distance—and often out of sight—as you slab around the ridges above. At mile 3.0 the trail descends to just above the creek, and at last you can easily reach the water. Swift Camp Creek will never be an Olympic diving venue, but it should have pools deep enough for a good dunking.

Don't wait too long to take a dip because soon—at mile 3.2—the trail leaves the creek and begins climbing toward KY 715. Be alert for the turn; it's easy to miss. A white arrow painted on a large rock points left to a narrow set of steps heading away from the stream. Take the steps, cross a small feeder stream named Sons Branch, and begin climbing westward along a ravine.

The first part of the climb is steep but brief. Soon the trail levels off, and it remains that way as you walk through young pines. The trail ends at a trailhead parking lot for Swift Camp Creek and Rough Trails. Your car is an easy walk of 1.3 miles south on KY 715.

Key Points

1.7 Swift Camp Creek Trail (219).

3.0 Swift Camp Creek.

Options: For a longer trip, take Rough Trail (221) west from KY 715; it goes for about 7 miles, ending at KY 77. If you take Swift Camp Creek Trail from its beginning at Rock Bridge and continue on Rough Trail to KY 77, the total distance is about 14 miles; you would, of course, have to arrange a shuttle back to Rock Bridge. To reach Rock Bridge by car, take exit 40 off the Bert T. Combs Mountain Parkway. Travel northeast on combined KY 15 and KY 715 for 1 mile, where the two routes split. Follow KY 715 to the right, driving 1 mile north and turning right onto gravel Rock Bridge Road (FR 24), which dead-ends in 3 miles at a picnic area.

26 Rock Bridge

A beautiful loop hike that is dog-friendly and short enough for children, it goes by a rock house, a waterfall, and a true natural bridge with a picturesque creek flowing beneath it.

Start: Rock Bridge Picnic Area
Distance: 1.3-mile loop
Hiking time: About 1 hour
Difficulty: Moderate
Best seasons: Any
Other trail users: None
Canine compatibility: Dogs permitted
Land status: National forest
Nearest town: Campton
Fees and permits: Vehicle pass required for overnight parking. Passes are sold at USDA Forest Service offices and area stores; see www.fs.usda.gov/main/r8/passes-permits/recreation for a list of outlets.
Maps: Forest Service map of Red River Gorge; USGS Pomeroyton
Trail contact: Gladie Visitor Center, Cumberland Ranger District, Daniel Boone National Forest, (606) 663-8100
Parking and trailhead facilities: There's plenty of parking space, as well as restrooms and picnic tables.

Finding the trailhead: From exit 40 off the Bert T. Combs Mountain Parkway, take combined KY 15 and KY 715 northeast for 1 mile, where the two routes split. Follow KY 715 to your right, driving 1 mile north and turning right onto gravel Rock Bridge Road (FR 24), which dead-ends in 3 miles at a picnic area. Rock Bridge Trail (207) begins at the edge of the road on the south side of the picnic area. GPS: N37 46.209' / W83 33.941'

The Hike

The route takes you to two Red River Gorge landmarks. The first is Creation Falls, a beautiful waterfall with a sandy beach at the base. The second is Rock Bridge, the area's only true natural bridge because it has a stream—Swift Camp Creek—flowing beneath it.

Rock Bridge Trail (207) is a 1.3-mile loop designed as a self-guided nature trail and is, for a portion of the way, covered with asphalt. It is one of the most scenic walks in the gorge, and a great one for families.

Taking the southern leg of this loop path, you descend quickly on steps into a lush ravine of ferns and rhododendrons and in 0.3 mile pass a rock house. Soon you are following a picturesque little stream, Rockbridge Fork, to Creation Falls, a waterfall with a sandy beach. It's a beautiful spot, and I've often found families wading and sliding here on the smooth surface of the rocks below the falls when the water levels are extremely low.

After the falls the stream meets Swift Camp Creek; just beyond, at mile 0.6, is Rock Bridge, both graceful and craggy at the same time. Lumbermen used to float logs beneath it downstream to the Red River. The arch was formed when a waterfall

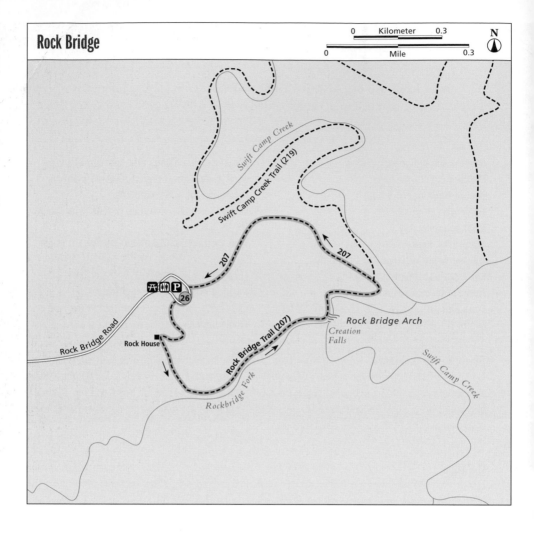

Rock Bridge

eroded the soft interior rock but not the hard limestone layer on top. It's the only example in the Red River Gorge of a waterfall arch. It was formed when water flowing over the limestone layer cut through the other, softer rock layers and washed them away.

Beyond the arch the creek jogs east and Rock Bridge Trail goes north to the start of Swift Camp Creek Trail (219). At this junction, which you reach at mile 0.8, Rock Bridge Trail turns west and climbs back to the picnic area. This northern leg of the loop is 0.6 mile long.

Key Points

0.3   Rock house.
0.6   Creation Falls and Rock Bridge.
0.8   Junction with Swift Camp Creek Trail (219).

Spanning Swift Camp Creek, Rock Bridge is the area's only real natural bridge.

Options: You can easily turn this day hike into a longer day trip or even an over-nighter. Hike north into Clifty Wilderness on Swift Camp Creek Trail, along which you can hike another 8 miles to a trailhead parking area along KY 715.

Swift Camp Creek Trail north of the arch is worth exploring. It goes through a beautiful gorge that gives the trail a more remote feel than the stretch featured in the Swift Camp Creek hike.

27 Natural Bridge and Hood Branch

This hike combines a visit to Kentucky's best-known rock arch with a walk through the backcountry of Natural Bridge State Resort Park.

Start: Parking lot near lodge complex at Natural Bridge State Resort Park
Distance: 5.8-mile lollipop
Difficulty: Moderate
Best seasons: Any
Other trail users: None
Canine compatibility: No dogs allowed
Land status: State park
Nearest town: Slade
Fees and permits: None

Maps: Natural Bridge State Resort Park trail pamphlet; USDA Forest Service map of Red River Gorge; USGS Slade
Trail contact: Natural Bridge State Resort Park, (606) 663-2214 or (800) 325-1710
Special considerations: Backcountry camping not allowed in park
Parking and trailhead facilities: There's plenty of parking space, and nearby are a snack bar, a swimming pool, 2 campgrounds, and a lodge with a restaurant and overnight accommodations.

Finding the trailhead: From exit 33 off the Bert T. Combs Mountain Parkway, take KY 11 south. In 2 miles, pass a right-hand turn into the park's Hemlock Lodge; this is the main park entrance. Continue for 0.5 mile, then turn right onto a road marked for various park features, including trails and the swimming pool. Park in the large lot 0.2 mile beyond. A paved path at the lot's north end leads to all trails. GPS: N37 46.537' / W83 40.720'

The Hike

Natural Bridge State Resort Park joins the southern end of the Forest Service's Red River Gorge Geological Area. The park has been a popular tourist attraction for decades and is highly developed. There's even a chairlift to whisk you to Natural Bridge so you don't have to hoof it up the steep hill. Likewise, most of the trails in the park are short and close to the busy lodge area. This hike and the Natural Bridge Park Perimeter hike are exceptions: Both range into the park's little-used backcountry for long, pleasant walks across deserted ridges and hollows. The park's interior scenery is, for the most part, not spectacular. But it offers plenty of streams, wildflowers, rock outcroppings—and quiet.

This hike combines a stop at the park's main attraction—Natural Bridge—with a walk along Upper Hood Branch, a major drainage of the park. The park totals about 2,300 acres, including a 1,500-acre nature preserve.

Taking the paved path at the north end of the parking lot, you quickly come to a fork. Go right and you are at the start of Original Trail (1), a wide, heavily used, steep path of sand and gravel that gets you from the lodge area to the base of Natural Bridge at mile 0.6. This sandstone arch measures 78 feet in length and 65 feet in

Sunset along the Original Trail near the top of Natural Bridge.

height. It's not the area's biggest; Gray's Arch is 2 feet longer and almost as tall, and Whittleton Arch just north of the park spans 100 feet. But Natural Bridge is definitely impressive, not just for its size but for its graceful lines as well. And the view from its top at 1,280 feet is stunning.

To get there, ease yourself through the narrow passageway (known as Fat Man's Misery) on the left side of the arch, and climb the steps. The top seems as long and wide as an airport runway. But it has no railings, so watch children. The best view is north across the valley of the Middle Fork of the Red River, the stream that runs along KY 11.

There are a number of other short trails to nearby park landmarks, like Lover's Leap, Devil's Gulch, and Balanced Rock. (See the park trail pamphlet.) But on this hike you leave all of that behind and head south on Hood Branch Trail (6), a 3.7-mile-long dirt path that starts at the base of Natural Bridge and ends on the park's north side near the lower terminus of the Skylift, the park's chairlift, and the miniature golf course.

From the southeastern end of Natural Bridge, Hood Branch Trail descends through rhododendrons, then winds along the base of a cliff well above Upper Hood Branch. At mile 1.0 (measured from the parking lot), cross a small feeder stream on a bridge—the first of a number that you will encounter—and walk west before making a sharp turn

Natural Bridge is the park's most well-known sandstone arch, measuring 78 feet long and 65 feet high.

south. The trail continues snaking east and west as it follows a level contour to the south. At mile 2.0 descend to the stream, cross it, and reach a fork. The main Hood Branch Trail turns right (north), but you turn left onto a side trail that makes a westward loop to a large rock shelter. This side trail—called the Upper Loop—is just less than a mile in length and is included in the total 5.8 miles listed for this hike.

Turning left onto the side trail, go a short distance before bearing left again, this time at the beginning of the loop itself. After climbing up a ravine and turning north, the side trail passes beneath a huge sandstone rock shelter at mile 2.4, which makes an interesting rest spot. This cave-like structure was formed when soft interior rock eroded away, leaving a top layer of hard sandstone standing. From the rock shelter, the side trail crosses a footbridge and passes along a cliff face to a smaller rock shelter. Then descending, you return to the start of the loop, and in short order reconnect with the main Hood Branch Trail at the streamside fork.

Heading north, the main trail generally follows the level creek bottomland. At mile 3.4 cross the stream on a bridge and immediately recross it. The trail then passes a shelter built in the 1930s by the Civilian Conservation Corps and begins following

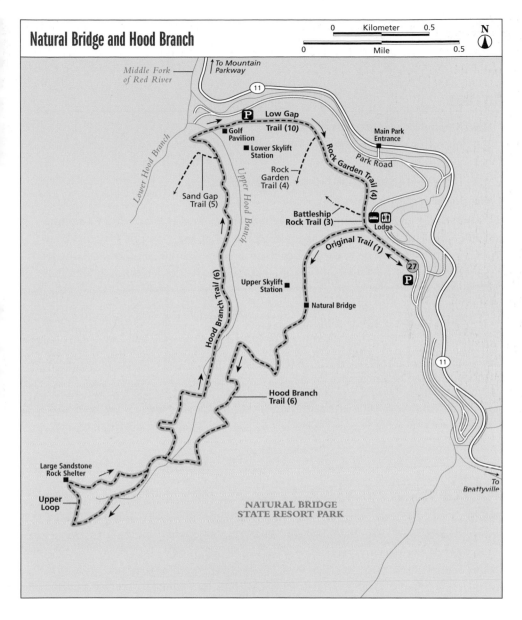

Natural Bridge and Hood Branch

0   Kilometer   0.5

0   Mile   0.5

N

Middle Fork
of Red River

To Mountain
Parkway

11

Lower Hood Branch

Upper Hood Branch

P   Low Gap
         Trail (10)
Golf
Pavilion
Lower Skylift
Station

Rock
Garden
Trail (4)

Main Park
Entrance

Park Road

Rock Garden Trail (4)

Sand Gap
Trail (5)

Battleship
Rock Trail (3)

Lodge

Original Trail (1)

27

P

Hood Branch Trail (6)

Upper Skylift
Station

Natural Bridge

Hood Branch
Trail (6)

11

Large Sandstone
Rock Shelter

To
Beattyville

Upper
Loop

NATURAL BRIDGE
STATE RESORT PARK

an old roadbed. Pass a turnoff for Sand Gap Trail (5) shortly before descending to the end of Hood Branch Trail at mile 4.3. The chairlift parking lot and a miniature golf course are to your right. The golf pavilion has a snack bar.

From the parking lot, go east on Low Gap Trail (10), which the park added in 2002 so walkers could avoid the park road between the lodge and chairlift. Low Gap Trail climbs and ends at Rock Garden Trail (4) at mile 4.8. Bear left onto Rock Garden Trail and head south through what park naturalist Zeb Weese considers one of the park's prettiest sections, full of native plants and birds. Rock Garden Trail dead-ends into Battleship Rock Trail (3) just above the lodge. Turn left onto Battleship Rock Trail, which quickly delivers you to Original Trail near the hike's starting point at mile 5.8.

Key Points

- **0.6** Natural Bridge and Hood Branch Trailhead.
- **2.0** Upper Loop side trail to large rock shelter.
- **2.4** Large rock shelter.
- **4.3** End of Hood Branch Trail and beginning of Low Gap Trail.
- **4.8** Left turn onto Rock Garden Trail.

Option: An alternative at the end of Hood Branch Trail is to take the 11-minute chairlift ride up to Natural Bridge and walk down to the lodge area on Original Trail, the same way you went up at the start of the hike. The chairlift runs from 10 a.m. to 6:30 p.m. (7:30 p.m. on Saturday) from the last weekend of March through October; a fee is charged.

28 Natural Bridge Park Perimeter

This long walk along the boundary of 2,300-acre Natural Bridge State Resort Park offers a few good views from a ridgetop and lots of solitude.

Start: Parking lot for chairlift and miniature golf course at Natural Bridge State Resort Park
Distance: 9.8-mile loop
Hiking time: About 6 hours
Difficulty: Moderate
Best seasons: Any
Other trail users: None
Canine compatibility: No dogs allowed
Land status: State park
Nearest town: Slade
Fees and permits: None
Maps: Natural Bridge State Resort Park trail pamphlet; USDA Forest Service map of Red River Gorge; USGS Slade

Trail contact: Natural Bridge State Resort Park, (606) 663-2214 or (800) 325-1710
Special considerations: No backcountry camping is allowed in the park, so this has to be a day hike—and it may be too long for some people. However, you can knock 2.3 miles off the total by using the chairlift; see option. Also, the Sand Gap Trail can be much harder to navigate during the fall and winter due to downed leaves and snow; take a compass or GPS device.
Parking and trailhead facilities: There are plenty of parking spaces; restrooms and a snack bar are available at the golf pavilion.

Finding the trailhead: From exit 33 off the Bert T. Combs Mountain Parkway, take KY 11 south for 2 miles and turn right at the state park's main entrance. The lodge is straight ahead, but make an immediate right and, in 0.7 mile, park in the lot near the chairlift and miniature golf course. Walk west across the field to the trailhead sign for Sand Gap and Hood Branch Trails at the edge of the woods just beyond the golf course. GPS: N37 46.908' / W83 41.482'

The Hike

This hike is for people who enjoy walking a long distance through pleasant woods and don't require lots of dramatic sights along the way to keep them going. The ridgetop section of this trek is thoroughly enjoyable and has several good vistas, but much of the scenery is pretty tame. Even if their young legs are up to it, children are likely to be bored on this one.

The guts of the hike are found along the park's Sand Gap Trail (5). The name is misleading because the trail doesn't go across a sand gap—and while there is a Sand Gap Arch just outside the park, you don't see it. What the trail does do, for much of its length, is follow the park boundary through an area that very few visitors ever see. Indeed, while the trail is easy to follow, it is used little enough that low-lying sections near Lower Hood Branch may be overgrown. In the fall and winter, fallen leaves and fresh fallen snow can make following it a challenge in some areas.

The park trail guide assumes you will start near Natural Bridge and hike clockwise, ending up at the miniature golf course and lower chairlift station. I recommend the

Gladie Cabin in Sky Meadow is a reconstructed log home and a wonderful place for a picnic lunch after a morning hike.

reverse. The part of the hike near the golf course and chairlift is more difficult and less rewarding than the ridgetop boundary portion, and better tackled when you're fresh.

Sand Gap Trail and Hood Branch Trail (6) leave together from the edge of the miniature golf course and climb briefly but steeply. Sand Gap Trail, which you take, soon splits off to the right, heading initially west and then south to shadow the upstream path of Lower Hood Branch. The trail stays on the ridge side in a forest of pines and hardwoods until it descends to cross the creek at mile 1.3. The trail climbs along the creek bed and then settles into a lengthy level period as it winds north and then west. At mile 3.5 you cross a stream that feeds into Lower Hood Branch, then climb west out of the valley on an old road.

At mile 3.9 you are on top of the ridge along the state park boundary, and here the character of the trail changes noticeably. Instead of thick vegetation, the woods are open and the trail is wide, flat, and attractively covered with pine needles. Going southeast, you get views of distant ridges to the south and west. Soon you see Forest Service signs marking a Daniel Boone National Forest tract on the right. The views peter out, but the walking is delightful—the kind that lets you put your feet on

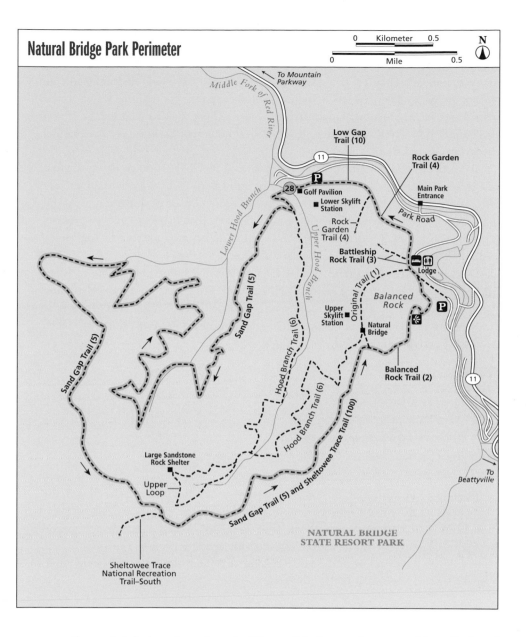

0   Kilometer   0.5

0   Mile   0.5

N

To Mountain Parkway

Middle Fork of Red River

Low Gap Trail (10)

Rock Garden Trail (4)

11

Main Park Entrance

P

28   Golf Pavilion

Lower Skylift Station

Park Road

Lower Hood Branch

Rock Garden Trail (4)

Sand Gap Trail (5)

Upper Hood Branch

Battleship Rock Trail (3)

Lodge

Original Trail (1)

Balanced Rock

P

Upper Skylift Station

Natural Bridge

Hood Branch Trail (6)

Balanced Rock Trail (2)

11

Sand Gap Trail (5)

Hood Branch Trail (6)

Sand Gap Trail (5) and Sheltowee Trace Trail (100)

To Beattyville

Large Sandstone Rock Shelter

Upper Loop

NATURAL BRIDGE STATE RESORT PARK

Sheltowee Trace National Recreation Trail–South

autopilot and sink deep into thought. The trail is frequently on an old roadbed and veers back and forth across the park's legal boundary line.

At mile 5.4 the trail dead-ends into another wide forest track; make a sharp left. In addition to Sand Gap Trail, you are now also on Sheltowee Trace National Recreation Trail (100), a long-distance hiking route through the Daniel Boone National Forest blazed with the likeness of a turtle. *Sheltowee*, the Indian name for Daniel Boone, means "big turtle." If you were to head right at this junction instead of left, in less than a mile you'd walk across a narrow ridge and the top of Whites Branch Arch.

After joining the Sheltowee, the trail narrows into a path. It heads east and then north with little change in elevation before coming to an overlook with a fine panorama that includes Natural Bridge. At mile 7.5, just past the overlook, Sand Gap Trail ends at the park's Balanced Rock Trail (2), which you take for 0.8 mile down to the lodge area. At this junction Natural Bridge is just a short walk to your left (north); if you haven't yet seen this arch, the side trip is definitely worthwhile. (See the Natural Bridge and Hood Branch hike.)

To complete this hike, turn right onto Balanced Rock Trail and go down the first of a series of stairways that are long and steep enough to make you thankful you are not coming up. The path goes north along a massive cliff of pockmarked rock and soon descends to Balanced Rock—a rounded boulder that, thanks to uneven erosion, is perched atop a small pedestal of rock in apparent defiance of gravity. The trail passes a rock shelter and ends near the lodge at mile 8.3.

From here you follow a series of trails back to the chairlift parking lot. Take Original Trail (1) and climb toward Natural Bridge. At the fork, bear right onto Battleship Rock Trail (3), and in a short distance turn right onto Rock Garden Trail (4). At mile 9.3, where Rock Garden Trail bends left, turn right onto Low Gap Trail (10), which descends to the chairlift parking lot at mile 9.8.

Key Points

1.3 Lower Hood Branch crossing.

3.9 Top of the ridge.

5.4 Sheltowee Trace National Recreation Trail.

7.5 End of Sand Gap Trail and beginning of Balanced Rock Trail.

8.3 Lodge area.

Option: You can shorten this hike by more than 2 miles by using the Skylift, the park's chairlift, to return to the parking lot. At the end of Sand Gap Trail, turn left (instead of right) onto Balanced Rock Trail. This will quickly take you to Natural Bridge and the upper chairlift station. The chairlift operates from 10 a.m. to 6:30 p.m. (7:30 p.m. on Saturday) from the last weekend of March through October; a fee is charged.

29 Pilot Knob

If you want a magnificent view west and north into the Kentucky Bluegrass region, this hike to the top of Pilot Knob is perfect.

Start: Parking lot at end of Brush Creek Road in community of Westbend
Distance: 3.65-mile lollipop
Hiking time: About 2.5 hours
Difficulty: Moderate
Best seasons: Any (but pick a clear day so you can enjoy the view)
Other trail users: None
Canine compatibility: No dogs allowed
Land status: State nature preserve
Nearest town: Clay City

Fees and permits: None
Maps: Pilot Knob map from Kentucky State Nature Preserves Commission; USGS Levee
Trail contact: Kentucky State Nature Preserves Commission, (502) 573-2886
Special considerations: No camping or off-trail activities, including climbing, are allowed in the Pilot Knob nature preserve.
Parking and trailhead facilities: There's space for about 6 cars, but no facilities.

Finding the trailhead: From exit 16 off the Bert T. Combs Mountain Parkway near Clay City, take KY 15 north, and in 3 miles turn right onto Brush Creek Road, the only paved road to the right in the community of Westbend. There is a historical marker noting Daniel Boone's supposed visit to Pilot Knob on KY 15 just before the turn. Brush Creek Road immediately crosses over the parkway; in 1.5 miles the pavement ends. Park in the gravel area on your right. Be aware that this parking lot is also a turnaround for school buses, so be sure to allow space if visiting during the school week. GPS: N37 54.720' / W83 56.715'

The Hike

Pilot Knob affords visitors a vista made famous in history books, as the point where famed Kentucky explorer Daniel Boone is said to have gotten his first view in 1796 of the storied rolling, fertile hills of Kentucky's Bluegrass region from the aptly named "Boone's Overlook," on the southeastern end of the 730-foot-tall sandstone outcropping. While there is no definitive evidence that Boone did in fact stand at that exact spot on the most obvious promontory along the line of knobs marking the western entrance to the more rugged hills of eastern Kentucky, historians believe it is highly likely.

What is certain is that this 1,440-foot lookout provides a good lesson in Kentucky geography. Behind you, to the east and south, are the forested ridges and high country of the Cumberland Plateau. In front of you, to the west and north, begins the relatively flat farmland of central Kentucky.

The top of Pilot Knob is only 1 mile from the parking area, but this loop trail allows you to explore more of this lovely 741-acre preserve. The loop is 1.9 miles long and is included in this hike's total of 3.65 miles.

From Pilot Knob the Bluegrass region of Kentucky unfolds to the north and west, while to the south lie the Cumberland Mountains.

From the parking area, take the old gravel road northeast. In a short distance you cross a creek, climb wooden steps on the far side, and pass through a metal gate. From here follow the well-trod Oscar Geralds Jr. Trail to the north. Just after the trail curves east, you come to a boxed sign-in sheet and a turnoff on the right for Millstone Quarry Trail. This side trail is a half mile and leads to a site where pioneers once quarried and shaped millstones.

Continuing eastward on Oscar Geralds Jr. Trail, climb steeply and at mile 0.5 reach the turnoff for Sage Point Trail. This trail, which is well marked with red paint, makes a loop to the south before rejoining the Oscar Geralds Jr. Trail 0.25 mile from the top of Pilot Knob.

Turning right onto Sage Point Trail, go south and then west on a shoulder before climbing to the top of Sage Point, a 1,110-foot-high knob with views west into the central Kentucky countryside. Turning around, you see Pilot Knob's rocky pinnacle above you. From here the trail descends southward and, after crossing a power-line clearing and a small stream, turns northeast to parallel the streambed. The trail is well marked.

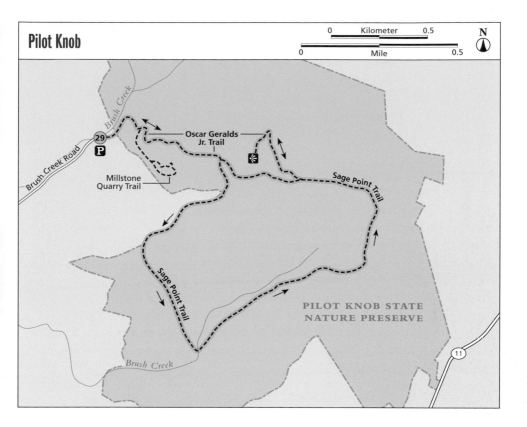

At the end of the streambed, make a short but steep climb to a gravel road used to service two communications towers west of the preserve. Turning left (north), follow the road less than 0.1 mile before a trail sign directs you back into the woods. The trail slabs around a hill and then climbs steeply westward before dead-ending into the Oscar Geralds Jr. Trail. At this point you have come 2.1 miles from the parking lot.

Turning right onto Oscar Geralds Jr. Trail, walk northwest before turning sharply south to reach the top of the knob and its rocky overlook at mile 2.65. Be careful near this unprotected drop-off. The views are to the west, north, and south. On a clear day you can see the water tower in the city of Richmond and the buildings of Eastern Kentucky University. This is a spot to enjoy. Return on Oscar Geralds Jr. Trail and reach your car at mile 3.65.

Key Points

0.5 Turn right onto Sage Point Trail.

2.4 Intersection with Oscar Geralds Jr. Trail.

2.65 Overlook atop Pilot Knob.

Lower Rockcastle

The Lower Rockcastle River—the stretch from just west of London to its entry into the Cumberland—flows through a beautiful, secluded section of the state that tends to get little attention from hikers. Perhaps that's because the recreational focus here is on the water. The Rockcastle and Cumberland, both swollen by backwater from Lake Cumberland's Wolf Creek Dam, are large streams, and Laurel River Lake is nearby. In few parts of Kentucky do boaters and anglers have as many opportunities as they do here.

But the Lower Rockcastle region is ideal for hikers as well. The river's last 16 miles have been designated a Kentucky Wild River, and the ridges and ravines along the largely untouched shore offer a number of good hikes. The area is within the Daniel Boone National Forest, and the USDA Forest Service maintains numerous trails and campsites. Recreation use fees are in effect at some locations. The London Ranger District (606-864-4163) has jurisdiction and can provide information. Also, see the Daniel Boone National Forest website at www.fs.usda.gov/main/r8/home.

The Cumberland River just above its confluence with the Rockcastle River. The rivers converge before flowing into Lake Cumberland (hike 34).

30 Laurel River Lake

Quiet tree-lined inlets along the peaceful Laurel River Lake are the setting for much of this stroll in the Daniel Boone National Forest.

Start: Flatwoods recreation area on Laurel River Lake
Distance: 3.4-mile lollipop
Hiking time: About 2 hours
Difficulty: Easy
Best seasons: Any
Other trail users: Mountain bikers
Canine compatibility: Dogs permitted, but must be leashed when in developed recreation area or campground
Land status: National forest
Nearest town: London or Corbin

Fees and permits: Vehicle pass required for cars parked at boat ramp but not for cars left at picnic area. Passes are sold at Forest Service offices and area stores; see www.fs.usda.gov/main/r8/passes-permits/recreation for a list of outlets.
Maps: Map #7 from London District of Daniel Boone National Forest; USGS Vox
Trail contact: London Ranger District, Daniel Boone National Forest, (606) 864-4163
Parking and trailhead facilities: You'll find parking spaces for several dozen cars, as well as restrooms.

Finding the trailhead: From exit 38 off I-75 at London, take KY 192 west for 8.4 miles and turn left (south) onto KY 312. In 3.5 miles, at a stop sign in the town of Keavy, turn right onto KY 3430; 1.7 miles later, turn right onto Flatwoods Road. In 2.6 miles, just beyond a right-hand turn for the Flatwoods picnic area, bear right to the Flatwoods boat ramp and park in the lot. Flatwoods Trail (470) starts on the lake bank by the ramp. (From Corbin, take KY 770 west for 1.2 miles and turn right (north) onto KY 312. In 0.5 mile, turn left onto KY 3430 and in 2 miles turn left onto Flatwoods Road. Follow the directions above to the boat ramp trailhead.) GPS: N36 57.147' / W84 12.433'

The Hike

The Laurel River was dammed in the early 1970s by the US Army Corps of Engineers to create a 5,600-acre lake for hydroelectric power and other purposes. Thanks at least in part to a prohibition on private homes and businesses within 300 feet of the waterline, the resulting Laurel River Lake is tree-lined and free of visible commercialization. It is also relatively deep for a man-made lake—about 260 feet. In short, it's a quiet (except for the motorboats) and appealing body of water.

This hike takes you along several small inlets on the multifingered lake's eastern shore. The path is shaded by pines and hardwoods, and ranges from running directly along the water to rising a good distance above it. The hike leads you by a number of spots good for a swim on a hot day. Of course, you are on your own: There are no lifeguards.

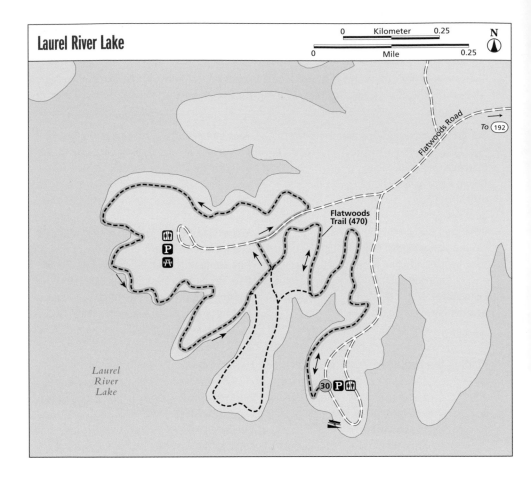

0   Kilometer   0.25

0   Mile   0.25

N

To 192

Flatwoods Road

Flatwoods
Trail (470)

Laurel
River
Lake

30

The Laurel River is a tributary of the Cumberland River, not the Rockcastle. But the Laurel is just east of the Rockcastle and part of the Lower Rockcastle area.

Flatwoods Trail (470) begins next to the water at the southwest end of the ramp parking lot and follows a long inlet north. The trail gradually rises above the shore and continues north around the streambed that feeds this finger before turning south down the other side of the ravine. At mile 0.8 the trail comes to an intersection; turn right onto a path climbing north. After 0.1 mile you come out on a paved road next to restrooms in the Flatwoods picnic area (mile 0.9). Turn right onto the road and walk 0.1 mile east to the parking area on the road's other side, where you find a sign marking the continuation of Flatwoods Trail. The path ducks back into the woods, initially going north and then curving west to follow another finger of the lake. Ferns make this a particularly attractive section.

At mile 1.4 pass a side trail coming in on your left from the end of the picnic area road. Bear right, continuing to follow the shoreline, and at 1.5 miles reach a spot just above the rocky shore that makes a pleasant, convenient place to stop for a swim.

At mile 1.9, after the trail curves around several small inlets, cross an old roadbed at the water's edge and then climb above the water. At mile 2.6 you come to a fork and bear right. While you may not recognize it from this direction, the left prong of the fork is the path you took up to the picnic area road early in your hike. This means that in another 0.8 mile, after retracing your steps, you are back at the boat ramp and your car.

Key Points

0.9 Picnic area.

1.5 Good lakeside spot.

Option: You can avoid the need to purchase a car pass by parking in the picnic area. If you do just the loop part of the hike, starting and ending at the picnic area, the mileage is 1.8.

31 Cane Creek

A secluded creek in the Daniel Boone National Forest, this hike passes several pretty streamside spots perfect for wading.

Start: Bald Rock picnic area
Distance: 5-mile out-and-back
Hiking time: About 3 hours
Difficulty: Easy
Best seasons: Any
Other trail users: Mountain bikers
Canine compatibility: Dogs permitted, but must be leashed when in developed recreation area or campground
Land status: National forest

Nearest town: London
Fees and permits: None
Maps: Map #1 from London District of Daniel Boone National Forest; USGS London SW
Trail contact: London Ranger District, Daniel Boone National Forest, (606) 864-4163
Parking and trailhead facilities: There's space for 15 to 20 cars, along with restrooms, drinking water, and picnic tables.

Finding the trailhead: From exit 38 off I-75 in London, take KY 192 west for 10.5 miles and turn right into the Bald Rock picnic area. The trail starts just beyond the restrooms at the edge of the woods. GPS: N37 01.949' / W84 13.338'

The Hike

Cane Creek, a tributary of the Rockcastle River, is a lazy little stream lined with rocky banks and small cliffs that make a walk along it thoroughly enjoyable. Except for a steep drop to the streambed at the beginning and a climb at the end, this hike is level as it follows the creek's path.

The Bald Rock picnic area was once the site of a fire lookout tower. Its use was discontinued in 1970 and the structure torn down. You won't find a bald rock in the picnic area either; that's the name of a nearby community.

From the picnic grounds, follow Sugar Tree Hollow Trail (407) north into the Cane Creek valley. It's a loop trail, and you can take it in either direction. The longer eastern leg, which I recommend for the trip down to the Cane Creek Trail, starts just behind the restrooms. It's a pleasant, narrow path that descends north along a ravine. At mile 0.7 the trail comes to a fork. Go right onto Cane Creek Trail (410), which winds its way to the creek and then follows its flow northwest. (The left prong of the fork leads 0.5 mile back up to the picnic area.) If there is no sign identifying Cane Creek Trail, just remember that Cane Creek Trail is the only path that runs off the Sugar Tree Hollow loop.

Beyond the junction Cane Creek Trail crosses the national forest boundary for a brief stretch across private property. You can see farm buildings below on the right. Go north, cross a small feeder stream, and follow it briefly on what appears to be an

Vanhook Falls along Cane Creek. The narrow stream plummets nearly 40 feet over a rock shelter to form the falls. PAM GIBSON

old road. When you come to a fork, go left; a right would take you to a barn. At mile 1.2, after skirting a farm field, you see Cane Creek about 20 feet below on your right. Some parts of the trail between Sugar Tree Hollow Trail and Cane Creek may be hard to find; the area is confused by old farm roads. Just be sure to go north and keep the field on your right.

Soon after reaching the creek side, the trail crosses a red-painted boundary line that shows you are back on national forest land. At mile 1.6 a large rock in the water makes a good resting place, and there's another pretty spot at mile 1.9, where you cross a bridge over a feeder stream just as it empties into the creek.

Beyond the bridge the trail widens from a path into an old roadbed. At mile 2.4, after moving away from the creek and above it, the trail makes a sharp right and descends, bringing you once again to the water. At mile 2.6 the creek turns to the west and the trail dead-ends into it.

Directly across the creek is FR 121, which connects with KY 192. If there hasn't been a lot of rain, you could easily wade across and pick up a shuttle car. The Forest Service cautions hikers not to try to cross the creek during high water. Assuming you

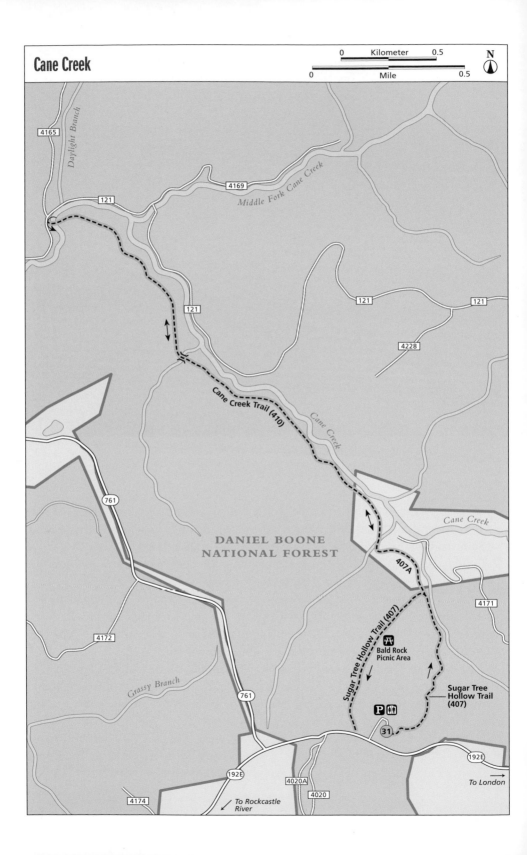

Cane Creek

0   Kilometer   0.5
0   Mile   0.5

N

4165

Daylight Branch

121

4169

Middle Fork Cane Creek

121

121

121

4228

Cane Creek Trail (410)

Cane Creek

761

Cane Creek

407A

DANIEL BOONE
NATIONAL FOREST

4171

4172

Sugar Tree Hollow Trail (407)

Bald Rock
Picnic Area

Sugar Tree
Hollow Trail
(407)

Grassy Branch

761

P

31

192E

To London

192E

4020A

4174

4020

To Rockcastle
River

have no shuttle, turn around and retrace your steps along the creek to the intersection with Sugar Tree Hollow Trail. At the trail junction, take a right onto the loop's western leg, which climbs steeply and comes out on the western side of the picnic grounds at mile 5.

Key Points

1.2 Reach the creek bank.

1.6 A pleasant streamside stop.

1.9 A second pleasant streamside spot.

2.6 Trail's end across from FR 121.

32 Rockcastle River

A beautiful hike that leads to multiple waterfalls and a river chute known as the Narrows of the Rockcastle River.

Start: Roadside clearing at the fork of KY 192 and KY 1193
Distance: 10.9-mile lollipop
Hiking time: About 6 hours
Difficulty: Moderate
Best seasons: Any
Other trail users: Mountain bikers
Canine compatibility: Dogs permitted
Land status: National forest
Nearest town: London

Fees and permits: None
Maps: Map #3 from London District of Daniel Boone National Forest; USGS Ano
Trail contact: London Ranger District, Daniel Boone National Forest, (606) 864-4163
Parking and trailhead facilities: There's space for 15 cars, but no facilities at the trailhead; water and restrooms are available at Bee Rock Campgrounds 4 miles west on KY 192.

Finding the trailhead: From exit 38 off I-75 in London, take KY 192 west for 15.5 miles to a spot where the road turns sharply right and KY 1193 forks to your left. Park in the off-road clearing left of this junction near the signboard. The trail starts immediately across KY 192 from the parking area. GPS: N36 59.872' / W84 16.992'

The Hike

Just before it flows into what was once the Cumberland River and is now officially Lake Cumberland, the Rockcastle River makes a tight loop to the east. On a map it looks like a big ear. Here tall cliffs on both sides force the stream into a thin chute called the Rockcastle Narrows that is popular with kayakers. This hike takes you down to and along the Narrows before catapulting you up the steep banks at the northern tip of the ear.

But first, the hike takes you on one of the prettiest paths you will find in Kentucky—the stretch from the parking area down into the Cane Creek valley. You descend through an area full of little streams and lovely waterfalls; it's worth a hike just by itself. This 2.6-mile section is part of Sheltowee Trace National Recreation Trail (100), the long north–south hiking route through the Daniel Boone National Forest. You also take this segment of the Sheltowee to return to your car at the end of the hike; it's the only backtracking on what is otherwise a loop.

From KY 192 the Sheltowee descends gently along a ravine that soon develops into a stream. After several stream crossings, you walk through a stand of pines. The stream you are following flows into Pounder Branch, which you follow north until it flows into Cane Creek. The first waterfall along the way is a small one just to the

Cascades along Bark Camp Creek near the Sheltowee Trace Trail. PAM GIBSON

right of the trail at mile 1.3. The water flows off a large rock into a pool and makes a fine spot for a refreshing dip in summer.

At mile 2.2 the trail crosses a large rock and turns sharply right to descend into a gorge where Pounder Branch and Cane Creek meet. Cross a bridge over Pounder and then immediately another, longer bridge across Cane, which by this point has grown from the lazy little flow featured in the Cane Creek hike into an adult-size stream. From here the Sheltowee continues north along a wall of rock and, after climbing to the northeast, comes to a good view of Vanhook Falls. The trail doesn't lead directly to the waterfall, but it's possible to scramble over to it; the Forest Service puts its height at 40 feet. Cross Vanhook Branch and, at mile 2.6, reach a trail junction. The Sheltowee goes right (north), while you go straight (west) on Rockcastle Narrows East Trail (401).

At the three-way fork, take a left and begin winding your way west at a level grade along the ridge side above Cane Creek. At mile 3.4 the trail makes a sharp left and

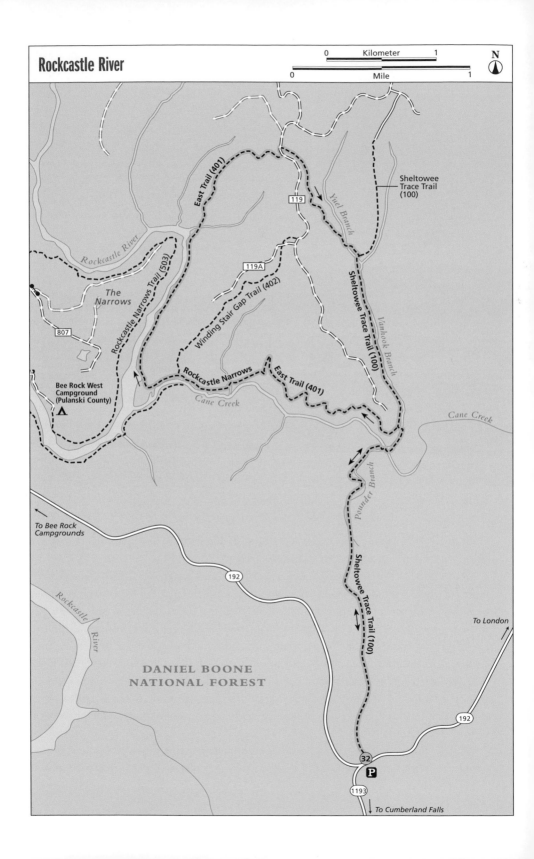

Rockcastle River

0 Kilometer 1

0 Mile 1

N

East Trail (401)

Sheltowee Trace Trail (100)

Yuel Branch

119

119A

Rockcastle River

The Narrows

Rockcastle Narrows Trail (503)

807

Winding Stair Gap Trail (402)

Sheltowee Trace Trail (100)

Vanhook Branch

Bee Rock West Campground (Pulanski County)

Rockcastle Narrows

East Trail (401)

Cane Creek

Cane Creek

Powder Branch

To Bee Rock Campgrounds

192

Sheltowee Trace Trail (100)

Rockcastle River

DANIEL BOONE NATIONAL FOREST

To London

192

32

P

1193

To Cumberland Falls

drops to near the creek. A mile later, shortly after passing a nice streamside spot with a good-size pool and sandy shore, you come to Winding Stair Gap Trail (402) on your right. Winding Stair Gap Trail runs 1.2 miles northeast to FR 119, which connects back to the Sheltowee Trace Trail.

Continuing on Rockcastle Narrows East Trail, at 4.6 miles you reach the Rockcastle River. Turn right and begin following the river through the Narrows. This unmarked turn can be momentarily confusing because there is also a path to your left, which ends in a short distance at a makeshift campsite. Cane Creek flows into the Rockcastle just beyond the trail but, at least when the foliage is out, their confluence is not visible.

The Rockcastle River stays below the trail, but there are numerous side paths to the boulder-strewn banks. The large rocks make a good place for sunning yourself. The yellow rings you see on trees along the river mark the boundary of a state wildlife management area. At the upper end of the river's loop, keep your eye out for the spot where the trail turns right, away from the water (GPS: N37 02.463' / W84 18.217'). The turn is marked by a white diamond painted on a tree, but it's easily missed because a more distinct path continues along the river. The turn comes about 1.5 miles beyond the Winding Stair Gap Trail junction and less than 0.1 mile after you cross a small stream. Just remember that if you find yourself following the riverbank west, you've missed the turn.

From the turn, climb steeply northeast to a cliff face, turn left, and climb some more. It's a tough haul to the top. Once there, the trail turns right onto an old roadbed and, at mile 6.5, dead-ends into gravel FR 119. Go left (north) on the road and in about 300 feet, at the trail marker, turn right. The path descends gently to the south, crosses Yuel Branch, and comes to Sheltowee Trace Trail at mile 7.1. From here you take the Sheltowee south to your car. The first 1.2-mile segment, which is new to you, follows Vanhook Branch back to the Rockcastle Narrows East Trail junction. From there you retrace your steps for 2.6 miles to KY 192.

Key Points

1.3 First waterfall.

2.3 Cane Creek.

2.6 Rockcastle Narrows East Trail junction.

4.6 Rockcastle River.

6.5 Trail dead-ends on FR 119.

7.1 Rejoin Sheltowee Trace Trail.

33 Rockcastle Narrows and Bee Rock

This walk along the western side of the Rockcastle River, past the striking Rockcastle Narrows, leads to Bee Rock with an overlook with a view of the river valley.

Start: Bee Rock West Campground
Distance: 4.5-mile loop
Hiking time: About 3 hours
Difficulty: Moderate
Best seasons: Any
Other trail users: None
Canine compatibility: Dogs permitted, must be leashed when in developed recreation area or campground
Land status: National forest

Nearest town: London
Fees and permits: None for day use; fee for overnight campground use
Maps: Bee Rock trail map from London District of Daniel Boone National Forest; USGS Ano
Trail contact: London Ranger District, Daniel Boone National Forest, (606) 864-4163
Parking and trailhead facilities: You'll find parking for a dozen or so cars, along with restrooms, water, and campsites.

Finding the trailhead: From exit 38 off I-75 in London, take KY 192 west for 15.5 miles to a spot where the road turns sharply right and KY 1193 forks to the left. Continue on KY 192 for 4 miles to the bridge over the Rockcastle River. At the far end of the bridge, turn right into Bee Rock West Campground (not Bee Rock East Campground on the near side of the bridge). Drive 0.9 mile to the end of the campground road and park. The trail starts at the south end of the parking area. (The end section of the road is gated closed in winter. The Forest Service cautions against parking in front of the gate.) GPS: N37 01.512' / W84 18.984'

The Hike

This hike follows the Rockcastle Narrows on the west bank, just across from the Rockcastle River hike. But the two treks are different in character. On this side the trail and woods have a more open, less remote feeling, and the hike is capped by an excellent view of the valley below. This vista is from the top of a cliff known as Bee Rock, so named because years ago it was supposedly the home of a large throng of honeybees.

From the parking lot, head south on Rockcastle Narrows Trail (503), following the river upstream. You immediately notice that there are a number of other paths going the same direction. Don't worry; they all merge sooner or later. Rockcastle Narrows Trail is blazed with white diamonds.

Early in the hike the river beside you is wide. That's because once it leaves the Narrows, the Rockcastle is technically part of Lake Cumberland. The Rockcastle runs into the Cumberland River just south of here. Wolf Creek Dam affects the water levels of both, even though the dam that creates Lake Cumberland is miles away.

Soon the trail and riverbank curve east and then north. By the time you've walked about 1 mile from the trailhead, the river has become the thin, fast stretch of water

Bee Rock stands high above KY 192 and the Rockcastle River. PAM GIBSON

known as the Narrows. The tall cliffs that have squeezed it into a thin chute rise above you on both sides. The trail stays above the river the entire way, but there are side paths down to it. At about mile 1.5, you and the riverbank curve west. Here the trail broadens from a path into a pleasant old roadbed, which rises gently before dead-ending into a gravel road at mile 2.0.

Turn left onto the gravel road, which climbs to FR 807 on top of the ridge. You will cross FR 807 later in the hike, but now you turn right, away from FR 807, and take the gravel road as it descends closer to the river and ends in less than 0.2 mile. Take an unmarked path to the left, climbing the riverbank until you reach another path on the left, this one marked with a sign that says 503, the number for Rockcastle Narrows Trail. Take the left trail and begin climbing west on switchbacks.

After leveling off, the trail slabs along the ridge side for a short distance and then climbs steeply to a cliff face. Go right, circle the cliff, and continue west. The trail then jogs south, traveling briefly through heavy vegetation that can make the way hard to find; just keep going up and you should have no problem. After winding through boulders and climbing wooden steps, the trail levels off just before reaching FR 807 at mile 3.0.

The trail continues across FR 807 and shortly dead-ends into a track of grass and dirt. This is Bee Rock Loop Trail (529), which runs from the campground up the ridge and back down to the campground. Take Bee Rock Loop Trail to the left, walking south and then southeast. At mile 3.6, almost immediately after passing a side trail

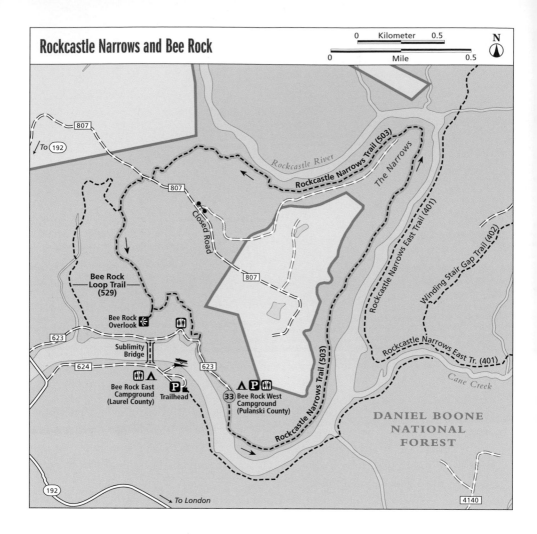

Rockcastle Narrows and Bee Rock

0   Kilometer   0.5

0   Mile   0.5

N

807

To 192

Rockcastle River

Rockcastle Narrows Trail (503)

The Narrows

807

Closed Road

807

Rockcastle Narrows East Trail (401)

Winding Stair Gap Trail (402)

Bee Rock
Loop Trail
(529)

Bee Rock
Overlook

623

Sublimity
Bridge

624

Bee Rock East
Campground
(Laurel County)

Trailhead

623

Rockcastle Narrows East Tr. (401)

Cane Creek

Rockcastle Narrows Trail (503)

33 Bee Rock West
Campground
(Pulanski County)

DANIEL BOONE
NATIONAL
FOREST

192

To London

4140

to the left, you come to the Bee Rock Overlook and a fine view of the river below and ridges to the south and east.

The hike's final leg is all downhill, some of it steeply so. Return to the side path you passed just before the lookout—it's now on your right—and take it a short distance to a railing. From here, wind your way down the cliff side, at one point passing through a cave-like opening. You'll reach the campground road at mile 4.2; your car is 0.3 mile to your left.

Key Points

1.0 Rockcastle Narrows.

3.0 Reach FR 807.

3.6 Bee Rock Overlook.

34 Rockcastle-Cumberland Confluence

A view of the confluence of the Rockcastle River and the Cumberland are highlights of this level walk along the Cumberland's upstream shoreline. In the spring, wildflowers make this especially lovely.

Start: Unpaved parking area on KY 3497 southwest of London
Distance: 9.1-mile loop
Hiking time: About 6 hours
Difficulty: Easy
Best seasons: Spring
Other trail users: Mountain bikers
Canine compatibility: Dogs permitted, but must be leashed when in developed recreation area or campground

Land status: National forest
Nearest town: London
Fees and permits: None
Maps: Map #5 from London District of Daniel Boone National Forest; USGS Sawyer
Trail contact: London Ranger District, Daniel Boone National Forest, (606) 864-4163
Parking and trailhead facilities: There's space for 4 cars, but no facilities.

Finding the trailhead: From exit 38 off I-75 in London, take KY 192 west for 15.5 miles to a spot where the road turns sharply right and KY 1193 forks to the left. Turn left onto KY 1193, and in 0.7 mile curve right onto KY 3497. After 3.8 miles, turn right into the small, unpaved parking area for Ned Branch Trail (405). The trail starts at the edge of the woods. GPS: N36 57.544' / W84 19.538'

The Hike

Lake Cumberland is the largest man-made lake east of the Mississippi River in terms of water volume. One reason is that it's deep—90 feet on average. Another is that it's long—101 miles. In all, Lake Cumberland has 1,255 miles of shoreline. The widest part—the part that on a map looks like a real lake—is the 50-mile stretch from the dam east to Burnside. But the dam affects the river's water level all the way to Cumberland Falls, and so the remaining 50-mile section, a portion of which you explore on this hike, is also officially a lake, even though it's snake-shaped like a river. This hike takes you to an overlook above the Rockcastle's confluence with the Cumberland and then follows the Cumberland shoreline upstream for 4 miles.

From the parking area, Ned Branch Trail (405) descends north to the Rockcastle River though a lush area of pines, ferns, and rhododendrons. On the way down, you skirt rock outcroppings and make several easy stream crossings. Just before the river, the trail divides. Lakeside North Trail (411) goes straight, following the Rockcastle north for 0.7 mile. Ned Branch Trail, which you continue to follow, turns left and crosses Ned Branch.

Just beyond the crossing, the little stream makes an elbow-shaped turn that backs up the water, creating a pool and a scenic rest spot. From here the trail parallels the

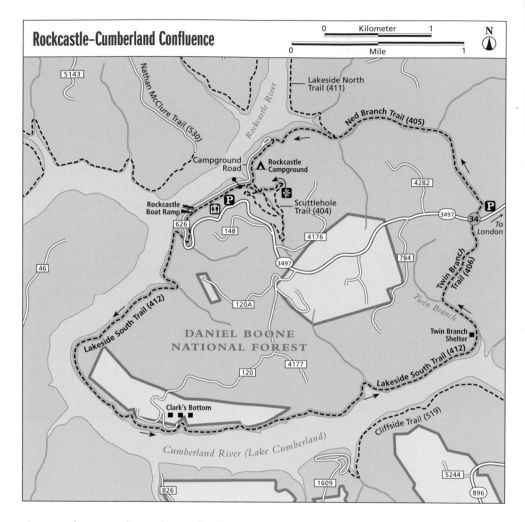

river southwest and at mile 1.9 dead-ends into a paved road running through Rock-castle Campground. This Forest Service fee facility has restrooms, drinking water, and twenty-four campsites.

Follow the road along the river for 0.4 mile, then turn left (south) onto Scuttle-hole Trail (404), which is marked by a sign. In 0.1 mile Scuttlehole Trail turns left and climbs steeply eastward to the base of a cliff. Bear right and go up a steep wooden stairway with lots of steps (127 according to the Forest Service). Be careful; these are slippery even in dry weather. At the top, turn left (a right would take you to KY 3497) and curve west. At 0.3 mile from the road, you reach an overlook with a stone fence in front of the drop-off. If you continue along the cliff, you come to two more over-looks in quick succession. All three have good views southwest to the point where the Rockcastle flows into the Cumberland. But the third vista is the best, because it also allows a look north up the Rockcastle. This view, at mile 2.6, is well worth the climb.

Return to the campground road and continue southwest along the Rockcastle. After leaving the waterfront, the campground road becomes KY 3497. Continue on it for 0.4 mile to a sign on your right marking the beginning of Lakeside South Trail (412) at mile 3.8. For the next 4.2 miles, this trail takes you along the Cumberland River/Lake Cumberland shore, almost all on level ground.

If you expect to find a swimming spot, you will probably be disappointed. The riverbank is often muddy and lined with flotsam in this area. The walking is nice, however, and the trail stays in the woods, a short distance from the water. In about 2 miles, pass through a collection of cottages; this is Clark's Bottom, a private summer community. At mile 7.9 you come to Twin Branch Shelter, a well-maintained, three-sided overnight facility for backpackers. It sits about 50 feet above the water and can sleep six comfortably. There are a number of suitable tent sites nearby.

Just beyond the shelter, Lakeside South Trail curves away from the river and becomes Twin Branch Trail (406). The trail climbs steeply and then descends to small, clear Twin Branch. After crossing the stream, make a steady ascent almost all the way back to KY 3497. It's the only time on the hike that you have to work. At mile 9.1 you reach the road across from the parking area.

Key Points

2.6 Overlook.

3.8 Cumberland River.

7.9 Twin Branch Shelter.

Cumberland Falls Area

On February 12, 1780, Zachariah Green and three fellow hunters boating down the Cumberland River had quite a surprise. It turned out that the rumbling they heard wasn't their stomachs. Green, his brother, and two companions are believed to have been the first non–Native Americans to discover the existence of Cumberland Falls. It was a tough lesson indeed, but they were lucky enough to make it ashore before being swept over the huge cascade.

Plunging 68 feet and spanning 125 feet, the waterfall is a powerful, beautiful, and, yes, noisy force of nature that has been impressing visitors ever since Zachariah and his hapless hunting party first reached it. But while the "Niagara of the South," as the waterfall has long been promoted, is the main attraction, the area has lots of other intriguing scenery and terrain. In addition to the 1,657–acre Cumberland Falls State Resort Park (606-528-4121 or 800-325-0063), the hikes in this section explore two nearby attractions in Daniel Boone National Forest—the Natural Arch Scenic Area and the Beaver Creek Wilderness. The Stearns Ranger District (606-376-5323) has information on both.

A moonbow often appears at the base of Cumberland Falls during the full moon (hikes 35 and 36).

35 Dog Slaughter Falls

This walk takes you from magnificent Cumberland Falls to a far smaller but delightful waterfall downstream. The return leg is on trails noted for wildflowers.

Start: Gift shop at Cumberland Falls State Resort Park
Distance: 7.2-mile lollipop
Hiking time: About 5 hours
Difficulty: Moderate
Best seasons: Spring and early summer
Other trail users: Lots of non-hiking tourists at Cumberland Falls overlooks at hike's start
Canine compatibility: Leashed dogs permitted
Land status: State park, national forest, state nature preserve

Nearest town: Corbin
Fees and permits: None
Maps: Cumberland Falls State Resort Park visitor guide; Map #6 from London District of Daniel Boone National Forest; USGS Cumberland Falls
Trail contact: Cumberland Falls State Resort Park, (606) 528-4121 or (800) 325-0063
Parking and trailhead facilities: You'll find lots of parking space, as well as restrooms, water, a snack bar, and a gift shop.

Finding the trailhead: From exit 25 off I-75 near Corbin, take US 25W south for 7 miles and turn right (west) onto KY 90. In 7.5 more miles, KY 90 passes the entrance to the Cumberland Falls State Resort Park lodge and begins a steep, winding descent to the Cumberland River. At the bottom of the hill—0.6 mile from the lodge entrance—turn right at the sign for the park gift shop. The trail begins in front of the gift shop. GPS: N36 50.367' / W84 20.723'

The Hike

This hike takes you from the state park overlooks at Cumberland Falls down the Cumberland River to a 15-foot-high waterfall on Dog Slaughter Creek. In comparison to its mighty neighbor, Dog Slaughter Falls is a mere trickle—but it's a lovely trickle in a picturesque setting of rocky cliffs and big boulders. There's another difference as well. The Cumberland Falls viewing area is paved with concrete and full of people. At the pint-size falls, chances are it will just be you.

To return from the falls, you can retrace yours steps along the Cumberland; this stretch of the river has lots of rapids and sandy beaches that make the trip enjoyable a second time. The loop hike described here, however, returns through the park interior on trails noted for their wildflowers. Park naturalist Bret Smitley says that violets, trilliums, and irises are plentiful in spring. But be aware that the interior route is longer and more difficult. If you're tired or it's not wildflower time, you might consider taking the level riverside trail. Also, in summer when the leaves are out, there are no good views from the ridgetops along the interior trails.

From the gift shop, two sidewalks head north. Take the one closer to the river; it goes to a series of overlooks with good views of Cumberland Falls and signs explaining the area's geological and human history. At the fifth and last overlook,

Dog Slaughter Creek, a tributary to the Cumberland River, tumbles 15 feet to form Dog Slaughter Falls. PAM GIBSON

turn around and go back toward the gift shop until you come to a concrete ramp to the left. Take this and, at its end, turn left and begin walking north. This is Moonbow Trail, which runs downstream 10.6 miles to where the Laurel River flows into the Cumberland (see option). Moonbow Trail carries the numerical designation of (1) in the park trail list. Moonbow Trail is also the long-distance Sheltowee Trace National Recreation Trail (100). The name Moonbow has long been associated with the falls because on full-moon nights, a "moonbow" can be seen in the mist generated by the plunging river.

The turn onto the Moonbow is at mile 0.3. Initially, you are above the river. Shortly, however, after passing two separate entrances to the park's Wildflower Loop Trail (12), Moonbow Trail makes a sharp left and descends on wooden steps to just above the river. The large boulders between the trail and the water make a good place to stop and watch the fast-moving Cumberland. Not to disturb your reverie, but the building on the bluff above you is the park sewage treatment plant. If you look for it, you will see a pipe discharging liquid—fully treated, I was told—into the river.

At mile 0.8, after crossing a rock area at the base of a cliff, the trail comes to the first of a series of nice beaches. At mile 1.0 turn onto the Rock House Trail (7); just a few feet into that trail, a trickle of water cascades off a tall cliff, providing a refreshing shower on a hot day. According to Pam Gibson, park maintenance supervisor, the 0.5-mile Rock House Trail has become a permanent reroute for this particular section of the Moonbow Trail. The stretch of riverside this trail bypasses is frequently washed out. This trail takes hikers up and over that trouble-prone spot. The Rock House Trail will dead-end back into the Moonbow Trail.

For the next little while, the Moonbow alternates between rocky stretches over outcroppings and flat, low areas with heavy vegetation. At mile 1.7 it passes the beginning of Cumberland River Trail (2), which you will take later on the return route.

Continue on the Moonbow across more nice beaches as well as a small stream on a bridge. Where the river makes a distinct turn to the west, the trail turns east along a large stream. This is Dog Slaughter Creek, and in just a few feet, you come to the junction with the USDA Forest Service's Dog Slaughter Trail (414). (You left the state park and entered the national forest 0.25 mile before the creek.)

Take Dog Slaughter Trail to the right. After a climb of 0.2 mile over rocks along a cliff face, you reach the base of Dog Slaughter Falls at mile 2.8. Be careful: The large rocks lining the pool at the bottom of the falls are slippery. Ease yourself onto them and enjoy a great rest spot. From the falls Dog Slaughter Trail heads east about 4 miles in the Daniel Boone National Forest and reaches FR 195 about 3.5 miles from KY 90, as well as again at a point about a mile from KY 90.

When you're ready to move on, retrace your steps to the mouth of the creek and take Moonbow Trail back to its junction with Cumberland River Trail (2). From here on you meander over ridges in the park's interior. Turn left onto Cumberland River Trail and climb switchbacks to the east and then the south. At mile 4.5 Cumberland River Trail meets Anvil Branch Trail (11). Turn right onto Anvil Branch Trail and begin winding southward. (The Cumberland River Trail turns left and makes a long trek east to KY 90 and then south to the river.) You eventually descend to cross a small, pretty stream with mossy logs at mile 5.2 and then climb toward KY 90. Just before the road, the trail turns north and descends to a dead end at Rock House Trail (7).

Turn left onto Rock House, cross a brook, and turn right onto Wildflower Loop Trail (12). Wildflower Loop follows a long cliff face west and then north before crossing the park road to the sewage plant. From there, descend to Moonbow Trail at mile 7.0. The gift shop is 0.2 mile to the left on a path parallel to the one you took to the falls overlooks at the beginning of the hike.

Key Points

0.1 Cumberland Falls.

1.7 Pass Cumberland River Trail (2).

2.8 Dog Slaughter Falls.

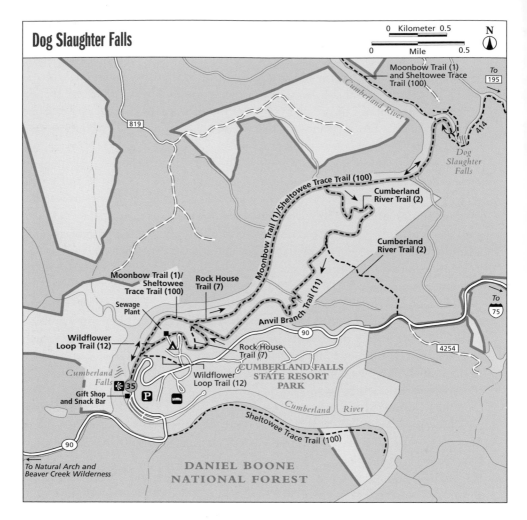

Dog Slaughter Falls

0 Kilometer 0.5

0 Mile 0.5

N

Moonbow Trail (1) and Sheltowee Trace Trail (100)

To 195

Cumberland River

819

414

Dog Slaughter Falls

Moonbow Trail (1)/Sheltowee Trace Trail (100)

Cumberland River Trail (2)

Cumberland River Trail (2)

Moonbow Trail (1)/ Sheltowee Trace Trail (100)

Rock House Trail (7)

Sewage Plant

Anvil Branch Trail (11)

Wildflower Loop Trail (12)

Rock House Trail (7)

90

To 75

4254

Cumberland Falls

35

Gift Shop and Snack Bar

P

Wildflower Loop Trail (12)

CUMBERLAND FALLS STATE RESORT PARK

Cumberland River

90

Sheltowee Trace Trail (100)

To Natural Arch and Beaver Creek Wilderness

DANIEL BOONE NATIONAL FOREST

Option: For a one- or two-night backpack trip, you can continue on Moonbow Trail from Dog Slaughter Creek to the Mouth of Laurel boat ramp on KY 1277. The total distance from Cumberland Falls is 10.6 miles. There are two overnight shelters along the trail, at about 5 and 7 miles from the falls. There is no easy way, however, to devise a loop route back to the falls, so you would have to arrange a shuttle.

KENTUCKYTRAIL TOWNS

Under the leadership of two-term Democratic governor Steve Beshear (2007–2015) and with the enthusiastic support of his wife, First Lady Jane Beshear, an avid equestrian, Kentucky began to invest heavily in its adventure tourism economy. Governor Beshear created the Adventure Tourism Office and his wife crisscrossed the state to promote Kentucky's recreation assets, while encouraging communities and the legislature to invest in infrastructure including trails and public campgrounds. The Kentucky State Park system has added recreation attractions that range from sanctioned rock-climbing routes to zip lines, and even the state's first scuba-diving refuge at Greenbo Lake (see hike 1). To help communities recognize and take advantage of the economic opportunities linked to tourism, the state has encouraged communities to become certified Kentucky Trail Towns.

More than a dozen Kentucky towns have joined the growing list of designated Trail Towns with more than thirty others in some phase of the application process at the end of 2015. Trail Towns are recognized for serving as gateways to popular outdoor recreation areas and have businesses that meet the needs of these tourists. The first town to become certified under the initiative in 2013 was Governor Beshear's hometown of Dawson Springs. Located in the Pennyrile area of the state along the scenic Tradewater River, the small community is surrounded by hunting, fishing, hiking, biking, horseback riding, and paddling destinations (see hike 80).

Other Trail Towns include Morehead, which is noted for its proximity to Cave Run Lake, a renowned muskie fishing locale. A center for Appalachian culture, it is close to the hiking and equestrian trails of the Daniel Boone National Forest (see hikes 7–9). Livingston, in the heart of the Daniel Boone National Forest, is near the midway point of the more than 300-mile Sheltowee Trace National Recreation Trail. London, known for its world-class cycling routes, is also a launching point for water sports on the Rockcastle River, the Laurel River, and Laurel River Lake (see hikes 30–34).

Stearns, sandwiched by both the Big South Fork Recreation Area and the Daniel Boone National Forest, is in the heart of McCreary County, which has sixty-one documented natural arches. The region is noted for its hiking, biking, paddling, and horseback riding and for the Stearns Historic Railway, which takes visitors into the gorge along the Big South Fork (see hikes 41–47). In the center of northeast Kentucky's Olive Hill, the Trailhead Depot is steps from a put-in to Tygarts Creek and serves as an access point for trails to Carter Caves State Resort Park and the city's Lake Trail System (see hikes 3–6).

(continued on next page)

KENTUCKY TRAIL TOWNS (continued)

Elkhorn City, the newest Trail Town, along the banks of the Russell Fork River, is a destination not only for whitewater kayakers, but also for cyclists traversing the US 76 Trans-America Bike Route. Hikers also flock to Elkhorn en route to a variety of Pine Mountain trails (see hikes 10–13).

The cities of Benham, Cumberland, and Lynch, known as Harlan County's Tri-Cities, are all historic mining towns and provide access to some of the area's best hiking and outdoor recreation areas. The Pine Mountain Scenic Trail, Kingdom Come State Park, the Looney Creek Trail System, and Kentucky Summit Bike Route, which takes cyclists to the top of Black Mountain, Kentucky's highest peak, are a short distance from this trio of mountain hamlets (see hikes 15–20).

36 Eagle Falls

This short hike gives you great cliff-side views down onto Cumberland Falls, plus a visit to beautiful Eagle Falls.

Start: Parking area along KY 90 across Cumberland River from state park

Distance: 2.2-mile lollipop

Hiking time: About 1.5 hours

Difficulty: Strenuous

Best seasons: Any

Other trail users: None

Canine compatibility: No dogs allowed

Land status: State nature preserve within a state park

Nearest town: Corbin

Fees and permits: None

Maps: Cumberland Falls State Resort Park visitor guide; USGS Cumberland Falls

Trail contact: Cumberland Falls State Resort Park, (606) 528-4121 or (800) 325-0063

Special considerations: During times of high water, the side trail to the base of Eagle Falls may be impassable. If in doubt, check with park personnel.

Parking and trailhead facilities: There are designated spaces for 6 cars and room for 6 more to squeeze in. No facilities are available at the trailhead, but restrooms, water, and a snack bar are at the state park gift shop next to the main Cumberland Falls viewing area, located 0.6 mile east on KY 90.

Finding the trailhead: From exit 25 off I-75 near Corbin, take US 25W south for 7 miles and turn right (west) onto KY 90. In 7.5 miles, KY 90 passes the entrance to the Cumberland Falls State Resort Park lodge and begins a steep, winding descent to the Cumberland River. Continue west across the river and pull into a parking area on the right shoulder 0.3 mile from the end of the bridge. The trailhead is just up the hill from the parking area and on the same side of the road. GPS: N36 50.209' / W84 20.734'

The Hike

This is a short hike, but beware: It's not an easy one. It has more ups and downs per mile than most walks. It also has more scenic rewards.

Hundreds of years ago, according to a history of the area by Jeannie McConnell, Eagle Falls was sacred to the Native Americans, and it's easy to see why. Though just a thin ribbon of water, Eagle Creek plunges an impressive 44 feet onto the rocky Cumberland River shoreline, creating a scene that is Mother Nature at her most pleasing. As a bonus, the hike takes you past several overlooks that offer the best views of Cumberland Falls in the park.

From the north side of KY 90, take Eagle Falls Trail (9) north, paralleling the Cumberland River. Almost immediately the trail begins climbing, and you are soon looking down on the swirling river just before it tumbles over Cumberland Falls. In a few more minutes, you are directly above the falls. From this vantage point, more

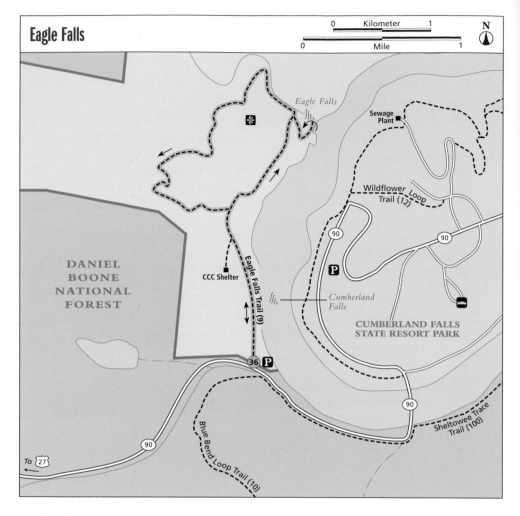

so than from the main falls observation area across the river, you can actually feel the power of the falling water.

The striking views continue as you climb. At mile 0.3 a trail branches off to your left, rising sharply on steps to a shelter built in the 1930s by the Civilian Conservation Corps (CCC). The shelter provides an overlook across the river during the winter, when Pinnacle Knob Watch Tower can be seen. Otherwise in the summer, vegetation obscures the view. The climb to the shelter is about 0.1 mile. The property immediately behind the shelter is private and monitored by cameras.

Continuing north on Eagle Falls Trail, you soon come to a fork and the beginning of the loop portion of the hike. Turn right at the fork, and at mile 0.6, after a brief descent, make a sharp right onto a side trail. This side trail, which is marked with a sign for Eagle Falls, descends toward the river on a series of wood-and-stone stairways steep enough that there is a cable to use as a banister. The boulder-lined riverbank is at the bottom. The trail here isn't marked; just follow the river downstream, and at mile 0.8 reach the base of Eagle Falls. This is a fine spot for a picnic; the creek water makes a nice pool before flowing into the river, and large rocks provide plenty of good reclining opportunities.

When you're ready to continue, retrace your steps to the main Eagle Falls Trail at 1.0 mile, and go right. The trail descends gently and, at mile 1.1, reaches Eagle Creek above the falls. Though you can't see the water cascading over the rocks, you are now at the top of the falls. According to Pam Gibson, park maintenance supervisor, rare snails live in this part of the creek. Hikers should be cautious not to disturb them.

From here the trail follows the creek upstream to another falls, this one small but also picturesque. After making your way through a patch of rhododendrons, leave the stream and begin climbing to the south, steeply in places. On the way up, the trail jogs around a couple of cliffs before reaching the ridgetop at mile 1.5. From there it's a short, mostly level walk back to the fork where the loop began. Turn right and retrace your steps down to the parking area.

Key Points

0.3 Side trail to CCC shelter.

0.6 Side trail to falls.

0.8 Base of falls.

1.0 Junction with Eagle Falls Trail.

Option: If you're up for more walking, you will find the trailhead for the Blue Bend hike just across KY 90 from the parking area.

37 Blue Bend

This leisurely hike along a serene stretch of the Cumberland River upstream of the falls includes a number of attractive riverside spots.

Start: Parking area on side of KY 90 near state park
Distance: 4.3-mile loop
Hiking time: About 3 hours
Difficulty: Easy
Best seasons: Any
Other trail users: None
Canine compatibility: No dogs allowed
Land status: State nature preserve within a state park, national forest
Nearest town: Corbin
Fees and permits: None

Maps: Cumberland Falls State Resort Park visitor guide; USGS Cumberland Falls
Trail contact: Cumberland Falls State Resort Park, (606) 528-4121 or (800) 325-0063
Parking and trailhead facilities: There are designated spaces for 6 cars and room for 6 more to squeeze in. No facilities are available at the trailhead, but you'll find restrooms, water, and a snack bar at the state park gift shop next to the main Cumberland Falls viewing area, located 0.6 mile east on KY 90.

Finding the trailhead: This hike starts just across the road from the Eagle Falls hike. From exit 25 off I-75 near Corbin, take US 25W south for 7 miles and turn right (west) onto KY 90. In 7.5 more miles, KY 90 passes the entrance to the Cumberland Falls State Resort Park lodge and begins a steep, winding descent to the Cumberland River. Continue west across the river and pull into the parking area on the right shoulder 0.3 mile beyond the end of the bridge. The trailhead is across the road and just up the hill from the parking area. GPS: N36 50.195 '/ W84 20.755'

The Hike

The Cumberland River above the falls is wide, smooth, and peaceful, an altogether different stream from the fierce, boulder-strewn flow below the falls. This hike takes you along the serene Cumberland—from its sharp westward turn, known as Blue Bend, to the KY 90 bridge just above the falls. This stretch of just over 2 miles is perfect for the early evening hours or any other time you feel like taking a quiet, relaxing stroll.

Delightful rest spots dot the riverbank and invite wading. But be careful: Preserve personnel warn that despite the river's surface calm, the current can at times be swift. Backcountry camping is not allowed on preserve property.

To reach the river, take the state park's Blue Bend Loop Trail (10 on new park maps), which starts on the south side of KY 90 opposite the parking area. Marked with blue paint on trees and the letters "BB" on signposts, the trail follows an old roadbed as it climbs steadily but easily to the south. At mile 0.4 it reaches a clearing and makes a sharp turn left (east). You are now on the top of the ridge, and from here

The Blue Bend area of the Cumberland River. PAM GIBSON

the hike is almost entirely level. From KY 90 to the riverbank, the distance is just less than 2 miles.

Although designated a state nature preserve, the terrain in this first segment is unspectacular. The ridgetop was logged in the early 1990s, and small trees and brush predominate. Also, the remnants of old roads can be confusing. After passing a metal gate at mile 0.8, the trail splits in two; follow the left-hand fork. At mile 1.2 there is a signpost directing a right turn around a marshy area.

Continuing east, reach a sign announcing that the long-distance Sheltowee Trace National Recreation Trail (100) lies 0.6 mile ahead. The Sheltowee, which runs north–south through much of the state, begins following the Cumberland just south of the park. At mile 1.8, after a sharp but brief descent to the southeast, Blue Bend Loop Trail dead-ends into the Sheltowee at the riverbank. Turn left onto the Sheltowee and begin following the Cumberland downstream toward the KY 90 bridge, officially known as Gatliff Bridge (the name used on the trail signs).

At mile 2.5 there is a group of large shoreline rocks perfect for sitting and enjoying the scene. If you want a softer perch, you'll find a small beach just beyond the rocks.

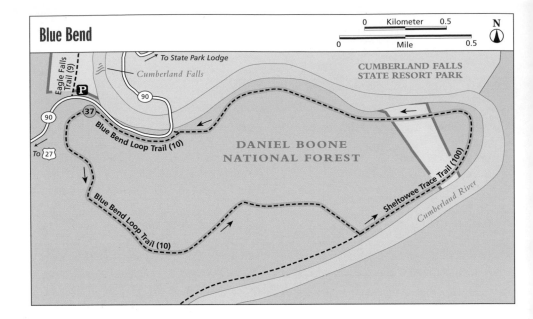

As you head west, the river seems to gradually pick up steam. The trail also becomes a bit rougher as it passes along a tall cliff. Shortly before reaching the bridge at mile 3.9, the trail veers away from the river, crosses a ravine, and climbs steeply up stone steps. You briefly parallel the river's course from on high before the trail ends at the KY 90 bridge. If you walk out on the bridge, you get a good view of the rapids that form just upstream.

The Sheltowee follows the bridge across the river, but you follow KY 90 back to your car, an uphill walk of 0.4 mile. Be careful on the highway. The shoulder is nonexistent in places, and cars come barreling down the big hill at high speeds. If you have children with you, take their hands.

Key Points

0.4 Sharp left turn.

1.8 Sheltowee Trace Trail and Cumberland River.

3.9 KY 90 bridge.

38 Natural Arch

Natural Arch is one of Kentucky's largest and provides a dramatic send-off for this walk along streams and through woodlands.

Start: Natural Arch Scenic Area in Daniel Boone National Forest
Distance: 6-mile lollipop
Hiking time: About 3 hours
Difficulty: Moderate
Best seasons: Any
Other trail users: None
Canine compatibility: Dogs permitted
Land status: National forest
Nearest town: Whitley City
Fees and permits: Day-use pass required in Natural Arch Scenic Area. You can pay at the entrance or buy a tag at USDA Forest Service offices; see www.fs.usda.gov/dbnf.
Maps: Forest Service map of Natural Arch area; USGS Nevelsville
Trail contact: Stearns Ranger District, Daniel Boone National Forest, (606) 376-5323
Special considerations: The trail crosses Cooper Creek 2 miles into the hike. This good-size stream can be impassable in high water. If in doubt, check with the Stearns Ranger District.
Parking and trailhead facilities: You'll find space for about 30 cars, plus a large picnic area with tables, restrooms, and water.

Finding the trailhead: From the intersection of KY 90 and US 27, about 20 miles south of Somerset, take US 27 south for 0.5 mile and turn right (west) onto KY 927. In 1.7 miles, turn right onto a paved road that dead-ends in 0.2 mile at a parking lot for Natural Arch. The trailhead is the concrete walkway at the north end of the lot. GPS: N36 50.522' / W84 30.756'

The Hike

Natural Arch is either 50 feet (in height) by 90 feet (in length) or 60 feet by 100 feet depending on what publication you consult. The Forest Service generally cites the former figures, but whatever the exact dimensions of this sandstone arch, it is definitely one of Kentucky's largest. (Natural Bridge, in comparison, is 65 feet by 78 feet.) It's also one of the most impressive, and in 1961 it and 945 surrounding acres were given special protection as a scenic area. This hike makes a loop through the arch and along the area's perimeter on a series of paths and forest roads left over from the days when homesteaders farmed the stream bottoms.

Even if there were no arch, this would be a walk well worth taking, through a lovely forest and along several attractive streams. In some places, including a parcel adjacent to the parking lot, numerous trees were downed by severe winter storms in 1994 and 1998. An infestation of southern pine beetle has also taken a toll. The damage is still evident but does not overshadow the scenic rewards. I took the hike on a rainy July day and consider it one of the most pleasing in this part of the state.

Natural Arch is one of Kentucky's largest.

The scenic area is restricted to day use. However, backcountry camping is allowed east of FR 5266 and north of Cooper Creek, making an overnight trip possible. Roughly, the scenic area's boundaries are FR 5266, Cooper Creek, and KY 927.

The hike starts on the concrete walkway near the middle of the parking area on the right. But if you want a panorama of where you will be going, take the concrete walkway at the center of the parking lot. In less than 0.1 mile, it delivers you to an overlook with a fine vista of the arch and scenic area.

Returning to the parking lot, take the concrete walkway past the picnic shelter to the asphalt walkway, Natural Arch Trail (510). It heads north on the ridgetop to another observation point, this one with more limited views. From here descend on a series of log-and-stone steps to an intersection at mile 0.2 with Buffalo Canyon Trail (508), also known as 5-Mile Loop Trail. This is the path you'll take through the scenic area; it's well marked with white diamonds. There is no Buffalo Canyon in the area, at least none that Forest Service personnel know of, and the origin of the trail name seems to be lost to history.

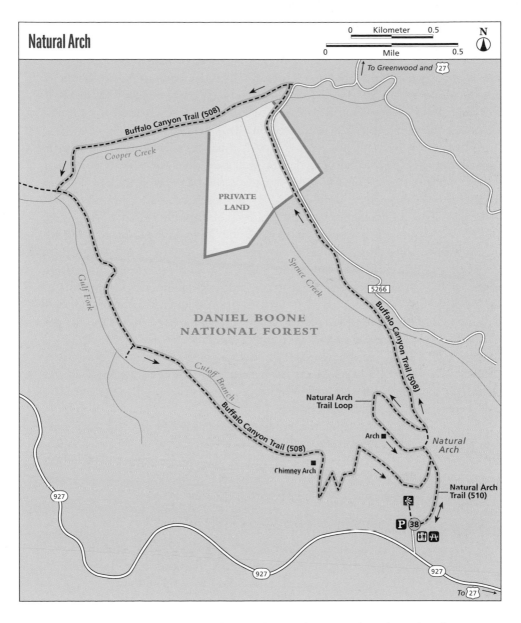

Natural Arch

0   Kilometer   0.5

0   Mile   0.5

N

To Greenwood and 27

Buffalo Canyon Trail (508)

Cooper Creek

PRIVATE LAND

Spruce Creek

Gulf Fork

5266

Buffalo Canyon Trail (508)

DANIEL BOONE NATIONAL FOREST

Cutoff Branch

Buffalo Canyon Trail (508)

Natural Arch Trail Loop

Arch ■

Natural Arch

Chimney Arch ■

Natural Arch Trail (510)

927

P 38

927

927

To 27

At the intersection, turn right and follow the Natural Arch Trail, still paved, to near the base of the arch at mile 0.4. Follow Natural Arch Trail to the right and climb to the entrance of the arch. This is a spot to linger over. Like other sandstone arches, Natural Arch was formed as water and weather eroded away softer rock, leaving the harder top strata behind. The tall surrounding cliffs add to the otherworldly beauty of the site. The arch is considered sacred to the Cherokee tribe. To protect it, the Forest Service constructed the fence of red cedar—a tree honored by the Cherokee—that you see at the base. You can walk through the arch, but stay out of the fenced area.

Is this the state's biggest arch? Wilson Francis, naturalist at Natural Bridge State Resort Park, says the question is unresolved. That's because arches vary in size and shape, and there's no agreement on how to measure them. By height? By span? By the size of the opening? Certainly Natural Arch is one of the largest arches in Kentucky. For the national title, there does seem to be agreement: Utah's Rainbow Bridge is, at 290 feet tall and 275 feet long, the largest natural bridge not just in the United States, but also in the world, according to the National Park Service.

When you're ready to move on, follow Natural Arch Trail, now a dirt path, through the arch, and bear left along the cliff wall. Bear right at the trail junction and follow Buffalo Canyon Trail. You begin descending through an area full of downed trees, victims of the winter storms. Gradually the forest becomes more robust and inviting. At mile 0.9 the trail crosses Spruce Creek, and at mile 1.8 it joins FR 5266. Go left on this pleasant, little-used gravel road. The houses you pass on your left are on a privately owned parcel within the national forest.

At mile 2.5 the road reaches Cooper Creek and fords the stream on concrete planks; as the sign notes, this crossing may not be passable in flooded conditions. On the other side of the creek, FR 5266 turns right (east) toward the community of Greenwood on US 27. Turn left onto an old dirt road and head west, with Cooper Creek on your left, flowing toward the Cumberland River. Disregard the small road coming in on the left and continue west through the pines. At mile 3.5, shortly after curving south, the trail forks. Take the left prong, which crosses Cooper Creek and begins climbing to the east and then southeast—the first uphill since the arch. The trail is now following Gulf Fork upstream.

At mile 4.2, after leveling off, the trail passes the north end of a trail (Gulf Bottom Spur Trail) now closed because of a slide. It used to lead to an overlook on KY 927 west of the Natural Arch parking lot. Continuing southeast, Buffalo Canyon Trail climbs and crosses Cutoff Branch before coming to Chimney Arch at mile 5.1. This arch, surrounded by a cliff, is about 30 feet in height and makes an interesting rest stop.

From the arch, follow the ridgetop for a short distance before descending and then traversing another damaged area. At mile 5.8, after a series of ups and downs and sharp turns to avoid cliffs, the trail meets Natural Arch Trail and the start of the loop. Turn right, climb the steps, and you are back at your car at mile 6.0.

Key Points

0.4 Natural Arch.

0.9 Spruce Creek crossing.

1.8 Left on FR 5266.

2.5 Cooper Creek crossing.

3.5 Cooper Creek second crossing.

5.1 Chimney Arch.

39 Three Forks of Beaver Creek

Hike to where the three forks of Beaver Creek meet in the lush bottomland of this wilderness area.

Start: Parking area at Three Forks of the Beaver Trailhead in Beaver Creek Wilderness area, 7 miles off US 27
Distance: 3.3-mile partial loop
Hiking time: About 2 hours
Difficulty: Moderate
Best seasons: Fall through spring
Other trail users: Equestrians
Canine compatibility: Dogs permitted

Land status: National forest
Nearest town: Somerset
Fees and permits: None
Maps: USDA Forest Service map of Beaver Creek Wilderness; USGS Hail
Trail contact: Stearns Ranger District, Daniel Boone National Forest, (606) 376-5323
Parking and trailhead facilities: There's space for about 20 cars, but no facilities.

Finding the trailhead: From the intersection of KY 90 and US 27, about 20 miles south of Somerset, take US 27 north for 4.1 miles and turn right onto gravel Bauer Road (FR 50). In 2.2 miles, turn right onto Bowman Ridge Road (FR 51). In 0.7 mile, turn into the parking area on your right at the Three Forks of Beaver trail sign. If you face the woods with your back to the road, the trailhead is at the left-hand corner of the parking lot. GPS: N36 54.365' / W84 26.943'

The Hike

The Beaver Creek Wilderness, the smaller of Kentucky's two federal wilderness areas (the other is the Clifty Wilderness in the Red River Gorge), encompasses 4,877 acres strung along Beaver Creek and its three forks: Hurricane, Middle, and Freeman. This hike heads first to an overlook on the edge of the wilderness area above the spot where the three forks meet, and then descends into the wilderness area to the junction itself.

The Beaver Creek area, which was acquired by the Forest Service in the 1930s and given wilderness status in 1975, is by no means untouched by the hand of humankind. The old roadbeds that crisscross the area are evidence of the coal mining, logging, and homesteading that used to take place here. (For thousands of years before that, the creek valley and its steep cliffs were home to Native Americans.) Nevertheless, this Cumberland River tributary is remote enough to make you feel sufficiently removed from civilization, and the junction of the three forks is a spot of quiet beauty. In length, this walk is definitely a day hike. But the creek bank offers good camping opportunities, making this a nice overnighter, especially for families with small children.

From the left end of the parking area, take Three Forks Loop Trail (512) and head southeast. The trail is actually two separate paths that parallel each other to make a

Leisurely flowing Beaver Creek after a January snow. PAM GIBSON

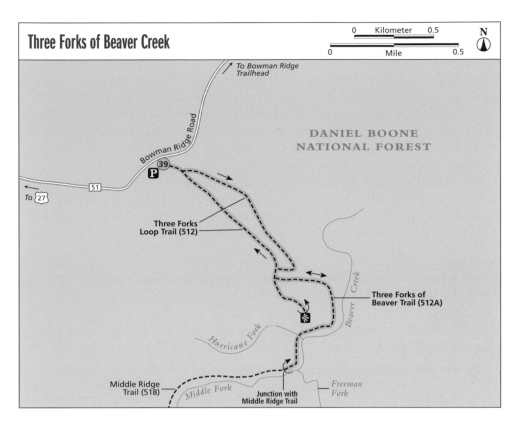

Three Forks of Beaver Creek

0 Kilometer 0.5

0 Mile 0.5

N

To Bowman Ridge Trailhead

Bowman Ridge Road

DANIEL BOONE
NATIONAL FOREST

39

P

51

To 27

Three Forks
Loop Trail (512)

Three Forks of
Beaver Trail (512A)

Beaver Creek

Hurricane Fork

Middle Ridge
Trail (518)

Middle Fork

Junction with
Middle Ridge Trail

Freeman
Fork

narrow loop. You can take either path; I chose the one on the left—the longer of the two—for the outbound leg of the hike, and followed the other on my return trip. The left-hand path descends gradually through a forest of hardwoods and pines, and at mile 0.5 passes a natural lookout point on the left with limited views into the Beaver Creek drainage. The path then weaves west and, at mile 0.8, intersects the other half of the loop.

At this point you take a left and walk south, following the sign indicating a wildlife-viewing area ahead. Just past the intersection, there's an old roadbed to your left; ignore it for now and continue south, sloping gently down to a stone-fenced observation point at mile 1.0. From here there are excellent vistas south and west across the Beaver Creek valley. You can't see the stream itself, but you can see the cuts in the forest floor made by the three forks flowing toward their meeting point.

From the overlook, retrace your steps to the old roadbed. This is Three Forks of Beaver Trail (512A), which descends to Beaver Creek. Turn right onto the trail. In 0.1 mile pass a sign marking the wilderness area boundary. The roadbed narrows and becomes steeper and, in places, overgrown. Continue downhill and, at mile 1.8, reach the creek bank at the point where Hurricane Fork flows into the main stream. It's a lovely spot, with a small sandy area and an inviting pool for wading.

The trail now becomes harder to see, but it crosses Hurricane Fork and follows Beaver Creek upstream for about 0.1 mile to the spot where Freeman Fork flows into Middle Fork. This is a quiet site full of pine trees and rhododendrons—and flat spots for tenting. However, be aware that the Forest Service requires primitive campsites in the wilderness area to be 300 feet from any stream or road and out of sight of any trail.

The trail dead-ends into the Middle Ridge Trail (518) at 1.9 miles. It's time to turn around and retrace your steps up to the ridgetop. The Middle Ridge Trail follows Middle Fork upstream for 6.5 miles all the way to FR 839 near the community of Greenwood on US 27.

From the creek bank, return on Three Forks of Beaver Trail to the intersection, taking the other leg of Three Forks Loop Trail north to the parking lot. This leg is an old dirt-and-grass road. Before reaching the parking lot, it jogs northeast around a field created for wildlife by Forest Service personnel.

Key Points

0.8 Intersection with other half of loop.

1.0 Overlook.

1.8 Meeting point of Beaver Creek and Hurricane Fork.

1.9 Turnaround spot.

Option: For another nearby walk to Beaver Creek, see the Bowman Ridge hike.

40 Bowman Ridge

Cross the Beaver Creek Wilderness from one ridgetop to another, crossing the Beaver Creek as it winds toward the Cumberland River.

Start: Parking area at end of FR 51 in Beaver Creek Wilderness area, 8.7 miles from US 27
Distance: 3.2-mile out-and-back
Hiking time: About 2 hours
Difficulty: Moderate
Best seasons: Fall through spring
Other trail users: None
Canine compatibility: Dogs permitted
Land status: National forest

Nearest town: Somerset
Fees and permits: None
Maps: USDA Forest Service map of Beaver Creek Wilderness; USGS Hail
Trail contact: Stearns Ranger District, Daniel Boone National Forest, (606) 376-5323
Parking and trailhead facilities: There's space for 5 cars, but no facilities.

Finding the trailhead: From the intersection of KY 90 and US 27, about 20 miles south of Somerset, take US 27 north for 4.1 miles and turn right onto gravel Bauer Road (FR 50). In 2.2 miles, turn right onto Bowman Ridge Road (FR 51). After 2.4 miles, turn into the parking area on the left just before the road dead-ends. The trailhead is at the parking area's north end. GPS: N36 55.265' / W84 25.855'

The Hike

This hike takes you from Bowman Ridge on the west side of the Beaver Creek Wilderness to Swain Ridge on the east side. In between you cross Beaver Creek downstream of the Three Forks of Beaver Creek hike. Here the stream is clear, wide, and lined with lush vegetation and wading spots, a perfect place to enjoy nature and solitude. The stream runs into the Cumberland River, about 3 miles farther north.

From the north end of the parking lot (the end away from the road), take the old grass track north 200 feet to a gate, which you can get around easily. On the other side of the gate, a trail marked both 514 and 532 branches off to the right (east). For this hike follow 514, the Bowman Ridge Trail.

Turning right onto the trail, you enter an open woodland with a number of downed trees. The path itself can be hard to see here, but there are enough white diamond blazes on trees that you should have no trouble. There was once a coal mine nearby, and the landscape remains changed by that human activity.

At mile 0.2 the trail splits, with 532 going left. Bear right on 514 and drop gently down to an old roadbed, which you take the rest of the way and is easy to follow. After a short detour into the woods to avoid a large tree fallen across the trail, pass the wilderness boundary marker and curve first north, then southeast and southwest

The pinnacles of Bowman Ridge high above Beaver Creek. PAM GIBSON

as you descend into the valley. At mile 0.9 you reach Beaver Creek and a wooden-floored bridge that crosses it.

Just downstream from the bridge, there is a tiny but nice little beach. You will find a larger beach about 50 yards upstream on the other side. There are also a number of well-used camping spots, some obviously in violation of the Forest Service rule that camps be 200 feet from a stream. The forest includes pines and hardwoods, and ferns dot the floor.

Continue on 514, crossing the bridge and heading in a generally southerly direction up Swain Ridge. The trail on this side of the creek is also an old road, but the forest here is more robust and inviting. There are some nice views of the creek below and across the valley to Bowman Ridge. At mile 1.6, shortly after leaving the wilderness area, you come to the Swain Ridge parking lot at the end of FR 52. The road is accessible from KY 90 near Cumberland Falls State Resort Park. Turn around and retrace your steps to your car.

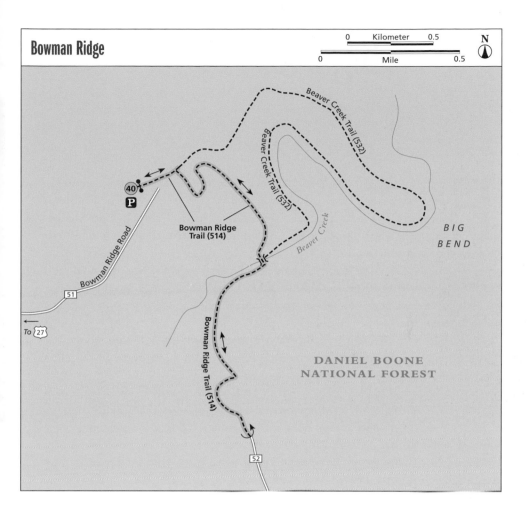

Key Points

0.2 Right turn at junction.

0.9 Beaver Creek.

1.6 End of trail at FR 52.

Big South Fork

From its origins in northern Tennessee, the Big South Fork of the Cumberland River cuts a deep gorge through the Cumberland Plateau as it flows north to join the main stem of the Cumberland in Kentucky near Somerset. Despite heavy logging and coal mining in the first half of the twentieth century, the rugged terrain of Big South Fork today makes it one of the finest hiking areas in the state. The vistas along the gorge are dramatic, and the land is dotted with beautiful creeks, waterfalls, and sandstone arches. Long isolated by the river and gorge, the area still retains the rustic feel of the frontier. You can easily walk miles without seeing another soul.

Prodded by Kentucky and Tennessee lawmakers, Congress in 1974 created the Big South Fork National River and Recreation Area to give the stream and shoreline special protection and to encourage use by visitors. Managed by the National Park Service (NPS), the 125,000-acre Big South Fork area is a cross between a national park and a national forest. It offers fewer creature comforts than a park but has a greater focus on hiking, camping, horseback riding, rafting, kayaking, and other outdoor activities than a typical national forest. Altogether, the Big South Fork area has more than 150 miles of hiking trails. The larger portion is in Tennessee, but the Kentucky section has a number of beautiful walks.

A permit is required for backcountry camping within the NPS area; the cost depends on the size of the group. Permits can be purchased at either of two Big South Fork visitor centers and from certain local vendors. The Kentucky center (606-376-5073) is south of Whitley City on KY 92; the Tennessee center (423-286-7275) is 14 miles west of Oneida on TN 297 at Bandy Creek. Hours of operation vary by season. Information on the web is at www.nps.gov/biso. Camping in the recreation area is prohibited within 100 feet of main roads, 200 feet of a developed area or parking lot, and 25 feet of any trail, road, cave, cemetery, or the rim of the gorge. Because of black bears, campers are required to hang their food at night.

The following Big South Fork hikes are all in Kentucky, although not entirely within the boundaries of the NPS-administered recreation area. Some of the trails are on adjacent Daniel Boone National Forest land overseen by the Stearns Ranger District (606-376-5323). Backcountry camping permits are not required in the national forest. The Stearns Ranger District requires campsites to be at least 300 feet from any trail, road, lake, or river. The terrain itself is indistinguishable between the recreation area and national forest, but trails are marked using graphic symbol signs and color-coded blazes.

Symbols of all uses allowed on trails are mounted on wooden posts and placed at the beginning of trails and at all trail junctions. The primary trail use symbol is displayed on the top of the sign, with other trail uses displayed below. Symbols represent a horseback rider, hiker, mountain bike, and a wagon wheel for the trails accessible to horse-drawn wagons. In addition to the graphic symbol, the trail use is reinforced with a color code: red for horse and wagon trails, green for foot trails, blue for biking trails, and orange for multiple-use trails. For more information on signage and blazing in the area, visit www.nps.gov/biso/planyourvisit/trail-blazing-and-signing.htm.

A cautionary note: Although the Big South Fork area is administered by the park service, hunting is allowed in accordance with state seasons. So think twice about hiking during deer season, and if you do, wear blaze orange.

Lick Creek, a tributary of the Big South Fork, tumbles over a rock outcropping to form Lick Creek Falls (hike 46).
PAM GIBSON

41 Yahoo Falls

Kentucky's highest waterfall, a 70-foot-wide natural arch, and a walk along Big South Fork are included on this hike through a part of the Big South Fork Recreation Area.

Start: Yahoo Arch Trailhead parking area
Distance: 8.5-mile loop
Hiking time: About 5 hours
Difficulty: Moderate
Best seasons: Any
Other trail users: None
Canine compatibility: Dogs permitted, but must be leashed on national park land
Land status: National park, national forest
Nearest town: Whitley City
Fees and permits: Permit required for backcountry camping in Big South Fork National River and Recreation Area. Permits can be purchased at Big South Fork visitor centers and from certain local vendors.
Maps: USDA Forest Service map of Yahoo Arch and Markers Arch trails; USGS Nevelsville and Barthell; Trails Illustrated map of Big South Fork area
Trail contacts: Big South Fork National River and Recreation Area, (606) 376-5073 or (423) 286-7275; Stearns Ranger District, Daniel Boone National Forest, (606) 376-5323
Parking and trailhead facilities: There's space for 3 cars, but no facilities. If there's no room at the trailhead, go 100 yards west and park on the left shoulder.

Finding the trailhead: From the intersection of US 27 and KY 478 at Whitley City, take US 27 north for 1.8 miles and turn left (west) onto KY 700. Continue straight at an intersection with KY 1651 and, in 3 miles, park at the sign for Yahoo Arch Trail (602). GPS: N36 45.396' / W84 30.730'

The Hike

This hike starts and ends in the Daniel Boone National Forest, but most of the walking is in the Big South Fork National River and Recreation Area. The main attraction is the 113-foot drop that Yahoo Creek takes just before it flows into Big South Fork. This is said to be the highest waterfall in Kentucky. Be warned that Yahoo Creek is not a big stream, and in rainless periods it can dry up completely. Even so, the hike is worthwhile.

The trail follows Big South Fork for 4.3 miles and crosses several scenic tributaries as they empty into the bigger stream. A pleasant campground—Alum Ford—is located just about halfway through the loop. It has tent sites, picnic tables, and portable toilets but no treated water supply or other facilities. There is a small per-site fee.

From KY 700, Yahoo Arch Trail (602) heads northwest on an old roadbed across a level ridgetop. You immediately pass a side trail on your right leading 0.5 mile to minor Markers Arch. Continuing northwest on Yahoo Arch Trail, you have a few limited views east and west through the thin forest of hardwoods and evergreens. After descending on switchbacks and stone steps, you come first to a weathered rock

At 113 feet, Yahoo Falls is thought to be the highest waterfall in Kentucky.

outcropping to the left of the trail and then, at mile 0.8, to Yahoo Arch. The arch is 17 feet high and 70 feet wide and, with the surrounding cliff, makes an interesting rest stop.

Continuing on Yahoo Arch Trail, follow the base of the cliff and pass from the national forest into the Big South Fork National River and Recreation Area. The trail curves more to the west and descends on switchbacks to a fork of Yahoo Creek, which you follow downstream toward Big South Fork. The forest here is fuller and more pleasing than on top of the ridge. At mile 1.5 you come to a fork in the trail and a sign indicating that the Yahoo Falls parking lot is straight ahead.

This is the beginning of the Yahoo Falls Scenic Area. At the sign take the right-hand fork. This trail descends and then heads west along the base of a cliff—the same cliff over which Yahoo Creek makes its 113-foot plunge. At mile 1.7 walk behind the falls and beneath a tall rock overhang. A sign on the other side of the falls explains how this kind of rock shelter is formed, and how it was used for shelter by Native Americans thousands of years ago.

Before reaching the falls, you'll pass a turnoff, which would take you down to another fork of the creek. Beyond the falls you'll pass another turnoff that descends farther into the gorge. Continuing straight, you'll come to yet another fork at mile 1.9. Go right onto Sheltowee Trace National Recreation Trail and follow Yahoo Creek to Big South Fork. The Sheltowee is a north–south route approximately 319 miles long; one spur of the trail ends just south of the state line in Tennessee's Pickett State Park, adjacent to the Big South Fork area. *Sheltowee* means "big turtle," the Indian name for Daniel Boone, and thus the trail is blazed with the outline of a turtle.

Taking the Sheltowee, you reach Big South Fork at mile 2.0 and curve left to begin following the river upstream. Cross a wooden bridge spanning a beautiful rocky drainage area festooned with rhododendrons and ferns. The cliff towering above on the left adds to the feeling of isolation. The Sheltowee soon jogs briefly away from the river to cross another streambed.

As you walk along Big South Fork, you'll cross a number of small streams flowing into the river through interesting rock formations, with several producing delightful waterfalls in the process. Initially the Sheltowee stays close to the river, and although there are no established side trails down to the water, you can easily reach the riverbank if you wish. The trail then turns away from the stream and, at mile 3.4, comes out onto KY 700 shortly before the road dead-ends into the river at the Alum Ford boat ramp. Turn right onto KY 700 and follow it a short distance to a gravel road branching off to the left. Take the gravel road up the hill and reach Alum Ford Campground at mile 3.6. The boat ramp and river are directly below you but difficult to see.

The gravel road ends at the campground, and the Sheltowee once again becomes a forest path as it continues following Big South Fork southward. Periodically the river and trail veer away from each other, at times putting the water completely out of sight. The walking is generally level, although there is a good climb at mile 5.6. After a pronounced jog inland, the Sheltowee crosses Cotton Patch Creek at mile 5.9, and at

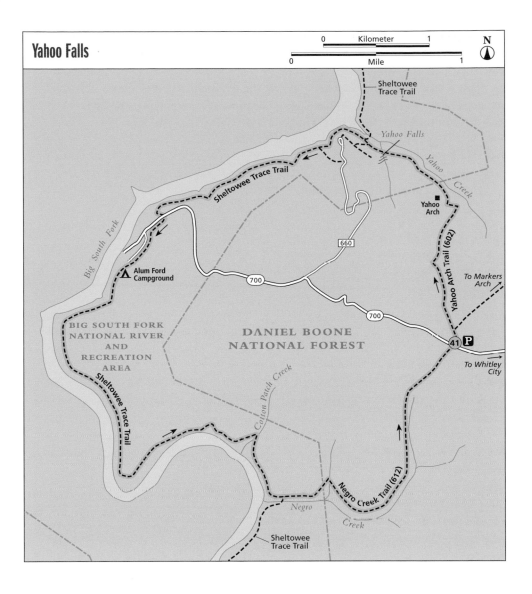

0   Kilometer   1

0   Mile   1

N

Sheltowee
Trace Trail

Yahoo Falls

Sheltowee Trace Trail

Yahoo Creek

Yahoo Arch

Yahoo Arch Trail (602)

Big South Fork

660

700

Alum Ford
Campground

To Markers
Arch

700

BIG SOUTH FORK
NATIONAL RIVER
AND
RECREATION
AREA

DANIEL BOONE
NATIONAL FOREST

41

P

To Whitley
City

Sheltowee Trace Trail

Cotton Patch Creek

Negro Creek Trail (612)

Negro
Creek

Sheltowee
Trace Trail

mile 6.3 it meets Negro Creek Trail (612), an old name that is jarring today. In *Hiking the Big South Fork*, the authors say that the origin of the name is uncertain, but a local historian believes an African-American family—a rarity in this part of Kentucky at the time—lived at the mouth of the creek in the 1800s.

The Sheltowee crosses Negro Creek and continues south along the riverbank, but you turn left onto Negro Creek Trail and head east, paralleling the creek. At first the walking is level, but shortly you begin climbing through evergreens. As the trail turns north and crosses a branch of the creek, it passes over several old dirt roads that might be confusing. Keep a close lookout for the trail's white diamond markings.

Winding along the ridge side, Negro Creek Trail follows the creek's main stem north, sometimes climbing steeply. At mile 8.1, beneath a power line, you reach the base of a rock outcropping. Using footholds chipped into the rock, climb the outcropping; at the top, turn left onto the gravel road in the power-line clearing. Follow the gravel road north to KY 700, now gated to prevent dumping, which you reach at mile 8.5. Your car is a minute's walk to your right (east).

Key Points

0.8 Yahoo Arch.

1.7 Yahoo Falls.

2.0 Big South Fork.

3.6 Alum Ford Campground.

5.9 Cotton Patch Creek.

6.3 Negro Creek Trail.

42 Blue Heron

On this hike you walk along the rim of the Big South Fork gorge and visit a re-created coal-mining camp.

Start: Blue Heron Loop Trailhead parking area in Big South Fork National River and Recreation Area
Distance: 6.6-mile loop
Hiking time: About 5 hours
Difficulty: Moderate
Best seasons: Any
Other trail users: Equestrians
Canine compatibility: Leashed dogs permitted
Land status: National park
Nearest town: Whitley City
Fees and permits: Permit required for back-country camping in Big South Fork National River and Recreation Area. Permits can be purchased at Big South Fork visitor centers and from certain local vendors.

Maps: National Park Service map of Blue Heron trails; USGS Barthell; Trails Illustrated map of Big South Fork area
Trail contact: Big South Fork National River and Recreation Area, (606) 376-5073 or (423) 286-7275
Parking and trailhead facilities: There's space for several cars. No facilities are available at the trailhead, but you'll find restrooms, water, a telephone, and a seasonal snack bar at the Blue Heron visitor complex, which is 2.5 miles away by road. Also, water, showers, electricity, and telephone are available at Blue Heron Campground just north of KY 742. There are also facilities at the nearby Blue Heron Overlook Trailhead.

Finding the trailhead: From the intersection of US 27 and KY 92 south of Whitley City, take KY 92 west past the Big South Fork National River and Recreation Area visitor center and, in 1.3 miles, turn left (south) onto KY 1651. In 0.4 mile, turn right onto KY 741; in another 0.7 mile, turn right onto KY 742. Take KY 742 west for 5.2 miles and bear left at the fork, following the sign to the overlooks. In 0.4 mile, pull into the parking area on the left side of the road at the sign for Blue Heron Loop Trail parking. GPS: N36 40.633' / W84 31.839'

The Hike

Blue Heron was a coal-mining town built in 1937 on the banks of Big South Fork by the Stearns Coal and Lumber Company. Disappointed with production, Stearns closed the mining operation in 1962, and the town was abandoned. Now, as a major attraction of the Big South Fork National River and Recreation Area, Blue Heron has been re-created to give visitors an idea of what life was like in the self-contained company towns that once dominated the coal-mining economy of eastern Kentucky.

Unfortunately, except for the huge coal tipple, none of the original Blue Heron buildings survived. As a result, the re-creation is dotted with new metal-frame structures that are supposed to represent the church, company store, school, homes, and other buildings that no longer exist. The recorded first-person accounts of Blue

The Blue Heron Overlook provides a spectacular view of the Big South Fork gorge.
PAM GIBSON

Heron life by former residents are authentic and interesting, and the full-size mock-up of a mine opening is also well done.

Because the tour of Blue Heron is self-guided, how much time you spend there is entirely up to you. Distance-wise, the Blue Heron visit is only a small fraction of the total hike. Most of the walking is in the woods and along the river bottom. The loop starts on the rim of the Big South Fork gorge above Blue Heron and descends to the town; from there you follow the river past a narrow, rocky stretch called Devils Jump before climbing back up the ridge.

From the parking area on the west side of KY 742, take the path heading west into the woods. It immediately dead-ends into Blue Heron Loop Trail. Turn right and go north through a forest of hardwoods, evergreens, and mountain laurel. For about the first mile, the trail parallels KY 742, which comes into and out of view on your right. The road ends at the Blue Heron Overlook.

Where the dirt path turns into pavement, there is an unmarked fork. Take the left prong and reach the Devils Jump Overlook at mile 0.7. Below, you see the river and the narrow, rocky stretch of rapids known as Devils Jump. In their book *Hiking the Big South Fork*, the authors say the name may stem from the 1800s when men who floated logs downstream—known as "raft devils"—had trouble with this dangerous section. At one point the US Army Corps of Engineers wanted to build a dam at Devils Jump, a proposal that helped stimulate support for legislation to protect the gorge area.

From the lookout, return to the fork and take the other prong, which passes in front of the overlook parking area. The walking surface changes back to dirt as the trail reenters the woods near a sign that tells you you're heading toward something called Cracks in the Rock. Walking northwest and then west, follow the base of a cliff on your right; the edge of the gorge is on your left. After a sharp right turn around the end of the cliff, reach a side trail to the right. It climbs in a little more than 0.1 mile up to the Blue Heron Overlook at mile 1.4. The climb is not difficult, but the view is similar to the one you had from the Devils Jump Overlook.

Continuing on the main loop trail, descend gently to the beginning of a long, steep set of wooden steps that takes you down a large rock. Be careful here: The steps can be dangerous, especially for small children. Just beyond the bottom of the stairway, you come to Cracks in the Rock—a huge rock with holes cut by nature through three of its sides. The trail goes through the rock and begins winding its way down to Blue Heron.

Reach the entrance to the mining town at mile 2.1. A free pamphlet is available to help guide you. You can take either of the two paved walkways that go south through the exhibits. The walkway on your left takes you to the mine opening and tipple, the one on your right to various "ghost" structures with cutout figures and buttons that activate recorded oral histories. At one, for example, a woman's voice explains that as a girl she entertained herself by reading all of the Nancy Drew books. You also learn that courtship consisted of walking a member of the opposite sex home from church. The train station and more exhibits are located below the tipple near the parking lot. (Blue Heron can be reached by car by taking the right-hand prong of the fork on KY 742 on top of the ridge.)

Just south of the tipple, the paved path forks. Go left, following a sign marking the continuation of Blue Heron Loop Trail. Heading south, pass the snack bar and picnic pavilion, descend concrete steps, cross the parking lot, and come to a fork at mile 2.4. The right prong is a gravel path leading a short distance down to the river. Go left on a dirt path that parallels the river and quickly comes to a sign telling you that Devils Jump is 0.4 mile ahead and Laurel Branch 1.7 miles.

Following the riverbank but staying slightly above it, pass several side trails down to the water's edge. For the best view of Devils Jump, take the second side trail, which you reach at mile 2.8. It leads to large rocks that offer nice spots for watching the water.

Back on the main trail, continue along the riverbank for a short distance until the trail forks. Go right and climb north away from the river through a cleared area. At mile 3.1 you reach the bottom of a flight of wooden steps that take you up to a broad bench in the ridge. This bench once carried a rail line used in the mining operation; it now serves as a horse path, which you take to your right (east). There are good views of the river below, and the black you see in the cliff side is testament to the mining that once went on here. At mile 3.3 the loop trail leaves the horse path, dropping off to the right and crossing an attractive rocky area.

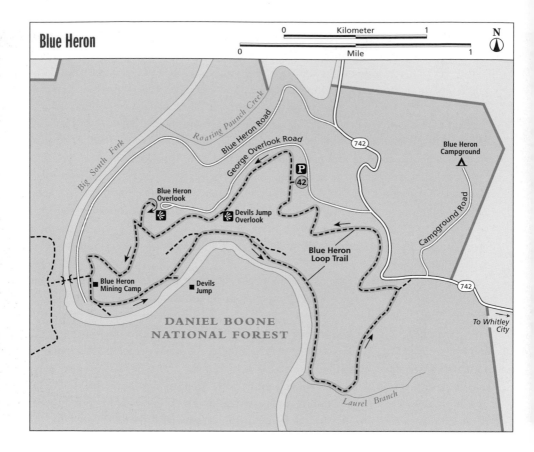

After passing over several small wooden bridges, the trail returns to the riverside and broadens into what appears to be an old roadbed. There are several nice resting spots above the water. At a cleared area the trail turns away from the river and climbs east to a sign at mile 4.3. The sign points straight ahead to Laurel Branch, an attractive creek just 350 feet away at mile 4.4. Blue Heron Loop Trail turns left at the sign and takes a series of steps and switchbacks up the ridge side. Winding your way generally northward, you reach the top of the ridge and enjoy a level stroll with limited views as you near KY 742.

At mile 5.2, just before KY 742, the trail forks; the right-hand prong goes north to the road, coming out near the entrance to Blue Heron Campground. Turn left and parallel KY 742 back to the hike's starting point, which you reach at mile 6.6.

Key Points

0.7 Devils Jump Overlook.

1.4 Blue Heron Overlook.

2.1 Entrance to Blue Heron mining camp.

2.8 Side trail to Devils Jump.

4.4 Laurel Branch.

The Big South Fork of the Cumberland River tumbles through the narrow 600-foot gorge visible from the Blue Heron Overlook. PAM GIBSON

Options: See the Big Spring Falls hike for another walk in the Blue Heron area. Also, for a change of pace, how about a train excursion? In season you can ride the Big South Fork Scenic Railway from the attractive little town of Stearns to Blue Heron. For the cost and schedule of the three-hour, round-trip run, call (800) 462-5664 or visit www.bsfsry.com. Stearns, which was built by the Stearns Company as headquarters for its now-defunct coal-and-lumber business, is located just off KY 92 a mile west of US 27.

43 Big Spring Falls

This excursion on the west side of the Big South Fork gorge ends at a 90-foot-high waterfall and a ravine full of rhododendrons and ferns.

Start: Blue Heron mining town in Big South Fork National River and Recreation Area
Distance: 7.2-mile out-and-back
Hiking time: About 4 hours
Difficulty: Moderate
Best seasons: Any
Other trail users: None
Canine compatibility: Leashed dogs permitted
Land status: National park
Nearest town: Whitley City
Fees and permits: Permit required for backcountry camping in Big South Fork National River and Recreation Area. Permits can be purchased at Big South Fork visitor centers and from certain local vendors.
Maps: National Park Service map of Blue Heron trails; USGS Barthell; Trails Illustrated map of Big South Fork area
Trail contact: Big South Fork National River and Recreation Area, (606) 376-5073 or (423) 286-7275
Parking and trailhead facilities: There's ample parking space, along with a snack bar (open seasonally), restrooms, water, a telephone, and soft drink machines. A campground with showers and electricity is located at the top of the gorge just north of KY 742.

Finding the trailhead: From the intersection of US 27 and KY 92 south of Whitley City, take KY 92 west past the Big South Fork National River and Recreation Area visitor center and, in 1.3 miles, turn left (south) onto KY 1651. In 0.4 mile, turn right onto KY 741; in another 0.7 mile, turn right onto KY 742. Take KY 742 west for 5.2 miles and bear right at the fork, continuing 2.5 miles to the parking lot at the re-created Blue Heron mining town. The hike starts above the parking lot at the east end of the tipple and bridge. GPS: N36 40.109' / W84 32.883'

The Hike

The center of activity in the Blue Heron mining town was the tipple, where raw coal was dumped, sorted, and loaded into waiting railcars for shipment. Connected to the tipple was a bridge that allowed motorized trams to bring coal from mines on the west side of Big South Fork as well as on the east side. This massive tipple-and-bridge structure, standing about 100 feet above the river, was considered leading-edge technology when it was built in the 1930s. Today it is open to pedestrian use, permitting access to hiking trails across the river from Blue Heron. (See the Blue Heron hike for more about the Blue Heron mining community.)

This hike follows a scenic west-side route called the Kentucky Trail, first to an overlook and then to two waterfalls on Big South Fork tributaries. The first waterfall is uncertain in rainless periods, but the second is likely to be flowing even in the driest of weather.

The Nancy's Grave area of the Blue Heron mining camp. PAM GIBSON

As you walk across the bridge to the river's west side, take in the various exhibits that help explain how the mining operation worked. The old mine maps on the left wall of the bridge are particularly interesting. At the far end of the bridge, turn left and head south on a broad, dirt roadbed cut into the side of the ridge. This was the tram road for the old mining operation and is now part of the Kentucky Trail, a 27-mile north–south route through the Kentucky portion of the Big South Fork National River and Recreation Area. The trail runs from the Yamacraw (KY 92) Bridge, located 8 miles north of Blue Heron, to the Peters Mountain Trailhead, 19 miles to the south.

At the west end of the bridge, the trail sign tells southbound hikers they are headed toward the Ledbetter Trailhead and Oil Well Branch, both farther south than this hike goes, and to the Catawba Overlook, which is your first destination. The trail curves west, and you follow the base of a cliff on the right as you gradually climb up Three West Hollow, passing through a lovely grove of evergreens. The hollow was named for the number three mine opening, which was on the west side of the river.

Turning south, cross Three West Creek at mile 0.5, and on the other side, climb initially southeast, then northeast, and finally south. There are limited views of the Blue Heron community below. At mile 1.0, after reaching the base of a tall cliff with a rock shelter, climb a set of steep wooden steps. At mile 1.2 the trail merges briefly with a horse path coming in from the right. After a few steps the foot trail leaves the horse path, branching left into a pleasant area of rocks and rhododendrons.

At mile 1.6 a short side trail descends to a wooden platform. This is the Catawba Overlook, named for a type of rhododendron. To the north you have a good view of the cliff lining the ridgetop above the Blue Heron community. You also see the Devils Jump and Blue Heron Overlooks (visited in the Blue Heron hike) as well as the Blue Heron bridge you just crossed.

Leaving the overlook, Kentucky Trail heads northeast and then drops south toward a small stream flowing out of an area known as Dick Gap. Along the way you pass over an unusual bridge. Instead of a stream, it crosses the trunk of a downed tree that has continued to live despite its horizontal attitude. Just after the tree bridge, descend a flight of wooden steps and at mile 2.2 come to a sign pointing left to Dick Gap Falls. I was at the falls in a dry period, and there wasn't so much as a drip of water. Nevertheless, the abundance of ferns, rhododendrons, and moss-covered rocks made this a delightful spot.

From Dick Gap Falls you descend gently, with the streambed on the left, and at mile 2.5 run into an old road running along the ridge side high above Big South Fork. To your left the road is blocked off. That stretch used to be part of the Kentucky Trail but is now considered unsafe because of unstable coal waste, according to the authors of *Hiking the Big South Fork*. Turning right, follow the road south and then west over level terrain. At mile 3.3 cross Big Spring Creek on a bridge.

From the bridge the path climbs to a fork. Turn right and at mile 3.4 come to a sign pointing right to a side trail that leads to Big Spring Falls. Head west on this

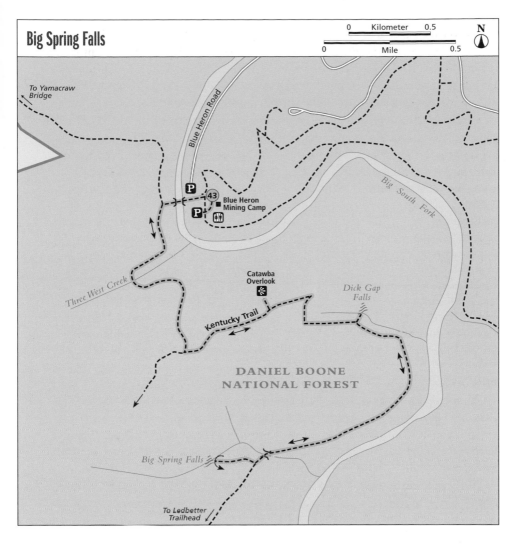

0   Kilometer   0.5

0   Mile   0.5

N

To Yamacraw
Bridge

Blue Heron Road

P

43   Blue Heron
Mining Camp

P

Three West Creek

Catawba
Overlook

Dick Gap
Falls

Big South Fork

Kentucky Trail

DANIEL BOONE
NATIONAL FOREST

Big Spring Falls

To Ledbetter
Trailhead

side trail; at mile 3.6, shortly after the trail mounts a boardwalk, you reach a fenced observation area. Just beyond, water falls over a massive cliff approximately 90 feet high and into a ravine blanketed with rhododendrons and ferns. From this pleasant scene, retrace your steps to the Blue Heron parking lot.

Key Points

0.5 Three West Creek.

1.6 Catawba Overlook.

2.2 Dick Gap Falls.

3.6 Big Spring Falls.

Option: You can easily lengthen the trip by continuing south on the Kentucky Trail, but you will have to either arrange a shuttle or retrace your steps.

44 Buffalo Arch

This hike climbs from a creek bottom up to the ridgetop, then levels out as it approaches a large, graceful arch just north of the Tennessee line.

Start: Trailhead parking area on FR 137 south of Whitley City

Distance: 4.5-mile out-and-back

Hiking time: About 2 hours

Difficulty: Moderate

Best seasons: Any

Other trail users: None

Canine compatibility: Dogs permitted

Land status: National forest

Nearest town: Whitley City

Fees and permits: None

Maps: USDA Forest Service map of Parker Mountain and Buffalo Arch Trails; USGS Barthell SW (TN/KY) and Sharp Place (TN/KY)

Trail contact: Stearns Ranger District, Daniel Boone National Forest, (606) 376-5323

Special considerations: Just before reaching the trailhead, you must drive on a narrow, gravel forest road that fords two small, bridgeless streams. Signs warn motorists not to attempt to cross the streams in high water. If the weather has been rainy, check with the Stearns Ranger District before setting out.

Parking and trailhead facilities: There's room for 3 cars on the shoulder. No facilities are available, but Great Meadows Campground, 3 miles north on FR 137, has restrooms and water (from mid-Apr to mid-Nov).

Finding the trailhead: From US 27 south of Whitley City, take KY 92 west for 6 miles to the Yamacraw Bridge over Big South Fork. At the far end of the bridge, turn left onto KY 1363 and go south for 11 miles. Here the pavement ends and the road forks; go right on FR 564. In 1.2 miles, turn left onto FR 137, following the sign for the Hemlock Grove picnic area and Great Meadows Campground. In 7 miles—after passing the picnic and campground sites and fording two small streams with warning signs—park on the left shoulder across the road from the Parker Mountain Trailhead (634) sign. Your total driving distance from the Yamacraw Bridge is 19.2 miles. GPS: N36 36.228' / W84 44.433'

The Hike

Buffalo Arch is 18½ feet high and, at its base, 81 feet wide. Native Americans hunting buffalo used to stand on top to look for their prey, hence its name. Or so the story goes. What is definite is that this large, impressive sandstone structure makes a rewarding destination. The arch, located at the end of a cliff, slopes gracefully west, sheltering a wide swath of ground beneath its span. In his book *The Historic Cumberland Plateau*, author Russ Manning likens this arch to "a flying buttress holding up the hillside"— an apt description.

This is a remote corner of the state, but this hike is surprisingly easy. Most of the walking is on top of a level ridge. From FR 137 just north of Rock Creek, take Parker Mountain Trail (634) north and begin climbing up the Rock Creek valley wall. You immediately notice a large number of downed trees, the victims of two

An eastern box turtle along a wooded trail in the Big South Fork area. Sadly, these turtles are becoming a threatened species.

severe storms in 1998—a heavy snow that winter and a tornado in the spring. The damage throughout this section of the national forest was significant, and you will see more of it as you make your way to the arch. You also see the results of a massive effort to clean up the mess and repair the trail. It will be years before the scars are healed but, thankfully, this hike does not suffer appreciably from them.

The narrow dirt path, marked by white plastic diamonds, curves west as it continues climbing the ridge side, providing views to the east and south. After reaching the base of an attractive, fern-sprouting cliff, climb stone steps to the southwest and wind your way up a break in the cliff wall. Next is a metal stairway, which takes you up to a good view of the valley to the south. Continuing to climb, but more gradually, head northwest and reach the top of the ridge at mile 0.5.

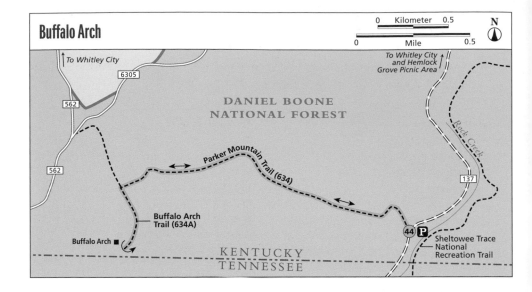

From here on, the trail is generally flat, most of the ups and downs slight enough to be unnoticeable. The ridgetop woods are pleasant enough but without remarkable features. At mile 1.8 the trail comes into a clearing and meets a dirt road. Parker Mountain Trail follows the road to the right and heads north toward FR 562 about 0.4 mile away. Turn left onto the road and head south. The turn marks the beginning of Buffalo Arch Trail (634A), which immediately leaves the clearing and goes into the woods, sloping down gently. After curving right the road comes to a fork and you bear right. After the fork the trail narrows once again into a path, turns west, descends, and reaches the arch at mile 2.2.

Retrace your steps to your car.

Key Points

0.5 Top of ridge.

1.8 Buffalo Arch Trail.

2.2 Buffalo Arch.

Options: See the Gobblers Arch hike for a walk in this same corner of the national forest. Great Meadows Campground, located nearby on Rock Creek, is an exceptionally nice, no-fee camping spot. The two sections—one on each side of FR 137—have a total of eighteen tent sites; there's no electricity.

45 Gobblers Arch

A variety of ridges and hollows make attractive terrain for this forest walk that includes a stop at a stocky, 12-foot-high arch.

Start: Hemlock Grove picnic area on FR 137
Distance: 4.8-mile loop
Hiking time: About 3 hours
Difficulty: Moderate
Best seasons: Any
Other trail users: Mountain bikers, equestrians
Canine compatibility: Dogs permitted
Land status: National forest
Nearest town: Whitley City

Fees and permits: None
Maps: USDA Forest Service map of Parker Mountain and Buffalo Arch Trails; USGS Bell Farm
Trail contact: Stearns Ranger District, Daniel Boone National Forest, (606) 376-5323
Parking and trailhead facilities: You'll find space for about 20 cars, along with restrooms, picnic tables, and a pavilion.

Finding the trailhead: From US 27 south of Whitley City, take KY 92 west for 6 miles to the Yamacraw Bridge over Big South Fork. At the far end of the bridge, turn left onto KY 1363 and go south for 11 miles. Here the pavement ends and the road forks; go right onto FR 564. In another 1.2 miles, turn left onto FR 137, following the sign for the Hemlock Grove picnic area and Great Meadows Campground. In 2.6 miles, park at the picnic area, which is on the left side of the road. GPS: N36 38.697' / W84 42.682'

The Hike

Gobblers Arch is a squat, solid structure 50 feet wide at the base and just under 12 feet in height. It lacks the grace of Buffalo Arch and instead personifies brute strength. It could be a linebacker for the Green Bay Packers. This loop (cobbled together from several trails) does take you to Gobblers Arch, but its real attraction is the variety of terrain and forest that you sample along the way.

Severe storms in 1998 damaged the Hemlock Grove picnic area and disrupted trails in the immediate vicinity. The picnic facilities have since been reconstructed and the trails reopened. But the decreased tree canopy permits more ground vegetation, and as a result, the trailhead for this hike—which is just outside the developed picnic area—can be difficult to find. From the parking area, walk southwest along FR 137 to an old roadway on the edge of the picnic area. You will see a turtle marker, the trail sign for the Sheltowee Trace National Recreation Trail.

Follow the trail to Rock Creek and ford it. This is a substantial stream and there's no bridge; if it's been raining, you may get your feet wet. Once you're on the other side, continue southwest, and at mile 0.1 (from the parking area), you come into a field with another sign for Sheltowee Trace National Recreation Trail. Brush along the creek bank may make the field difficult to see, but don't give up. I had trouble until I found an old farm track, barely visible, leading from the stream to the field.

At 12 feet high, Gobblers Arch is not the tallest standstone formation along the trail, which is lined with bluffs. PAM GIBSON

The Sheltowee is a long-distance trail that starts at the north end of the Daniel Boone National Forest and passes through Hemlock Grove on its way to its ending point in Tennessee. From the trail sign, take the Sheltowee west—but not for long. At mile 0.2, turn left (south) onto Gobblers Arch Trail (636) and begin a climb from the Rock Creek valley floor up the ridge. Initially the incline is gentle, but it soon becomes steep.

At mile 0.5 you come to a rock outcropping and begin paralleling the base of the ridge-side cliff, first going south and level, then southwest and up a small, inviting ravine lined with evergreen trees and rhododendrons. Near the top of the ridge, the trail turns northeast before curving again to the south. At mile 1.4 reach a lookout with good views to the west across the Rock Creek valley. The lookout, located just to the right of the trail, makes a nice rest spot, but be sure to watch small children and dogs carefully.

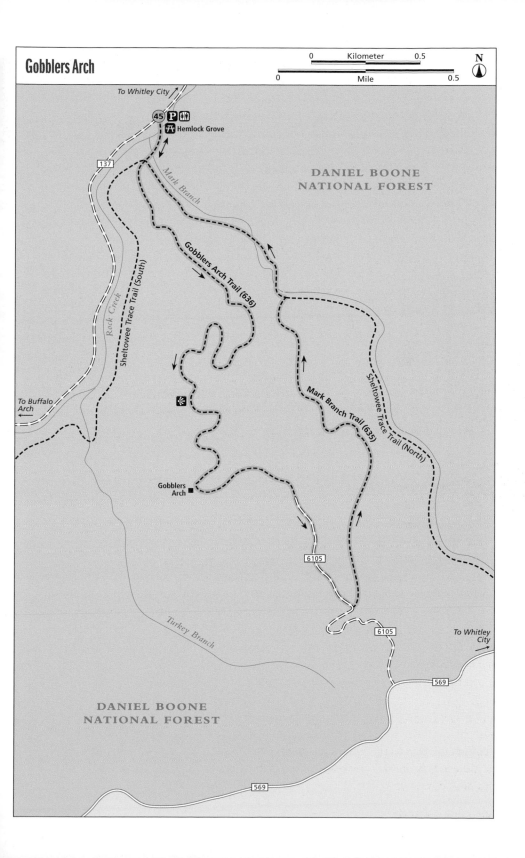

Gobblers Arch

0 Kilometer 0.5
0 Mile 0.5

N

To Whitley City

45 P 🚻
🏕 Hemlock Grove

137

DANIEL BOONE
NATIONAL FOREST

Mark Branch

Gobblers Arch Trail (636)

Rock Creek

Sheltowee Trace Trail (South)

To Buffalo
Arch

Mark Branch Trail (635)

Sheltowee Trace Trail (North)

Gobblers
Arch

6105

6105

To Whitley
City

Turkey Branch

569

DANIEL BOONE
NATIONAL FOREST

569

At mile 2.0, after winding through several drainages, you reach Gobblers Arch, a perfect place for lunch. The trail proceeds through the arch opening and climbs to the top of the ridge that houses the arch. Go northeast over level terrain until you meet FR 6105 at 2.2 miles. This is where Gobblers Arch Trail ends.

Follow FR 6105 south for 0.6 mile to Mark Branch Trail (635), which will take you north back toward the picnic grounds. FR 6105 starts out as a wide, pleasant forest path but grows into a full-fledged gravel road by the time you leave it at the top of a slight rise. The left-hand turn onto Mark Branch Trail at mile 2.8 is marked by a sign. However, both the trail and sign are far enough off the road that you could miss them if you're not on the lookout. FR 6105 continues south to FR 569, which connects with roads leading to the Yamacraw Bridge and Whitley City.

Mark Branch is a small stream that runs into Rock Creek at the Hemlock Grove picnic area. But the trail of the same name doesn't reach the stream for 1.3 miles. From FR 6105, Mark Branch Trail winds northward through several lovely hollows and across a number of small streambeds that may be dry. At mile 3.7 the trail begins its descent toward Mark Branch, gradually at first and then steeply. At mile 4.1, just before reaching the stream, Mark Branch Trail dead-ends into the Sheltowee Trace Trail. Turn left onto the Sheltowee. Cross Mark Branch, recross it twice in rapid succession, and in another 0.1 mile cross it again. Heading north with the stream below you, descend gently and at mile 4.7 reach the open field where you found the Sheltowee Trace Trail sign at the beginning of the hike. Retrace your steps across Rock Creek; you're back at your car at mile 4.8.

Key Points

0.1 Sheltowee Trace Trail.

0.2 Gobblers Arch Trail.

2.0 Gobblers Arch.

2.2 FR 6105.

2.8 Mark Branch Trail.

4.1 Sheltowee Trace Trail.

46 Lick Creek

A striking waterfall awaits at the end of this picturesque hike along a Big South Fork tributary.

Start: Roadside parking area on edge of Whitley City
Distance: 5.6-mile out-and-back
Hiking time: About 3 hours
Difficulty: Easy
Best seasons: Any
Other trail users: None
Canine compatibility: Dogs permitted
Land status: National forest

Nearest town: Whitley City
Fees and permits: None
Maps: USDA Forest Service map of Lick Creek/Lick Creek Falls Trails; USGS Whitley City and Barthell
Trail contact: Stearns Ranger District, Daniel Boone National Forest, (606) 376-5323
Parking and trailhead facilities: There's room for 5 or 6 cars, but no facilities.

Finding the trailhead: From US 27 in Whitley City, take KY 478 west for 0.1 mile to the stop sign, turn left onto KY 1651, and in 0.9 mile turn right onto FR 622, which is the first paved road after the school bus lot. Park in the gravel trailhead parking lot. Do not block the driveway to the private residence. GPS: N36 42.925' / W84 28.869'

The Hike

Lick Creek, a tributary of Big South Fork, is a picturesque stream lined with interesting rock formations and full of pleasant pools. This hike descends into the Lick Creek valley, follows the stream a short distance, and then climbs along a feeder stream to a beautiful waterfall named for the creek.

Most of the hike is on Lick Creek Trail (631), which starts in a residential area not far from the center of Whitley City. From FR 622, the trail initially follows a dirt road. Heading south at first but turning to the northwest, the road crosses a flat ridgetop that was replanted following the southern pine beetle epidemic, and the trees are still relatively small. After the first half mile, however, the forest becomes more substantial, and there are limited views to the east.

At mile 1.0, just after starting to descend, the dirt road narrows into a path. It then turns left (west) and goes down a set of stone steps. Next you negotiate a metal stairway, followed by a second, bringing you at mile 1.2 to the base of a cliff. The trail follows the cliff north, and along the way passes beneath a number of impressive rock overhangs. Children especially will like these interesting rock formations. At one point you feel as if you're in a tunnel; a cliff flanks you on one side, a huge boulder on the other.

The trail descends gradually and, after following stone steps around a large outcropping, crosses a small tributary and comes to Lick Creek. The banks of this lovely

Princess Falls along Lick Creek is named for Cherokee princess Cornblossom. Pam Gibson

stream are covered with tall evergreen trees and rhododendrons. You should have no trouble finding a nice lunch spot here.

Follow the creek downstream and, at mile 2.2, come to a side trail branching off to the left. Although there may be no sign identifying it—as thieves often steal it—this is Lick Creek Falls Trail (631A). Turn left onto this trail; the main trail continues to follow Lick Creek to Sheltowee Trace National Recreation Trail a little more than a mile away. The Sheltowee, a long-distance trail through the Daniel Boone National Forest, runs along Big South Fork.

Climbing south, Lick Creek Falls Trail comes to a fork at mile 2.4. The right-hand prong, which goes back down to Lick Creek Trail, is for hikers continuing to the Sheltowee after visiting the falls; that way they don't have to completely retrace their steps. Bear left at the fork and, at mile 2.8, after following the base of a tall cliff, reach the falls. The water comes down over a V-shaped overhang, making it possible to walk behind the falls without getting wet. The entire area seems to be dripping with water. Lush ferns and mossy rocks cover the bottom of the narrow ravine.

From the falls, retrace your steps to your car.

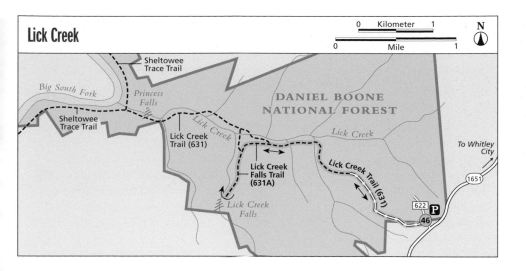

Lick Creek

Key Points

1.0 Dirt road ends; path begins.

1.2 Bottom of second metal stairway.

2.2 Lick Creek Falls Trail.

2.8 Lick Creek Falls.

Option: For a longer hike, continue on Lick Creek Trail to Sheltowee Trace Trail, which connects north to the Yahoo Falls area (see the Yahoo Falls hike). Just before reaching the Sheltowee, Lick Creek Trail passes Princess Falls, named for Princess Cornblossom, a Cherokee princess in the late 1700s. The one-way distance of the full Lick Creek Trail, including the detour to Lick Creek Falls, is 4 miles.

47 Laurel Creek

Wildflowers, ferns, and rhododendrons line the banks of this easily accessible stream that is the centerpiece of this hike near Whitley City.

Start: Trailhead parking on shoulder of Pigskin Road (696) just outside Whitley City
Distance: 8.8-mile out-and-back (4.4 miles one way, if you have a shuttle)
Hiking time: About 4 hours
Difficulty: Moderate
Best seasons: Any
Other trail users: Mountain bikers
Canine compatibility: Dogs permitted
Land status: National forest
Nearest town: Whitley City
Fees and permits: None

Maps: USDA Forest Service map for Laurel Creek Trail; USGS Whitley City
Trail contact: Stearns Ranger District, Daniel Boone National Forest, (606) 376-5323
Special considerations: If you want to make this a one-way hike, there is a parking area on KY 478 at the far end of the trail where you can meet a shuttle.
Parking and trailhead facilities: There's room on Pigskin Road for about 5 cars, but no facilities.

Finding the trailhead: From Whitley City, take US 27 south for 2 miles and turn left (east) onto Pigskin Road (696). Disregard the numerous side streets and, in 2.2 miles, just after the road surface changes from pavement to gravel, park on the shoulder by the sign for Laurel Creek Trail. GPS: N36 42.906' / W84 25.851'

The Hike

Even in the driest weather, you can count on finding water flowing in Laurel Creek. The banks of this robust stream make a refreshing walk any time of year. There are numerous wading spots as well as an abundance of wildflowers, ferns, rhododendrons, and interesting rock outcroppings.

Located only minutes off US 27, the trailhead is unusually easy to reach. Some may not see this as an attribute. At the north end of the hike, there is apt to be traffic noise from KY 478. And midway along the creek, a power line passes overhead several times, each passing accompanied by a clearing that interrupts the forest. Despite these distractions, I felt far from civilization.

This hike is entirely on Laurel Creek Trail (620), which runs between Pigskin Road and KY 478. The trail doesn't intersect any roads or other trails, and so there is no way to avoid retracing your steps unless you have a shuttle. Either end of the trail will do just fine as the starting point. For no good reason, these directions are from the southern trailhead.

From the south side of Pigskin Road, the trail heads south on an old dirt road across a ridgetop timbered in the 1980s. As with the Lick Creek hike, this initial stretch is not attractive, though it does offer vistas of mountain ridges to the southeast.

Laurel Creek flows toward the Cumberland River below the falls. Pam Gibson

Descend gradually at first and then more steeply. At mile 0.5, just after leaving the cut area and entering a forest of evergreens and mountain laurel, you come to Laurel Creek. Turn northeast and follow it downstream; the trail now narrows into a path.

Unlike the other streams encountered on hikes in this area, Laurel Creek does not flow into Big South Fork. Instead, after mingling with other creeks, its waters make their way into the main stem of the Cumberland River south of Cumberland Falls. Not only was the Laurel Creek watershed hit by the 1998 storms that damaged so much of this part of the Daniel Boone National Forest, but it also suffered a wildfire in 1999. You can still see the scars, including some blackened splotches, but the stream retains enough beauty and solitude to overcome those negatives, and Mother Nature is slowly but surely healing the forest here.

Except for a few gentle ups and downs, the trail follows the creek's gradual descent—so gradual it's undetectable. On this hike there are no obvious features to point out, like a waterfall or sandstone arch. But at mile 1.7 a tall cliff towering above the trail and a pooling in the creek make a particularly nice rest spot. There's another nice spot at mile 2.8, where tall pines line the creek bank. I found the middle third of the creek-side hike the prettiest.

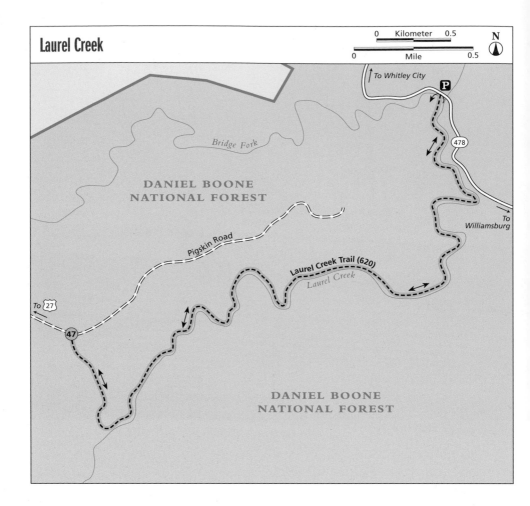

Just before reaching KY 478, the trail crosses a bridge and climbs wooden steps to a paved parking area on the south side of the highway. This is the end of the trail. Turn around and return to your car the same way you came.

Key Points

0.5 Laurel Creek.

4.4 KY 478.

Central Kentucky—North

The northern half of central Kentucky is a beautiful area. It includes the famous Bluegrass region—the gently rolling countryside surrounding Lexington where thoroughbreds romp on exquisite lawns in front of handsome old mansions surrounded by gleaming white fences. Yes, these perfect scenes really do exist—and you will see some of them as you drive to the hikes outlined in the following pages. This part of Kentucky has a number of parks and wildlife areas that offer quiet walks through moderate terrain. These public areas, however, are relatively small in size, and consequently the following are all day hikes of fairly short duration. For the most part, this is easy walking along stream bottomlands and low-lying ridges.

Two forks of Raven Run come together at what was once the site of Evans Mill (hike 53).

48 Middle Creek: Two Loops

This hike consists of two separate but nearby loops on wooded ridges with wildflowers and some limited views across the Ohio River valley.

Start: Parking areas at Boone County Cliffs and Dinsmore Woods State Nature Preserves
Distance: 3.4 miles for both loops (1.7 miles for each loop)
Hiking time: About 2 hours for both (1 hour for each)
Difficulty: Easy
Best seasons: Any
Other trail users: None
Canine compatibility: No dogs allowed
Land status: State nature preserves
Nearest town: Florence
Fees and permits: None

Maps: Kentucky State Nature Preserves Commission maps of Dinsmore Woods and Boone County Cliffs State Nature Preserves; USGS Rising Sun and Lawrenceburg (IN/KY)
Trail contact: Kentucky State Nature Preserves Commission, (502) 573-2886
Special considerations: These two short loops are near each other but in separate nature preserves, making a short drive necessary to get from one loop to the other.
Parking and trailhead facilities: The first loop parking area has room for 5 cars, but no facilities. At the second loop, you'll find room for two-dozen cars and a portable toilet.

Finding the trailhead: From exit 181 off I-75 at Florence, take KY 18 west. For the first loop, turn left in 10.9 miles onto Middle Creek Road; 1.7 miles farther, park on the left in the lot for the Boone County Cliffs State Nature Preserve. The loop starts at the lot. GPS: N38 59.603' / W84 47.068'

 For the second loop, return to KY 18, turn left, and in 0.3 mile turn left again into the parking area for Middle Creek Park. The second loop, in the Dinsmore Woods State Nature Preserve, starts on the north side of KY 18 directly across from the park entrance. There is a flashing crosswalk sign at the entrance to this paved lot. GPS: N38 59.953' / W084 48.918'

The Hike

Together, these two short loop walks in the rolling Middle Creek area of Boone County make a pleasant, leisurely half-day escape from the urban bustle of northern Kentucky. Both are easy rambles up wooded ridges covered with wildflowers and offering views—though limited by the surrounding trees—across the Ohio River into Indiana. Unfortunately, the two walks must be interrupted by a 2-mile drive because they are in separate preserves with no connecting trail. The trails are jointly managed by the Boone County Parks Department and the Kentucky State Nature Preserves Commission.

 The first loop is in the Boone County Cliffs preserve, a 74-acre wooded tract bordering Middle Creek, a lively little stream that empties into the nearby Ohio River.

The nineteenth-century Dinsmore homestead is open to the public, including the home, which was completed in 1842.

The trail climbs a ridge above the creek, circles the head of a ravine, and descends along a brook that flows into Middle Creek just south of the parking lot.

From the sign, walk northwest to the little feeder stream, follow it north for a short distance, and then climb the log steps to the east. The trail is marked with red-and-white metal signs and the number 1. At mile 0.2 you come up to a level ridge-side spot that provides an overlook of the wooded valley below from a rock outcropping. There are several benches along the trail. Continuing up, pass one of several old side trails that have been closed to prevent erosion. The trail is quiet and serene, and in the late spring awash with the scent of honeysuckle blooming.

After rounding the head of the ravine, the trail turns southwest, initially staying on the level ridgetop. At mile 1.4 descend and cross the small Middle Creek tributary just north of Middle Creek Road. Follow the road east, and you are back at the parking lot at mile 1.7.

The second loop is in Dinsmore Woods, a 106-acre preserve that includes mature maple, oak, and ash trees. The tract was once part of a farm belonging to a prominent Boone County family, the Dinsmores, and has never been logged commercially. The

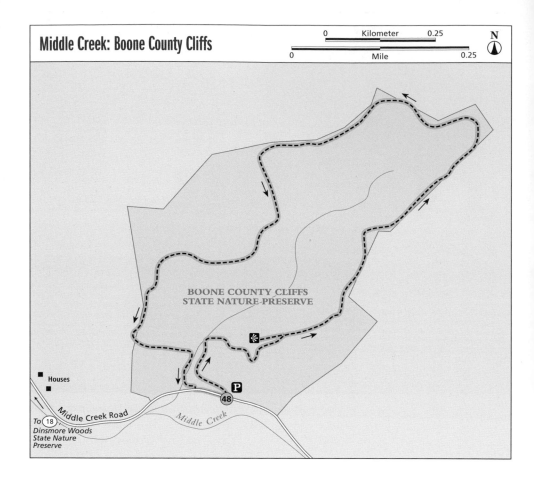

BOONE COUNTY CLIFFS
STATE NATURE PRESERVE

Houses

To 18,
Dinsmore Woods
State Nature
Preserve

Middle Creek Road

Middle Creek

nineteenth-century Dinsmore homestead, separately administered by a private foundation, is adjacent to the preserve and open to the public.

From the preserve sign on the north side of KY 18, take a narrow dirt path ascending northwest. The mileages that follow are figured from this trailhead. After curving northeast, you come to a level area that includes the walled Dinsmore family cemetery and then climb north to the beginning of the loop at mile 0.3. Continuing to climb, you reach the ridgetop at mile 0.5, where there are limited views west. In March, here and at other spots along the trail, the ground is white with spring beauties.

After winding along the ridge, the trail curves east and descends partway down the hillside toward KY 18 before turning south and following a level contour. You have views across the Middle Creek valley. You also have noise from the considerable truck traffic on the highway below. Circle back to the beginning of the loop (mile 1.4), and from there retrace your steps to the KY 18 trailhead at mile 1.7.

Middle Creek: Dinsmore Woods

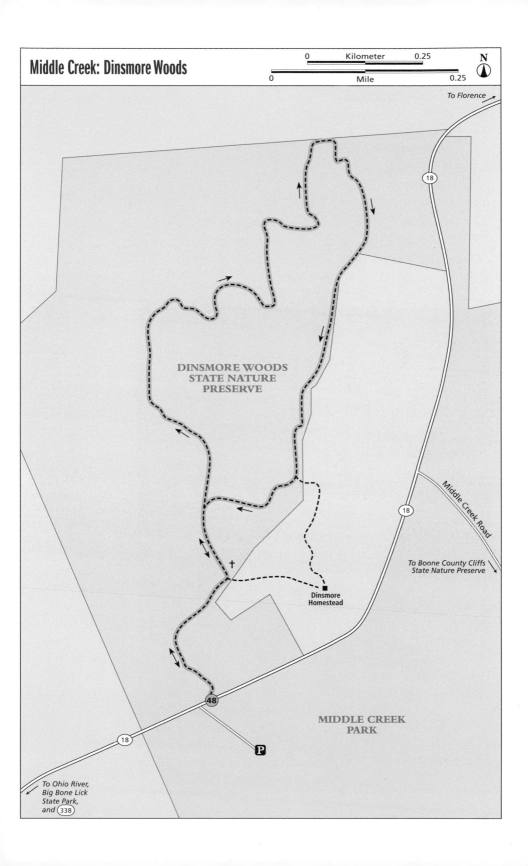

0   Kilometer   0.25

0   Mile   0.25

N

To Florence

18

DINSMORE WOODS
STATE NATURE
PRESERVE

Middle Creek Road

18

To Boone County Cliffs
State Nature Preserve

†

Dinsmore
Homestead

48

MIDDLE CREEK
PARK

18

P

To Ohio River,
Big Bone Lick
State Park,
and 338

Key Points

Boone County Cliffs loop

0.2 Overlook.

0.7 Head of ravine.

1.7 Arrive back at parking lot.

Dinsmore Woods loop

0.3 Beginning of loop.

0.5 Views from ridgetop.

1.2 Circle back to beginning of loop, which is at mile 1.4.

1.7 Arrive back at KY 18.

Option: Big Bone Lick State Park, which has several short hiking trails, is just a few miles south via KY 18 and KY 338.

Middle Creek comes to life after a heavy summer rain.

49 General Butler State Park

This pleasant hike through woods and open meadows includes a side trip to a stone lookout that provides a view of the confluence of the Kentucky and Ohio Rivers.

Start: Fossil Trailhead, at south end of parking lot off General Butler Park Road
Distance: 4.3-mile loop
Hiking time: About 2.5 hours
Difficulty: Moderate
Best season: Any
Other trail users: Mountain bikers
Canine compatibility: Leashed dogs permitted
Land status: State park
Nearest town: Carrolton
Fees and permits: None

Maps: State park map available online or at park
Trail contact: General Butler State Resort Park, (502) 732-4384, www.parks.ky.gov
Parking and trailhead facilities: You'll find space for about 20 cars, but no facilities. A full-service lodge with restaurant is just down the hill. The park also has a 111-unit campground with shower houses in addition to a conference center and golf pro shop.

Finding the trailhead: From Florence, take I-71 south to KY 227 at Carrollton (exit 44). Turn right and follow KY 227 north for 2 miles to the General Butler State Park entrance and road on your left. Follow the park road 1.2 miles until you reach the turnoff for the Stone Overlook on the right. Immediately turn left into the parking lot. The trailhead is on the southwest end of the parking lot. GPS: N38 40.219' / W085 09.684'

The Hike

General Butler State Park, one of Kentucky's first parks, is named for General William O. Butler and includes a 300-acre tract of former farmland owned by him. The park preserves the old Butler family home, which was built in 1859 and is now open for tours. The family cemetery and final resting place of the general are nearby. Butler was a well-known soldier and statesman. He served in the War of 1812 and the Mexican-American War. He was a congressman and ran unsuccessfully for governor of Kentucky and vice president of the United States.

This loop hike traverses wooded hillsides and crosses open meadows as it wanders through the northwest side of the park. A short detour takes you to the stone lookout tower built in the 1930s by the Civilian Conservation Corps (CCC). From the tower views stretch northward to historic Carrollton and the confluence of the Kentucky and Ohio Rivers.

The hike begins at the southwestern end of the parking lot; a wooden sign describing the hike sits just off the edge of the pavement. Almost immediately you reach a junction with the trail going to the right or left. I went left, in order to finish the hike with the short detour to the overlook. The trail begins gradually descending through the woods heading in a southwesterly direction before it turns and begins heading

This CCC-built stone structure provides views of downtown Carrollton at the confluence of the Kentucky and Ohio Rivers.

north. In 0.1 mile reach the junction of the Boy Scout trail, a steep 0.25-mile trail that leads to the General Butler mansion and cemetery. The trail levels out with gentle ups and downs, and at 0.5 mile passes under a power line in a small clearing. The trail then ascends and in 0.1 mile crosses a rocky wash. Through the trees, at the bottom of the hill, you can see houses and a road below you, but the traffic noise is not invasive.

At mile 0.8 the trail makes a series of sharp switchbacks before coming out of the woods onto a level grassy mowed path. The trail passes between two hills here and is lined with thistle, Queen Anne's lace, and a healthy crop of stinging nettle. At mile 1.0 the trail begins to ascend and heads back into the woods. In 0.1 mile it passes some water gates and water lines and comes back out into another section of meadow.

Follow the wooden directional signs and quickly pass over a little wooden bridge and head back into the woods. At mile 1.5 pass under a set of telephone and power lines, and at 1.6 miles you reach a small pond, before crossing under the power lines again at mile 1.8.

At mile 1.9 come to a junction with a short spur trail to the left, which leads up to the conference center. The trail is fairly level in this area and just inside the edge of the woods. At mile 2.4 cross another wooden bridge, and at mile 2.5 the trail comes

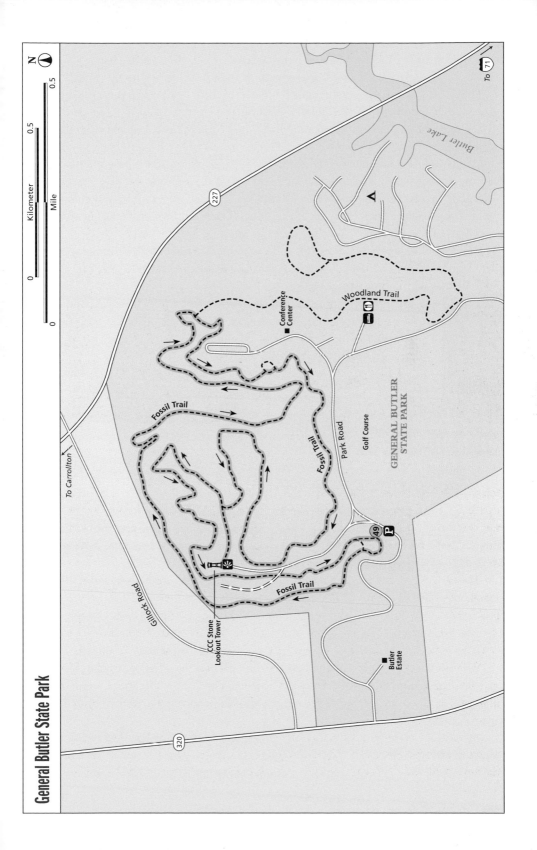

General Butler State Park

N

Kilometer
0   0.5   0.5

Mile
0   0.5

To 71

Butler Lake

To Carrollton

Gillock Road

320

227

Fossil Trail

Fossil Trail

Fossil Trail

Fossil Trail

Conference Center

Woodland Trail

Park Road

Golf Course

GENERAL BUTLER STATE PARK

CCC Stone Lookout Tower

49

P

Butler Estate

out onto a cleared ridgetop where it passes a large storage tank before turning right and descending the hill on a wide grassy path. It then heads back into the woods.

The forest has a large population of ash trees, which the park service has been systematically removing in the wake of finding the emerald ash borer, an invasive species, in the park in 2013. The mature hardwood forest also includes large poplars, beech trees, and several species of oak and hickory.

At mile 3.0 the trail reaches another clearing and, after a few feet, comes to an unmarked junction. The path to the left leads uphill 0.1 mile to the stone lookout tower. The shaded stone tower is a wonderful place to sit and rest for a few minutes while taking in the sweeping vistas of the Ohio River and Indiana farmland to the north.

Retrace your steps to the junction and continue downhill on the mowed grassy path. At mile 3.5 the trail again heads back into the woods and quickly passes another side trail back to the lookout tower.

At mile 4.1 cross a small footbridge in a clearing under a utility line and continuing ascending to a deeply rutted gravel road. After crossing the road, the trail passes back into the woods and continues climbing. At mile 4.3 you reach the end of the loop. Retrace your steps back to the parking lot.

Key Points

0.1   Junction with Boy Scout trail.

1.9   Spur trail to conference center.

3.1   CCC stone lookout tower.

4.1   Cross gravel road.

50 Quiet Trails State Nature Preserve

This unspoiled spot on the banks of the Licking River offers good views of the rolling river valley.

Start: Small parking area on Pugh's Ferry Road
Distance: 1.8-mile lollipop
Hiking time: About 1 hour
Difficulty: Easy
Best seasons: Any
Other trail users: None
Canine compatibility: No dogs allowed
Land status: State nature preserve

Nearest town: Cynthiana
Fees and permits: None
Maps: Kentucky State Nature Preserves Commission map of Quiet Trails; USGS Claysville
Trail contact: Kentucky State Nature Preserves Commission, (502) 573-2886
Parking and trailhead facilities: There's room for 6 cars, but no facilities.

Finding the trailhead: From Cynthiana, take US 27 north about 10 miles and turn right onto KY 1284. Drive 2.8 miles to the town of Sunrise. At the four-way stop, go straight on gravel Pugh's Ferry Road; in 1.8 miles, turn right into the small parking area for the nature preserve. GPS: N38 33.409' / W84 13.627'

The Hike

The name of this small preserve along the Licking River may sound a bit trite, but it's accurate. These 165 acres, tucked away in the rural northeast corner of Harrison County, are tranquil indeed. Most of the preserve is former farmland donated to the state in the early 1990s. From the fields you get good views of the Licking River valley. This hike also takes you to a pretty riverside spot that was once the site of a trading post for river travelers. Now it's just you and the fish.

From the parking area, go through the gate. To your left is a box that should contain trail maps and a sign-in sheet. A loop trail takes you through the preserve. The first leg is Deep Hollow Trail, which starts just inside the gate on the right.

Deep Hollow Trail heads south and then east as it follows the preserve boundary downhill toward the river. Initially you are on a mowed grass path, a line of young hardwoods to the right. But you soon enter more mature woods on an old roadbed that follows a drainage area downhill. Disregard the connector trail that goes off to your left at 0.1 mile into the preserve interior, unless you want a shorter loop back to the parking lot. At mile 0.5, after crossing a small drainage, Deep Hollow Trail ends at its intersection with Challenger Trail. Note the old fence made of stones placed vertically instead of horizontally, an arrangement said to be more stable.

Turn right onto Challenger Trail and head east, with a good view of a beautiful rolling pasture in the distance. At mile 0.7 enter a large clearing with a pavilion and picnic table. This is the site of the trading post. Continue east, keeping the woods on

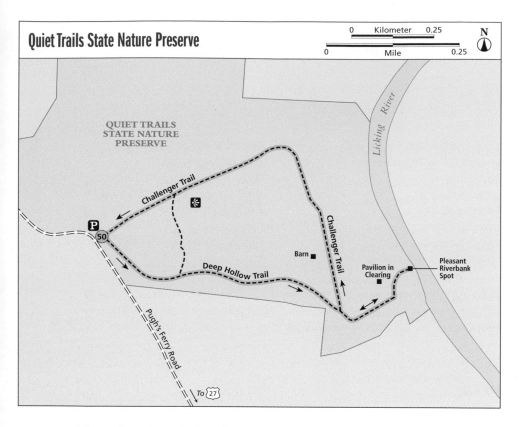

QUIET TRAILS
STATE NATURE
PRESERVE

Challenger Trail

P
50

Challenger Trail

Deep Hollow Trail

Barn ■

Pavilion in
Clearing ■

Pleasant
Riverbank
Spot ■

Licking River

Pugh's Ferry Road

To 27

0   Kilometer   0.25

0   Mile   0.25

N

your right, and go through the tall grass, where you find a set of wooden steps down to the river. There are rocks along the water where you can sit and watch the stream flow lazily to meet the Ohio River at Covington.

Return to the clearing and backtrack to the Deep Hollow Trail intersection, where you turn right onto Challenger Trail. Follow Challenger Trail uphill to the north, passing a barn on the left. Continue on Challenger Trail until, at mile 1.5, you reach the top of the hill. The trail jogs west here.

Follow the now well-defined farm road west past a small pond. Just beyond the pond a sign points left to the Prairie Vista at mile 1.7. From this vantage point in an open field a few steps off the trail, you can enjoy a wonderful view southeast across the Licking River valley. From the overlook return to the trail. The parking lot is just ahead at mile 1.8.

Key Points

0.8 Licking River.

1.7 Vista.

An eastern tiger swallowtail butterfly sips on nectar from a purple coneflower. Both the butterfly and coneflowers are common in Kentucky grass- and woodlands.

51 Kleber Wildlife Management Area

This walk on an attractive old roadbed follows a modest creek and makes a short side trip to a hilltop vista.

Start: Parking area on gravel road just off KY 368
Distance: 4.6-mile out-and-back
Hiking time: About 2 hours
Difficulty: Easy
Best seasons: Spring and fall
Other trail users: Equestrians; hunters in season
Canine compatibility: Dogs are permitted; must be leashed Mar 1 through the third Sat of Aug to protect ground-nesting wildlife
Land status: State wildlife management area

Nearest towns: Frankfort, Owenton
Fees and permits: None
Maps: Kleber Wildlife Management Area map; USGS Switzer and Stamping Ground
Trail contact: Kleber Wildlife Management Area, (502) 535-6335
Special considerations: Several days each year, the Kleber area is closed for special hunts.
Parking and trailhead facilities: You'll find space for about 6 cars, but no facilities.

Finding the trailhead: From Frankfort, take US 127 north for about 15 miles and turn right (southeast) onto KY 368. From Florence, take I-75 south to KY 330 west (exit 144), travel 1.5 miles, and then take KY 607 west for 18 miles to US 127 south. In 0.7 mile, turn left onto KY 368.

Travel KY 368 for 5 miles. When you come to a metal building on the right, which is the office for the wildlife area, go 0.1 mile farther and turn left onto the narrow gravel road, which ends in 0.2 mile at a gate. Park near the gate, which is where the hike begins. GPS: N38 21.644' / W84 46.774'

The Hike

The state's John A. Kleber Wildlife Management Area covers 2,605 acres of hills and bottomlands in rural Owen and Franklin Counties about halfway between Frankfort and Owenton. The rolling terrain is covered with a mixture of brush, grassland, and woods—a habitat that attracts a variety of birds along with deer, raccoons, and groundhogs. The wildlife area is named for a Frankfort resident who left money in his will to help the state buy the initial acreage in the early 1950s.

For the most part, this hike follows an old roadbed along a little stream called Elm Fork. It's all fairly level, except for a short detour up a grassy hilltop to enjoy a 360-degree view of the rolling countryside. There is nothing spectacular about the creek or the scenery along it, and in hot weather this is likely to be sticky, buggy territory. But in spring and fall, this is a delightful walk along a quiet country road.

From the gate go east on the old two-track dirt road, which is an extension of the gravel road you followed from KY 368. Beyond the gate travel is restricted to foot and horseback. On the right, between you and the creek, is a field covered with grass,

A steady summer rain falls on the Elm Fork of Cedar Creek.

scrub bushes, and small trees; on the left is a cedar forest. The vegetation lining both
sides of the road, however, soon becomes more substantial and attractive. As you head
upstream, the road veers alternately toward and away from the creek, putting you one
minute on the bank and the next on a wooded ridge above the stream. At both mile
1.0 and 1.3, the road climbs a good way from the creek.

At mile 1.6 pass a line of rocks lying across the creek to make a ford for horses.
On the other side a path goes up the bank and heads south to Oakland Branch Road
near the hamlet of Elmville on KY 368—a distance of about 1.5 miles. Continuing
east on the creek-side roadbed, pass the mouth of Minors Creek and come into an
area of open fields. For a nice break from the bottomland, take the old farm track
that veers off to your left at mile 1.9 (GPS: N38 21.723' / W84 44.893'). The rough
roadbed climbs steadily northwest and then northeast for 0.2 mile to a treeless hilltop
field with a grand view of the ridges that surround the Kleber area. This is an especially nice spot at sunset.

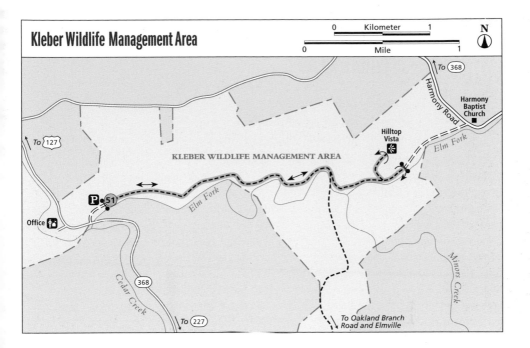

Kleber Wildlife Management Area

0   Kilometer   1

0   Mile   1

N

To 368

Harmony Baptist Church

To 127

Hilltop Vista

KLEBER WILDLIFE MANAGEMENT AREA

Harmony Road

Elm Fork

P 51

Office

Elm Fork

Cedar Creek

368

Minors Creek

To 227

To Oakland Branch Road and Elmville

After returning to the creek-side road, continue east and at mile 2.5 come to a gate that marks the eastern end of the hike. Beyond the gate a rough gravel road leads 0.4 mile to Harmony Road and Harmony Baptist Church, an attractive white structure built on land donated for the church in 1851. Between the gate and Harmony Road is a shooting range open to the public. At the gate turn around and take the creek-side road back to your car, which you reach at mile 4.6.

Key Points

1.6   Rock ford across Elm Fork.

1.9   Left turn onto old farm track leading up to hilltop vista.

2.5   End of trail and turnaround point.

52 Clyde E. Buckley Wildlife Sanctuary and Life Adventure Center

Enjoy a mix of open fields and wooded areas, plus a stop at a small pond, on this easy walk—an especially good one for young children.

Start: Sanctuary parking lot off Germany Road
Distance: 3-mile loop
Hiking time: About 1.5 hours
Difficulty: Easy
Best seasons: Any
Other trail users: None
Canine compatibility: No dogs allowed
Land status: Privately owned wildlife sanctuary
Nearest town: Frankfort
Fees and permits: Day-use fee (honor system; put money in well next to parking lot)
Maps: Buckley Wildlife Sanctuary map; USGS Frankfort East

Trail contact: Clyde E. Buckley Wildlife Sanctuary and Life Adventure Center, (859) 873-3271, www.lifeadventurecenter.org
Special considerations: Clyde E. Buckley Wildlife Sanctuary and Life Adventure Center is open Wed through Fri from 8:30 a.m. to 4 p.m. and Sat and Sun from 9 a.m. to 6 p.m.; closed Mon, Tues, and holidays. The invasive emerald ash borer caused heavy damage to the center's native ash trees, which were removed in early 2015, temporarily closing the Yellow and Red Trails.
Parking and trailhead facilities: There's space for several dozen cars, along with water, restrooms, a picnic shelter, and nature center.

Finding the trailhead: The sanctuary is 6.5 miles from the intersection of I-64 and US 60 at Frankfort. Going east on US 60, just beyond the interstate, turn right onto KY 1681 (McCracken Road). In 2.5 miles, turn left onto KY 1659. In 1.6 more miles, turn right onto KY 1964 (Watts Ferry Road), and after 1.1 miles, turn right onto Germany Road. Take Germany Road for 1.3 miles and turn left at the Buckley Wildlife Sanctuary sign. Drive to the end of the road and park in the gravel lot. The trailhead is just north of the lot, up the incline. (Coming from Lexington or Versailles on US 60, turn left onto KY 3360 and follow the signs to the sanctuary.) GPS: N38 08.099' / W84 51.332'

The Hike

The trails on this small, privately owned preserve near the Kentucky River are geared to families. The distances are short, the terrain level, and the interpretive materials easy to understand. For families with little ones, this is a perfect place for an afternoon hike. But even if you don't have children—or maybe you just want to get away from some—these 374 acres can provide a couple of hours of pleasant walking. You will find a good mix of woods and open fields, and a lovely little pond.

The hike combines the sanctuary's three longest trails—the Red, Yellow, and Blue—into one loop. The total length is 3 miles, but that can easily be reduced to

A quiet pond usually inhabited by waterfowl and ringed with violet cow vetch is a delightful resting spot along the Blue Trail.

accommodate little legs by taking just the Red or Blue segment. For each of its trails, the sanctuary has a written guide explaining plants and environmental conditions you see along the way. You can borrow a copy to take with you on the hike. Copies are kept at the end of the message board next to the well. Signage with plant names is also located along the trails.

The sanctuary was founded in the 1960s when a Lexington woman, Mrs. Emma E. Buckley, set aside this farm as a memorial to her late husband, Clyde E. Buckley. The handsome beige farmhouse near the parking lot, now the Emma E. Buckley Center, is the sanctuary's nature center and gift shop. The grounds and trails are closed on Mondays, Tuesdays, and holidays.

This hike starts with the Red Trail, which begins on the rise north of the parking lot beyond a large maintenance building. The trail, marked by red-painted cutouts of a fox, heads north on a broad dirt path into a thin forest along the edge of a field. You soon emerge into an open field and follow a fence west before turning north along a tree line separating two fields.

Where the Red Trail curves west, a 0.5-mile-long path—the Yellow Trail—forks off to the right and continues north before looping south and meeting up again with the Red Trail. After completing the Yellow Trail and rejoining the Red, head south along the edge of the field and then into the woods. The Kentucky River is below on the right; you can't see the river through the trees, but as you move south, you can see the palisades above the river.

The trail winds south and then east above the Elk Lick Branch and joins a section of another sanctuary trail—the White Trail—before reaching the northwest edge of

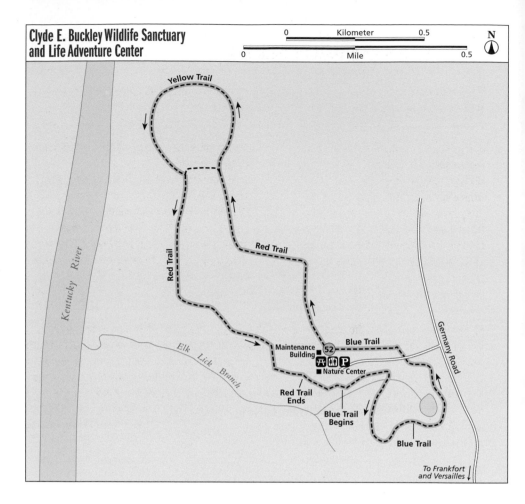

Kilometer
0   0.5

Mile
0   0.5

N

Yellow Trail

Red Trail

Red Trail

Kentucky River

Red Trail

Elk Lick Branch

Maintenance Building

52

Blue Trail

Germany Road

Nature Center

Red Trail Ends

Blue Trail Begins

Blue Trail

To Frankfort and Versailles

the parking lot at mile 2.0. Skirting the lot's south side along the woods, you quickly come to the beginning of the Blue Trail.

Following the Blue Trail, descend southeast into the woods and take a power-line clearing east a short distance before turning south and crossing a fork of Elk Lick Branch. Wind eastward to the south end of a 1.5-acre pond lined with cattails. The trail guide says the pond also has ducks and muskrats.

Continuing to the pond's north end at mile 2.7, climb easily to the north and follow a power-line clearing west to the sanctuary's entrance road. Go west a few steps along the road and then cross it to continue west along a tree line. At mile 3.0 you come to a grass lawn east of the nature center and near the redbrick home of the sanctuary manager. Your car is just a few steps away.

Key Points

2.0 Blue Trail.

2.7 North end of the pond.

53 Raven Run Nature Sanctuary

This wooded walk outside Lexington goes to a fine overlook above the Kentucky River before descending into a scenic creek gorge.

Start: Gate just north of sanctuary office
Distance: 4.1-mile loop
Hiking time: About 3 hours
Difficulty: Moderate
Best seasons: Any
Other trail users: None
Canine compatibility: No dogs allowed
Land status: City/county nature preserve
Nearest town: Lexington
Fees and permits: None

Maps: Raven Run Nature Sanctuary trail map; USGS Coletown
Trail contact: Raven Run Nature Sanctuary, (859) 272-6105
Parking and trailhead facilities: You'll find space for about 50 cars and picnic tables at the parking lot, along with restrooms and drink and vending machines at the new nature center.

Finding the trailhead: From exit 99 off I-75, take US 25/421 (Old Richmond Road) north toward Lexington; after 5 miles, turn left onto Jacks Creek Road. Stay on Jacks Creek Road through several sharp turns and a change in its numerical designation, and in 5 miles turn left at the sign for Raven Run Nature Sanctuary. In 0.4 mile, turn right into the visitor parking lot; only employees are allowed to drive beyond this point. From the lot, take the paved walkway 0.2 mile northwest, then northeast, to the sanctuary office. The trail starts at the gate just north of the office. GPS: N37 53.378' / W84 23.740'

The Hike

The 730-acre Raven Run Nature Sanctuary gets its name from a scenic creek that meanders through southeastern Fayette County and empties into the Kentucky River just below a 100-foot bluff. The area was originally settled and farmed two centuries ago; a house built by the Prather family in the late 1700s on a Revolutionary War land grant still stands.

Today, run by the Lexington-Fayette Urban County government, the sanctuary is exactly that—a delightful wooded area where you can get away from almost all signs of urban life. It has deer, wild turkeys, more than 300 species of wildflowers, and a well-developed system of trails totaling about 10 miles. For the most part, this hike follows the longest trail—the Red Trail—in a counterclockwise loop that takes you to the bluff overlooking the Kentucky River and then down into the Raven Run gorge at the site of a nineteenth-century gristmill. A trail map available at the office includes information about the mill and other historical points along the way. (To make it easier to read, the map in this book purposely excludes some of the shorter trails.)

The drystone field fences found at Raven Run are common across this area of central Kentucky.

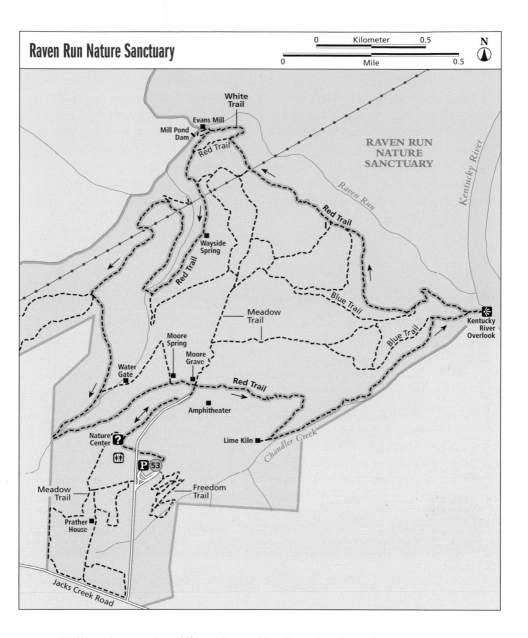

Raven Run Nature Sanctuary

0   Kilometer   0.5

0   Mile   0.5

N

White Trail

Evans Mill

Mill Pond Dam

Red Trail

RAVEN RUN NATURE SANCTUARY

Kentucky River

Raven Run

Red Trail

Wayside Spring

Red Trail

Blue Trail

Meadow Trail

Kentucky River Overlook

Moore Spring

Moore Grave

Water Gate

Red Trail

Blue Trail

Amphitheater

Nature Center

Lime Kiln

Chandler Creek

P 53

Meadow Trail

Freedom Trail

Prather House

Jacks Creek Road

Follow the paved trail from the parking lot 0.1 mile to the nature center, crossing over a paved access road on your way. All trails start behind the nature center and office. Follow a wide mulched path for another 0.2 mile, passing a series of storage buildings and an old barn. Turn right (east) onto the Red Trail at 0.4 mile and follow the sign for the overlook. Following a fence built of fieldstones in the 1800s, the dirt path soon begins a gentle descent through a young forest, then makes a sharp right turn, followed at mile 0.7 by a sharp left turn. At the latter there's a trail marker labeled A.

From marker A the trail follows the ravine carved by Chandler Creek on its way to the Kentucky River. At marker B the Blue Trail intersects on the left; continue to follow the Red Trail, which curves right and comes to a set of stairs. At the bottom you come to marker C and a short side trail leading right to a rock outcropping at mile 1.2. This is the Kentucky River Overlook, and it would be hard to find a better rest spot. The view of the river below makes you feel like a soaring bird. Just to the north you see the mouth of Raven Run. In the fall the trees covering the riverside cliff make a handsome tapestry of oranges, yellows, and browns.

Returning to marker C, take the Red Trail west as it follows the level ridgeline above Raven Run to marker D, where the Red Trail goes left and the Yellow Trail descends right.

Following the Red Trail, the path soon climbs as it heads south and reaches an intersection with the Blue Trail on your left at mile 1.5. The Red Trail continues straight with relatively flat walking through the large second-growth forest before ascending slightly and crossing a small wooden bridge. At mile 1.6 it reaches yet another intersection with the Blue Trail; the Red Trail continues heading northwest and at mile 1.8 reaches a junction with the Yellow Trail, which rejoins it from the right. The Red Trail turns left, heading northwest, and quickly reaches a junction with the Black Trail. Continue following the mostly level Red Trail, which features numerous benches in this area for sitting and resting. The Kentucky River is far below you.

At mile 2.1 reach the intersection of the White Trail; follow it to the right to make a detour into the gorge to the gristmill. At mile 2.2 reach the banks of Raven Run and a small viewing platform overlooking the old foundation of the gristmill built in 1820. Raven Run flows over rocks and is a beautiful place to stop and rest.

From the creek the White Trail makes a short climb back up the gorge to rejoin the Red Trail. From here it continues south and passes beneath the power line a second time and, at mile 2.5, crosses a branch of Raven Run. Follow the streambed northeast to another meeting with the power line. At mile 3.0, after crossing beneath the power line twice more and turning southwest, skirt a meadow and drop down to cross the same branch of Raven Run that you crossed less than a mile earlier. You now head northeast and, at mile 3.6, turn right to retrace your steps to the nature center and on to the parking lot at mile 4.1.

Key Points

1.2 Kentucky River Overlook.

2.2 Old gristmill site on Raven Run.

54 Kentucky River Palisades

This short walk down to the banks of the Kentucky River allows you to admire the towering palisades that line both sides of the river.

Start: Parking area for Tom Dorman State Nature Preserve off KY 1845 south of Nicholasville
Distance: 2-mile loop
Hiking time: About 1 hour
Difficulty: Moderate
Best seasons: Any
Other trail users: None
Canine compatibility: No dogs allowed

Land status: State nature preserve
Nearest town: Nicholasville
Fees and permits: None
Maps: Tom Dorman State Nature Preserve brochure; USGS Wilmore
Trail contact: Kentucky State Nature Preserves Commission, (502) 573-2886
Parking and trailhead facilities: There's space for 10 cars, but no facilities.

Finding the trailhead: From Nicholasville, take US 27 south for about 10 miles and, after crossing the Kentucky River, turn right onto KY 1845. Go 0.9 mile and turn right onto the narrow road by a small church. Drive another 0.7 mile—making sure to go straight at the fork—and park in the paved lot at the end of the road. GPS: N37 45.914' / W84 37.628'

The Hike

In the early evening the tops of the Kentucky River Palisades gleam in the setting sun. This is a good hike anytime, but it's especially nice when the last rays of the day are lighting up the 200- and 300-foot cliffs that line the river. This short hike takes you from the top of the gorge on the river's south side down to what used to be a ferry landing, although nothing is now left except the remains of a house. Most of the walking is on old roadbeds, and despite the elevation change, the grades are not severe.

Originally this approximately 817-acre area was called the Palisades State Nature Preserve. It was renamed in 1999 to honor a former director of the Kentucky River Authority.

One end of the loop starts at the west end of the parking lot, the other at the east end. You can take either; the west half of the hike is a bit steeper. These directions start from the east end. The trail is not blazed, but it is well-trod and easily followed.

Follow an old roadbed east before turning northeast onto a grass path and entering a forest of young trees. As the trail curves north, the woods become more mature. You are descending, gradually at first. But when the trail, now an old dirt road, turns west, the going gets steeper. It's at this point that you also get your first good view of the palisades along the opposite shore. At mile 0.9, just after the grade becomes gentle

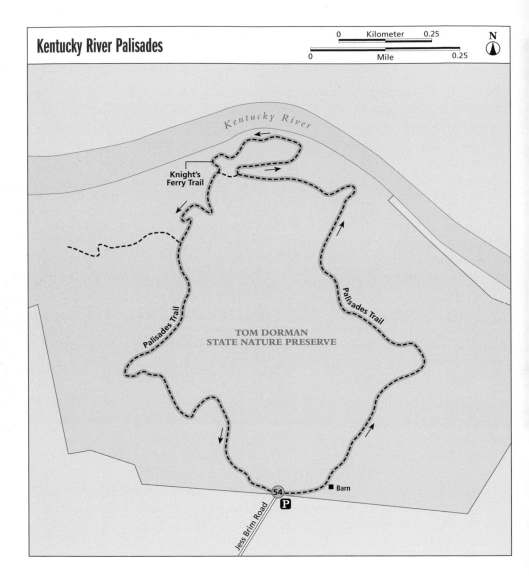

once again, you come to a sign on the right for Knight's Ferry Trail, which loops to the river and rejoins Palisades Trail a few steps farther west.

Turning right onto Knight's Ferry Trail, pass stone ruins that were once the home of a family who ran the ferry and farmed these bottomlands, according to a state nature preserve official. The trail winds east and comes to the riverbank at mile 1.0. It then turns west to parallel the river for a short distance before returning to Palisades Trail.

Back on the main trail at mile 1.2, continue west for only a few steps before turning left and beginning the climb up the side of the gorge. The trail is steep at first but tapers off. When it turns southwest, you even enjoy a level stretch. Dip down twice

The palisades of the Kentucky River stretch more than 100 miles.

to cross drainages before the final uphill push, which gets you to the west side of the parking lot at mile 2.0.

Key Points

0.9 Knight's Ferry Trail.
1.0 Kentucky River.

55 Central Kentucky Wildlife Management Area

Fields and wooded areas full of birds, small game, and flowering plants are the attractions of this do-it-yourself hiking area. There are no established trails; you compose your own route on mowed paths and horse tracks.

Start: Just about anywhere you want along Muddy Creek Road
Distance: How ambitious do you feel today?
Hiking time: Ditto
Difficulty: Easy
Best seasons: Fall (definitely not July and August)
Other trail users: Equestrians, hunting dogs and their owners participating in field trials, hunters
Canine compatibility: Dogs permitted but must be leashed Apr 1 through the third Sat of Aug unless in an authorized field trial

Land status: State wildlife management area
Nearest towns: Richmond, Berea
Fees and permits: None
Maps: USGS Moberly and Bighill
Trail contact: Central Kentucky Wildlife Management Area, (859) 986-4130
Parking and trailhead facilities: There's room at the parking area I used (one of several along Muddy Creek Road) for half a dozen cars; there are no facilities.

Finding the trailhead: From Richmond, take US 421 south for about 9 miles; at Kingston, turn left onto Dreyfus Road. Go 2 miles and turn right onto Muddy Creek Road. From Berea, take KY 1016 northeast to US 421 and turn right (south). Take US 421 for 1.4 miles and turn left (north) onto Muddy Creek Road, which intersects Dreyfus Road in 2.4 miles.

This unit of the wildlife management area extends along both sides of Muddy Creek Road for about 1 mile south of Dreyfus Road. The 2.2-mile route shown on the map begins at the parking area on the west side of Muddy Creek Road 0.4 mile south of Dreyfus Road. GPS: N37 37.775' / W84 12.095'

The Hike

Fall is the best time to hike this 1,690-acre state wildlife area. The grasses and stalks that cover the fields are golden brown, and the trees that line them are rich in oranges and yellows. Bugs are one reason you don't want to come in the heat of summer, and another is that there are no mowed swaths through the fields, so hiking is difficult.

The mowing, which starts in late August, produces a labyrinth that lets you go just about anywhere in the wildlife area you want. On a gorgeous October afternoon, Michael Brown, the author of earlier editions of this book, walked to two picturesque barns near the south boundary. With a GPS unit, he pinpointed the barns before starting out. Then, following mowed paths, horse tracks, and tree-lined streambeds, worked his way toward them from the parking area, a round-trip of 2.2 miles.

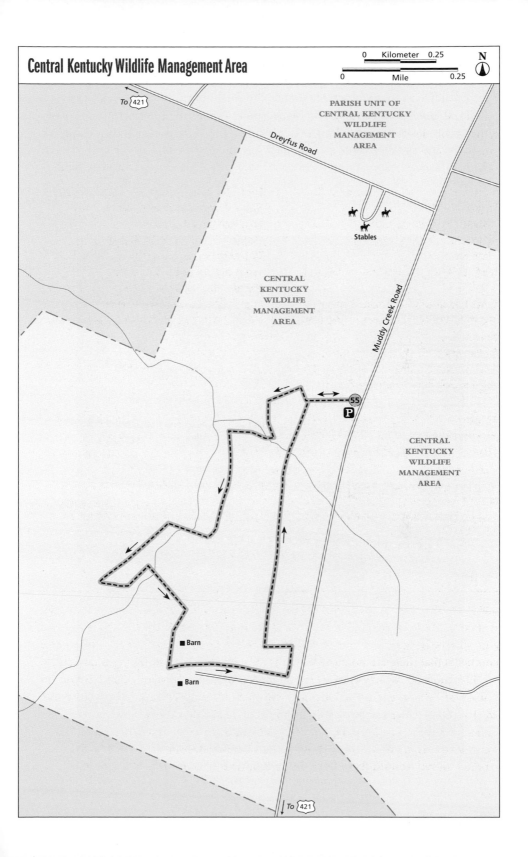

Central Kentucky Wildlife Management Area

0   Kilometer   0.25

0   Mile   0.25

N

To [421]

Dreyfus Road

PARISH UNIT OF
CENTRAL KENTUCKY
WILDLIFE
MANAGEMENT
AREA

Stables

CENTRAL
KENTUCKY
WILDLIFE
MANAGEMENT
AREA

Muddy Creek Road

55
P

CENTRAL
KENTUCKY
WILDLIFE
MANAGEMENT
AREA

■ Barn

■ Barn

To [421]

He included a map of his route as an example of what you can do here. The terrain is flat and without points of special note. The enjoyment here is walking, watching for wildlife, and soaking up the sounds and smells of rural central Kentucky.

The Central Kentucky Wildlife Management Area is used heavily for dog trials. Hunting for doves, squirrels, deer, turkey, and some waterfowl is allowed.

At the information stand, you can pick up a free copy of a list of birds seen at the wildlife area—from common wrens to rare hawks and waterfowl. The stand is located next to the stables on the right side of Dreyfus Road, just before the turn onto Muddy Creek Road.

Kentucky has more than thirty native species of goldenrod, the official state flower. Locust borers, also native, are often found on them.

56 Berea Forest

Five different overlooks connected by this moderate ridgeline trail provides striking views of rolling central Kentucky farmland. This is a great hike for a clear, sunny day and appropriate for families with children.

Start: Indian Fort Theater parking area on edge of Berea Forest
Distance: 6.6-mile lollipop
Hiking time: About 4 hours
Difficulty: Moderate
Best seasons: Any
Other trail users: None
Canine compatibility: Leashed dogs permitted
Land status: Privately managed college forest
Nearest town: Berea

Fees and permits: None
Maps: Berea College map of Indian Fort trails; USGS Bighill
Trail contact: Berea College forestry office, (859) 985-3587
Special considerations: The trails are open only during daylight hours.
Parking and trailhead facilities: You'll find a large parking lot with space for dozens of cars, picnic tables, and restrooms.

Finding the trailhead: From exit 76 off I-75, take KY 21 east through the city of Berea. In 4.3 miles, turn left and park in the large parking lot. The trail starts at the north end of the lot at the wooden gate. GPS: N37 33.260' / W84 14.470'

The Hike

Located in the town of the same name, Berea College is a highly rated liberal arts school that gives a tuition-free education to promising youths from Appalachia and beyond. In fact, inability to pay is a requirement for admission; students work instead. In addition to the pleasant campus, the college manages some 8,000 acres of forestland, much of it donated in the early 1900s to give the college timber income and forestry demonstration sites. Included in these holdings is Indian Fort Mountain, a popular hiking area full of cliffs and overlooks. It's a tradition that on one beautiful day each autumn, the college cancels classes and the students troop out to Indian Fort Mountain for hikes and fellowship. The area is open to the public, but camping is not allowed. This hike takes you to the most impressive of the observation points.

Indian Fort Mountain is crisscrossed by many trails that are well cared for by Berea forestry staff and underwent some major renovations and signage updates in late 2015. This hike takes you on several of the most popular trails in this gem of a forest. From the north end of the parking lot, head north on the asphalt walkway through an area used for outdoor crafts fairs. In 0.2 mile you come to Indian Fort Theater, an amphitheater, on your right. The restrooms are located here. Here the path, named Indian Fort Trail, becomes gravel and dirt, and a sign explains that humans roamed this area in the period from 100 BC to AD 400. In 2015 this trail was relocated back

Davis Hollow lies far below the West Pinnacle of Berea Forest.

onto an existing pathway, which was closed twenty years prior but was updated with improved drainage and reopened.

As you climb gradually, notice that the forest is dominated by oak and hickory, with some pines and yellow poplars. Much of this land was farmed at one time, and the hardwoods are tall but thin.

At 0.6 mile reach the three-way junction of the Sacred Shadow Trail, the Indian Fort Trail, and the East Pinnacle Trail. Turn right and follow the East Pinnacle Trail to the east. After 0.2 mile of easy walking, the trail begins to climb. At mile 1.2 reach a bench at the edge of a meadow clearing and a junction with the Lookout Trail. Turn right and continue following the East Pinnacle Trail east, then quickly reach a series of quick switchbacks. At mile 1.4 reach the ridgeline, which has numerous well-worn side trails to lookouts on both sides and at the end of the trail, giving the hiker sweeping views to the east, south, and north.

Retrace your steps back to the junction with the Lookout Trail and follow it up another series of switchbacks to another junction at mile 2.3, this one with the Indian Fort Lookout to the north, West Pinnacle to the west, and Robe Mountain Trail, which leads to Buzzards Roost/Eagles Nest to the northeast. Turn right and follow the Robe Mountain Trail to the northeast. At mile 2.6 reach a fork; turn left to go to Buzzards Roost, right to go to Eagles Nest. Both provide spectacular views.

After visiting both lookouts, retrace your steps back to the three-way junction and follow the trail to Lookout Trail to the north. At mile 4.2 you will pass the turnoff to Devils Kitchen Trail, which literally passes beneath the Lookout Trail. Be on the lookout for the metal bars in the trail that keep hikers from falling into the rock house below. At mile 4.4 reach the Indian Fort Lookout and take in views that sweep across the farmland below to Berea and Richmond beyond.

From here the trail follows the edge of the cliff line to the West Pinnacle. If you are walking with small children, take their hand in this section. A number of paths snake across this well-used area and can be confusing. But simply follow the cliff edge southward, keeping the drop-off on your right, and you soon come to another overlook, this one with good views looking south.

Here it's easy to get stumped, because the trail to West Pinnacle—your next destination—is hard to find. The only path immediately visible goes northeast back toward Indian Fort Lookout, which you don't want. But if you closely examine the boulders on the west edge of the overlook, you will find a steep dirt path—almost a chute—cutting down through the rocks on the west side of the cliff. This is what you take (GPS: N37 33.834' / W84 14.077'). You will need both hands, but it's not dangerous, and you quickly reach the bottom. Be sure to pause at the bottom to take in views to the south, including one of two lakes owned by the college. (You saw the other from the East Pinnacle.)

You are now on the Main Dome Trail. Heading west on the dirt path, level at first, you soon climb up one side of a wooded peak and down the other. After passing a narrow side trail leading off to the left, you make your way northwest over a rocky section and, at mile 5.1, come to a mushroom-shaped tower of rock called West Pinnacle. There is a way to get on top, although at first you may not think so. Midway up the west side of the huge rock, there's a ledge. Put your feet on the ledge and, holding the top of the rock with your hands, inch your way to the middle of the west side. There you will find a large hole running down the rock that looks as if it were made by a giant corkscrew. Bracing your body against the inside of the hole, you can push yourself up and come out on the flat top of West Pinnacle. You will feel like a true climber. Children should not try it on their own, however; a fall could cause serious injury. The view is worth the small rock scramble, and the top of the rock is wide and flat.

This is an excellent vantage point that on a clear day affords views of Lexington 36 miles to the northwest.

From here retrace your steps to the narrow side trail you passed shortly before West Pinnacle. Take this trail, now on your right, and descend initially west and then south to a wider path. Turn left onto this wider path at mile 5.4; almost immediately you come to another trail and again turn left onto the Sacred Shadow Trail. Heading south and then east, this trail takes you through a level stretch of large hardwoods before intersecting two trails at mile 6.0, both going southwest. Turn right onto the first trail, a sharper right, which is Indian Fort Trail, the main route back to the parking lot. Pass the trail to East Pinnacle that you took at the beginning of your hike. Continuing southwest past the amphitheater, you are back at your car at mile 6.6.

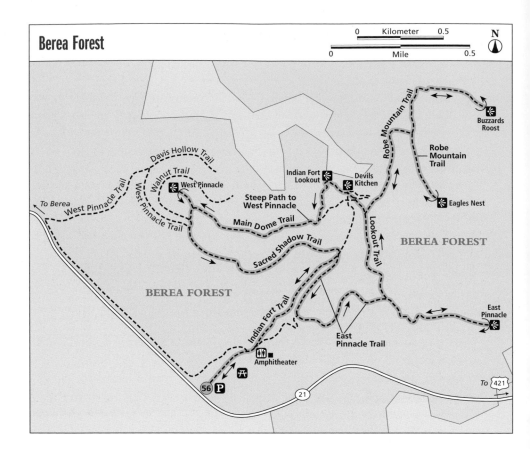

Berea Forest

Berea Forest

To Berea

West Pinnacle Trail

Davis Hollow Trail

Walnut Trail

West Pinnacle Trail

West Pinnacle

Steep Path to West Pinnacle

Main Dome Trail

Sacred Shadow Trail

Indian Fort Lookout

Devils Kitchen

BEREA FOREST

Robe Mountain Trail

Robe Mountain Trail

Eagles Nest

Buzzards Roost

Lookout Trail

BEREA FOREST

East Pinnacle

Indian Fort Trail

East Pinnacle Trail

Amphitheater

56 P

21

To 421

Key Points

1.4 East Pinnacle.

2.8 Eagles Nest.

3.2 Buzzards Roost.

4.2 Turnoff to Devils Kitchen.

4.4 Indian Fort Lookout.

5.1 West Pinnacle.

57 Shaker Village of Pleasant Hill

This stroll from the historic center of Shaker Village down to Shaker Landing on the Kentucky River travels part of the way on a roadbed built by Shakers in the early nineteenth century.

Start: Shaker Village admission booth
Distance: 3.4-mile out-and-back
Hiking time: About 2 hours
Difficulty: Moderate
Best seasons: Any
Other trail users: None
Canine compatibility: Leashed dogs permitted
Land status: Private land
Nearest town: Harrodsburg
Fees and permits: None
Maps: Shaker Village trail card; USGS Wilmore
Trail contact: Shaker Village of Pleasant Hill, (859) 734-5411 or (800) 734-5611, www .shakervillageky.org

Special considerations: Shaker Village is a restored National Historic Landmark owned by a private nonprofit educational organization. It charges a fee to tour the historic village center and farm but allows hikers to use the trails free of charge. Be aware that the buildings and most of the grounds are for paying visitors.
Parking and trailhead facilities: There's room for numerous cars; restrooms are found near the parking lot. Restaurant and hotel accommodations are available in the village.

Finding the trailhead: From Harrodsburg, take US 68 northeast for 7 miles and turn left at the Shaker Village entrance directly across from KY 33. Park in the first lot. Directions for this hike start from the red admission booth just north of the lot. GPS: N37 49.078' / W84 44.418'

The Hike

The Shakers were members of a religious sect that began in England in the early 1700s and came to America about the time of the Revolution, settling first in New York and then spreading to other states. The Pleasant Hill community, located on a plateau above the Kentucky River, started in 1805 and grew to 500 people before dying out in the early 1900s due to many complex factors, including Civil War trade embargos and the industrial revolution. Still, it was a fate not too surprising given the group's teachings against marrying and having children.

Nonetheless, the Shakers—the name comes from their movements during religious observance—were an industrious lot, and this handsomely restored village is a testament to their talents. Thirty-four historic buildings have been restored. Several buildings are used today to house exhibitions and daily programming.

Among their many talents, the Shakers were successful traders, and they moved their wares to the marketplace on the Kentucky River. This hike follows the route the Shakers took to get their goods from the hilltop village down to the river landing. As you descend into the cliffs of the Palisades, you may choose between a paved country

Purple coneflower, liatris, and asters are abundant along the trail during the summer months.
PROVIDED BY SHAKER VILLAGE

lane and the rocky path that the Shakers cut out of the cliff side in 1826. I, of course, choose the rocky path.

At the Kentucky River, there is a Shaker-built barn with exhibits and a paddle-boat, the *Dixie Belle*, that (for a fee) will take you on a one-hour river excursion from spring to fall. Tickets are available at the admission booth.

From the parking lot, go north to the admission booth and take the gravel path running east down the main village street. Follow the gravel road between two pad-docks and cross a turnstile at a historic stone fence. At mile 0.3 you reach the east end of the village. Walk southeast toward US 68 and, using caution, cross it.

Take the narrow road on the other side and go downhill (southeast). Though paved, the road is little-used and pleasant, but there is traffic coming to and from the *Dixie Belle* riverboat. An old stone fence lines the left side, and rolling farmland is all around. This was originally a toll road built by the Shakers in 1861 as a replacement for the more rudimentary version they constructed in 1826, which you will soon use.

In the stone fence near two small ponds, there is another turnstile. A trail marker should be here on the left side of the road. Take the path that leads to the 1826 road-bed. Initially the path is a mowed swath through a grassy field lined with wildflowers. The trail narrows and runs along the base of a rocky cliff. This is the roadbed dating back to 1826. The cliff is on your left, and the paved road on your right far below. The drop-off to the road is severe enough in certain spots that you will want to take the hands of small children.

As the path turns sharply left and parallels the Kentucky River, you get a good view of the beautiful, tall cliffs of the Palisades that line the river. You also get a good view of a railroad bridge spanning the river gorge high above you. This is High Bridge, a well-known landmark. The original bridge, 275 feet tall, opened in 1877

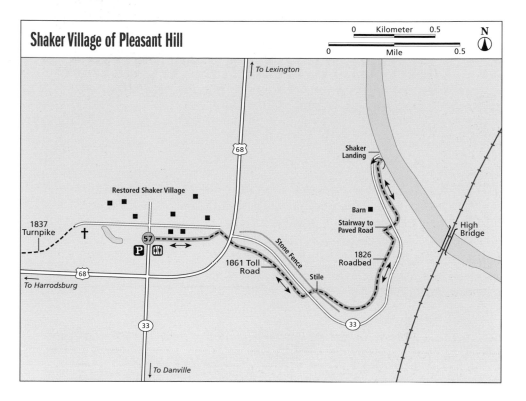

Shaker Village of Pleasant Hill

To Lexington

Restored Shaker Village

Shaker Landing

Barn

Stairway to Paved Road

High Bridge

1826 Roadbed

1837 Turnpike

57

1861 Toll Road

Stone Fence

Stile

68

To Harrodsburg

33

To Danville

and ranked for a time as the highest railroad bridge in the world. It was replaced by the current structure in the early 1900s.

At mile 1.4 you come to a metal stairway that takes you down to the paved road. Following the road, you soon pass an 1866-built barn. After passing the foundation of a Shaker warehouse, you'll come to the river landing at mile 1.7. If it's not out on a sightseeing trip, the stern-wheeler *Dixie Belle* will be moored here. She takes passengers about 2.5 miles upstream, passing beneath High Bridge.

Return to Shaker Village the same way you came.

Key Points

0.3 East end of the village.

1.4 Stairway down to the road.

1.7 Shaker Landing.

Options: The Preserve at Shaker Village contains nearly 40 miles of trails, which are also open to mountain bikers and equestrians. There are two other trails in the park that are open to dogs. Staff naturalist Don Pelly's recommendations include the Shawnee Run Trail, a 5-mile loop through fields and woods west of the village. Another possibility is the 1837 Turnpike—a gravel road extending west 1.5 miles from near the village cemetery. See www.shakervillageky.org for a map of the trail network and more information on guided hikes and other programs.

Central Kentucky—South

The southern half of central Kentucky is dominated by public parks, and the following hikes explore the best of the offerings—three state parks built on the banks of man-made lakes and the national park land above Mammoth Cave. These areas are larger and not quite as tame as the public tracts available in the northern half of central Kentucky. Consequently, these hikes are longer and a bit more demanding than those in the previous section. You should find the walking entirely enjoyable.

Visitors to Mammoth Cave exit via the natural entrance. Tours of the longest known cave system in the world are offered year-round and are an excellent addition to any hiking trip at the national park.

58 Green River Lake

This hike takes you across the low ridges bordering Green River Lake, stopping first on a bluff overlooking the lake and later at a shoreline point with a view of the dam.

Start: Trailhead off Robin Road on edge of Green River Lake State Park
Distance: 6.1-mile lollipop
Hiking time: About 3.5 hours
Difficulty: Moderate
Best seasons: Any
Other trail users: Mountain bikers and equestrians
Canine compatibility: Leashed dogs permitted
Land status: State park
Nearest town: Campbellsville

Fees and permits: None
Maps: Green River Lake State Park trail guide; USGS Campbellsville
Trail contact: Green River Lake State Park, (270) 465-8255
Parking and trailhead facilities: There's space for three dozen cars. No facilities are available at the trailhead, but you'll find drinking water, restrooms, and a campground nearby in the state park. The park entrance is 0.3 mile farther east on KY 1061.

Finding the trailhead: From Campbellsville, take KY 55 south for 4 miles and turn left (east) onto KY 1061. In 1.2 miles—where KY 1061 makes a sharp right turn—go straight on Robin Road. In 0.4 mile, turn right into the lot marked for trailhead parking. (From the south, turn right onto KY 1061 off KY 55 when you're 14 miles north of Columbia.) GPS: N37 16.962' / W85 20.774'

The Hike

The Green River is one of Kentucky's major streams. In the 1960s, as part of the flood-control plan for the Ohio and Mississippi Rivers, the US Army Corps of Engineers dammed the Green River just south of Campbellsville, 300 river miles from where it empties into the Ohio near Henderson. The resulting 8,200-acre reservoir snakes 25 miles through low-lying ridges in the rolling farmland of Taylor and Adair Counties. This hike loops through the 1,331-acre park developed by the state in the early 1970s on the west side of the lake at one of its widest sections.

The park terrain is not spectacular, but this is an enjoyable walk through a good mix of easily maneuvered ridgetops and bottomlands, including visits to two attractive lakeside spots. The park has lots of birds as well as deer and wild turkeys. The ridgetops were farmed before the reservoir was built and so are now thinly wooded with cedars and young hardwoods. But more mature growth covers the low-lying areas around the lake. Park personnel and volunteer groups of hikers, equestrians, and mountain bikers have developed an ambitious system of trails totaling nearly 30 miles. Indeed, there are so many trails going in so many directions, it can all be a bit confusing. For clarity, the accompanying map leaves out park trails that are not part of the loop route.

From the parking lot, head southeast into the low-lying woods on an old roadbed called Wildcat Trail. At mile 0.2, turn left onto a narrower path called North Trail, which goes north at first and then northeast. There are no blazes, but the path is well worn and impossible to lose. Disregard the unmarked horse trail on the left and another on the right.

At mile 1.0, as you begin to descend gradually, pass one end of Turkey Bluff Trail on the left, and in a few minutes North Trail ends at a three-way junction. To the left is the other end of Turkey Bluff Trail, straight ahead is Rocky Bluff Spur, and to your right is Devil's Canyon Trail. Take Rocky Bluff Spur, a trail of less than 0.25 mile that ends at an overlook about 70 feet above the lake at 1.2 miles. You get a good view of the lake and the land directly across called Goat Island. Partway out to the bluff, there is a spot where you can easily drop down to the shoreline.

After your waterside rest, retrace your steps to the junction and turn left onto Devil's Canyon Trail, which leads into a shallow but scenic ravine. Going west, cross two rock-bottomed streams at mile 1.7 just before they join together for their final dash to the lake. This is another pretty spot, although rainfall and the lake's level will affect the robustness of the streams.

From the streams Devil's Canyon Trail climbs steeply up the ridge side and dead-ends into Deer Creek Trail. Turn left onto Deer Creek Trail, which for the next mile remains at a fairly constant elevation as it follows the ridge contour first south, then north, and once again south. This last leg brings you at mile 2.9 to the park road just across from a parking lot, which is the park's trailhead for mountain bikers.

Cross the road, and on the south side of the parking lot, you will find two trails going into the woods. These are the two ends of Lakeshore Trail, which loops down to the lakeshore at a spot called South Point. For no good reason, take the left-hand leg (the one to the east). Disregard the trail you pass on the left a few steps from the parking lot and continue south. The trail is initially level, but at mile 3.3 begins to descend. At mile 3.5 you come to a cliff above the water. Turn right and parallel the shoreline. At mile 3.7 you arrive at a point of land with flat rocks that go down to the water just like steps. This is a fine place for sunning, and you have a view south to the dam.

From here Lakeshore Trail leaves the shore and heads north and west as it winds around two inlets. Climb back up the ridge, curve north, and reach the parking lot at mile 4.8. From the lot take the path going west along the south side of the park road. This is the Marina–Main Trail, which runs between the boat ramp and campground on the park's east end and the marina on the west end. Initially on the open shoulder, the trail soon turns into the woods, and you hardly know the road is there. This is a nice stretch.

At mile 5.4 you approach the park office and maintenance building, and after crossing the driveway, turn right onto the North Trail. Take the North Trail across the park road and rejoin the Wildcat Trail, which returns you to your car at mile 6.1.

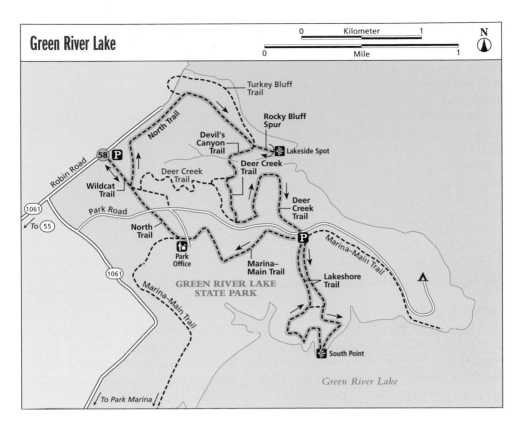

Green River Lake

Kilometer
0   1

Mile
0   1

N

Turkey Bluff
Trail

Rocky Bluff
Spur

North Trail

Devil's
Canyon
Trail

Lakeside Spot

Robin Road

58 P

Deer Creek
Trail

Deer Creek
Trail

Wildcat
Trail

Deer
Creek
Trail

1061

Park Road

To 55

North
Trail

P

Marina–Main Trail

Park
Office

Marina–
Main Trail

Lakeshore
Trail

1061

Marina–Main Trail

**GREEN RIVER LAKE
STATE PARK**

South Point

Green River Lake

To Park Marina

Key Points

1.2 Rocky Bluff.

3.5 Starting here and extending for about 0.2 mile, lakeshore at South Point.

4.8 Marina–Main Trail.

59 Lake Cumberland

You get grand views of Lake Cumberland on this hike, which explores one of Kentucky's most popular state parks.

Start: Lure Lodge at Lake Cumberland State Resort Park
Distance: 3.8-mile loop
Hiking time: About 2.5 hours
Difficulty: Easy
Best seasons: Any
Other trail users: None
Canine compatibility: Leashed dogs permitted
Land status: State park
Nearest town: Jamestown

Fees and permits: None
Maps: Lake Cumberland State Resort Park's visitor guide; USGS Jamestown
Trail contact: Lake Cumberland State Resort Park, (270) 343-3111 or (800) 325-1709
Parking and trailhead facilities: There's virtually unlimited parking space. Restrooms, drinking water, a restaurant, and overnight accommodations are available at the lodge; the park campground is nearby.

Finding the trailhead: From exit 62 off the Cumberland Parkway at Russell Springs, take US 127 south for 13 miles and turn left onto the state park entrance road, which is marked by a sign for Lure Lodge, the park's main overnight facility. Drive 5 miles and park in the lot by the lodge. (From the south, starting at KY 90, take US 127 north for 16.5 miles and turn right onto the park road.) GPS: N36 55.755' / W85 02.431'

The Hike

This hike is a lot like walking through a city park, because you are never far from roads, buildings, and cars. But this loop route offers something you won't find in many other parks of any kind: a huge lake. With a length of 101 miles and a shoreline totaling 1,255 miles, Lake Cumberland is one of the largest man-made bodies of water in the eastern United States. This stroll through Lake Cumberland State Resort Park takes you along an unspoiled ridge overlooking the 52,250-acre reservoir at one of its widest points. You then meander through the park's developed area to a rock outcropping at the water's edge, and end up at a commanding lake overlook. You're in one of Kentucky's most popular parks, so don't expect wilderness. What you do get is a chance to see and enjoy one of the state's premier attractions.

Lake Cumberland was created by damming the Cumberland River. Work on the project started in the early 1940s in response to devastation from the river's all-too-frequent flooding. The Wolf Creek Dam, completed by the US Army Corps of Engineers in 1951, is 240 feet high and slightly more than a mile long. US 127 runs on top of the dam 4 miles south of the state park road. Lake Cumberland is deep—200 feet in some spots—and as a result it ranks as the largest man-made lake east of the Mississippi in terms of water volume, although not in surface acreage. In the latter category, for example, Kentucky Lake and Lake Barkley in western Kentucky are both bigger.

At 52,250 acres, Lake Cumberland is one of the state's most popular summer recreation spots.
Wade Franklin

The 3,117-acre Lake Cumberland State Resort Park was built in the early 1950s to take advantage of what was then the new reservoir. This hike is entirely on the park's Lake Bluff Nature Trail, which starts just south of Lure Lodge next to the nature center. Go down the steps in front of the nature center, turn right at the bottom, then left, and descend more steps. Here you come to the first of a series of signs and plaques that you may appreciate the next time you play Trivial Pursuit. What is the Kentucky state tree? The answer, you learn on this hike, is the tulip poplar, the tallest hardwood species in North America.

From the nature center, the trail heads south above a small inlet of the lake. The trees here are young, but the area is attractive. After crossing a bridge over a drainage area and passing what may or may not be a waterfall, depending on rainfall, the trail forks. The right prong climbs to a store on the park road; bear left to begin an easy climb up a ridge running along the main stem of the lake. On top, follow the sign

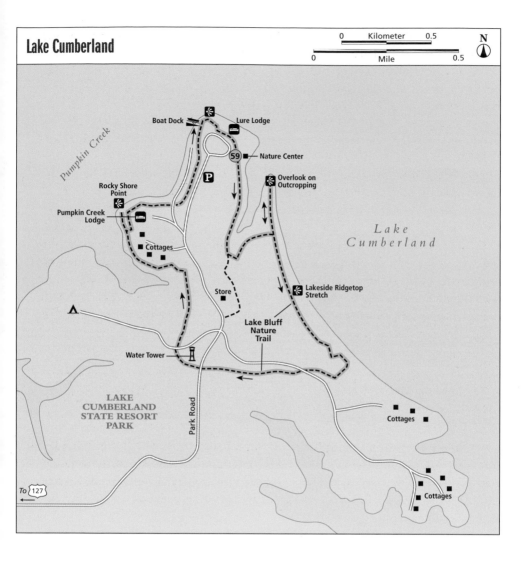

Lake Cumberland

0 Kilometer 0.5

0 Mile 0.5

N

Pumpkin Creek

Boat Dock

Lure Lodge

59 Nature Center

P

Rocky Shore Point

Overlook on Outcropping

Pumpkin Creek Lodge

Cottages

Lake Cumberland

Store

Lakeside Ridgetop Stretch

Lake Bluff Nature Trail

Water Tower

LAKE CUMBERLAND STATE RESORT PARK

Park Road

Cottages

To 127

Cottages

pointing left a short distance to an overlook on a rock outcropping. You get a good view northeast across the lake as well as an inviting lunch spot. But be careful; you are high above the water, and there are no railings.

From the overlook retrace your steps to the main trail and walk south on the wooded ridgetop along the water. This is the prettiest stretch of the hike. It ends at mile 1.4 with a turn right (west) away from the lake and a climb up to a park road leading south to cottages. Cross the road and, on the other side, follow it west, keeping watch for a nature trail sign directing you away from the road and into the woods. At the sign the trail descends to cross a shallow drainage; at mile 2.1 it crosses the main park road.

On the other side of the road, the trail climbs northwest past a water tower and across the campground road. Go north into the woods, descend to cross another drainage, and at mile 2.6 come to an old road. A sign for Pumpkin Creek Lodge points left down the road, and you follow it. The lodge, named for the creek that it overlooks, was the park's original lodge; it is still used for guests.

Following the road, pass between a finger of the Pumpkin Creek inlet far below on your left and park buildings above on your right. When the road comes to a fork, bear left and descend on shale and rock to the shoreline at 2.8 miles. How easy this descent is will depend on the water level. In dry periods the water may be too far below to reach. Still, this rock outcropping makes an enjoyable waterside rest spot.

Return to the fork and head north on the other prong. Disregarding a path up to the cottages, walk along the side of the bank and round the promontory on which Pumpkin Creek Lodge sits. At mile 3.3, after climbing to a point near the lodge, the trail crosses the road that descends to a large boat dock. You immediately climb up to the main park road and follow it to a sidewalk that leads to a fenced overlook on the bluff near Lure Lodge at mile 3.6, where you look down on the dock and have a good view of the lake. From the overlook take the walkway east to the lodge and nature center at mile 3.8.

Key Points

0.8 Reach the lakeside ridgetop.

2.8 Lakeshore.

3.6 Overlook.

Option: The park has one other trail, Baugh Branch Trail, which runs 1.6 miles from the park road to a lake overlook. The trailhead is 3.6 miles from Lure Lodge back on the park entrance road. The trail is relatively level with gentle grades except for the end of the trail, which leads up an incline to an overlook of the lake and Baugh Branch.

60 Dale Hollow Lake

This forested walk takes you to the tip of an isolated ridgetop jutting into the lake. It includes a side trip to a secluded cove on a short but unofficial trail.

Start: Lodge at Dale Hollow Lake State Resort Park
Distance: 5-mile out-and-back
Hiking time: About 3 hours
Difficulty: Easy
Best seasons: Any
Other trail users: Mountain bikers and equestrians
Canine compatibility: Leashed dogs permitted
Land status: State park, US Army Corps of Engineers reservoir
Nearest town: Burkesville

Fees and permits: None
Maps: Dale Hollow Lake State Resort Park's trail guide; USGS Frogue and Dale Hollow Reservoir SE (TN)
Trail contact: Dale Hollow Lake State Resort Park, (270) 433-7431 or (800) 325-2282
Parking and trailhead facilities: You'll find seemingly unlimited parking space; restrooms, drinking water, a restaurant, and overnight accommodations are available in the lodge. The park's campground is off KY 1206.

Finding the trailhead: From the junction of US 127 and KY 90, north of Albany, go west on KY 90 for 10 miles. Turn left (south) onto KY 449, and in 4.5 miles turn left onto KY 1206. In 4 miles you could enter the park—but continue instead for another mile on KY 1206, turning right at the sign for the Mary Ray Oaken Lodge. Go 0.9 mile and park in the lot at the end of the road near the lodge complex. The hike starts on the west side of the parking lot. (From Burkesville, take KY 90 east and turn right onto KY 449.) GPS: N36 38.339' / W85 18.000'

The Hike

Dale Hollow Lake State Resort Park, Kentucky's second largest, opened in 1978, and the lodge (named for a deceased state park official) opened in 1997. This hike follows an old roadbed that was around long before either. Along the way, you pass the remnants of one of the homesteads that years ago dotted these isolated hollows and ridgetops on the Kentucky-Tennessee border.

Dale Hollow Lake is a flood-control reservoir built by the US Army Corps of Engineers in the early 1940s by damming the Obey River, a tributary of the Cumberland. The dam is near the Tennessee town of Celina. The shoreline of this 27,700-acre impoundment is largely undeveloped, and this hike takes you to a bluff at the tip of one of the isolated fingers of land that jut into the water. This peninsula is called Boom Ridge, and to get there you cross onto Corps property in Tennessee. You also pass the entrances to several side trails that follow small ridges shooting off Boom Ridge.

These side trails are not included in the 5-mile round-trip distance listed for the hike. The mileage does include a short, steep detour down to the lake shoreline. Otherwise the hike is entirely on the ridgetop, and it's about as flat a walk as you will find anywhere. Backcountry camping is not allowed in the state park; it is permitted only at designated sites on Corps property in Tennessee.

From the west side of the parking lot—directly across from the main lodge entrance—a path goes about 50 feet up a small hill and into the woods. Just inside the trees, this little path dead-ends into Boom Ridge Trail. To your right, Boom Ridge Trail goes through scraggly woods and across mowed areas to the entrance to the park campground about 1.5 miles away. To your left, which is the way you go, it follows an attractive old dirt roadbed through a forest made up largely of beech, cedar, oak, and walnut that's home to a large number of deer.

Initially Boom Ridge Trail goes south, but it soon curves west. Disregard the first side trail you see on your left. The trail then turns northward briefly, and at that point a side trail spouts to your right at 0.5 mile and heads down Short Ridge for 0.5 mile. (All side-trail mileages are state park measurements.)

At mile 0.6, after once again heading south, the trail comes to Brushy Ridge Trail on your right (0.8 mile long), followed at mile 0.9 by Groce Ridge Trail on your left (0.6 mile long). You then head west again, passing the remains of a stone-and-brick foundation. After the trail again curves back to the south, you come to Buck Ridge Trail on your left at 1.4 miles. This side trail is 0.2 mile long, according to the park, but I found that it went twice that distance before petering out on a bluff with a view south over the lake.

While the trees along the trail are generally young, there are definitely some senior citizens still around. At mile 1.5 a large beech stands guard just before the trail passes the boundary marker separating the state park from Corps property. This is also the line between Kentucky and Tennessee. Just before the boundary, Wolf Ridge Trail branches northwest off the main trail.

At mile 1.7 the trail curves southwest, and at this point (GPS: N36 37.337' / W85 18.800'), there is a short unmarked path down to the lakeshore. It's the best opportunity you'll have on the hike to get to the water—a welcome stop on a hot summer day. To reach the lake, go southeast instead of southwest, and at the edge of the ridge, take the shale-covered path. The drop is extremely steep at first but quickly moderates. The "beach" is shale, but even so, this secluded inlet makes a nice waterside picnic spot.

Retracing your steps up to the ridgetop, you are back on Boom Ridge Trail at mile 2.1 and making the turn southwest. From here on, I found the trail more difficult to follow, in part because of storm damage. Also, for the most part, the trail is now just a path, not a roadbed.

At mile 2.5 (GPS: N36 37.197' / W85 19.104'), the trail curves right (west). Shortly after the turn westward, the trail passes rock outcroppings on the right and then makes another right turn before reaching the end of the ridgetop at mile 2.7. The lake is far below and provides excellent views south across the water. They are best during winter, spring, and fall. The vista is no doubt diminished by summer foliage.

Return to the lodge parking lot the way you came.

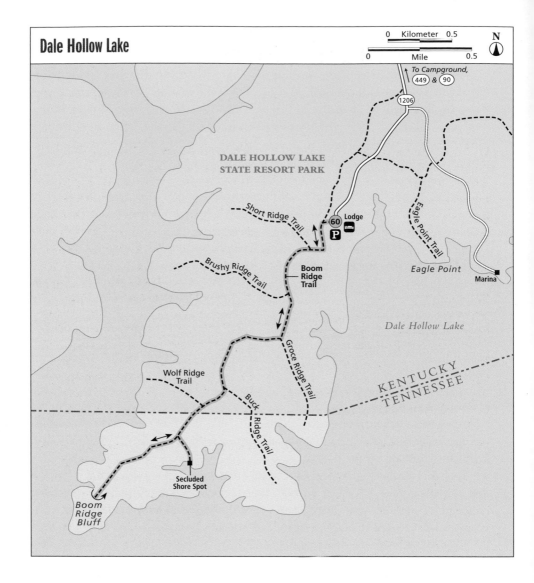

Dale Hollow Lake

DALE HOLLOW LAKE
STATE RESORT PARK

Short Ridge Trail

Brushy Ridge Trail

Boom Ridge Trail

Wolf Ridge Trail

Groce Ridge Trail

Buck Ridge Trail

Secluded Shore Spot

Boom Ridge Bluff

Eagle Point Trail

Eagle Point

Marina

Lodge

Dale Hollow Lake

KENTUCKY
TENNESSEE

To Campground, 449 & 90

1206

60

P

0 Kilometer 0.5

0 Mile 0.5

N

Key Points

0.5 Short Ridge Trail turnoff.

0.6 Brushy Ridge Trail turnoff.

0.9 Groce Ridge Trail turnoff.

1.4 Buck Ridge Trail turnoff.

1.5 State line.

1.7 Side trail to lakeshore.

1.9 Lakeshore.

2.7 Bluff at the end of Boom Ridge.

61 Mammoth Cave Big Hollow Loop Trails

These loop trails offer quiet contemplative walking in a less visited area of Mammoth Cave National Park.

Start: Maple Springs parking lot and trailhead
Distance: 11.0-mile double loop
Hiking time: About 5 hours
Difficulty: Moderate
Best seasons: Any
Other trail users: Equestrians and mountain bikers
Canine compatibility: Leashed dogs permitted
Land status: National park
Nearest town: Cave City
Fees and permits: Free permit, issued at visitor center, required for backcountry camping, which is limited to designated sites
Maps: Park backcountry map and guide; USGA Rhoda
Trail contact: Mammoth Cave National Park, (270) 758-2180, www.nps.gov/maca

Special considerations: The Green River may be crossed via the park's ferries when in operation. When ferries are out of service, access to the park backcountry is by bridge at Brownsville or at Munfordville. Call (270) 758-2166 for the current status of ferries. Ferries cannot transport buses or RVs; low water levels may also restrict traffic of long trailers. Ferries are free and operate daily from 6 a.m. to 9:55 p.m.
Parking and trailhead facilities: There is room for about 20 cars and horse trailers, horse tie-ups, 2 pit toilets, numerous picnic tables, and a dumpster. The nearby Maple Springs Group Campground is used largely by equestrian groups and must be reserved ahead of time. The park hotel, restaurant, and main campground are found near the visitor center.

Finding the trailhead: Mammoth Cave National Park is off I-65 about 25 miles north of Bowling Green and 85 miles south of Louisville. From the north, take I-65 exit 53 and go west on KY 70. In 3 miles, bear right onto KY 255 and, in 4.2 miles, turn right onto the park's Mammoth Cave Parkway. In 0.7 mile, turn left and go 1.2 miles to the Green River Ferry landing. The 2-minute ferry ride is free. (To reach the visitor center, continue on Mammoth Cave Parkway another 0.6 mile.) Approaching the park from the south, take I-65 exit 48, turn left onto KY 255, and follow the signs toward the park visitor center. When KY 255 enters the park, the name changes to Mammoth Cave Parkway.

Once on the other side of the river, drive north (the park road here is named Green River Ferry Road) for 2.2 miles and turn left onto the road for Maple Springs. Go about a mile to the trailhead parking area. GPS: N37 12.332' / W86 08.369'

The Hike

Mammoth Cave, the most extensive cave system in the world, has more than 365 miles of known underground passageways and possibly hundreds more that are not yet discovered. Mammoth Cave National Park wasn't fully established until 1941, but is one of the oldest tourist attractions in the United States.

The park's 53,000 aboveground acres—37 square miles—are a lesser-known attraction but cover scores of wooded hollows and ridges above the Green River.

The Green River Ferry is the quickest way to reach the park's Maple Springs hiking area.

The river itself is a popular destination for paddlers and anglers. The park contains 66 miles of trails, many of them open to hikers, mountain bikers, and equestrians. In the spring the wooded hillsides are painted with a variety of colorful wildflowers, and small creeks with numerous waterfalls are active.

This hike follows the relatively new Big Hollow North Loop and South Loop trails along wooded ridges above the Green River. The woods are composed of some second-growth trees. Along the hike you will see some impressive yellow poplars, along with smaller oak, sycamore, and beech trees.

Access to the loop trails is via the Maple Springs Trail. The trailhead is located at the east side of the Maple Springs parking area. Turn left onto the gravel path beyond the fence, at the site of a kiosk and map. The trail is multiuse, so be on the lookout for equestrians and mountain bikers.

The 1-mile walk to the Big Hollow trailhead is easy and flat along a wide gravel path. At 0.1 mile pass the turnoff to a trail leading to the campground. In another 0.1

mile the Maple Springs Trail turns sharply to the left (north), while the Maple Springs Research Center trail splits off to the right (south).

At 1.0 mile the Mill Branch Trail continues straight (northwest), but turn right (east) to begin walking on Big Hollow Trail. A kiosk and map mark the beginning of the trail, which becomes a single-track dirt path. At mile 1.25 the trail crosses Green River Ferry Road and then quickly comes to the intersection of the trail's North Loop and South Loop at mile 1.3 Follow the trail to the South Loop.

Weaving its way through thicker forest, the trail crosses a number of wet-weather washes, lined neatly with rocks in this area. Just past the 3-mile point is the junction of the North Loop shortcut. Continue straight to the South Loop. The sign indicates the beginning of the South Loop is 0.1 mile ahead. When you reach that intersection at mile 3.1, take the right fork and continue on the Big Hollow South Loop Trail.

Lots of different types of mushrooms and fungi decorated the trail the day I visited, appearing in a virtual rainbow of colors from white to bright red to dusty purple and vivid blue. The variety and abundance of fungi along the trail, I was told by park rangers, could be attributed to the unusually wet summer and the composition of the soil within the park. I counted dozens of varieties on my visit.

The trail traverses a series of small hills several feet in elevation over the next couple of miles and turns to gravel for a small section. The South Loop is a lollipop hike, and you can complete the loop by going either clockwise or counterclockwise. On this hike I went right (counterclockwise), which takes you southwest toward the Green River. The trail gradually descends and you pass the 1.5-mile marker, which indicates the distance hiked on the South Loop, not the distance you have walked. You have walked 4.1 miles. For clarity, I do not reference the mile markers along the trail, but instead the mileage walked.

The trail makes a number of splits around some islands of large rocks in this area that would make excellent seating for a lunch break or short rest. The forest is more open here, but dense summer foliage hides the Green River far below.

After another 0.25 mile, the trail begins to ascend but stops short of the ridgetop as it continues to weave back and forth along the hillside, which drops steeply off the right side of the trail. Over the next 0.5 mile, the trail turns to the north and gains additional elevation. You have walked a distance of 4.85 miles. This area is littered with lichen- and moss-covered rocks and wet-weather runs over the next 0.75 mile. During the spring and winter, this area offers your best opportunity for seeing the Green River.

The trail then curves around the ridge and heads eastward, as it makes a number of quick climbs and drops over the next 0.25 mile. The trail curves, following the ridge, and ascends to reach the top, before it turns and heads westward and then north toward the intersection of the loop. At this point you have hiked 5.9 miles. Bear to the right and retrace your steps 1 mile back toward the North Loop.

At the intersection of the North Loop bear to the right (west) to follow the North Loop toward the North Loop shortcut. In 0.1 mile the trail descends gradually.

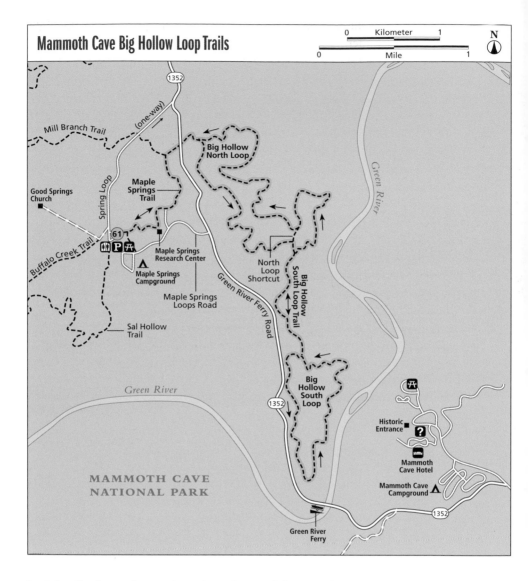

Big Hollow
North Loop

Mill Branch Trail

(one-way)

1352

Spring Loop

Good Springs
Church

Maple
Springs
Trail

Buffalo Creek Trail

61

P

Maple Springs
Research Center

Maple Springs
Campground

Green River

Green River Ferry Road

North
Loop
Shortcut

Big Hollow
South Loop Trail

Maple Springs
Loops Road

Sal Hollow
Trail

Green River

Big
Hollow
South
Loop

1352

Historic
Entrance

?

Mammoth
Cave Hotel

MAMMOTH CAVE
NATIONAL PARK

Mammoth Cave
Campground

1352

Green River
Ferry

In 0.5 mile the trail ascends to the ridgetop, following the contours of the landscape as it climbs. In another 0.25 mile the trail descends, rounds the corner of the ridge, and heads west. The walking is fairly easy, and the trail well maintained and used, continuing with its patterns of small ups and downs.

Pass the North Loop shortcut, bearing right, to finish the North Loop. You have now walked 8 miles. The trail curves to the northwest and is flat in this area. Watch for mud in this section, and look for small sinkholes forming on the sides of the trail. The trail curves back and forth in this area, turning north, then west, then east, before heading back in a north and west direction.

The trail then steadily descends, again the ridge falls steeply away to the right of the trail. The path then turns decidedly to the south and southwest and crosses a number of wet-weather runs before turning north and west and gradually ascending.

The trail then heads southeast and descends again, then turns toward the north and east. The hillside continues to drop off steeply to the right. After another series of sharp turns, the trail levels out and continues to weave and turn directions quickly as it approaches the end of the North Loop at your mile 10. Turn right and retrace your steps back to the intersection of the Maple Springs Trail and then on to the parking lot.

Key Points

1.0 Right turn onto Big Hollow Trail.

1.3 Right turn to follow the Big Hollow North Loop counterclockwise.

3.1 Right turn at junction of South Loop and North Loop to follow Big Hollow South Loop Trail.

4.1 Right turn to follow the Big Hollow South Loop counterclockwise.

6.9 Right turn to retrace steps along Big Hollow South Loop Trail back to Big Hollow North Loop.

7.9 Right turn at junction of South Loop and North Loop trail.

10.0 Left to retrace steps along Big Hollow North Loop back to Mill Springs Trail and on to parking lot.

62 Mammoth Cave Turnhole Bend

This is a nice stroll down well-worn, shaded trails to a quiet campsite above a bend in the Green River.

Start: Maple Springs parking lot and trailhead
Distance: 5.8-mile out-and-back
Hiking time: About 2 hours
Difficulty: Easy
Best seasons: Any
Other trail users: Equestrians and mountain bikers
Canine compatibility: Leashed dogs permitted
Land status: National park
Nearest town: Cave City
Fees and permits: Free permit, issued at visitor center, required for backcountry camping, which is limited to designated sites
Maps: Park backcountry map and guide; USGA Rhoda
Trail contact: Mammoth Cave National Park, (270) 758-2180, www.nps.gov/maca

Special considerations: Green River maybe crossed via the park's ferries when in operation. When ferries are out of service, access to the park backcountry is by bridge at Brownsville or at Munfordville. Call (270) 758-2166 for the current status of ferries. Ferries cannot transport buses or RVs; low water levels may also restrict traffic of long trailers. Ferries are free and operate daily from 6 a.m. to 9:55 p.m.
Parking and trailhead facilities: There is room for about a 20 cars and horse trailers, horse tie-ups, 2 pit toilets, numerous picnic tables, and a dumpster. The nearby Maple Springs Group Campground is used largely by equestrian groups and must be reserved ahead of time. The park hotel, restaurant, and main campground are found near the visitor center.

Finding the trailhead: Mammoth Cave National Park is off I-65 about 25 miles north of Bowling Green and 85 miles south of Louisville. From the north, take I-65 exit 53 and go west on KY 70. In 3 miles, bear right onto KY 255 and, in 4.2 miles, turn right onto the park's Mammoth Cave Parkway. In 0.7 mile, turn left and go 1.2 miles to the Green River Ferry landing. The 2-minute ferry ride is free. (To reach the visitor center, continue on Mammoth Cave Parkway another 0.6 mile.) Approaching the park from the south, take I-65 exit 48, turn left onto KY 255, and follow the signs toward the park visitor center. When KY 255 enters the park, the name changes to Mammoth Cave Parkway.

Once on the other side of the river, drive north (the park road here is named Green River Ferry Road) for 2.2 miles and turn left onto the road for Maple Springs. Go about a mile to the trailhead parking area. GPS: N37 12.332' / W86 08.369'

The Hike

This hike is a leisurely out-and-back walk along old roadbeds to a campsite above a bend in the Green River. The walking is mostly level, and the campsite at the end is a popular destination. A short bushwhack downhill from the campsite is needed to reach the riverbank, which offers excellent fishing. This trail can easily be combined with others in the area to offer a multiple-night backpacking trip.

The trail to Turnhole Bend follows a series of old forest roads through lush second-growth forest to a campsite.

If planning an overnight trip, you should be aware that backcountry camping is only allowed in designated campsites or on the banks of the Green and Nolin Rivers. Permits are required, and campsite permits are site-specific, with each site limited to eight people per night. This means during busy seasons you may not get your first choice. The earlier in the day you show up at the visitor center, the better your chances. Campsites are in pleasant places, but are primitive. They offer a fire ring, horse tie-ups, and level places for tents. All water within the park must be treated, and many of the streams are intermittent. In dry periods it is smart to check with rangers on availability beforehand.

According to Ranger Vickie Carson, the park is in the process of updating all of its trail signage, which will soon include a two-letter abbreviation of the trail name and a number so users in trouble can call in and give their location to park officials. Main trails will also be blazed in blue and side trails to campsites in orange, according to Carson.

The trailhead for the Buffalo Creek Trail is located on the west side of the Maple Springs parking lot. Follow the wide dirt and gravel Buffalo Creek Trail southwest for 1.1 miles to its intersection with the Dry Prong Trail. The Turnhole Bend Trail begins here. Turn left and head south on the Turnhole Bend Trail; there is a sign at the intersection. The Turnhole Bend Trail is wide and easily followed and begins to climb gradually. A small stream comes in from the west and follows the trail for a short distance here, but then quickly turns away from the trail.

After 0.6 mile the Sal Hollow Trail crosses the Turnhole Bend Trail. There is a campsite here with a fire ring and tie-ups for horses. The Turnhole Bend Trail continues straight (south) for another 1.2 miles before reaching the campsite at Turnhole Bend. The trail here is lined with lots of large second-growth beech trees and gradually ascends to the top of the ridge, which has some open meadow areas that on my visit were thick with bee balm in bloom.

Just beyond the trail on the eastern side, the ridge drops steeply away and in some areas has a series of exposed sandstone bluffs. Be careful in this area if you decide to bushwhack for a view of the river far below. On my hike I spotted a number of large deer along the path.

As you approach the campsite, the trail narrows to a single-track path, makes a quick turn to the east, and then dips down into a small valley before quickly climbing a second ridge and reaching the campsite. The campsite features horse tie-ups, a fire ring, and ample space for tents. There are orange blazes in this area marking the campsite, which is ringed by large trees. A quick bushwhack downhill to the south, east, or west from the campsite will lead to the Green River.

Retrace your steps back to the Buffalo Creek Trail and the Maple Springs parking lot.

Key Points

1.1 Junction of the Buffalo Creek, Dry Prong, and Turnhole Bend Trails. Turn left (south) onto Turnhole Bend Trail.

1.7 Campsite and intersection of Sal Hollow Trail.

2.9 Turnhole Bend campsite.

Option: For a multi-night hike, retrace your steps back on the Turnhole Bend Trail 1.5 miles to its intersection with the Sal Hollow Trail. Follow the Sal Hollow Trail west for 3.3 miles along the winding wooded ridgeline above the Green River to the Sal Hollow campsite. From the Sal Hollow campsite, follow the trail northeast

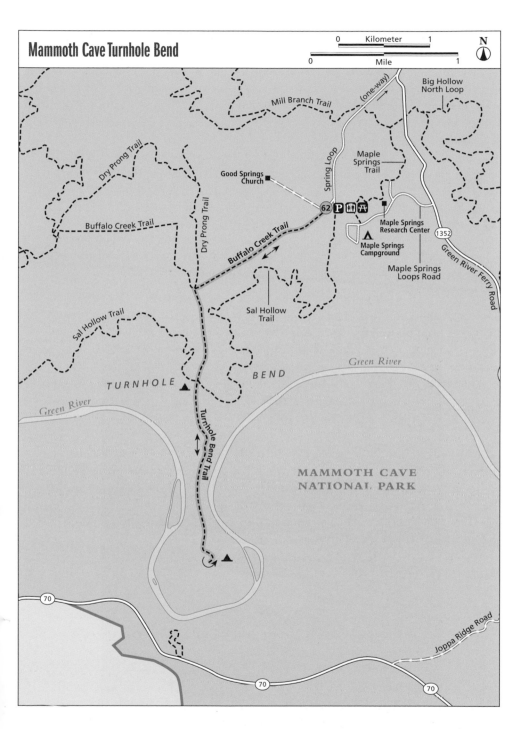

Mammoth Cave Turnhole Bend

for another 1.4 miles until you reach its intersection with the Buffalo Creek Trail. Follow it east for 2.4 miles back to the Maple Springs parking area.

Louisville Area

A number of good hiking opportunities surround Kentucky's largest city. The following walks are all within about an hour's drive of downtown—with the exception of the Yellowbank Wildlife Area, which is a little farther. Wooded ridges and hollows of moderate grade dominate the area, so you can expect gentle ups and downs. As a corollary, you can also expect few overlooks or dramatic views. What you will find are enjoyable rambles that take you far from the hurly-burly of urban life.

The Tiago Falls tumble in a series of cascades 130 feet down Muldraugh Hill. The Tioga Falls trail is located on Fort Knox but is open to the public (hike 66).

63 Bernheim Forest

Deer, wildflowers, and a good number of ups and downs are your companions on this long day hike across quiet ridgetops and hollows in a handsome hardwood forest.

Start: Guerilla Hollow picnic area of Bernheim Forest
Distance: 13.8-mile loop
Hiking time: About 7 hours
Difficulty: Moderate
Best seasons: Late fall to early spring
Other trail users: None
Canine compatibility: Leashed dogs permitted
Land status: Private land owned by a nonprofit corporation
Nearest town: Shepherdsville
Fees and permits: Vehicle entrance fee charged Sat and Sun; free admission Mon through Fri
Maps: Bernheim Arboretum and Research Forest trail map; USGS Shepherdsville

Trail contact: Bernheim Arboretum and Research Forest, (502) 955-8512
Special considerations: The forest is open from 7 a.m. to sunset daily except Christmas and New Year's Day. Users of the Millennium Trail, the trail featured in this hike, are asked to register at the visitor center, open daily 9 a.m. to 5 p.m., and to return and sign out when they are finished. Camping is not allowed in the forest, so this has to be a day hike. To cut the mileage, see option.
Parking and trailhead facilities: You'll find spaces for at least a dozen cars, along with picnic tables and cooking grills. The visitor center has vending machines and restrooms.

Finding the trailhead: From Louisville, take I-65 south for 25 miles to exit 112, turn left (east) onto KY 245, and in 1 mile turn right into Bernheim Forest. Just past the entrance, the road splits to form a large circular drive through the park's developed area. Bear left and follow the road (Visitor Center Drive) a short distance to the parking lot for the visitor center on your right. After registering at the center for Millennium Trail, get back in your car and continue on the circular road (now named Arboretum Way) for about 0.5 mile to the road on the left marked by a sign for Guerilla Hollow. Take this road for 0.2 mile and bear right where it turns into a one-way loop. In another 0.2 mile—just before the loop curves sharply left—pull into the parking strip on your right by the picnic area. The hike starts 50 yards farther down the road on the right side near the chain gate. A small Millennium Trail sign marks the trailhead. GPS: N37 54.574' / W85 39.966'

After the hike, turn left on the circular entrance road (Arboretum Way) for the quickest way back to KY 245.

The Hike

Isaac W. Bernheim (1848–1945) was a German immigrant who settled in Kentucky and became a successful whiskey distiller under the I. W. Harper brand. In 1929, full of gratitude for his good fortune, he established Bernheim Forest and dedicated it to the education and enjoyment of the Kentucky public. His gift has become one of the top outdoor attractions in the Louisville area.

A small, carefully manicured section of Bernheim Forest—the part you drive through immediately after entering—consists of an arboretum, gardens, and lawn, all of it sprinkled with statues and other artwork. But most of the nearly 15,000 acres are covered with wooded ridges and hollows, and it is this natural area that provides the best hiking. Most of the land was farmed before 1929, so the forest is still not fully mature. In addition to art displays, the visitor center has educational materials.

For decades Bernheim Forest offered hikers only relatively short paths, most of them less than 2 miles. In the year 2000, however, Bernheim redesigned its trail system to add a 13.8-mile loop named, appropriately, the Millennium Trail. It combines several old trail segments with three short road sections and a number of newly developed paths to take you into the forest's interior. The walk is a sequence of level legs along ridgetops and bottomlands interrupted by fairly short climbs and descents, so you can expect a good number of ups and downs but none strenuous. The park has since added other trails, including the new 5-mile Elm Lick Trail.

On any of the park's trails, you can expect to see deer and, in season, lots of wildflowers. Oak, beech, and maple dominate the woods. A walk along the Millennium Trail is most interesting after a rain when the little wet-weather streams that crisscross the hollows come alive, creating small, attractive waterfalls. If there has been no rain, you may not find even a drop of water; there are no permanent streams. In summer this can be a dry, hot environment—and a buggy one. When the heat index is 90°F and above, the park closes the trail to visitors. Call ahead in the summer. Also, be aware that while in winter there are some limited views, you can see very little from the ridgetops when the leaves are out in the summer. What you get on the Millennium Trail is a pleasant walk in quiet woods, not dramatic scenery.

The hike starts on the edge of Guerilla Hollow, so named because Confederate guerrillas supposedly operated out of it during the Civil War. Both Bernheim and the USGS map use the less common spelling of the word. The Millennium Trailhead sign is located about 50 feet from the road—on the other side of the chain fence, just across the small wet-weather streambed. The trailhead sign is purposely difficult to see from the road; Bernheim wants only registered hikers to know about it. If you hike the loop clockwise, the trail is marked by little yellow rectangles. Going counterclockwise, it's yellow triangles. Whichever way, keep a close lookout for the marks; otherwise, it's easy to stray onto one of the old footways that frequently intersect the Millennium Trail.

At the trailhead, step over the chain gate and cross the small streambed. If it's been raining, you may need to walk on top of the small concrete dam to keep your feet dry. Head northwest on an old double-track road that quickly peters out into a path, then cross a grass field and enter the woods. At mile 0.3 you come to a small meadow at the south end of 32-acre, man-made Lake Nevin; make a sharp right turn and cross a feeder stream on a wooden bridge. On the other side, a short climb takes you up to an old asphalt road now open only to cyclists and walkers; turn right (south) and follow this paved strip.

The 5-acre cypress-tupelo swamp serves as a natural filter for Bernheim's Lake Nevin.

Without the yellow disks, this initial part of the hike through Bernheim's developed section would be impossible to follow. In 0.3 mile the trail makes a well-marked right turn off the asphalt strip, cuts through the woods, and at mile 0.9 crosses Guerilla Hollow Road just before the beginning of the one-way loop. On the other side of the road, you quickly come to the Magruder family cemetery. Archibald Magruder, a member of the Maryland militia during the American Revolution, was one of the area's original landowners, and the old tombstones make interesting reading.

From the cemetery you briefly go southeast before making a sharp turn left (north) and starting to climb the first ridge of the hike. The small fenced plot you pass at the turn encloses what was a cemetery for the Magruders' slaves. At mile 1.2 you reach the ridgetop—and a gate in the wire-mesh fence designed to keep deer out of Bernheim's developed section. Go through the gate, turn left, and follow the fence northeast.

Initially you descend into a hollow, then you climb again. At mile 1.7, after an easy downhill stretch, cross Forest Hill Drive (formerly Tower Hill Road), which takes motorists to the trailheads for most of Bernheim's short hikes and to an old fire tower that is open on weekends. At the road you leave the deer fence behind and climb north to another ridgetop—and the trail's 2-mile marker.

Here pay special attention to the yellow disks. Just past the mileage sign, the trail turns sharply right (south)—away from a broader path that tempts you to continue straight ahead. The Millennium Trail crosses over to the other side of the ridge and then turns north to follow the level ridgeline toward KY 245. At mile 2.5 jog around a small clearing and begin following a pleasant old roadbed gently down and around the north end of the ridge. This is easy, delightful walking, marred only by the truck noise from the highway and the steady humming of a nearby distillery operation, one of a number that populate this part of Kentucky.

At mile 2.9 the trail leaves the old roadbed, turning sharply right into the woods. This turn—another that is easily missed—comes just before the road intersects a power-line clearing. From the woods the trail parallels the clearing in a southeasterly

FOLLOW KENTUCKY'S BOURBON TRAIL

There are more barrels of bourbon in Kentucky than there are citizens to drink it. Kentucky boasts a population of 4.4 million, but according to the Kentucky Distillers' Association, in 2015 more than 5.7 million barrels of the spirit were aging in the state. Kentucky produces 95 percent of the United States' only native spirit, as declared by Congress in 1964. There are more than twenty distilleries in Kentucky, including nine of the most recognizable brands in the industry that can be found within an 80-mile radius of one another in central Kentucky: Bulleitt Frontier Whiskey, Evan Williams, Four Roses, Heaven Hill, Jim Beam, Maker's Mark, Town Branch, Wild Turkey, and Woodford Reserve. As you explore Kentucky's hiking trails, you will almost certainly pass one or more of these fabled distilleries. In fact, the entrance to Bernheim State Forest (hike 63) is adjacent to the Jim Beam Distillery. For more information, visit www.KyBourbonTrail.com.

direction before crossing the clearing and descending—at mile 3.3—to the often-dry bed of a stream named Rock Run. KY 245 is just above you.

From intermittent Rock Run—which eventually drains into the Salt River, a tributary of the Ohio—climb southeast through ferns and, at mile 3.8, reach the top of a ridge. Here a side trail to your right leads to an "overlook" named in honor of Robert Paul, Bernheim's first executive director. This level path ends in 0.1 mile at a little clearing—said to be Mr. Paul's favorite spot in the forest. You will find a picnic table built by the Boy Scouts, the only accommodation on the trail. But especially when the trees are full, you won't find much of a view; you just barely see the tops of distant ridges through the leaves.

Returning to the main trail, walk first east and then south to reach—at mile 4.9—the cemetery of the Jackson family, another of the early settlers. Just beyond the cemetery, an unmarked trail to your right leads a short distance down to Forest Hill Drive. It comes out near a parking lot for Jackson-Yoe Loop, one of the short Bernheim hikes.

Continuing southeast, the Millennium Trail comes to a fork and goes left; the unmarked right prong is another remnant of Bernheim's old trail system. Wind northward, following a small drainage downhill to its intersection with a streambed. At the intersection the trail turns right and follows the streambed east for a short distance. At mile 5.8 the trail crosses the streambed and, immediately on the other side, hits Old Headquarters Road. Turn right and follow this tree-shaded dirt and-gravel road for 0.2 mile—to just beyond the spot where it crosses the streambed. Here the trail turns left into the woods and begins an easy climb to intersect gravel Ashlock Hollow Road on the ridgetop, just east of the loop end of Forest Hill Drive. This spot—which is where Old Headquarters Road also intersects Ashlock Hollow Road—marks the hike's halfway point at 6.9 miles.

Crossing Ashlock Hollow Road, you begin a stretch to the south, initially on the level ridgetop and then dropping down into bottomland and crossing a series of wet-weather streambeds. The forest here is completely quiet—and in spring full of blooming dogwoods. Climb another ridge and, at mile 9.1—after descending to cross still another of Bernheim's ephemeral streams—come up to a gravel road just as it splits into two: Wilson Creek Fire Road going left (south) and Yoe Trace Fire Road heading right (west).

The trail crosses Wilson Creek Fire Road and enters the woods just south of Yoe Trace Fire Road. After passing a small pond and crossing a few wet-weather stream-beds, the trail crosses the Yoe Trace Fire Road and reenters the woods at mile 10.1. The trail dips down to cross another drainage and, at mile 11.5, begins climbing the first of a series of four ridgetop knobs that in winter offer limited views northeast to the next ridgeline.

Descend southwest to cross Guerilla Hollow and climb up the other side of the hollow. At mile 13.4, after a short descent, you come once again to the deer fence—and a gate that lets you back into Bernheim's developed section. Pass through the gate,

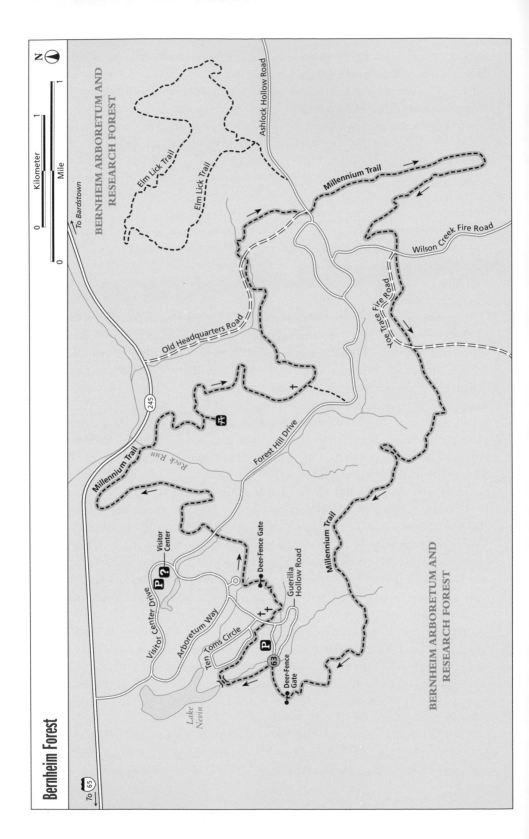

turn right, and follow the grass-and-dirt track along the fence. At mile 13.7 the fence ends; in a few steps you will once again meet the trail's beginning leg. Turn right onto the old double-track road. Almost immediately you are back at the trailhead near the loop road where you left your car.

Key Points

1.2 Deer-fence gate into natural area.

1.7 Forest Hill Drive.

3.8 Side trail to picnic table on ridgetop.

6.9 Ashlock Hollow Road, hike's halfway mark.

9.1 Wilson Creek Fire Road.

11.5 Ridge with limited views northeast.

13.4 Return gate into Bernheim's developed section.

Option: If you want a shorter hike, I suggest the Elm Lick Trail. This moderate hike begins off Ashlock Hollow Road, 0.25 mile from where the Millennium Trail crosses the road at mile 7 near Paul's Point Circle. Elm Lick opened in 2015 and is a loop hike on the northeastern edge of the forest. In the summer, mowed paths through the prairie make for some good, easy, 1- to 2-mile walking first thing in the morning, before the heat of the day.

64 Vernon-Douglas State Nature Preserve

This walk through mature second-growth forest takes you to a bluff that overlooks farms and houses lining the peaceful flats along Younger Creek.

Start: Parking area on the side of Audubon Trace Road
Distance: 3.1-mile lollipop
Hiking time: About 2 hours
Difficulty: Moderate
Best seasons: Any
Other trail users: None
Canine compatibility: No dogs allowed
Land status: State nature preserve

Nearest town: Boston
Fees and permits: None
Maps: Nature preserve trail map; USGS Nelsonville
Trail contact: Kentucky State Nature Preserves Commission, (502) 573-2886
Parking and trailhead facilities: You'll find space for a dozen vehicles, but no facilities.

Finding the trailhead: From Louisville, take I-65 south for about 32 miles to exit 105. Go south on KY 61 and, in 4 miles in the town of Boston, turn right (west) onto combined US 62/KY 61. In 3.8 miles, turn left (south) onto KY 583, and in 2 miles—immediately after passing over the Blue Grass Parkway—turn right (west) onto Audubon Trace Road. In 0.6 mile, turn into the gravel parking lot on the left side of the road. GPS: N37 44.023' / W85 42.475'

The Hike

Central Kentucky is dotted with knobs, and this hike explores one of these large hills—one covered with mature second-growth hardwoods, mainly maple, beech, tulip poplar, oak, and hickory. Unlike Bernheim Forest, this 730-acre preserve is not well known. Most likely you will see no one else as you make your way through Hall Hollow and then climb the ridge to the Pinnacle, the local name for a bluff overlooking the pastoral Younger Creek valley. The only intrusion on your solitude—and in some spots it definitely is an intrusion—is the swish-swish of traffic on the nearby Blue Grass Parkway. Even so, the attributes of this preserve, including its many wildflowers, more than compensate for that one drawback.

The Douglas family owned the land before donating it to the National Audubon Society in 1972. The Vernons owned it before the Douglases. Both families were careful to leave the land undisturbed. It has never been commercially logged, at least not in the last ninety years, according to the Kentucky State Nature Preserves Commission. The Audubon Society gave the property to the state in 1991.

The trail—the preserve has only one—starts at the south end of the parking lot at the gate in the fence. There are blazes identifying the trail, which is easily followed. Heading south, cross several split-log bridges over small drainages before angling up a ridge known as Hall Hill. You don't go to the top but rather, at mile 0.6, come up

A towering canopy provided by the preserved forest at Vernon-Douglas bathes the forest in green light during the summer months.

to a saddle between Hall Hill and an unnamed hilltop just to the south. Here a signpost announces the beginning of a 2.5-mile-long loop through the preserve. (This mileage is no longer correct due to recent trail reroutes. Using a handheld GPS unit, I measured the trail at 3.1 miles total.) You can go either way, but I suggest a counterclockwise approach.

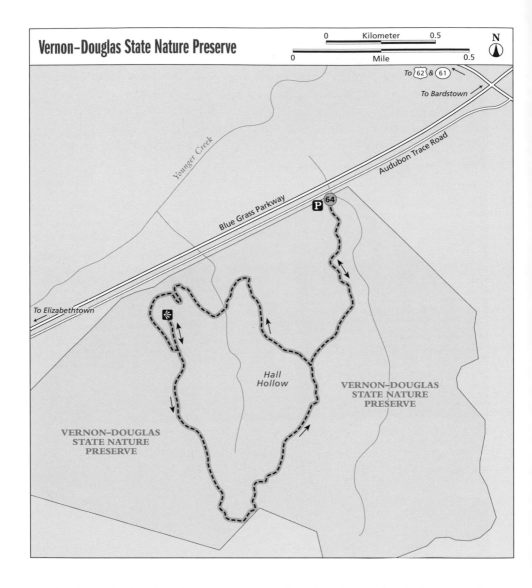

Younger Creek

To 62 & 61

To Bardstown

Audubon Trace Road

Blue Grass Parkway

P 64

To Elizabethtown

Hall Hollow

VERNON–DOUGLAS STATE NATURE PRESERVE

VERNON–DOUGLAS STATE NATURE PRESERVE

Turning right (west) at the signpost, descend gently on a broad path that no doubt at one time was a dirt road, and at mile 1.0 come down into Hall Hollow. After crossing a small creek on rocks, begin climbing—initially northwest, but shortly making a sharp turn left, followed by a sharp turn right. The grade here is steep but eased considerably by a series of switchbacks. Soon the path curves west and begins an almost-level slabbing of the ridge side parallel to the parkway below. At mile 1.5, after turning southeast away from the parkway, you reach the top of the ridge.

Here the trail goes right, but instead turn left and follow a side path 0.2 mile north through pines and cedars to a bluff at the end of the ridge at 1.7 miles—a spot known locally as the Pinnacle. You look down on farms and houses lining the flats along Younger Creek. It's a peaceful scene, but trees along the ridgetop constrict the view. In summer the view is especially limited.

From the Pinnacle return to the junction and take the main trail south along the ridgetop. The large trees make a pleasing canopy. As you near a farm field sprouting a tall communications tower, the trail curves east and then north to circle Hall Hollow. At mile 2.3 the trail begins descending; at mile 2.5 you are back at the signpost marking the beginning of the loop. Retrace your steps and reach the parking lot at mile 3.1.

Key Points

0.6 Beginning of loop.

1.0 Hall Hollow.

1.7 Pinnacle overlook.

2.5 End of loop.

65 Jefferson Memorial Forest

Pleasantly wooded ridges and hollows with limited views north toward the Ohio River and Indiana are the terrain for this day hike south of Louisville.

Start: Jefferson Memorial Forest Welcome Center on Mitchell Hill Road
Distance: 13.4-mile out-and-back (6.7 miles one way with shuttle)
Hiking time: About 6 hours for round-trip
Difficulty: Moderate
Best seasons: Any
Other trail users: None
Canine compatibility: Leashed dogs permitted
Land status: City/county forest
Nearest town: Louisville
Fees and permits: None

Maps: Forest map for Siltstone Trail/Scotts Gap; USGS Valley Station
Trail contact: Jefferson Memorial Forest, (502) 368-5404, www.memorialforest.com
Special considerations: The forest closes at dusk, and no camping is permitted along the trail.
Parking and trailhead facilities: There's space for 18 cars, along with restrooms, water, and vending machines. The welcome center is open 8:30 a.m. to 4 p.m. Mon through Sat and 10 a.m. to 3 p.m. on Sun.

Finding the trailhead: From downtown Louisville, take I-65 south to the Snyder Freeway (KY 841) and go west for 3 miles to exit 6, New Cut Road. Go south on New Cut Road and continue straight on Manslick Road. After traveling 1.8 miles from the freeway, turn right onto Mitchell Hill Road; after another 1.5 miles, turn left into the parking lot for the Jefferson Memorial Forest Welcome Center. (Don't be confused by a sign on Holsclaw Hill Road for another section of the forest. The welcome center is on Mitchell Hill Road 0.6 mile beyond Holsclaw Hill Road.) The trailhead is on the north side of Mitchell Hill Road at the parking lot entrance. GPS: N38 05.134' / W85 46.081'

The Hike

Local officials call the Jefferson Memorial Forest the nation's "largest public urban forest." Indeed, from one of the knobs you cross on this hike, you can see downtown Louisville. It's hard to believe that these 5,600 acres of wooded ridges and hollows are anywhere near the state's biggest city.

In fact, for generations this area of steep hills and winding roads was well isolated from the rest of Louisville and surrounding Jefferson County. Cut off by a swamp, it was a place for lumbering, moonshining, and other decidedly noncosmopolitan activities, according to one former manager of the forest. The welcome center—where you can pick up trail maps and other information about the forest—is a renovated two-room schoolhouse built in the early twentieth century when this was still an area very much unto itself. The first forest parcels were acquired for public use in 1946.

This hike, much of it on a ridgetop with partial views north toward the Ohio River and into Indiana, follows a 6.7-mile-long trail running east–west across the main section of the forest. Unfortunately there is no way to make a loop out of it; you must either retrace your steps or arrange for a shuttle at the western terminus on Scotts Gap Road. The trail crosses two other roads—Jefferson Hill Road at mile 2.2 and Bearcamp Road at mile 3.0. There are several steep climbs as you go up and down knobs, but they are all of short duration, and the exertion is more than offset by the long segments of flat ridgetop.

The entire hike is on the Siltstone Trail. The trail is marked by brown composite markers at key locations only. From Mitchell Hill Road, the Siltstone Trail heads west into tall hardwoods and evergreens, crosses a small creek on a bridge, and brushes the side of a road leading to Tom Wallace Lake, a popular recreation site. Almost immediately you begin climbing, steeply in places, and at mile 0.4 reach the top of a knob with a view of downtown Louisville's tallest buildings. Like other ridgetop vistas on this hike, this one is partially obstructed by trees, even in winter.

Following the ridgetop, the trail descends gently and then climbs to a saddle, bypassing the next hilltop. From the saddle the trail angles down the north side of the ridge and meets a concrete walk coming from Tom Wallace Lake. Crossing the walkway, climb west not quite all the way to the appropriately named Top Hill Road; you don't see the road, but you do see the houses perched on it. Walking north—and level—pass through a beautiful stand of evergreens. Turning west, leave the ridgetop and at mile 2.2 descend to Jefferson Hill Road just as it passes over a stream on a small bridge.

After crossing the road and stream, climb west over another knob called Pine Top and descend to cross Bearcamp Road at mile 3.0. You continue west and soon are climbing again, this time to the top of High Knob, the highest point of the hike. Just before reaching the top at mile 3.8, you get the first of numerous views—all limited by trees along the ridge—north to the Ohio River and into Indiana. Those tall smokestacks you see are the Louisville Gas and Electric Power Plant, which is in southwest Jefferson County on the Ohio River.

From High Knob the rest of the hike is for the most part on top of the ridge and level. The trail travels southwest, but then does a small stint to the northwest, before again turning southwest and starting down the ridge. After reaching the bottom and fording a small stream, turn northwest, go up a small hill, and cross a power-line clearing. From there descend to Scotts Gap Road at mile 6.7. The red-blazed trail on the other side of the road makes a 3.3-mile loop through an adjoining forest parcel. Assuming you don't want to add that mileage to your trip, this is where you hop in a shuttle car or turn around and begin retracing your steps to the welcome center.

Jefferson Memorial Forest

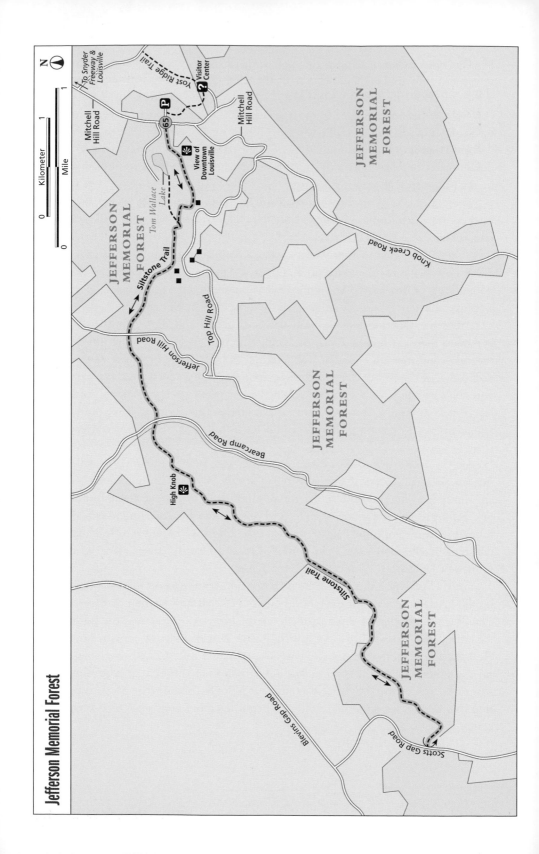

Key Points

0.4 Limited view of downtown Louisville.

2.2 Jefferson Hill Road.

3.0 Bearcamp Road.

3.8 Top of High Knob.

6.7 Scotts Gap Road.

Options: The park recently added a new 1-mile spur to its existing 2.2-mile Yost Ridge Trail. The spur now allows hikers to travel from the welcome center to the Paul Yost Recreation Area by foot, providing access to three additional loop trails in that area.

66 Fort Knox

This two-part hike on the Fort Knox reservation takes you to a dramatic multitiered waterfall and then on a shady stroll down the old Louisville–Nashville Turnpike across three Civil War bridges.

Start: Parking lot at the end of Louisville–Nashville Turnpike on edge of Fort Knox Military Reservation
Distance: 4.2 miles total for 2 hikes beginning at same trailhead, one a loop, one an out-and-back
Hiking time: About 2.5 hours
Difficulty: Easy
Best seasons: Any, but especially spring after a heavy rain when Tioga Falls is at its most robust
Other trail users: None
Canine compatibility: Leashed dogs permitted
Land status: US Army fort
Nearest town: West Point

Fees and permits: None
Maps: Fort Knox brochures for each of the trails; USGS Fort Knox
Trail contact: Fort Knox Cultural Resources Office, (502) 624-7431 or 624-6581
Special considerations: This hiking area is sometimes closed for military training and also for hunting. Check beforehand with the Cultural Resources Office. Also, be aware that the second of these two trails is on a paved surface.
Parking and trailhead facilities: You'll find room for about 30 cars and picnic tables, but no other facilities.

Finding the trailhead: From downtown Louisville, take I-65 south to the Snyder Freeway (KY 841) and go west for 10 miles to the freeway's end at US 31W (Dixie Highway). Turn left onto US 31W and travel 10 miles; in the town of West Point at the caution light, turn left onto a narrow road named the Louisville–Nashville Turnpike. In 0.7 mile, park in the gravel lot at the end of the road. GPS: N37 58.110' / W85 57.656'

The Hike

Fort Knox, famous as the nation's gold depository, is a 170-square-mile army training facility for tank and other armored crews. On a small corner of this huge base are two short trails open to the public, except during special training exercises and some hunting seasons. The two trails share a common parking area. I have paired them as one hike with a total distance of 4.2 miles. In character, however, the two are entirely different kinds of walks.

The first is mostly on a dirt path along a wooded ridge to a multitiered waterfall that is especially impressive after a big rain; this is Tioga Falls Trail, a 2-mile loop. The second follows a section of a nineteenth-century turnpike that linked Louisville and Nashville. Unfortunately, the original cobblestones were paved over as part of the development of Fort Knox, so this half of the hike is on a road. However, you are walking along a pleasant stream flanked by woods and ridges.

The road, closed to vehicles and called Bridges to the Past Trail, crosses three pre–Civil War stone bridges said to be among the oldest still standing in the state. The trail ends in 1.1 miles at a locked gate, making the total out-and-back distance of the paved portion 2.2 miles.

The Tioga Falls path leaves the west side of the parking lot and heads west, paralleling railroad tracks above on the left and an old paved road below on the right. The paved road was the original Dixie Highway, built in 1921 to connect Louisville with what was then Camp Knox. Replaced in 1942 by the current Dixie Highway, the old road, now called Railroad Trestle Road, is blocked off just beyond the hiking area.

Cross the East Fork of Tioga Creek on a bridge and begin climbing a ridge side. You are going up Muldraugh Hill, on which the developed portion of Fort Knox is located. From here to the falls, you are following old wagon roads. This area was full of farms and dirt roads before the military's acquisition of the land in 1918.

You reach the tracks at mile 0.4 and follow them westward for about 20 feet before crossing and turning south. Be careful here, because the tracks are still in use. They were originally built in 1873 and operated by various companies, including the Illinois Central, the Paducah & Louisville Railroad, and now CSX. This crossing spot was once the site of a small railroad station, though there is no sign of it now. Just to the west, the tracks go over Tioga Creek on a 130-foot-high trestle, which you will walk beneath on your way back to the parking lot. The trestle and the one visible from the parking lot were completed in 2015. The construction forced the closure of the trail for a number of years, and part of the loop trail had to be rerouted from a dirt path onto the old Dixie Highway. These new cement marvels replaced the original iron trestles.

From the tracks continue briefly up the wooded ridge side and then, after a short level stretch that offers a view north to the Ohio River and Indiana shore beyond, descend to the base of Tioga Falls at mile 0.9. Tioga Creek tumbles 130 feet down Muldraugh Hill, and after a heavy rain there are a number of separate gushes at various elevations, making an impressive multitiered cascade. From the falls the creek flows to meet the East Fork, and together they go into the Ohio.

In the 1800s, to escape malaria, wealthy families from the Deep South summered at the fine two-story Tioga Hotel just above Tioga Spring. Kentucky, which remained neutral in the Civil War, recognized slavery, and this was as far north as Southerners could come and still be accompanied by their slaves. The hotel is long gone.

After crossing Tioga Creek on rocks at the base of the falls, turn north, then east, and recross the stream to begin following it north toward old Dixie Highway. You shortly come to the stone walls of an old springhouse; just before these ruins, there is a large rock on the creek bank that makes a nice lunch spot. Walking on level ground along the creek, pass beneath the railroad trestle at mile 1.3.

Continue following the creek bottom, and in 0.1 mile run into old Dixie Highway. Turn right onto the paved road, which will lead you in 0.1 mile around a

The three stone bridges carried travelers across the East Fork of Tioga Creek on the Louisville–Nashville Turnpike before the Civil War.

cattle gate blocking the roadway and past a brick building built in the 1930s as a telephone company facility and now private property. You are back at the parking lot at mile 2.0.

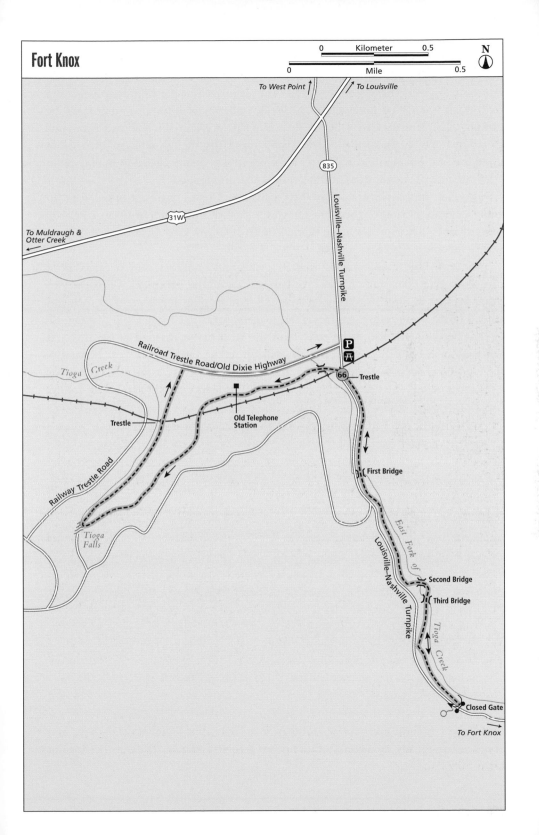

Fort Knox

The paved Bridges to the Past portion of the hike starts at the lot's south end beneath the railroad trestle and climbs steadily but easily up Muldraugh Hill toward Fort Knox proper. This was part of a toll road authorized by the Kentucky legislature in 1829. It connected Louisville to Nashville and was well traveled—especially by visitors to Mammoth Cave—before the Louisville & Nashville Railroad was completed in 1859. The railroad ended the road's popularity, though military forces made good use of it during the Civil War. This segment was finally closed to public use in 1919 because of danger from nearby artillery training ranges.

Heading south, follow the East Fork of Tioga Creek upstream. Initially it's on your right, but at mile 2.3 you cross it on the first of three arch bridges, which are more than 150 years old. During World War II the army used German prisoners of war to repoint the bridges' mortar.

The rock-bottomed stream is lively in spring, and large rock outcroppings above on the far side make this an attractive setting, despite the pavement. Cross the two other bridges in rapid succession at mile 2.8, and at mile 3.1 come to a spring—named Dripping Springs—on the right side of the road.

Just beyond, a locked metal gate across the road marks the end of the trail and the beginning of Wilson Road, which leads up to the buildings of Fort Knox. On the left side of the road just before the gate is Sieboldt Cave—named for the farmer who once owned the land. In the old days local farmers used the cave as an icebox for their dairy products.

Turn around and you are back at the parking lot at mile 4.2.

Key Points

0.9 Base of Tioga Falls.

2.0 Bridges to the Past trailhead.

3.1 Locked gate.

67 Otter Creek

A grand view of the Ohio River is the top prize of this hike on a bluff above the river valley.

Start: Nature center at Otter Creek Park
Distance: 5.3-mile loop
Hiking time: About 3 hours
Difficulty: Moderate
Best seasons: Any
Other trail users: Mountain bikers
Canine compatibility: Leashed dogs permitted
Land status: State owned, managed by Kentucky Fish and Wildlife
Nearest town: Brandenburg
Fees and permits: Day-use fee; children under 12 free. Fees must be paid at entry gate; annual passes are available online.

Maps: Otter Creek Park trail map; USGS Rock Haven
Trail contacts: Otter Creek Park, (502) 942-9171, www.fw.ky.gov; trail status hotline, (502) 942-5052
Special considerations: The park is closed to day use Mon and Tues, but is open to campers who are in the park by dusk on Sun.
Parking and trailhead facilities: You'll find room for about 25 cars; restrooms and water are inside the nature center (closed Mon and Tues), and picnic tables are outside. The park campground is nearby; the park also has cabin accommodations.

Finding the trailhead: From downtown Louisville, take I-65 south to the Snyder Freeway (KY 841) and go west for 10 miles to the freeway's Fort Knox exit at US 31W (Dixie Highway). Take US 31W south for 13.5 miles, turn right onto KY 1638, and in 2.8 miles turn right at the entrance sign for Otter Creek Park. In 1.3 miles, after passing the park office on the right, turn right into the parking lot for the nature center, which has maps and other park information. The trail starts at the south end of the nature center building. GPS: N37 56.452' / W86 02.910'

The Hike

Located in Meade County, the 2,600-acre Otter Creek Outdoor Recreation Area was once operated by the Louisville–Jefferson County metropolitan government. It's also home to a number of separate camps, including the YMCA's Camp Piomingo, a summer destination for generations of Louisville youngsters. However, in 2009 the city closed the park, which lost an estimated $500,000 annually. In 2010 Governor Steve Beshear announced that the park would reopen in early 2011 under the management of the Kentucky Department of Fish and Wildlife Resources.

Located on a ridge above the Ohio River at the mouth of Otter Creek, the park offers the hiker approximately 26 miles of trails, several leading to commanding views of the river and Indiana shore. This hike combines parts of three different loop trails to make a wide loop through the park, including a leg along the edge of the ridge above the river. The hike involves lots of ups and downs but of moderate grade and short duration. The park has plenty of deer, birds, and wildflowers. Be aware that Fort Knox is nearby, and so any booms you hear may well be artillery, not thunder.

The hike starts on the Valley Overlook Trail loop heading east from the nature center. Just beyond the south end of the building, the path cuts across a field and begins following the grass clearing above a buried natural gas pipeline. Heading southeast and east, the pipeline clearing parallels a paved park road on your left and soon crosses a gravel road leading right to the Pine Grove picnic area.

At mile 0.7, after passing through a stand of good-size hardwoods, the trail leaves the pipeline clearing and follows a path left (northeast) into the woods. This turn is marked by a sign for the Valley Overlook, which you reach at mile 0.9. The overlook is a small clear area on the right side of the trail with a view across the Otter Creek valley to the ridges on the other side. The creek is far below, so watch children carefully.

From the overlook you initially parallel the creek but soon veer to the north, crossing a park road and stream before climbing to a small utility building at mile 1.3. Continue on the level ridge side to another point overlooking the creek valley. According to park manager Charles Logsden, this next area is home to "acres of bluebells" when they are in season in early spring.

Descending at first to the west and then to the northeast, you come down to and cross an Otter Creek tributary at mile 2.1. On the other side, after a short climb, you come to another natural gas pipeline clearing, which you cross going north.

Beyond the pipeline clearing, you enter a pleasant wooded area and climb northward to reach the ridgetop at mile 2.5. Here the Valley Overlook Trail turns left and heads southwest back toward the nature center. Turn right instead and follow a connector trail north to an excellent Ohio River overlook at mile 2.7. This rock outcropping is above a wide bend in the river, and the upstream view is especially good. Just below, Otter Creek flows into the river. Otter Creek is a premier destination for trout fisherman during the winter months.

From the overlook it's possible to turn right onto the Otter Creek Trail and take it down the ridge to the creek and south to KY 1638. However, in flooded conditions, which are not unheard of along the Ohio, this lengthy stretch of the 8.1-mile-long Otter Creek Trail loop is impassable.

Instead, turn left onto the Otter Creek Trail and follow it west along the ridgetop, with views across the river into appealing Indiana farmland. Reach the first of several park cottages at mile 3.0, and at mile 3.6 cross a gravel road, then a paved road that goes north to the park's still-closed conference center. On the other side of the paved road, cross another connector trail and continue west on Otter Creek Trail.

You soon come to a bluff above a paved road running to a riverbank boat ramp. The trail parallels the road south and, after passing an old quarry, comes to a side path at mile 4.0 that descends to the boat ramp road and a streambed just below. Across the streambed is Morgan's Cave, which legend holds was used by John Hunt Morgan and his Confederate raiders during the Civil War. Morgan and his men certainly visited

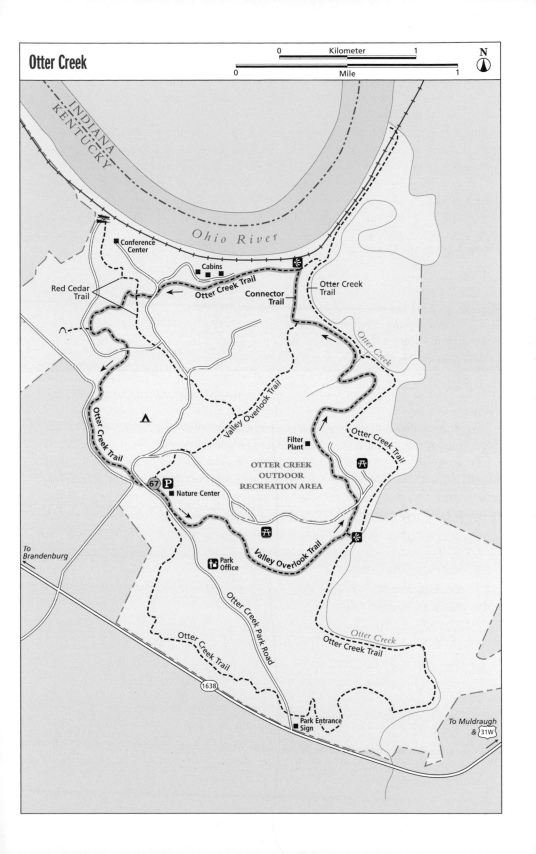

Otter Creek

Ohio River

INDIANA
KENTUCKY

Conference Center

Cabins

Red Cedar Trail

Otter Creek Trail

Connector Trail

Otter Creek Trail

Otter Creek

Valley Overlook Trail

Filter Plant

Otter Creek Trail

OTTER CREEK OUTDOOR RECREATION AREA

67

Nature Center

To Brandenburg

Park Office

Valley Overlook Trail

Otter Creek

Otter Creek Park Road

Otter Creek Trail

Otter Creek Trail

Otter Creek

1638

Park Entrance Sign

To Muldraugh & 31W

N

Farm fields dot the landscape along the Ohio River at Otter Creek.

what is now park property but probably not the cave itself. The cavern, which has water running out the opening, is gated shut except for special tours.

Back on the Otter Creek Trail, head southeast, cross the boat ramp road, and skirt around the park campground. Continuing south, proceed through a flat area full of cedars and pines, and at mile 5.1 cross the main park road. After traversing another pine grove, you are back at the nature center at mile 5.3.

Key Points

0.9 Otter Creek valley overlook.

2.7 Ohio River overlook.

4.0 Side trail to Morgan's Cave.

Option: Nearby Brandenburg's 2.2-mile Buttermilk Falls trail leaves the city's Riverfront Park and follows the old Buttermilk Falls road past large old-growth trees to a pair of waterfalls. The trail, which is fully wheelchair-accessible at present, also boasts views of the Ohio River and is noted for wildflowers in the spring. Although currently paved, Carole Logsdon with the Meade County Tourism Commission said the trail will soon be relocated closer to the ridge itself and will allow hikers to make a 4.4-mile loop trek versus an out-and-back hike. Parking is available at both Riverfront Park and at the Ronnie Commerce Road trailhead. For more information, contact Meade County Tourism at (270) 422-3967 or visit www.meadeky.com/buttermilk-falls-trail.

68 Yellowbank Wildlife Management Area

Quiet woods and open fields full of wildlife are the backdrop for this easy hike in an out-of-the-way stretch near the Ohio River.

Start: Trailhead parking lot on KY 259 near Yellowbank Creek, across the road from hunters' check-in station
Distance: 2.3-mile lollipop
Hiking time: About 1 hour
Difficulty: Easy
Best seasons: Spring and fall
Other trail users: Equestrians and hunters
Canine compatibility: Dogs permitted; must be leashed Mar 1 through the third Sat of Aug to protect ground-nesting wildlife
Land status: State wildlife management area

Nearest town: Brandenburg
Fees and permits: None
Maps: USGS Lodiburg (KY) and Rome (IN/KY)
Trail contact: Yellowbank Wildlife Management Area, (270) 547-6856
Parking and trailhead facilities: You'll find room for about 4 cars, but no facilities. There's additional parking across KY 259 at the hunters' check-in station and a primitive campground with pit toilets 0.2 mile north on KY 259.

Finding the trailhead: From downtown Louisville, take I-65 south to the Snyder Freeway (KY 841) and go west for 10 miles to the freeway's end at US 31W (Dixie Highway). Take US 31W south for 13.5 miles, turn right onto KY 1638, and, in 8.8 miles, turn right onto KY 448 toward Brandenburg. In another 1.2 miles, turn left onto KY 1051. After 2.3 more miles, turn left onto KY 79; 2.4 miles later, turn right onto KY 144. Continue on KY 144—making sure to bear right at Paynesville—for 15 miles to KY 259. Turn right onto KY 259 and, in 7.3 miles—after passing a paved road on the right to the Yellowbank office and crossing Yellowbank Creek—turn left into the small gravel lot marked for trailhead parking. The trail starts on the lot's east side. GPS: N37 58.282' / W86 30.494'

The Hike

Located along the Ohio River 60 highway miles west of Louisville, the state's Yellowbank Wildlife Management Area offers 6,675 acres of bottomlands and ridges covered by a combination of hardwood forest, open fields, and ponds. You can count on seeing lots of songbirds, including warblers, and most likely wild turkeys, quail, and doves. In the bottomlands, if you don't see frogs, you will certainly hear them. The sounds of nature are the only thing you hear on this hike.

Yellowbank definitely qualifies as remote. This was principally dairy farming land until 1976, when the state acquired the major hunk of acreage. Most of the farm buildings are now gone, but the old homestead sites are still recognizable.

The wildlife area gets its name from the creek that runs through its middle and empties into the Ohio River just north of the trailhead. The area is crisscrossed by gravel roads, horse trails, old footpaths, and a wide swath of grass running above a

A large pond is home to turtles and a variety of waterfowl.

buried Texas Gas natural-gas pipeline. There are also two designated hiking loops: Rockhouse Trail, a little over 2 miles, and the nearby 1-mile Black Knob hiking trail. The following hike follows the Rockhouse Trail, which has a number of ups and downs, but with the exception of a steep, brief descent near the end of the hike is moderate.

From the parking lot, head southeast on the grass-and-dirt track, passing through fields planted in corn and soybeans. Come to a large pond stocked for fishing, where on a sunny day you're apt to see dozens of turtles sunning themselves on rocks and tree limbs in the water. Turn right along the shoreline and, at mile 0.2, go around the south end of the pond on top of the levee. From there you follow a path northeast into the woods for about 150 yards and then start up the hill on an old roadbed.

At mile 0.4 bear right onto Rockhouse Trail. The trail is well-marked with a series of different markers including brown wooden arrows, blue blazes, and round metal blazes featuring a hiker.

After climbing gently to the northeast among hardwoods that get taller the farther you go, Rockhouse Trail intersects the pipeline clearing at mile 0.8. Crossing the clearing, you continue to the northeast, walking along the top of a small cliff with a ravine on your right. The trail name comes from a rock house in the side of the cliff below. At mile 1.0 the trail reaches the head of the ravine; if there has been a recent

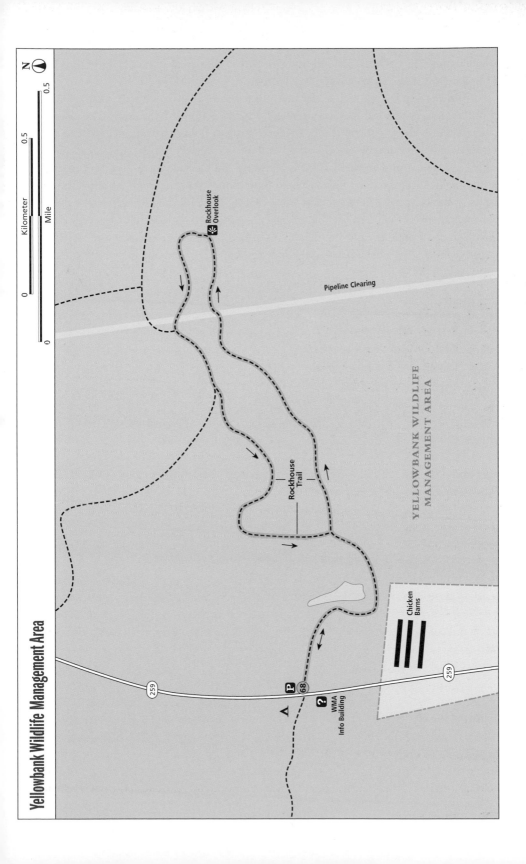

Yellowbank Wildlife Management Area

Rockhouse Overlook

Pipeline Clearing

YELLOWBANK WILDLIFE
MANAGEMENT AREA

Rockhouse
Trail

Chicken
Barns

259

259

68

P

WMA
Info Building

N

Kilometer
0   0.5   0.5

Mile
0   0.5

rainfall, you will be treated to the sight of water falling over the cliff side into the hollow below. This is a good spot for lunch.

From the top of the ravine, the trail climbs a short distance to a small wildlife pond, which you round in a counterclockwise direction. At the northwest corner, the trail leaves the pond and climbs northwest into a field that was once the site of a farmhouse. It then follows an old grass roadbed to intersect the gas pipeline clearing once again, this time at mile 1.2. After crossing the clearing again, the trail reaches an unmarked gravel road at mile 1.3. The Rockhouse Trail turns left (southwest) and quickly climbs to the top of a small wooded knoll. The trail then levels out as it passes through an area of large oaks and then descends through a grove of cedar trees. After passing a small pond at mile 1.5, the trail then begins descending down a wide grassy path. At mile 1.8 reach the end of the loop trail and retrace your steps back to your car at mile 2.3.

Key Points

0.4 Bear right onto Rockhouse Trail.

1.2 Right turn onto gas pipeline clearing.

1.3 Turn left onto an old gravel road.

1.8 End of loop portion of trail.

Western Kentucky

Western Kentucky offers a wide range of hikes—from a short stroll around Columbus-Belmont State Park to a multiday backpacking trip in Land Between The Lakes. It also offers what you won't find anywhere else in the state: vast cypress-sprouting sloughs that are far closer to the scenery and feel of the Deep South than the mountains of eastern Kentucky. In fact, from the Mississippi River bottomlands of Fulton County, you can drive to Tupelo, Mississippi, in about half the time it takes to get to Pikeville.

Western Kentucky is dominated by water—the Ohio and Mississippi Rivers on the north and west, and Kentucky Lake and Lake Barkley in the middle. Most of the following hikes are on or close to one of them. There is another common denominator. Western Kentucky is, for the most part, low and flat. If you get above 500 feet, you are mountain climbing in this part of the state. The elevation along several of the river-bottom hikes doesn't vary more than a few feet. So ignoring summer heat and mosquitoes—which, of course, you can't ignore—this is pretty easy walking. The one big exception is the Pennyrile Forest hike, where the multitude of ups and downs more than makes up for the gentleness of the terrain.

The liquid landscapes of western Kentucky sloughs attract thousands of migratory birds each year. The swampy wetlands feature a variety of flora and fauna including the American lotus (hike 70).

297

69 John James Audubon State Park

This hike loops through a hardwood forest with lots of songbirds and a small lake.

Start: State park welcome center and administrative offices
Distance: 3.6-mile loop
Hiking time: About 2 hours
Difficulty: Moderate
Best seasons: Spring and fall
Other trail users: None
Canine compatibility: Dogs not permitted on this hike; park does have a 0.9-mile pet trail (see option)
Land status: State park and nature preserve
Nearest town: Henderson
Fees and permits: None

Maps: Park trail map; USGS Evansville South (IN/KY)
Trail contact: John James Audubon State Park, (270) 826-2247
Parking and trailhead facilities: There is space for about 20 cars next to the office, which has restrooms and information. Additional parking is available by the nearby museum, which offers exhibits on the life and art of John James Audubon as well as a bird observation room (an entrance fee is charged at the museum). The park campground is 0.3 mile west on the park road just off US 41.

Finding the trailhead: From the junction of US 60 and US 41 on the northern outskirts of Henderson, take US 41 north for 1.7 miles and turn right at the entrance sign for John James Audubon State Park. In 0.4 mile, turn left at the sign for the nature center and museum and park in front of the first building, which is the administrative office. The hike starts a few steps east of the parking lot at the beginning of an old asphalt road closed to traffic. GPS: N37 52.923' / W87 33.449'

The Hike

Naturalist John James Audubon (1785–1851), famous for his realistic paintings of birds, lived in Henderson for nine years, roaming the woods and sketching wildlife. Born in what is now Haiti, the son of a French sea captain and his Creole mistress, Audubon came to Kentucky with a partner to establish a mercantile business. The enterprise proved successful, giving Audubon an opportunity to pursue his true passion, which was studying and painting birds.

The Ohio River community of Henderson was then—and is now—on a major flyway for migratory songbirds and waterfowl. Only after he left Kentucky did Audubon become famous, but the park—developed in the 1930s by the Civilian Conservation Corps (CCC) and one of the state's oldest—commemorates an important period in his development. The park museum claims to have the largest collection of Audubon memorabilia in the world.

For the hiker, the park offers a pleasant ramble through a mature beech and sugar maple forest to a small CCC-made lake lively with beavers, turtles, frogs, wood warblers, and waterfowl. Birds, not surprisingly, are the park's main focus, and late April through early May is the prime time for visiting birders. The park is an especially

Large second-growth trees, including yellow poplars and sycamores, line the trail.

good place to see rose-breasted grosbeaks, indigo buntings, scarlet tanagers, and other colorful species that, while not rare, are not your everyday robin either.

The park is relatively small—724 acres—but has plans to add 649 more. It is now all but surrounded by Henderson sprawl, but the park interior has been left in its natural state and has a greater away-from-it-all feel than many larger, more remote tracts.

It's been at least a hundred years since the park was timbered, so many of the trees are towering. Half the park—the half you will be hiking through—is a designated state nature preserve and strictly regulated. That's why pets are prohibited.

The hike starts at the entrance to an old asphalt road. Named Warbler Road, it is narrow and sufficiently lined with trees and wildflowers to make the paved surface unobtrusive. If you have children with you, you may want to start on King Benson Trail, an interpretive nature path that branches off into the woods at the beginning of Warbler Road. It parallels the road for less than 0.2 mile before crossing it and looping back to the parking lot.

Going east on Warbler Road, climb a hill—where Wilderness Lake Trail shoots off to your left—and then drop into a trough and go up a second hill. The string of large, private homes you see on the ridge to your right is just across the park boundary.

At mile 0.6 leave Warbler Road and take the switchback to your right, which marks the beginning of Back Country Trail. Reaching the top of the ridge, the trail continues east before turning north and descending. If it's winter and the trees are leafless, you get a good view of the Ohio River to the north. After crossing two small streambeds on bridges, climb back up the ridgetop near an electronics tower before descending to cross another drainage. After regaining the ridgetop once again, you enjoy a more extended stretch of level walking.

At mile 1.8 the trail curves west, and as you proceed, the noise of US 41 traffic may become noticeable—if not annoying. The highway, which crosses the Ohio just north of Henderson, is a key link to Indiana and the Hoosier city of Evansville. Descending the ridge, you reach the shore of Wilderness Lake at mile 2.1. This is the end of Back Country Trail.

The left fork of Wilderness Lake Trail goes to the lake's south end and beyond to Warbler Road. You, however, go right on Wilderness Lake Trail and cross the earthen dam at the lake's north end. From the dam the trail climbs up the ridge for a good view of the lake and, proceeding south, comes to a small stone pavilion at mile 2.5. Wilderness Lake Trail continues south.

From the pavilion follow Wilderness Lake Trail uphill to the right and a junction with two short trails—Kentucky Coffee Tree Trail and Woodpecker Trail—that go west to the office/museum area. Either will do. I took Kentucky Coffee Tree, which descends to a ravine at mile 3.3 and then follows the ravine south for a short distance before crossing it on a wooden bridge. Just before the bridge, Woodpecker Trail merges on the left.

Just beyond the bridge, Kentucky Coffee Tree Trail turns right and heads for the museum, and Woodpecker Trail bears left for Warbler Road. Take Woodpecker Trail. When you reach a service road beneath one of the largest yellow poplars in the county, turn left to take you to the paved Warbler Road at mile 3.5. Turn right and you are back at the parking lot at mile 3.6.

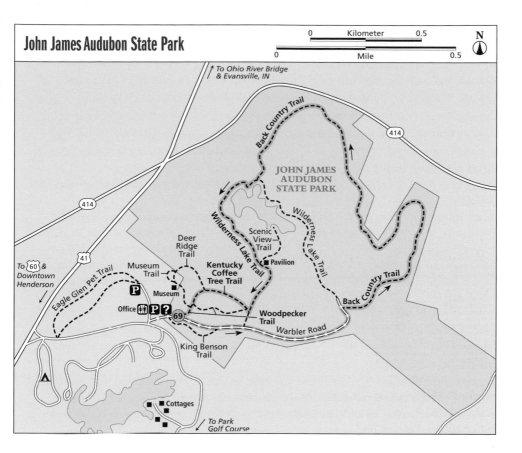

John James Audubon State Park

Key Points

0.6 Right onto Back Country Trail.

2.1 Shore of Wilderness Lake.

2.5 Stone pavilion.

Option: If Fido needs exercise, you will find the park's new 0.9-mile pet trail a short distance beyond the museum building.

70 Sloughs Wildlife Management Area

On this flat walk through wooded and open marsh, you are certain to see a variety of waterfowl and shorebirds as well as a handsome stand of bald cypress trees.

Start: Wildlife management area office/maintenance building off KY 268
Distance: 2.5-mile loop
Hiking time: About 1.5 hours
Difficulty: Easy
Best seasons: Spring and fall; this section of wildlife management area closed to public Nov 1 through Mar 15
Other trail users: Hunters
Canine compatibility: Dogs permitted; must be leashed Mar 1 through the third Sat of Aug to protect ground-nesting wildlife
Land status: State wildlife management area
Nearest town: Henderson

Fees and permits: None
Maps: Wildlife management area map; USGS Smith Mills
Trail contact: Sloughs Wildlife Management Area, (270) 827-2673
Special considerations: This hike is on a dirt road and a series of levees; there are no trails in this section of the Sloughs Wildlife Management Area. Also, be aware that much of this hiking route can be impassable in high water conditions.
Parking and trailhead facilities: There's room for about 10 cars, but no facilities. Camping is not allowed in the wildlife management area.

Finding the trailhead: From downtown Henderson, take US 60 west for 4 miles, turn right onto KY 136, and in 3 miles—in the community of Geneva—turn right onto KY 268. Take KY 268 for 6.5 miles and—after passing several wildlife-viewing stands on the left side of the road—turn left onto the narrow gravel lane marked by a sign for the Sauerheber Unit of the Sloughs Wildlife Management Area. Park near the metal building. The hike starts just west of the building. GPS: N37 51.560' / W87 46.783'

The Hike

A slough is a swamp or marsh, and the state's Sloughs Wildlife Management Area is well named indeed. These 10,600 acres along the Ohio River are oozing with flooded fields and woods. For anyone not familiar with this type of liquid terrain, a visit takes you into an intriguing new world—one where handsome bald cypress trees shoot out of the water and hundreds of shorebirds dart across the muddy flats. The Ballard Wildlife Management Area hike offers a similar experience.

The Sloughs area consists of six different tracts spread over northern Henderson and Union Counties. This hike is in the Sauerheber Unit, the most popular because of the number of migratory birds it attracts. Each winter this 3,000-acre tract, named for a former game warden, draws 15,000 migratory ducks and more than twice that many snow, white-fronted, and Canada geese.

Because Sauerheber serves as a waterfowl refuge, it's closed to the public in winter, when most of the migrants are in residence. The walking is delightful in early spring,

Cypress trees rise from the shallow water, a refuge for waterfowl.

after the tract is opened and before the western Kentucky sun begins blazing and insects begin buzzing. There are still sandpipers and other shorebirds to see, as well as some geese and ducks that stay year-round. If you're lucky, you may get a glimpse of bald eagles that make Sauerheber their home. Supervisor Charlie Plush reports that there are now three active bald eagle nests at Sauerheber.

Although Plush cautions that summer can be a trying time to hike because of mosquitoes and the heat, it still provides for some very good birding, as migrant songbirds are present during this time. Mid- to late October is also a great time to visit the Sloughs, particularly after a hard frost gets rid of the mosquitoes. During that time a large influx of early migrant waterfowl species visit the area, including green-winged teal, northern shoveler, northern pintail, American widgeon, and gadwall, along with many other species of marsh birds and shorebirds.

Sauerheber is completely level and has no trails. You simply go where you want to go, restricted only by the water. The following route, which I took on a sunny morning in late March, is a good one for sampling this swampy area. From the parking lot, walk to the far side of the metal building, which is both the office and maintenance barn for Sloughs. Just on the other side of the building, you will find a dirt road running parallel to the gravel lane you took in from KY 268. Turn left onto this narrow, little-used road and follow it south between a farm field on your left and woods on your right. Just where the water starts depends on the time of year and how much rainfall there has been. At some point, however, you will notice that the right side of the road is a swamp, and shortly you see cypress trees towering above you.

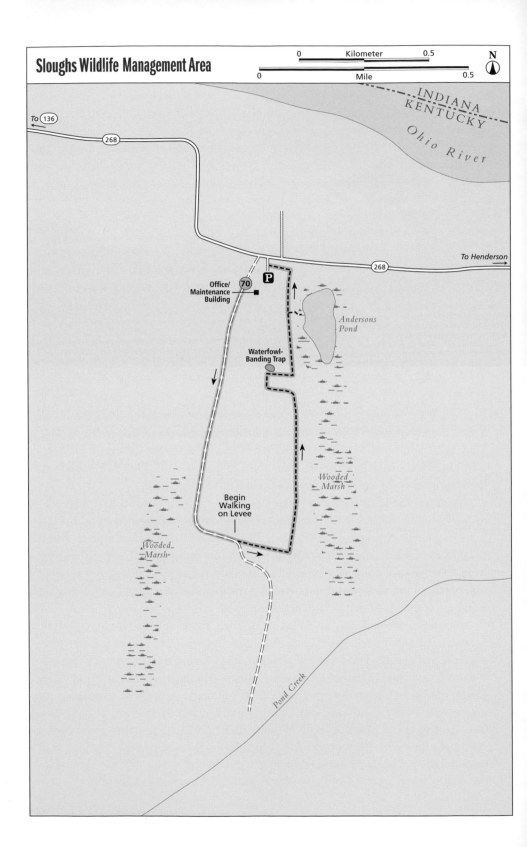

At mile 0.9 an unpaved boat launch slips into the swamp as the road curves east into the open field. Just beyond the curve the elevation drops an imperceptible few feet—but enough that, in the spring at least, water is likely to be lapping at your feet at about this point. The road continues a little less than a mile before dead-ending near Pond Creek, the source of the water around you. But from here on, the road is impassable for much of the year. It may be late May or early June before it dries out completely.

Instead of continuing on the road, at 1.0 mile climb up the earthen levee running parallel to the road and walk on it. The Sauerheber Unit is crisscrossed by a number of these grass-covered embankments; in winter they are used to control the water level for the benefit of the visiting waterfowl. In spring they make welcome bridges that keep hikers' feet dry.

The nearby road soon turns south again, but continue east on top of the levee. At mile 1.2, as you near trees marking the field's eastern boundary, the levee turns north. You turn with it, keeping the woods on your right. There are birds everywhere—shorebirds and mallards in the wet field, large birds in the trees. As I made my way, a kingfisher eyed me warily from a brambly bush growing out of the middle of the levee.

At mile 1.7 the levee turns west, and you follow it until it ends in a field. Here you take a path running north and, at mile 1.9, come to a small pond covered by a large wire contraption: a trap used to catch waterfowl so they can be banded for research purposes.

From the trap walk back east through the field—there are no levees here—to the edge of a soggy forest lining the east side of the field. Turn north and follow the line of trees toward KY 268. At mile 2.4, just before the fence along the highway, turn left onto the grass strip paralleling the road. It quickly takes you to the gravel drive leading to the maintenance building, and you are back at your car at mile 2.5.

Key Points

0.9 Dirt road turns east.

1.0 Begin following levee to avoid high water.

1.2 Turn north.

1.9 Waterfowl-banding trap.

Option: For a more traditional hike, the Sloughs Wildlife Management Area's Cape Hills Unit, south of the Sauerheber Unit, has a 1.2-mile trail (2.4 miles out and back) across a wooded ridge. There are no overlooks or special scenic rewards, though you are likely to see deer. The trail follows an old dirt track from near the town of Smith Mills north to a small stream and parking area along Martin Martin Road. It's an easy walk, with little elevation change. From Sauerheber take KY 268 west for 1.5 miles and turn south onto KY 136. Go 7.4 miles; in Smith Mills turn left onto Mill Street, and in 0.9 mile bear left at the fork and park at the top of the hill. The unmarked trail starts at the north end of the small parking area (GPS: N37 48.754' / W87 45.385').

71 Higginson-Henry Wildlife Management Area

Wooded ridgetops and bottomlands full of intermittent streams offer the hiker pleasant walking and a good chance to see wildflowers, turkeys, and deer.

Start: Parking area near Cap Mauzy Lake
Distance: 7.5-mile loop
Hiking time: About 5 hours
Difficulty: Moderate
Best seasons: Spring and fall
Other trail users: Equestrians and hunters
Canine compatibility: Dogs permitted; must be leashed Mar 1 through the third Sat of Aug to protect ground-nesting wildlife
Land status: State wildlife management area
Nearest town: Morganfield
Fees and permits: None

Maps: Higginson-Henry trail map; USGS Bordley, Waverly, and Morganfield
Trail contact: Higginson-Henry Wildlife Management Area, (270) 389-3580
Special considerations: Backpackers wanting to camp overnight should contact the Higginson-Henry office beforehand.
Parking and trailhead facilities: There's room for a dozen cars, but no facilities. Camping is allowed around the lake; there are no designated sites—and no drinking water. There is a convenience store 1.3 miles east at the KY 56/141 junction.

Finding the trailhead: From Morganfield, take KY 56 southeast for 5.3 miles and turn right onto the road marked by a sign for Mauzy Lake. In 0.4 mile, bear right at the fork, and in another 0.3 mile, turn left into the gravel parking area. (From the east, at the junction of KY 56 west and KY 141, turn left onto KY 141 and follow it 1.1 miles, then turn right onto Lake Mauzy Road. Follow it for 0.5 mile, then turn left on Daisy Mae Road. The gravel parking lot will be on your left after 1 mile.) The hike starts at the northwest end of the lot. GPS: N37 37.426' / W87 51.618'

The Hike

This wildlife area is on land that used to be part of an army training base named Camp Breckinridge. After World War II, the federal government closed the facility and sold off the level acreage to private buyers. The hilly part not suitable for farming was acquired by the state and turned into this 5,424-acre wildlife management area. Shaped in a long, thin rectangle, it stretches across a series of ridges and ravines, all of moderate grade. The area was named for two local sportsmen killed in a boating accident.

This hike uses a variety of paths and forest tracks to follow the rolling terrain across most of the Higginson-Henry area. The ridgetops offer some limited views north and west, but there are no good overlooks or other special points of interest. This is attractive but simple forestland. The bottomlands are full of small, intermittent streams likely to be flowing in spring. There are also lots of wildflowers, turkeys, and deer and, according to the state, some gray foxes and coyotes.

Cap Mauzy Lake teems with life and is a popular camping and fishing destination at Higginson-Henry Wildlife Management Area.

The loop starts and ends near Cap Mauzy Lake, an 80-acre impoundment built by the army for use in training and now a favorite of local anglers. It was named for a former game warden.

This is a popular horseback-riding area, and parts of the hiking route have been well trod by four-footed users, making it generally easy to follow. Indeed, some of the trail, especially near the lake, is badly eroded. The farther you get from the lake, the narrower and more pleasant the paths become.

From the parking area, take the northwesterly trail that's marked by horseback-riding signs. After passing through a beautiful stand of tall pines, cross the road just west of the parking area—and just east of the line where the road surface turns from pavement to gravel. After a dip the trail climbs gently through young hardwoods, passing two old concrete buildings that were once army latrines. At mile 0.4 the trail ends at the gravel road, above the spot where you crossed it just minutes before. Turn right and follow the road as it heads northwest and rises slightly. Make sure you continue straight on this road at its junction with another gravel road.

At mile 0.9 the road dead-ends in the woods, and you continue on a path to the northwest. Here and at various other high points throughout the hike, you can see north and northeast across the flat farmland extending toward the Ohio River. At mile 1.1, after descending the ridge, cross a small creek lined in spring with wildflowers and immediately climb up another ridge side. You repeat this up-and-down sequence several times before reaching KY 758. At mile 2.0 you come into a creek bottomland that may be confusing: There are two trails and nothing to identify the correct one. Take the trail going straight (west).

Just before KY 758, the trail dead-ends into a path running parallel to the road. Turn right and follow this path for about 30 yards to the road at mile 2.4. On the other side, make an easy climb to the ridgetop and follow it with few interruptions to an old fire tower at mile 3.2.

The tower, which anchors an antenna and is not climbable, is just off a gravel road that loops through the wildlife area from KY 56. From the tower a stone-and-dirt path runs south—away from the road. This is an unofficial shortcut used by horseback riders. It soon meets up with the main trail, but it's not marked and can be a bit confusing. To stay on the official route, turn left and walk west on the fire tower road. In 0.4 mile the trail leaves the left side of the road and runs south into the woods. The spot should be marked by a trail sign with the likeness of a horse's head.

(Shortly before you get to the turnoff, you will pass a trailhead on the right side of the road. This is a loop trail about a mile long that runs north, circles a lake, and returns to the fire tower road farther west. I have not been on that trail, but Scott Buser, foreman at Higginson-Henry, says it's a nice path that passes an old quarry with a good variety of songbirds.)

Proceeding south and then southeast from the fire tower road, stay on top of the ridge for about a half mile before dropping into an attractive bottomland where you meet the shortcut from the fire tower. After crossing a creek, the trail ends, and you turn left onto a swath of grass and mud made by workers to improve wildlife habitat and retard any fires that might develop. The trail climbs gently and joins an old dirt road that reaches KY 758 at mile 4.8.

On the other side of the road, jog right and immediately begin paralleling the road south to a forest track. Bear left on the track, which climbs southeast to the ridgetop and begins a relatively level stretch. To the left you can see the ridgeline you took on the hike's westward leg.

At about mile 6.5, as you near Cap Mauzy Lake, the trail formerly dipped into an attractive ravine. However, to keep horses out of the ravine, the trail was rerouted around it. The route now jogs south and then follows a gravel road north a short distance before descending through the woods, crossing a lake-access road, and reaching the shore at mile 7.3. A short side trail forks right to the water's edge; the main trail turns north, climbing through the pine grove to the parking area at mile 7.5.

Higginson–Henry Wildlife Management Area

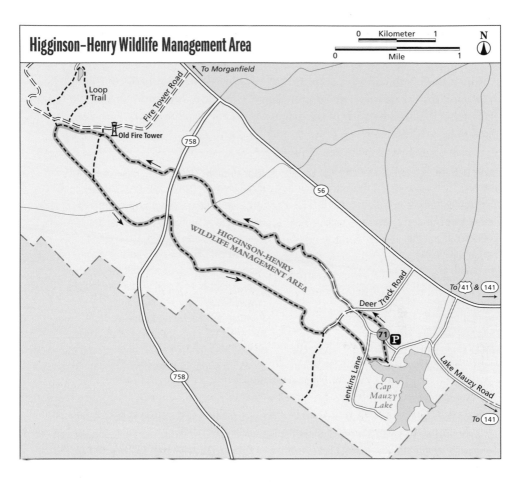

Key Points

0.4 Right turn onto gravel road.

2.4 Cross KY 758.

3.2 Old fire tower on gravel road.

4.8 Recross KY 758.

7.3 Lakeshore.

Option: At the eastern end of Higginson-Henry, there is a small tract developed for bird-watching. Called the Lee K. Nelson Wildlife Viewing Area, it's an attractive spot with a mile-long loop trail around a pond. From Lake Mauzy Road, take KY 56 east for 2.1 miles and turn left onto the gravel road. In another 0.4 mile, turn right and park.

72 Mantle Rock

A large natural arch and a beautiful stream-crossed bottomland make this little hike a real gem. You also learn about an unfortunate chapter of American history, the Trail of Tears, and follow a portion of the original route the Cherokee took between 1838 and 1839.

Start: Parking area off KY 133 near community of Joy
Distance: 2.75-mile lollipop
Hiking time: About 1.5 hours
Difficulty: Moderate
Best seasons: Any
Other trail users: None
Canine compatibility: No dogs allowed
Land status: Private land
Nearest town: Marion
Fees and permits: None
Maps: Mantle Rock map from the Nature Conservancy's Kentucky Chapter; USGS Golconda

Trail contact: The Nature Conservancy, Kentucky Chapter, (859) 259-9655, www.nature.org/ourinitiatives/regions/northamerica/unitedstates/kentucky/placesweprotect/mantle-rock-preserve.xml
Special considerations: Part of the preserve is open to hunting. Check with the Kentucky Department of Fish and Wildlife Resources (www.fw.ky.gov) for season dates.
Parking and trailhead facilities: There's room for about 10 cars, but no facilities. (Drivers should not attempt to take their cars on the gravel road that extends beyond the parking area.)

Finding the trailhead: From Marion, take US 60 west for 11.3 miles to the town of Salem and turn right onto KY 133. In 13 miles—2 miles beyond the community of Joy—turn left onto the narrow gravel road next to a historical marker for Mantle Rock. In 0.1 mile, park in the gravel lot. The hike starts at the south end of the lot. GPS: N37 21.608' / W88 25.439'

The Hike

This hike takes you to Mantle Rock, a large sandstone arch located in a beautiful stream-crossed bottomland. The walk offers scenic rewards to justify the drive to reach this corner of Kentucky.

Measuring 188 feet in length and 30 feet in height, Mantle Rock is one of the longest arches in the state. It is also part of one of the ugliest chapters in American history: President Andrew Jackson's expulsion of the Cherokee Indians from the eastern United States. In the winter of 1838–39, waiting for improved weather that would allow them to cross the Ohio River, many Cherokee on the forced trek west took shelter in Mantle Rock and nearby rock houses. Those who did not survive the brutal Kentucky winter were among the 2,000 to 4,000 Cherokee who perished in this unfortunate forced migration, known as the Trail of Tears.

The Cherokee were by no means the first Native Americans to use Mantle Rock. According to the Nature Conservancy, which owns the 367-acre preserve

Cherokee on the Trail of Tears are believed to have taken shelter beneath Mantle Rock and other nearby rock houses.

surrounding the arch, people were hunting and gathering food here 10,000 years ago. In addition to history, the Nature Conservancy says the area is significant for a number of plant species, including June grass, prickly pear cactus, and a rare kind of goldenrod.

From the parking area, walk south on the rough gravel road. It descends gradually through a field and into the edge of the woods. Here the gravel road ends, and you take a broad dirt path right into a forest of good-size hardwoods. At mile 0.1 you reach a sign directing you to the left (southeast) toward Mantle Rock, or right to take the original Trail of Tears. Follow the trail to Mantle Rock first, in order to hike the loop in a clockwise direction. In 2010, in partnership with the National Park Service, the Nature Conservancy opened this new loop trail, which retraces the steps Cherokee would have taken on their march to cross the Ohio River. It also highlights the preserve's sandstone glades and native prairie, both of which include rare plants.

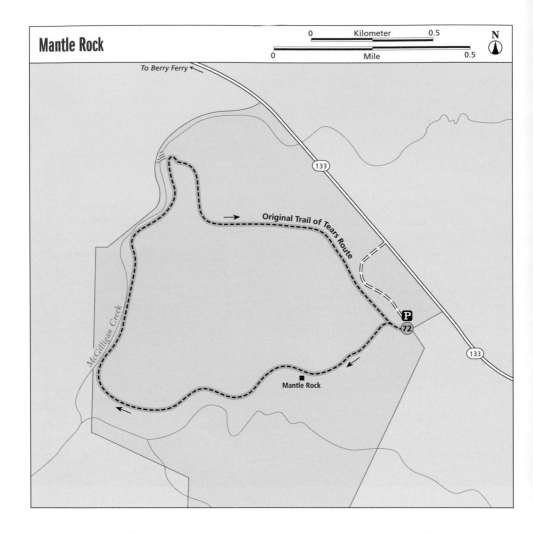

Kilometer

To Berry Ferry

133

Original Trail of Tears Route

McGilligan Creek

P
72

133

Mantle Rock

After passing through a gate and a kiosk, at 0.4 mile, immediately after the trail curves west, you will see a cliff about 40 feet to the right of the trail and, in front of the cliff, gracefully sloping Mantle Rock. In the spring a small, rock-bottomed stream with grassy banks runs along the arch, adding to the pleasantness of the scene. This is a spot to enjoy, but please stay off the top of the arch; the rare sandstone ecosystem there is extremely sensitive and easily damaged.

Follow the curve of the creek around the edge of the sandstone bluff and cross the small intermittent stream. The trail climbs here through a gap in the rock and then crosses another small wet-weather stream before climbing again through another narrow gap in the rock.

The trail follows the cliff line heading west, and on my visit was still dripping with water from recent rains. It created a soothing sound in the quiet woods. To your left far below you, McGilligan Creek rushes toward the Ohio River. After another 0.3

mile, the trail quickly drops down to the creek bank as it continues to weave its way through the forest to the west.

At mile 1.0 the trail begins to climb and then quickly levels out. Again the waters of McGilligan Creek are far below you; watch out in this area for the steep cliffs that drop off to your left. After crossing a number of intermittent streams, the trail turns to the north and then quickly drops down to follow another branch of the creek. This stretch is relatively level as it parallels the creek, passing a number of nice swimming holes and a small waterfall before reaching a sign at mile 1.8 announcing the end of this section of the hiking trail and the beginning of the 1-mile stretch of the original Trail of Tears route.

The trail makes a sharp left turn here and begins to head southeast, climbing up a rocky old roadbed. This is the area where the Cherokee camped during the winter of 1838–39, waiting for suitable weather to cross the Ohio River. The trail passes between two embankments lined with large trees. As it approaches a sandstone glade, the trail surface grows rockier, then takes another sharp turn and heads east. Passing under a large, old oak tree at mile 2.4 that no doubt was standing when the Cherokee camped along the road, the trail follows the edge of a native prairie, which is maintained with the use of fire. After 0.1 mile the trail heads back into a narrow strip of woods between two open prairie fields. At mile 2.6 reach the end of the loop and turn left to retrace your steps back to the parking lot.

Key Points

0.2   Gate and information kiosk.

0.4   Mantle Rock.

1.8   Original Trail of Tears route.

73 Ballard Wildlife Management Area

Cypress swamps and open fields combine to make this a lovely hiking area in the spring and fall.

Start: Wildlife-viewing platform on gravel road off KY 473
Distance: 5.8-mile loop
Hiking time: About 3 hours
Difficulty: Easy
Best seasons: Spring and fall; closed Oct 15 through Mar 15
Other trail users: Equestrians and hunters
Canine compatibility: Leashed dogs permitted
Land status: State wildlife management area
Nearest town: La Center
Fees and permits: None
Maps: Ballard Wildlife Management Area map; USGS Olmsted (IL/KY)

Trail contact: Ballard Wildlife Management Area, (270) 224-2244
Special considerations: The Ballard area has no trails; this hike is entirely on gravel roads. In the spring the area is subject to Ohio River flooding.
Parking and trailhead facilities: At the wildlife-viewing platform, there is room for 5 cars, but no facilities. The wildlife area office, with a restroom and information, is 0.5 mile north—just beyond Wildlife Lodge Road. There are primitive camping areas on Shelby and Big Turner Lakes.

Finding the trailhead: From Paducah, take US 60 west for 20 miles to La Center and turn right (north) onto KY 358. In 5.5 miles, turn left onto KY 473, and in 0.4 mile—at the four-way stop—go straight on Kentucky 1105. In 3.2 miles, bear right onto KY 473 (the same KY 473), and in 2.3 miles, turn left onto Wildlife Lodge Road, marked by a sign for the Ballard Wildlife Management Area headquarters. At the four-way intersection in 0.7 mile, turn left onto the gravel road, and in another 0.4 mile, pull into the dirt parking area on the right side of the road next to the wildlife-viewing platform. GPS: N37 10.639' / W89 01.861'

The Hike

Once a collection of more than twenty farms, the Ballard Wildlife Management Area is now a refuge for migratory waterfowl. Each winter this 8,373-acre, state-owned tract along the Ohio River gets hundreds of thousands of Canada, snow, and blue geese, plus thousands of mallards, wigeons, and other ducks. The wildlife area also has five resident pairs of eagles.

For the migrants' protection, the area is closed from October 15 through March 15. For the hiker the weeks just after the opening and just before the closing are a wonderful time to visit. While most—though not all—geese and ducks have gone, the cypress-filled lakes, wooded marshes, and open farm fields provide rich visual rewards. With the exception of the similar but smaller Sauerheber tract in the Higginson-Henry Wildlife Management Area, this is bottomland scenery you won't find elsewhere.

A thick layer of algae looks almost like a lush lawn as it covers the surface of shallow sloughs.

The Ballard area—which is as flat as a pool table—has no trails, and so the hike is entirely on gravel roads. They get little vehicle traffic and make fine walking paths—in early spring or fall, that is. During summer, hiking here would be hot and certainly buggy.

The following route offers a good mix of lakes, woods, and open fields. The Ballard area is broken up by small bodies of water, all naturally made and regularly flooded by the Ohio. Some are called lakes, some sloughs. There is not much difference between them. With only a few exceptions, most are between 5 and 10 feet deep, says Ballard manager Robert Colvis. Their level is controlled somewhat by a system of levees.

From the parking area, start southeast but immediately turn right onto the gravel road running southwest parallel to thin, shallow Turkey Lake. Indeed, the lake can be almost nonexistent. At mile 0.5 turn right onto the gravel road going across the south end of Turkey Lake. At mile 0.8, after cutting through a wooded marsh, you come to Big Turner Lake and one of Ballard's primitive camping areas. Big Turner is popular with anglers. In this and the other lakes, the catch includes bass, bluegill, crappie, catfish, and anything else found in the Ohio River.

At the campground the road turns southwest along Big Turner's cypress-studded shore. On your left a planted field gives way to a pond before the trail winds into a wooded area. At any point in the woods, take a short detour right and you quickly come to the edge of a handsome cypress swamp. Whether you are at the end of Big Turner Lake or the beginning of Butler Lake may be hard to tell. Whichever, it will be a perfect spot for a rest break.

At mile 2.2, at the end of Butler Lake, turn left onto Mitchell Lake Road and follow its packed-dirt-and-stone surface southeast, passing Castor Lake on your left. In the spring the woods here sparkle with blooming redbud trees. Ignore the first road you cross—Humphrey Creek Road—and continue southeast on Mitchell Lake Road as it cuts through a field and crosses the lower end of Mitchell Lake, another favorite of anglers.

At mile 3.2 turn left onto a gravel road—the first you come to after crossing the lake—and walk northeast between fields of grass and corn. In the spring patches of the ground are covered with the beautiful purple blooms of henbit. At a couple of picturesque old barns, the road jogs north, taking you closer to the lake. On a warm day you may see dozens of turtles sunning themselves on shoreline logs and deadheads. Even though most of the migratory waterfowl have gone or not yet come, you are also likely to see some ducks and geese plying the water.

At mile 5.0, just after passing three more barns, the gravel road dead-ends into KY 473 at a hairpin turn. Turn left onto the highway and then left again onto the gravel road going northwest into the wildlife area's interior. After crossing a slough, the road cuts through a wooded marsh and reaches the parking area at mile 5.8.

Key Points

0.5 Right turn at end of Turkey Lake.
2.2 Left onto Mitchell Lake Road.
3.2 Left onto first road south of Mitchell Lake.
5.0 Left onto KY 473, then left again onto gravel road.

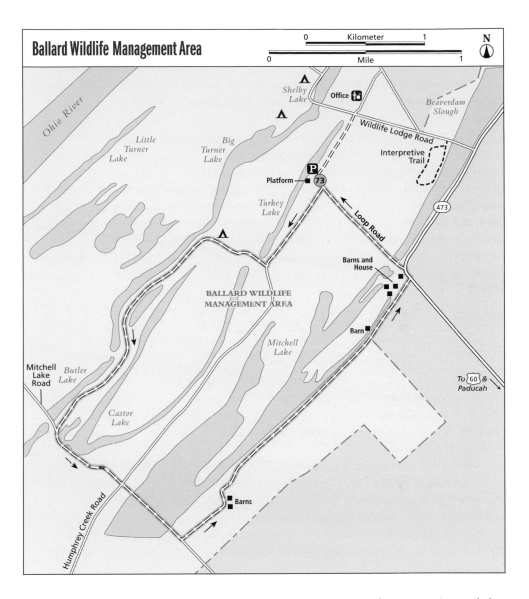

Ballard Wildlife Management Area

Option: The wildlife management area maintains a 1-mile interpretive trail that includes an elevated metal walkway over a slough. The trail is on the left side of Wildlife Lodge Road near the entrance.

74 Columbus-Belmont State Park

You get a magnificent view of the Mississippi River, and take in some impressive Civil War earthworks, on this little hike at the state's western tip.

Start: State park picnic area
Distance: 1.7-mile loop
Hiking time: About 1 hour
Difficulty: Easy
Best seasons: Any
Other trail users: None
Canine compatibility: Leashed dogs permitted
Land status: State park
Nearest town: Columbus
Fees and permits: None

Maps: Park map; USGS Arlington
Trail contact: Columbus-Belmont State Park, (270) 677-2327
Parking and trailhead facilities: There's room for two dozen cars, along with drinking water, restrooms, and, in summer, a snack bar. There is also minigolf here and a park museum. The park campground is 0.4 mile from the picnic area.

Finding the trailhead: From Bardwell, take KY 123 south for 10 miles to the town of Columbus and turn right onto Cheatham Street. (From Clinton, take KY 58 west to Columbus, turn right onto KY 123, and, in 0.1 mile, turn left onto Cheatham Street.) Cheatham becomes Park Road and ends in 0.8 mile at a parking lot for the picnic area. The hike starts at the west end of the lot. GPS: N36 45.932' / W89 06.619'

The Hike

This little hike takes you along a bluff high above the Mississippi River with stupendous upstream and downstream views. It is one of the most dramatic overlooks you will find anywhere in the state. Indeed, that's exactly why the little town of Columbus played a role in the Civil War.

In 1861, disregarding Kentucky's neutral status, Confederate troops fortified these bluffs to stop Union forces from using the Mississippi to penetrate the South. On November 7, 1861, under a then little-known brigadier general named Ulysses S. Grant, the Yankees attacked the Confederate camp at the Missouri town of Belmont just across the river from Columbus. The cannon fire from the Kentucky bluff helped turn back the Northern advance. Militarily the battle was inconclusive, but the aggressiveness shown by Grant's troops gave a significant boost both to Union morale and to his career. The next year, after the loss of strategic forts on the Tennessee and Cumberland Rivers, the Confederates abandoned Columbus.

This 156-acre state park was developed in the 1930s to commemorate the 1861 battle and preserve the extensive earthworks. Its main attribute, however, is the commanding vista of the Mississippi. The little park has only a few short trails, so this hike relies on a combination of paths, paved walkways, and Park Road.

The bluffs at Columbus-Belmont afford fantastic views of the Mississippi River.

From the end of the parking lot, where placards tell you about the battle, take the asphalt walkway north to a small picnic shelter and a sign marking the start of the Confederate trenches. With earthen mounds rising up on both sides, follow a dirt path along the trench floor. The depth gives you an immediate appreciation for just how much work it took Confederate soldiers to construct the fortifications. The trench curves right and then left as it circles northward, climbing gently. At mile 0.3, after jogging south on top of the earthworks, you come to Arrowhead Point and look out over a section of the trench system.

From the point, head northwest through woods to a modern metal fence, which you follow as it curves south. Taking log stairs, descend once again into the trench and circle back to the start of the trench loop. Bear right along the fence and climb steps leading up to the open bluff. Here the metal fence gives way to an older, wooden one more in keeping with the surroundings.

Follow the fence as it curves along the edge of the bluff to a large picnic pavilion and a grand view of the Mississippi. If you stay even a few minutes, you are likely

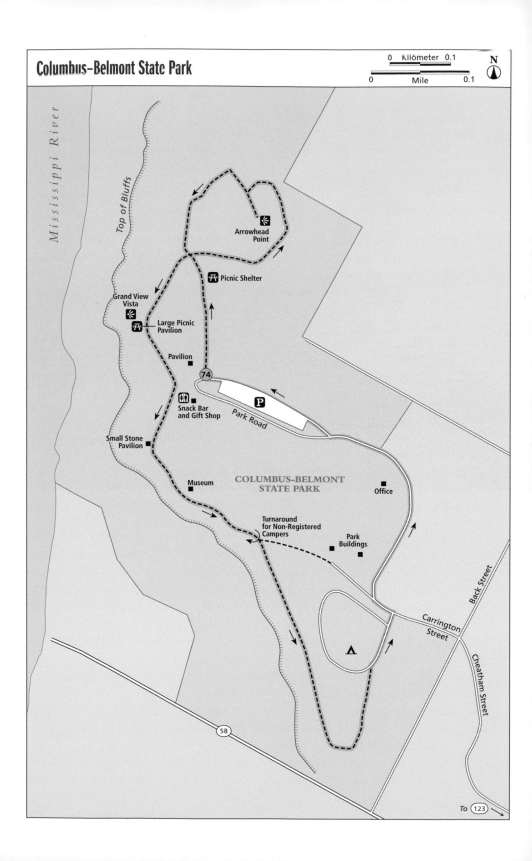

Columbus–Belmont State Park

0   Kilometer   0.1

0   Mile   0.1

N

Mississippi River

Top of Bluffs

Arrowhead Point

Picnic Shelter

Grand View Vista

Large Picnic Pavilion

Pavilion

74

P

Park Road

Snack Bar and Gift Shop

Small Stone Pavilion

Museum

COLUMBUS–BELMONT STATE PARK

Office

Turnaround for Non-Registered Campers

Park Buildings

Back Street

Carrington Street

Cheatham Street

58

To 123

to see a barge or two moving goods up or down the river. On display behind the pavilion is a section of a large chain that the Confederates ran across the river to stop Union gunboats.

Continuing along the bluff, you follow the wood fence and then take an asphalt walkway to a small stone pavilion at mile 0.6. Here you have the best river view of all. Stay on the walkway as it goes southeast, passing a building that served as a hospital for the Southern troops and is now the park museum (a small fee is charged). Just behind the museum is a redoubt that has been beautifully restored; it's worth a stop.

At mile 0.9, just after passing beneath a utility wire, turn right off the paved walkway onto a narrow, unmarked dirt path that climbs up to the bluff at the edge of the campground at 1 mile. Here you have another good view of the river. If you can't find the little path, just thread your way uphill through the trees, making sure to skirt the eroded, vine-filled gully on your right.

Cindy Lynch, the park manager, said the campground is off-limits to visitors who aren't registered campers; thus you may have to bypass this next stretch and retrace your steps back to the museum and parking lot. At the campground, walk along the edge of the open bluff to the start of another fortification. Follow the trench east to its end near the campground loop road. Taking the road north, you reach the campground entrance at mile 1.3. Turn left and follow Park Road back to the picnic area parking lot.

Key Points

0.3 Arrowhead Point and earthworks.

0.6 View of the Mississippi River from pavilion.

1.0 Bluff at campground.

75 Reelfoot National Wildlife Refuge

This short walk to the upper reaches of Reelfoot Lake ends at a quiet cove full of water lilies, bald cypress trees, and waterfowl.

Start: Wildlife-viewing platform 0.5 mile off KY 1282
Distance: 4-mile out-and-back
Hiking time: About 1.5 hours
Difficulty: Easy
Best seasons: Spring and fall; closed Nov 15 to Mar 15
Other trail users: Equestrians and vehicles (hike is on a gravel-and-dirt road, not a trail)
Canine compatibility: Leashed dogs permitted
Land status: National wildlife refuge

Nearest town: Hickman
Fees and permits: None
Maps: Refuge pamphlet; USGS Bondurant and Samburg (TN)
Trail contact: Reelfoot National Wildlife Refuge, (731) 538-2481, www.fws.gov/reelfoot
Special considerations: There is a 3-day deer hunt the second week of Nov.
Parking and trailhead facilities: You'll find room for about 10 cars, but no facilities.

Finding the trailhead: From Hickman, take KY 94 west for 4.5 miles and turn left onto KY 311. In 1.6 miles, turn right onto KY 1282, making sure to follow the sign for the Long Point Unit of the Reelfoot National Wildlife Refuge and not the refuge's visitor center, which is 6 miles south in Tennessee. After 2.6 miles on KY 1282, turn left onto the gravel road marked by a sign for the refuge. In 0.5 mile, park on the left of the road next to the wildlife-viewing platform. The hike starts at the platform. GPS: N36 30.881' / W89 19.237'

The Hike

In late 1811 and early 1812, the most severe series of earthquakes ever recorded in North America rocked the Mississippi River area where Kentucky, Missouri, and Tennessee meet. Known by the name of the Missouri town just north of the river, the New Madrid quakes literally changed the geography by rerouting streams and creating Reelfoot Lake.

Named for a Chickasaw chief born with a deformed foot, this long, shallow lake—5 feet deep on average—is mainly in Tennessee. But its upper reaches stretch into Kentucky, as does part of the 10,428-acre federal wildlife refuge established in 1941 around the northern shoreline. The refuge's Long Point Unit—named for a thin strip of land jutting into the lake's Upper Blue Basin—is accessible by car only from Kentucky.

This hike crosses the Long Point Unit, starting in marshland on the Kentucky side and ending in Tennessee at a scenic cove full of water lilies, bald cypress trees, and waterfowl. This part of the refuge has no trails; the hike is on a gravel-and-dirt road. Though little used, the narrow road is open to vehicles—meaning, of course, that you

White American lotus flowers blanket the water at Reelfoot Lake.

could drive to the lake. You would, however, miss a lovely walk—lovely, that is, in the cool of spring or fall. There is absolutely no shade to ward off the summer sun.

From the wildlife platform, follow the road south, passing a field on your left that in the spring looks more like a pond. The principal purpose of the refuge is to provide

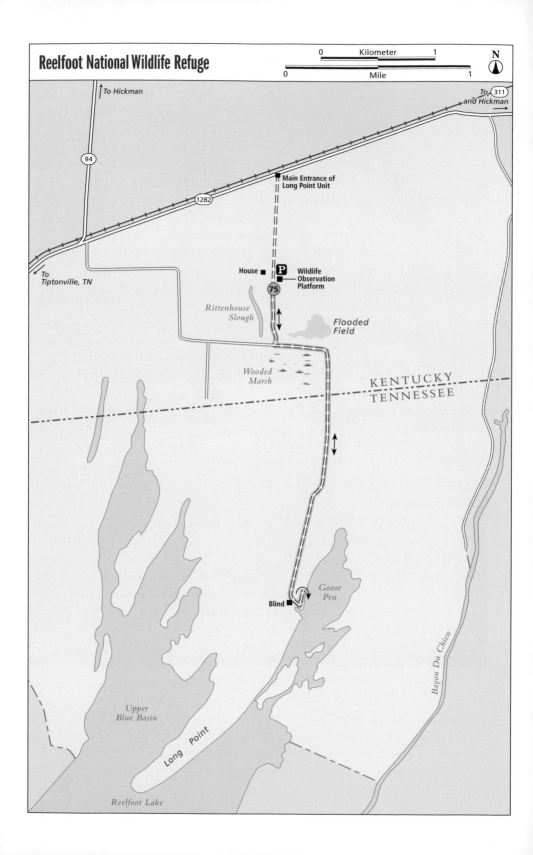

Reelfoot National Wildlife Refuge

To Hickman

94

To 311
and Hickman

1282

Main Entrance of
Long Point Unit

House ■ P Wildlife
Observation
Platform

75

To
Tiptonville, TN

Rittenhouse
Slough

Flooded
Field

Wooded
Marsh

KENTUCKY
TENNESSEE

Blind ■ Goose
Pen

Bayou Du Chien

Upper
Blue Basin

Long Point

Reelfoot Lake

food and habitat for waterfowl on the Mississippi Flyway, and levees allow the water level to be manipulated. During late fall and winter, the refuge is a sanctuary mainly for Canada geese and mallards. That's why the facility is closed for that part of the year. Bald eagles and marsh birds are also visitors. On the right side of the road, the ditch sprouting cypress trees is called Rittenhouse Slough.

At mile 0.3 the road comes to a T intersection and you turn left. (A right would take you 1.4 miles across open fields and swamp to the intersection of KY 94 and KY 1282 on the refuge's western boundary.) Going east, the road skirts a wooded marsh on your right and, at mile 0.6, turns south once again. At mile 0.8 cross the unmarked Kentucky-Tennessee line as the road continues through dry fields planted with corn or other crops. It's a quiet stretch, good for bird-watching.

At mile 2.0, as the road bends left, a sign prohibits further vehicle travel. The lake, dotted with cypresses and covered by water lilies and families of ducks, is just beyond. Going southeast, you quickly reach the grassy shore—a great place to watch nature.

This secluded body of water, which is connected by a couple of ditches to the lake's Upper Blue Basin, is known locally as Goose Pen. That's because years ago it was fenced off to make a home for crippled geese. Now, from time to time, refuge workers use it to trap ducks for banding. The bands allow researchers to track migration. The structure just beyond the road's end is the blind where workers operate the large net that traps the waterfowl.

When you've soaked up the scene to your content, turn around and retrace your steps to your car.

Key Points

0.3 Left turn at T intersection.

2.0 Road's end.

Option: Ranger Tara Dowdy recommends the 1-mile out-and-back Grassy Island Trail, located 17 miles from Union City, Tennessee. The easy walk takes about 30 to 45 minutes, begins on a wide gravel trail, and is dotted with interpretive signage and benches. This trail is shaded by lush vegetation, and the shallow waters make an excellent place to view snakes, turtles, herons, and other wildlife. The area is open and visitors can see farther into the bottomland and hardwood forest, thus making it an excellent place to bird.

76 Honker Lake

This day hike in Land Between The Lakes National Recreation Area follows the wooded shoreline of Honker Lake, a small reservoir adjacent to Lake Barkley that was created to attract geese and ducks.

Start: Woodlands Nature Station in Land Between The Lakes
Distance: 4.5-mile loop
Hiking time: About 3 hours
Difficulty: Easy
Best seasons: Spring and fall
Other trail users: None
Canine compatibility: Leashed dogs permitted
Land status: National recreation area
Nearest town: Calvert City
Fees and permits: None
Maps: Land Between The Lakes Honker Lake Trail Maps; USGS Mont
Trail contact: USDA Forest Service at Golden Pond, (270) 924-2000 or (800) 525-7077, www.LandBetweenTheLakes.us

Special considerations: Ticks are a problem throughout Land Between The Lakes from early spring to autumn. The Forest Service urges visitors to wear long pants and tuck pant legs into boots or socks and keep shirts tucked into pants, treat clothing with an approved tick repellent containing permethrin, and periodically check body and clothing to remove ticks.
Parking and trailhead facilities: There is space for about 45 cars. Restrooms and vending machines are available at the nature station, an environmental education facility with displays and live animals (entrance fee charged). More restrooms and additional parking are also found a short walk west on Silver Trail Road.

Finding the trailhead: From I-24 or US 62, southeast of Calvert City, take KY 453 south from Grand Rivers into Land Between The Lakes (LBL), where the highway loses its numerical designation and becomes Woodlands Trace National Scenic Byway. LBL's North Welcome Station, which has maps and other information, is 5 miles south of US 62. From the welcome station, continue south on Woodlands Trace and, in 8.8 miles, turn left onto Silver Trail Road. In 3 miles, park in front of the nature station. The trail starts on the parking lot's north side. GPS: N36 54.093' / W88 02.214'

The Hike

Land Between The Lakes (LBL) was created in the 1960s by the federal government to turn the remote hill country between two large man-made reservoirs—Kentucky Lake and Lake Barkley—into a multiuse recreation area that would attract people from across the country. Shaped in a long, thin rectangle, this 170,000-acre tract stretches from Kentucky into Tennessee and has 300 miles of shoreline. In addition to a multitude of boat-launch facilities and campgrounds, it offers 200 miles of hiking trails, some of which are shared with mountain bikers and equestrians.

Initially managed by the Tennessee Valley Authority but now under the auspices of the Forest Service, LBL is a rustic place with few amenities for visitors. Make sure you buy whatever food you need before you come. Also, be aware that LBL is notorious for its robust crop of ticks from March through October. Hikers are urged to wear long pants and apply tick repellent.

For backpacking in LBL, I recommend the North/South Trail hike and the Canal Loop hike. The Honker Lake hike is for visitors who don't have the time or inclination for an overnight trip but want to see a pleasant stretch of lakefront.

Honker Lake—the name comes from the sound made by Canada geese—was created by damming off an inlet of Lake Barkley. It's a reservoir within a reservoir. The purpose was to create a separate body of water whose level could be better controlled to accommodate geese and ducks. Honker Lake is a refuge for both migrant and resident waterfowl, and the surrounding shore is set aside as an environmental education area with special restrictions, including no camping. The Honker Lake Trail is open all year, but the lake itself is closed to boats during the winter because of its refuge function.

From the parking lot, descend north on wood-and-gravel steps to a dirt path and—just before reaching a gravel road—turn right. Shortly, Woodland Walk Trail branches right to begin a mile-long loop around the Woodlands Nature Station, and you turn left onto Honker Lake Trail.

Entering the woods, the trail goes northwest into a stand of tall hardwoods and climbs gradually up a hill, reaching the top at mile 0.6. After a level stretch, the trail, which is marked by posts with white-and-brown emblems, curves north and descends to cross a small stream at mile 1.4. Turning east, you come to an old gravel track; you can turn right onto this or continue on the path. Either way, at mile 1.6 you reach a thin strip of land running between Honker Lake on your right and an inlet of Lake Barkley—named Honker Bay—on your left. On both bodies of water, you are likely to see waterfowl and wading birds. Tall pines and the sound of croaking frogs contribute to the scene's attractiveness.

Continuing east, climb to the top of a small hill and descend to cross the narrow dam separating Honker Lake from its big brother. When Lake Barkley is at a high level, it can overcome this thin barrier, temporarily eliminating Honker's separate identity. The dam is a favorite with anglers, so you're apt to have company here.

Reaching the dam's eastern end at mile 2.1, curve northeast on gravel before turning into the woods and going south. After angling away from the lakeshore to avoid a low-lying wet area, the trail turns northwest toward the lake and then roughly follows the shoreline south, in the process crossing two small streams on bridges.

As you circle the lake's southern tip, you might hear the loud honking of geese. They like to congregate on a grassy field just across the lake. Curving north, cross a small stream and then take a long wooden bridge over Long Creek at mile 4.1. This is a scenic part of the hike, and a good place for a rest stop.

From the bridge the trail winds north and crosses a gravel road leading to the lake. On the far side of the road, you meet the other end of Woodland Walk Trail. Following the signs for the nature station, climb first northeast and then northwest.

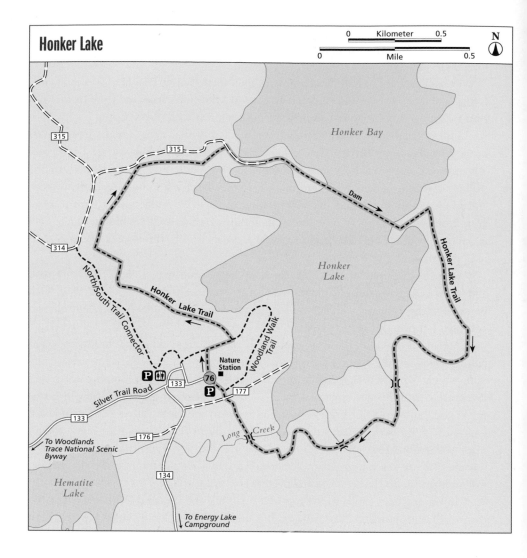

After passing the nature station's outdoor animal cages, you reach the building and parking lot at mile 4.5.

Key Points

1.6 Shoreline between Honker Lake and Lake Barkley.

1.9 Honker Lake dam.

4.1 Bridge across Long Creek.

77 North/South Trail

This long-distance hike in Land Between The Lakes takes you into isolated coves along Kentucky Lake and up to quiet ridgetops above the water.

Start: Golden Pond Visitor Center in Land Between The Lakes National Recreation Area
Distance: 31.2-mile shuttle
Hiking time: 1- to 3-night backpack
Difficulty: Moderate
Best seasons: Spring and fall
Other trail users: Mountain bikers
Canine compatibility: Leashed dogs permitted
Land status: National recreation area
Nearest town: Calvert City
Fees and permits: Permit required for back-country camping. Permits can be purchased at Golden Pond Visitor Center (open daily 9 a.m. to 5 p.m. year-round) and North and South Welcome Stations (open daily 9 a.m. to 5 p.m. Mar through Nov).

Maps: Land Between The Lakes North End of North/South Trail Map; USGS Birmingham Point, Mont, Fairdealing, and Fenton
Trail contact: USDA Forest Service at Golden Pond, (270) 924-2000 or (800) 525-7077, www.LandBetweenTheLakes.us
Special considerations: Ticks are a problem throughout Land Between The Lakes from early spring to autumn. The Forest Service urges visitors to wear long pants and tuck pant legs into boots or socks and keep shirts tucked into pants, treat clothing with an approved tick repellent containing permethrin, and periodically check body and clothing to remove ticks.
Parking and trailhead facilities: You'll find space for 50 cars, as well as restrooms, drinking water, vending machines, a telephone, maps, and other information.

Finding the trailhead: From I-24 or US 62, southeast of Calvert City, take KY 453 south into Land Between The Lakes (LBL), where the highway loses its numerical designation and becomes Woodlands Trace National Scenic Byway. LBL's North Welcome Station, which has maps and other information, is 5 miles south of US 62. From the welcome station, continue south on Woodlands Trace for 18.3 miles to the Golden Pond Visitor Center entrance on your left. Take the entrance drive 0.2 mile and park in front of the building. The trail starts on the west side of Woodlands Trace across from the visitor center entrance. GPS: N36 46.631' / W88 03.938'

The Hike

The North/South Trail runs the length of Land Between The Lakes (LBL)—from the South Welcome Station in Tennessee to the North Welcome Station in Kentucky. (For more information on LBL, see the Honker Lake hike.) This hike follows the trail's northern half, starting at Golden Pond Visitor Center about 10 miles north of the Tennessee line. According to LBL, the entire trail is 58.6 miles long, and this northern part totals 31.2 miles.

The trail is a lovely backpacking route along Kentucky Lake, with a good mix of shoreline stretches and ridgetop bluffs. There's also a good deal of bottomland walking along small streams that feed into the lake. Seven springs line this route, along with shelters for overnight camping.

Kentucky Lake, an impoundment of the Tennessee River, is the largest man-made reservoir east of the Mississippi in length and surface area. (Lake Cumberland is larger in water volume.) Kentucky Lake drains some 40,000 square miles and covers 160,300 acres. It's relatively deep and has the blue of a natural lake instead of the soupy green of many lesser reservoirs. It also has lots of barge traffic; the Tennessee River is a major commercial route to and from the Ohio River. Completed in 1944 for the purpose of flood control, navigation, and hydropower generation, the lake is operated by the Tennessee Valley Authority (TVA).

There is no way to make a loop out of the North/South Trail. As the name implies, this is a linear experience. Unfortunately, LBL has not yet spawned—at least as of this writing—a shuttle service to help hikers out, and Forest Service personnel say the nearest taxi is in Murray or Paducah, a good 25 to 30 miles away. This means that if you want to do the entire northern half of the trail, you need two cars.

Making life easy for backpackers, North/South Trail is lined with attractive, level camping spots. LBL allows camping just about everywhere—except inside cemetery boundaries and picnic areas, within 200 yards of Woodlands Trace and other major roads, and in certain posted sites, such as the environmental education area at Honker Lake. Warm-month backpackers, however, will have to contend with ticks. The critters are prevalent enough that the North Welcome Station sells a repellent to spray on clothing. That's one reason—heat and mosquitoes are two more—I recommend spring and fall hiking.

LBL trail maps show several sites with drinking water, but backpackers shouldn't count on this. All water from the lake, streams, and springs must, of course, be treated.

North/South Trail's northern half is divided into four sections. For northbound hikers, the first is 8.5 miles long. It starts at Golden Pond Visitor Center, which is named for what was once a settlement on LBL. Like other communities, it was eliminated and its residents resettled when the recreation area was developed in the 1960s.

The official trailhead is south of the parking area, but instead of spending time looking for it, simply take the entrance drive 0.2 mile west to Woodlands Trace. There you will find North/South Trail running along the west side of the road. Cross the road, turn right, and follow the shoulder for 0.2 mile to the underpass beneath US 68/KY 80. A short distance on the other side, the trail angles away from Woodlands Trace and into the woods. Here and throughout, the North/South Trail is well marked by white diamond blazes. (Side trails are blazed with yellow diamonds.)

Going north and then west, descend into sizable pines and hardwoods. At mile 2.3, after crossing several small streambeds on wooden bridges, you come to a large bottomland field and a side trail that leads south 0.5 mile to Brush Arbor Shelter—an overnight shelter and spring. Continuing west, follow a rock-bottomed creek bed for a short distance before crossing first it and then an unmarked dirt road. There are numerous good camping spots in this attractive area.

A quiet cove just off the main trunk of Kentucky Lake.

After climbing several hills, descend at mile 3.9 to the shore of Vickers Bay, the first in a series of secluded Kentucky Lake inlets that the trail passes on its way north. Crossing two creeks, you move counterclockwise around the head of Vickers Bay and then mount a series of ridges rimming the bay's north side. There are numerous ups and downs in this stretch, none of them strenuous but in the aggregate enough to qualify as a workout.

Turning north, you reach a small, unnamed bay. Again going counterclockwise, cross a stream in the bottomland at the head of the bay and then climb steeply northward to the top of a ridge. At mile 7.1 the trail turns right onto a dirt road, FR 337, and follows it for 0.4 mile before turning left off the road.

Continuing along the ridgetop, you come to a bluff overlooking Rhodes Bay before descending to just above the water's edge. Following the Rhodes Bay shoreline northeast, cross a stream and, at mile 8.4, come to FR 141, which marks the end of the trail's first section. A small trickle of water named Buzzard Wing Spring is 0.1 mile south on the east side of the road. The spring is designated a backcountry campsite, and has a fire ring and a small flat spot, but is uninviting.

The second section of the trail is 9.6 miles in length, according to the LBL mileage. Turning left (northeast) onto FR 141, follow it briefly before turning left and

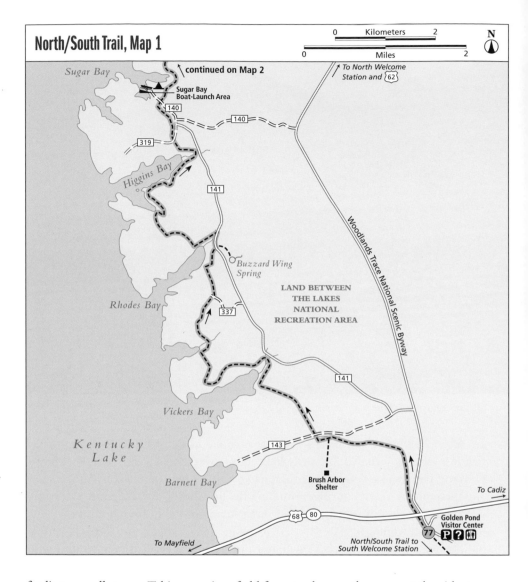

Kilometers 2

0 Miles 2

N

continued on Map 2

Sugar Bay

Sugar Bay
Boat-Launch Area

140

140

To North Welcome
Station and 62

319

Higgins Bay

141

Buzzard Wing
Spring

Rhodes Bay

337

**LAND BETWEEN
THE LAKES
NATIONAL
RECREATION AREA**

Woodlands Trace National Scenic Byway

141

Vickers Bay

143

Kentucky
Lake

Barnett Bay

Brush Arbor
Shelter

To Cadiz

68 80

Golden Pond
Visitor Center

77 P ? ♿

To Mayfield

North/South Trail to
South Welcome Station

fording a small stream. Taking a series of old farm tracks, you then mount the ridgetop and descend north to the shore of a finger of Higgins Bay at mile 10.0, another quiet lakeside spot. Following the level lakeshore, you pass a strange sight—a tiny island covered by a graveyard. The numerous graveyards you see along the trail are testament to the days when farms and small communities dotted the LBL countryside and the now-inundated Tennessee River banks.

After crossing several streambeds at the top of Higgins Bay, go north over a knob and come down to FR 319 at mile 12.4. Turn right onto this dirt road and go north for a short distance before turning left into the woods and crossing gravel FR 140 at mile 13.3. The Sugar Bay boat-launch area—with a backcountry campground,

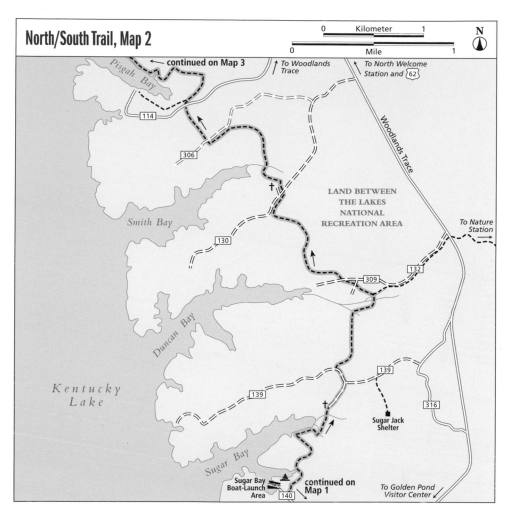

0   Kilometer   1

0   Mile   1

N

Pisgah Bay

← continued on Map 3

To Woodlands Trace

To North Welcome Station and 62

114

306

Smith Bay

LAND BETWEEN THE LAKES NATIONAL RECREATION AREA

To Nature Station

130

132

309

Duncan Bay

Kentucky Lake

139

139

316

Sugar Jack Shelter

continued on Map 1

Sugar Bay Boat-Launch Area

140

Sugar Bay

To Golden Pond Visitor Center

portable toilets, and picnic tables but no drinking water—is just a few steps north on the road. This would be a good turnaround point for anyone wanting to make this an out-and-back hike.

Going northeast, climb several ridges as you skirt a large inlet off Sugar Bay and then the end of the bay itself. At mile 15.6 the trail dead-ends into an old dirt road. To your left is a cemetery; turn right and follow the dirt track up to the top of the ridge. There you run into a gravel road, FR 139, at 16.2 miles. It's also known as County Line Road because it roughly follows the line between Lyon and Trigg Counties. Turn left onto FR 139 and take it for 0.3 mile to a sign directing you to branch right onto an old dirt track. (Another overnight shelter, Sugar Jack, is a short distance farther down FR 139 off a small side trail.)

After a level stretch, descend into a bottomland where you skirt a large farm field and, after crossing a creek, come to a side trail leading right 4.8 miles to the nature

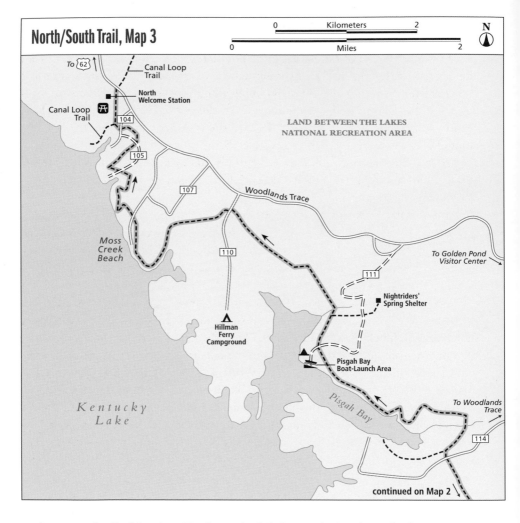

0   Kilometers   2

0   Miles   2

N

To 62

Canal Loop Trail

North Welcome Station

Canal Loop Trail

104

LAND BETWEEN THE LAKES
NATIONAL RECREATION AREA

105

107

Woodlands Trace

Moss Creek Beach

110

111

To Golden Pond Visitor Center

Nightriders' Spring Shelter

Hillman Ferry Campground

Pisgah Bay Boat-Launch Area

Kentucky Lake

Pisgah Bay

To Woodlands Trace

114

continued on Map 2

station on Lake Barkley (see Honker Lake hike). North/South Trail, after crossing a large creek on a substantial wooden bridge, curves left (west) and at mile 18.0 comes to Hatchery Hollow, marking the end of the trail's second section. Hatchery Hollow is so named because a building once there was the base of TVA efforts to reintroduce bald eagles into the area.

From the mileage sign, the trail crosses gravel FR 309. Winding northward, you climb to the top of the ridge and a view of Duncan Bay. At mile 19.7 the trail crosses gravel FR 130, followed in short order by a left turn onto a gravel road that dead-ends into the Gray family cemetery. Turn right onto a path and descend into the bottom-land at the tip of Smith Bay, an inlet said to be good for viewing eagles.

After crossing the Smith Bay drainage, climb a hill and turn left onto dirt FR 306. In 0.4 mile you leave the road, following a path that descends northwest to cross an asphalt road at mile 22.5. This is FR 114, which marks the end of the third section.

A side trail left leads about 1 mile to a boat-launch and camping area that is said to have drinking water.

On the other side of the road, North/South Trail follows a dirt track northeast along a field. After crossing an especially attractive stream, the trail turns west and comes to the end of thin Pisgah Bay. Running along a rocky beach littered with mollusk shells, this stretch is one of the most delightful of the hike. Just before reaching the Pisgah Bay boat-launch area at mile 25.1, the trail turns away from the lake and climbs north to cross gravel FR 111 at mile 25.3.

The trail then descends to another arm of Pisgah Bay. Just before crossing a stream at the end of the bay, a side trail branches right to Nightriders' Spring, a small overnight shelter 0.6 mile away.

From Pisgah Bay, North/South Trail climbs out of the bottomland, crosses a ridge, and enters an area marred by the repeated appearances of a scraggly power-line clearing. At mile 27.6 cross paved FR 110, which goes south to Hillman Ferry, one of the few developed campgrounds in LBL; it has drinking water, vending machines, and showers.

Winding southwest, the trail approaches but never crosses paved FR 107. Just before the road, drop south and follow a small, unnamed inlet to reach the rocky shoreline of Kentucky Lake at mile 28.9. This is the first time on the hike that you've been on the main body of the lake. It's also the only time, so if you want to take a dip in the lake itself, this is the place to do it. It's called the Moss Creek Day Use Area. The residential development you see across the lake is near the town of Benton.

After a brief stretch along the beach at mile 29.1, the trail veers right onto a paved road that climbs north to a bluff. Looking northwest, you can see the 8,422-foot-long dam that creates the lake. To the left is Kentucky Dam Village State Resort Park. The road then dips, and you leave it to turn left onto a path that climbs once again above the water.

After turning away from the lake to circle a couple of ravines, you descend to and cross gravel FR 105 near a boat-launch ramp at the end of a small inlet. Then, climbing to another bluff, you follow the ridgetop northeast and again cross FR 105. After skirting the power-line clearing, descend to and cross a paved road, FR 104, near the head of another small inlet. Turning north, pass the end of Canal Loop Trail on your left (you can hike this trail too; see Canal Loop hike) and, after crossing the power-line clearing and a wooded area, come to an asphalt walkway. Cutting across a picnic area, you reach North Welcome Station—with drinking water, restrooms, and vending machines—at mile 31.2.

Key Points

3.9 Shore of Vickers Bay.

8.4 FR 141 near Rhodes Bay.

10.0 Higgins Bay.

13.3 FR 140 near Sugar Bay boat launch.

16.2 FR 139.

18.0 Hatchery Hollow.

22.5 FR 114.

25.1 Pisgah Bay boat-launch area.

27.6 FR 110 near Hillman Ferry Campground.

29.1 Beach at Moss Creek area.

Options: To shorten this into an out-and-back hike and eliminate the need for a shuttle, simply stop at any of the shore points along the trail. The Sugar Bay area at FR 140—mile 13.3 when walking north from Golden Pond Visitor Center—makes a good overnight spot if you want a semideveloped campground with tables and portable toilets (but no drinking water).

78 Canal Loop

This long day hike or one-night backpack in Land Between The Lakes takes you along the shoreline of upper Kentucky Lake and Lake Barkley and to the canal that connects the two large reservoirs.

Start: Land Between The Lakes North Welcome Station
Distance: 11.8-mile loop
Hiking time: About 7 hours
Difficulty: Moderate
Best seasons: Spring and fall
Other trail users: Mountain bikers
Canine compatibility: Leashed dogs permitted
Land status: National recreation area
Nearest town: Calvert City
Fees and permits: Permit required for backcountry camping. Permits can be purchased at Golden Pond Visitor Center (open daily 9 a.m. to 5 p.m. year-round) and North and South Welcome Stations (open daily 9 a.m. to 5 p.m. Mar through Nov).
Maps: Land Between the Lakes Canal Loop Trail Map; USGS Birmingham Point

Trail contact: USDA Forest Service at Golden Pond, (270) 924-2000 or (800) 525-7077, www.LandBetweenTheLakes.us
Special considerations: On weekends, especially in nice weather, this trail is highly popular with mountain bikers. Also, ticks are a problem here from early spring to autumn. The Forest Service urges visitors to wear long pants and tuck pant legs into boots or socks and keep shirts tucked into pants, treat clothing with an approved tick repellent containing permethrin, and periodically check body and clothing to remove ticks.
Parking and trailhead facilities: You'll find space for 80 cars, along with restrooms, drinking water, vending machines, a telephone, maps, and other information.

Finding the trailhead: From I-24 or US 62, southeast of Calvert City, take KY 453 south into Land Between The Lakes (LBL), where the highway loses its numerical designation and becomes Woodlands Trace National Scenic Byway. LBL's North Welcome Station, which has maps and other information, is 5 miles south of US 62. The hike starts at the parking lot. GPS: N36 58.272' / W88 11.925'

The Hike

The northbound Tennessee River and the westbound Cumberland River come side by side in northern Tennessee and flow together through Kentucky to the Ohio River. In the mid–1960s, two decades after the Tennessee was dammed to make Kentucky Lake, the US Army Corps of Engineers finished damming the Cumberland just a few miles to the east. The result was Lake Barkley, named for the US senator from Kentucky who was vice president under Harry Truman.

Lake Barkley isn't nearly as big as its neighboring reservoir—nor, to my mind, as blue and appealing. (Lake Barkley has 1,004 miles of shoreline compared to Kentucky Lake's 2,380 miles.) Still, it's a sizable body of water with scores of secluded inlets. This hike takes you along the northern shorelines of both lakes—and to the edge of the canal that connects the two.

Though not as heavily used by commercial barges, the Cumberland River gets its share, and watching towboat captains pilot their cumbersome craft from one lake into the other through the canal is intriguing. The people who operate the two lakes try to ensure that the water levels are the same—354 to 359 feet, depending on the time of year.

This hike is a good compromise for backpackers who want to experience LBL but don't have time for the longer North/South Trail. But be aware that there is a difference between the two. While the northern half of the North/South is open to mountain bikes (the southern half is not), Canal Loop gets far more bike traffic. At least that's my judgment, and the trail erosion I saw in the early portions of this hike near the welcome station offers some supporting evidence. Maybe it's because Canal Loop is easily accessed, and the four connector trails that cut across it allow bikers to tailor the length of their trip to their endurance.

According to LBL, the entire loop—which this hike follows—measures 11.8 miles. (The loop plus all four connectors is said to total 14.2 miles.) LBL personnel say the mileages have been verified by odometer-equipped vehicles, and so as with the North/South Trail, those are what I'm using. LBL regulations allow backcountry camping just about anywhere along the trail. The lakeshore segments offer the most pleasant spots. You pass no water source other than the two lakes and a limited number of streams, all of which must be treated before using.

This is a loop and so, of course, you can go either way. I traveled counterclockwise, and these directions assume that approach. The trail is well marked with blue metal strips. From the welcome station parking lot, cross Woodlands Trace and, at the Canal Loop Trail sign on the shoulder, head north into the thin woods. Descending gently on a well-worn mud path, you parallel a small streambed and reach the tip of a Lake Barkley inlet at mile 0.5.

Veering west, climb to a gravel road and then curve back down to follow the inlet north toward the main lake body. Near the north end of the inlet, the trail climbs west across the little peninsula and turns south to follow the shoreline on the other side, away from the lake. The trees here are taller, the trail in better shape, and the area more secluded than the initial stretch.

At mile 2.1, just after the trail crosses a stream, the C connector trail splits off to the left. It rejoins the main trail on the south side of the loop near Kentucky Lake. Like the other connectors, it's marked with yellow strips. The main trail winds north along the inlet and at mile 2.8, after turning west and climbing, crosses gravel FR 102. The Nickell Branch boat launch and camping area is just to your right.

From the road the trail curves southwest and crosses an ugly power-line clearing before turning north and again reaching the lake. From a small inlet, you follow the shoreline around to the main lake body. This is one of the most pleasant stretches of the hike. From bluffs above the water, you have a view north of the dam and the Lake

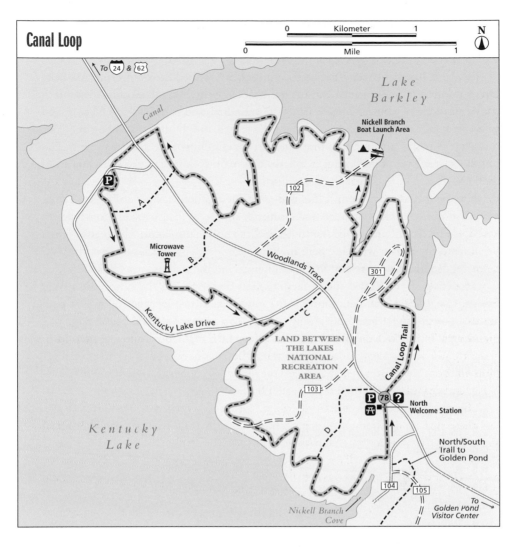

Canal Loop

To 24 & 62

Canal

Lake
Barkley

Nickell Branch
Boat Launch Area

P

102

A

Microwave
Tower

B

Woodlands Trace

301

Kentucky Lake Drive

C

Canal Loop Trail

LAND BETWEEN
THE LAKES
NATIONAL
RECREATION
AREA

103

P 78 ?

North
Welcome Station

Kentucky
Lake

D

North/South
Trail to
Golden Pond

104

105

Nickell Branch
Cove

To
Golden Pond
Visitor Center

Barkley end of the canal. Hopefully a barge will be coming out of or going into the canal so you can watch the captain maneuver the behemoth.

The trail continues winding along the shoreline to mile 4.7. There, near the canal entrance, it climbs a ridge and goes first west and then south as it circles a large field in the canal bottomland. This is the least scenic part of the hike. After dipping down to cross an old road and power-line clearing, the trail rises and dips a second time. Here, at mile 6.0, the B connector branches left. At mile 6.5, after winding north close to Woodlands Trace, you pass the A connector and shortly afterward come to the edge of the canal.

Turning left, pass under Woodlands Trace at mile 6.9 and, in rapid succession, cross paved Kentucky Lake Drive, circle a parking area, and veer northwest back toward the road. Instead of recrossing it, however, turn south and skirt a low-lying area on your right. After passing the other end of the A connector, climb and follow the ridgetop southeast to the other end of the B connector at mile 8.2; pass a tall microwave tower, which you no doubt began seeing miles earlier.

From the tower descend gradually through a wooded area to Kentucky Lake Drive at mile 8.9. Shortly after crossing the road, pass the other end of the C connector. At the edge of a power-line clearing, the trail turns south and follows a streambed to an inlet of Kentucky Lake. From the inlet climb to a bluff overlooking the lake. You then descend and circle another inlet before climbing once again to a bluff. The trail is especially pleasant here as it follows the main Kentucky Lake shoreline from high above.

The trail briefly runs along a dirt-and-gravel road, then leaves it to begin circling a number of small shoreline inlets and drainages, a process that involves several climbs and descents. At mile 10.8 pass the south end of the D connector, which goes north 0.9 mile to the North Welcome Station.

After descending to the bottom of another ravine, the trail follows Nickell Branch Cove north and crosses a drainage feeding into the cove. On the other side of the bridge, Canal Loop Trail runs into North/South Trail. Turn left and follow the path across a power-line clearing and wooded area to an asphalt walkway at the edge of a picnic area. North Welcome Station is on the far side of the picnic area at mile 11.8.

Key Points

0.5	Shore of Lake Barkley inlet.
2.1	C connector.
2.8	FR 102 at Nickell Branch boat launch area.
6.0	B connector.
6.5	A connector.
8.2	Microwave tower.
8.9	Kentucky Lake Drive.
10.8	D connector.

79 Lake Barkley State Resort Park

Exploring Kentucky's largest state park, this hike takes you to a nice spot on the Lake Barkley shoreline and into the surrounding woods.

Start: Park lodge
Distance: 5.6-mile loop
Hiking time: About 3 hours
Difficulty: Easy
Best seasons: Any
Other trail users: Mountain bikers
Canine compatibility: Leashed dogs permitted
Land status: State park
Nearest town: Cadiz

Fees and permits: None
Maps: Park trail map; USGS Canton
Trail contact: Lake Barkley State Resort Park, (270) 924-1131 or (800) 325-1708
Parking and trailhead facilities: You'll find a large lot with all but unlimited parking, along with overnight rooms, a restaurant, vending machines, restrooms, and drinking water.

Finding the trailhead: From Land Between The Lakes National Recreation Area, take US 68/KY 80 east for 2.5 miles and turn left onto KY 1489. In 2 miles, where KY 1489 turns right, continue straight on the park road. (From Cadiz, the nearest town of any size, take US 68/KY 80 west and turn right onto KY 1489. The lodge is 8 miles from Cadiz.) Following signs for the lodge, turn left in 0.6 mile, right in another 0.6 mile, and right again in 0.4 mile. Just before the main lodge building, take the ramp down to the parking area. The trail starts just east of the parking lot—near the playground at the end of the east wing of the lodge complex. GPS: N36 50.933' / W87 55.804'

The Hike

With 3,700 acres, this is the largest park in the state system. It's also one of the most popular. As the "resort" part of the name suggests, it has plenty of amenities, including a handsome wood-and-glass lodge overlooking Lake Barkley. So despite the name of one of the park trails—Wilderness Trail—this is not a place for rugged, backcountry hiking. If you want that, go west a few miles to Land Between The Lakes.

What this well-maintained park does offer is a stroll through lakeside woods with wildflowers and deer. Recent expansion of the park's trail system now lets you do this loop route almost entirely on footpaths and, except for one brief segment, avoid roads.

By the way, if you are from outside Kentucky and wondering why everything in this part of the state seems to be named Barkley, here's the reason. Alben W. Barkley, a Kentucky politician who went on to be a national player, was from nearby Paducah. Before being elected vice president with Harry Truman as president in 1948, Barkley served more than two decades in the US Senate; half that time he was the Senate's Democratic leader. After failing to receive his party's 1952 presidential nomination, he won a new Senate term two years later, and died two years after that at age 78.

Fishermen try their luck near the lodge at Lake Barkley and the start of the Wilderness Trail.

From the parking lot, walk down to the playground at the end of the east lodge wing. As you near the lakeshore, you will find a common trailhead for three trails: the Lena Madesin Phillips, Cedar Grove, and Wilderness Trails. Following the path south, you quickly come to a fork marking the entrance to the Phillips Trail, a short nature loop best saved for the end of the hike. Bear left and you come just as quickly to a second fork; to your right is the other end of the Phillips loop, but you go left. At mile 0.4, after crossing a creek bed likely to be dry, you come to a third fork. To your right is Wilderness Trail, which you will take on the return leg. Turn left onto Cedar Grove Trail. Appropriately named, the trail meanders north through a pleasant stand of tall cedars, climbing gently from the lakeside bottomland partway up the ridge. Where the cedars give way to hardwood trees, the trail turns left and begins to descend. This turn was unmarked when I took the hike—and easily missed, at least by me. If you go too far, as I did, you will run into the park road.

The trail descends through hardwoods into a drainage area and then climbs to the grass lawn in front of a picnic pavilion just off the park road. At the pavilion turn left and descend a short distance through the woods to the lakeshore at mile 1.3. Here, just a few feet off the trail, you will find a secluded rest spot on the rocky "beach." Trail signs give directions for bypassing this segment in high-water conditions.

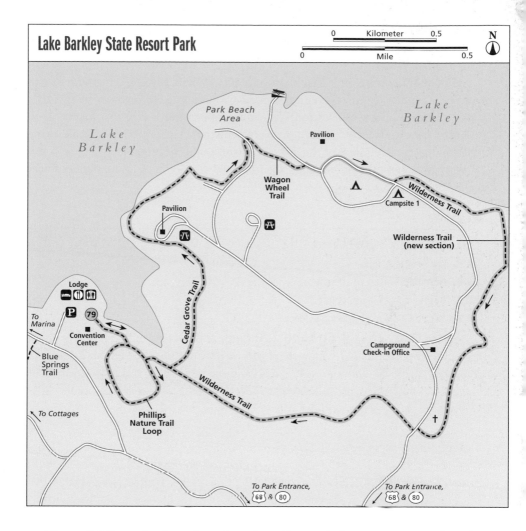

The trail follows the shore for only a short distance before veering away from the water and rising slightly. Just before you reach the start of the park's beachfront area, a plastic stake directs you southeast to a short, paved drive, which dead-ends into the park's beachfront road at mile 1.8. Turn left onto the road and follow it for 0.2 mile to the start of Wagon Wheel Trail on the right shoulder at 2 miles.

Wagon Wheel Trail climbs easily and, at mile 2.3, ends at an asphalt road in the campground. Across the road is a sign indicating that the Wilderness Trail begins at campsite 1. Turn right onto the paved road, then make an immediate left turn and follow it until you reach the first campsite on your left in 0.3 mile. Campsite 1 is on the right side of the trail, and the trail begins across from it. The lake is visible far below. This is where the Wilderness Trail begins. After crossing a streambed, the trail curves west around a small cemetery with gravestones dating to the 1800s and crosses the main park road. Now you are on an older section of the Wilderness Trail. This attractive, moss-covered path initially goes northwest on the ridgetop, but soon descends into a ravine. Here you follow—on your left—a small streambed full of ferns and wildflowers.

At mile 4.9 you pass the Cedar Grove Trail and then, turning left, come to one end of the Phillips nature trail. This interpretive loop, named in memory of a woman active in the business world, includes a wooden suspension bridge that jiggles when you walk over it—a feature certain to please children. A pamphlet—available at the lodge and at the beginning of the loop—explains points of interest.

At mile 5.5 exit the other end of the loop, and you are back at the trailhead near the lodge at mile 5.6.

Key Points

1.3 Beginning of lakeshore stretch.

1.8 Left onto park road.

2.0 Right onto Wagon Wheel Trail.

2.3 Beginning of Wilderness Trail.

4.9 Beginning of small nature trail loop.

Option: Blue Springs Trail, which starts south of the lodge, makes a loop of about 1.5 miles when combined with a short park road. I did not take this trail, but park personnel say the lakeshore portion is a good place to see deer and geese.

80 Pennyrile Forest

Small streams and waterfalls in isolated hollows make this long-distance forest trail ideal for backpacking.

Start: Parking lot at Pennyrile Forest State Resort Park lodge

Distance: 13.7-mile shuttle

Hiking time: About 8 hours

Difficulty: Strenuous

Best seasons: Spring and fall

Other trail users: Mountain bikers

Canine compatibility: Dogs permitted

Land status: State park and forest

Nearest town: Dawson Springs

Fees and permits: None

Maps: Kentucky Division of Forestry map of Pennyrile Nature Trail; USGS Dawson Springs and Dawson Springs SW

Trail contacts: Kentucky Division of Forestry, (270) 797-3241 (Pennyrile forest office) or

(270) 824-7527 (Madisonville district office); Pennyrile Forest State Resort Park, (800) 325-1711

Special considerations: This hike is a 13.7-mile shuttle. If you do not have two cars, contact Tradewater Canoes and Kayaks LLC for a shuttle, (270) 871-9475. The north terminus of the trail is located steps from the canoe and kayak rental shop along KY 109.

Parking and trailhead facilities: There is space for about 75 cars, as well as overnight rooms, a restaurant, a telephone, restrooms, and drinking water in the lodge. The park campground is off KY 398 just south of the lodge entrance.

Finding the trailhead: From Hopkinsville, take KY 109 north for 20 miles and turn left onto KY 398. In 1.7 miles, turn right at the main entrance to the Pennyrile Forest State Resort Park; 0.5 mile later, park by the lodge. (From the Western Kentucky Parkway, take the Dawson Springs exit, go south for 8 miles on KY 109, and turn right onto KY 398.) From the lodge parking lot, walk a few steps north and turn left onto the road to the park golf course. The trailhead is less than 0.1 mile on your right. GPS: N37 04.395' / W87 39.854'

The Hike

In the late 1990s state forestry staff set about to develop a hiking trail through the northern half of the 14,468-acre Pennyrile State Forest, the second-largest forest owned by Kentucky. The result is the Pennyrile Nature Trail (PNT), which this hike follows.

Running from the Pennyrile Forest State Resort Park to the town of Dawson Springs, the trail winds through numerous bottomlands that early in the year are flowing with attractive streams and dotted with small, picturesque waterfalls. Between the low-lying areas, the trail climbs constantly. For much of the way, you are on the ridge above the east shore of Lake Beshear—a 760-acre reservoir with a wiggly, natural-looking shoreline that belies its man-made status. None of these ups and downs is in itself a killer, but all together they take their toll by the second half of the hike, especially if you are carrying a backpack.

Be aware that the state forestry division does not provide for recreational activities but allows for them on land owned and managed by the Division of Forestry. Forester Timothy Crowell said the PNT does not have a strong group of volunteers who maintain it, and sections of the trail are in need of maintenance. Indeed on my visit, hiking with Crowell, sections of the trail were overgrown with briars, and blowdowns from recent storms caused us to take a number of detours. For that reason the early spring is the best time to visit, as Crowell and his team of volunteers—most often inmates from the nearby detention center—typically clear the trail for the season in late February.

Crowell added that the forest has been affected over the last ten years by a number of ice storms, a tornado, and the southern pine beetle. There is evidence of all three along the trail.

I suggest walking south to north because Pennyrile State Park is one of the state's nicest parks and it makes a good place to leave your car. The trail ends on the south side of Dawson Springs at a roadside parking space for about six cars with no facilities. The town center, with stores, restaurants, and telephones, is another 1.5 miles north on KY 109. The KY 398 turnoff to the state park is 5 miles south on KY 109.

Backcountry camping is prohibited in the state park, but only the first 1.5 miles of the trail is in the park. Beyond that you are in the state forest, where camping is allowed. There are no permit requirements or designated sites; all water must be treated.

Pennyrile Nature Trail starts together with Indian Bluffs Trail, a short park path. After about 1,000 feet, the nature trail splits off, heading north, then west, and then north once again. This first segment of the trail was relocated to accommodate expansion of the park golf course. As a result, you are initially walking in the woods between fairways. The way is marked by white diamonds. Indeed, when I did the hike, the entire trail was marked every 40 to 80 feet or so with signs.

As an interpretive plaque you see later in the hike explains, what is now Pennyrile Forest was hardscrabble farming country until the 1930s, when a New Deal resettlement program bought out the homesteaders. To help restore the land, the fields and pastures were planted with millions of pines. The bottomlands and slopes never farmed remain in hardwoods. Those pines became infested with the southern pine beetle in the early 2000s and subsequently have been harvested and replanted, according to Crowell.

At mile 1.5 the trail crosses FR 20, which marks the state park boundary. From here on you are in the state forest. From the road the trail follows an old dirt road along a creek into an appealing bottomland, with a waterfall on your right. This stream flows into a branch of Clifty Creek, which you cross and follow toward Lake Beshear in a valley lined with rock outcroppings. This can be a wet section, and your boots may get a bit soggy. The trail then begins a steep climb up the ridge side.

Steam rises off Lake Beshear during a summer rain.

Near the top of the ridge, you pass one of the old homesites. After a view of the lily-covered end of Lake Beshear down below, descend and follow a dry drainage away from the lake. Again climbing the ridge, you walk over several old gas-well pipes before descending to cross a creek at mile 4.1. On the other side, the trail goes up a rock-strewn area and follows the level ridgetop north, with views of the lake below on your left.

Follow a ravine southeast and, after crossing the stream in another appealing bottomland, begin winding your way northeast. At mile 6.0, shortly after passing another delightful falls on the left of the trail, cross gravel Clifty Shores Road just west of KY 109, marking the end of the hike's first—and easier—half.

The trail now takes a meandering, up-and-down route northwest, back toward Lake Beshear. After reaching the end of a small inlet, follow the shoreline from above on the ridge. At mile 7.9 the trail descends on an old roadbed to a point of land

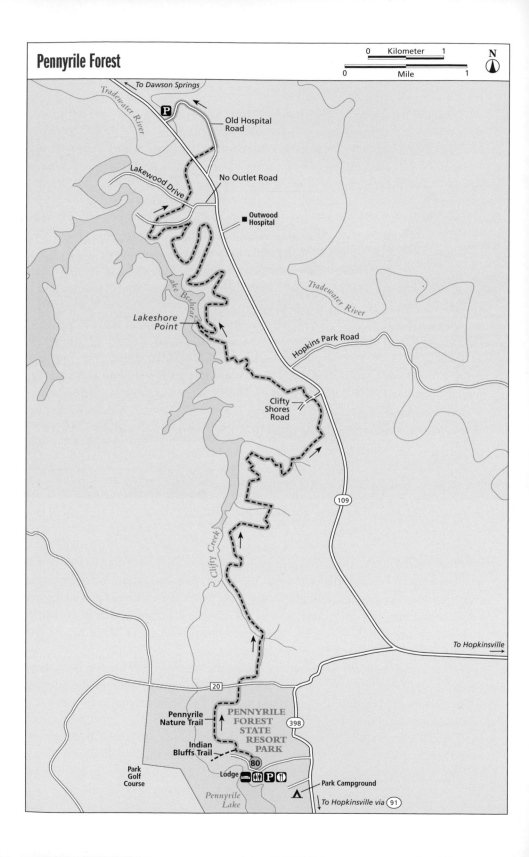

sticking out into the lake. This point, covered with grass and wildflowers, makes a great place for lunch or a rest. You can easily walk down to the water's edge, which is lined with large, flat rocks.

From the point retrace your steps about 300 feet up the hill and turn left (southeast). Following a stream on your left, walk along the steep slope above the stream before crossing it and climbing north. Here the trail begins a series of lengthy swings toward KY 109 as it circles streambeds and ravines draining into the lake. One of these eastward legs takes you close to the entrance to Outwood Hospital, a now-closed state facility for the mentally and developmentally disabled.

At mile 11.2, on the last of these spokes and just before the route reaches a paved road, the trail turns abruptly left (west) and descends into a lovely ravine lined with fern-covered rocks. On the left of the trail, you pass an overlook above a waterfall—another good rest spot, though be careful of the drop-off if small children are with you. After climbing back up the ridge and turning north, you cross the same road as earlier and then, at mile 12.1, Lakewood Drive.

Continuing north, cross KY 109 and a power-line clearing before following an old dirt road into a ravine and coming to a dilapidated asphalt road. This is Old Hospital Road (mile 13.2), which you take to your left. The road curves south and quickly brings you, at mile 13.7, to the Tradewater River and a pedestrian bridge. On the other side are KY 109 and the trail's end. The trail ends at a gravel parking lot and a small building that is home to Tradewater Canoes and Kayaks LLC. The company offers canoe and kayak rentals along with ferry service for boats and PNT hikers.

Key Points

1.5 FR 20, marking the beginning of the state forest.
6.0 Clifty Shores Road.
7.9 Lake point.
12.1 Lakewood Drive.
13.2 Old Hospital Road.

Appendix A: For More Information

Federal Government

Big South Fork National River and Recreation Area
Kentucky Visitor Center
HC 69, PO Box 1
Stearns, KY 42647-0001
(606) 376-5073

Tennessee Visitor Center
(423) 286-7275
www.nps.gov/biso

Cumberland Gap National Historical Park
PO Box 1848
Middlesboro, KY 40965-1848
(606) 248-2817
www.nps.gov/cuga

Daniel Boone National Forest
Forest Supervisor's Office
1700 Bypass Road
Winchester, KY 40391
(859) 745-3100
www.fs.usda.gov/dbnf

Gladie Visitor Center of the Cumberland Ranger District
3451 Sky Bridge Road, KY 715
Stanton, KY 40380
(606) 663-8100

Cumberland District Office
2375 KY 801 South
Morehead, KY 40351
(606) 784-6428

London District Office
761 South Laurel Road
London, KY 40744
(606) 864-4163

Redbird District Office
91 Peabody Road
Big Creek, KY 40914
(606) 598-2192

Stanton Office
705 West College Avenue
Stanton, KY 40380
(606) 663-2852

Stearns District Office
3320 US 27 North
Whitley City, KY 42653
(606) 376-5323

Fort Knox

Cultural Resources Office
Fort Knox, KY 40121
(502) 624-7431 or (502) 624-6581

Land Between The Lakes National Recreation Area

100 Van Morgan Drive
Golden Pond, KY 42211
(270) 924-2000 or (800) LBL-7077
www.LandBetweenTheLakes.us

Mammoth Cave National Park

Mammoth Cave, KY 42259
(270) 758-2180
www.nps.gov/maca

Reelfoot National Wildlife Refuge

4343 Highway 157
Union City, TN 38261
(731) 538-2481
www.fws.gov/reelfoot

US Army Corps of Engineers

Huntington District
(for Dewey, Fishtrap, Grayson, Paintsville, and Yatesville Lakes)
502 Eighth Street
Huntington, WV 25701
(304) 399-5211
www.lrh.usace.army.mil

Louisville District
(for Barren, Buckhorn, Carr Fork, Cave Run, Green River, Nolin, Rough River, and
Taylorsville Lakes)
600 Dr. Martin Luther King Jr. Place
Louisville, KY 40201-0059
(502) 315-6766
www.lrl.usace.army.mil

Nashville District
(for Barkley, Cumberland, Dale Hollow, Laurel, and Martins Fork Lakes)
PO Box 1070
Nashville, TN 37202
(615) 736-7161
www.lrn.usace.army.mil

Kentucky Government

Kentucky Department of Fish and Wildlife Resources
1 Sportsman's Lane
Frankfort, KY 40601
(502) 564-4336 or (800) 858-1549
www.kdfwr.state.ky.us

Kentucky Department of Parks
Capital Plaza Tower
500 Metro Street, Suite 1100
Frankfort, KY 40601-1974
(800) 255-PARK
www.parks.ky.gov

Kentucky Department of Travel and Tourism
Capital Plaza Tower
500 Metro Street, 22nd Floor
Frankfort, KY 40601
(800) 225-TRIP or (502) 564-4930
www.kentuckytourism.com

Kentucky Division of Forestry
627 Comanche Trail
Frankfort, KY 40601
(502) 564-4496
www.forestry.ky.gov

Kentucky Geological Survey
504 Rose Street
Room 228, Mining and Minerals Resources Building
University of Kentucky
Lexington, KY 40506-0107
(877) 778-7827 or (859) 257-5500
www.uky.edu/kgs

Kentucky State Nature Preserves Commission
801 Schenkel Lane
Frankfort, KY 40601
(502) 573-2886
www.naturepreserves.ky.gov

Lilley Cornett Woods
91 Lilley Cornett Branch
Hallie, KY 41821
(606) 633-5828

Local Governments

Lexington–Fayette County Parks and Recreation Department
469 Parkway Drive
Lexington, KY 40504
(859) 288-2900
www.lexingtonky.gov/index.aspx?page=198

Metropolitan Parks Department
(Louisville and Jefferson County)
PO Box 37280
Louisville, KY 40233-7280
(502) 456-8100
www.louisvilleky.gov/metroparks

Private Organizations

Bernheim Arboretum and Research Forest
PO Box 130
Clermont, KY 40110
(502) 955-8512
www.bernheim.org

Clyde E. Buckley Wildlife Sanctuary and Audubon Center
1305 Germany Road
Frankfort, KY 40601
(859) 873-5711

Nature Conservancy, Kentucky Chapter
642 West Main Street
Lexington, KY 40508-2018
(859) 259-9655
www.nature.org/kentucky

Pine Mountain Trail Conference
www.pinemountaintrail.com

Shaker Village of Pleasant Hill
3501 Lexington Road
Harrodsburg, KY 40330
(800) 734-5611
www.shakervillageky.org

Sierra Club, Cumberland Chapter
PO Box 1368
Lexington, KY 40588-1368
(859) 296-4335
www.kentucky.sierraclub.org

Appendix B: Further Reading

History

Aron, Stephen. *How the West Was Lost: The Transformation of Kentucky from Daniel Boone to Henry Clay.* Baltimore: Johns Hopkins University Press, 1996.

Caudill, Harry M. *Night Comes to the Cumberlands: A Biography of a Depressed Area.* Boston: Little, Brown, 1962.

Clark, Thomas D. *A History of Kentucky.* Ashland, KY: Jesse Stuart Foundation, 1992. Originally published by Prentice-Hall, 1937.

Coleman, J. Winston, Jr., ed. *Kentucky: A Pictorial History.* Lexington: University Press of Kentucky, 1971.

Harrison, Lowell H., and James C. Klotter. *A New History of Kentucky.* Lexington: University Press of Kentucky, 1997.

Hiking and Outdoors

Berry, Wendell. *The Unforeseen Wilderness: Kentucky's Red River Gorge.* San Francisco: North Point Press, 1991.

Bluegrass Group of the Sierra Club. *Hiking the Red: A Complete Trail Guide to Kentucky's Red River Gorge Including Natural Bridge State Park.* Louisville, KY: Harmony House, 2000.

Deaver, Brenda G., Jo Anna Smith, and Howard Ray Duncan. *Hiking the Big South Fork,* 3rd ed. Knoxville: University of Tennessee Press, 1999.

Erwin, Chris. *Camping Kentucky.* Guilford, CT: FalconGuides, 2014.

Manning, Russ. *100 Trails of the Big South Fork.* Seattle: The Mountaineers Books, 2000.

————. *The Historic Cumberland Plateau: An Explorer's Guide.* Knoxville: University of Tennessee Press, 1999.

Molloy, Johnny. *Exploring Mammoth Cave National Park.* Guilford, CT: FalconGuides, 2014.

Ruchhoft, Robert H. *Kentucky's Land of the Arches.* Cincinnati, OH: Pucelle Press, 1986.

Sides, Stanley D. *Guide to the Surface Trails of Mammoth Cave National Park.* St. Louis, MO: Cave Books, 1995 (revision in process).

Appendix C: A Hiker's Checklist

Always make and check your own checklist!

If you've ever hiked into the backcountry and discovered that you've forgotten an essential item, you know that it's a good idea to make a checklist and check the items off as you pack so you won't forget the things you want and need. Here are some ideas:

Clothing
- ☐ Dependable rain parka
- ☐ Rain pants
- ☐ Windbreaker
- ☐ Thermal underwear
- ☐ Shorts
- ☐ Long pants or sweatpants
- ☐ Wool cap or balaclava
- ☐ Hat
- ☐ Wool shirt or sweater
- ☐ Jacket or parka
- ☐ Extra socks
- ☐ Underwear
- ☐ Lightweight shirts
- ☐ T-shirts
- ☐ Bandanna(s)
- ☐ Mittens or gloves
- ☐ Belt

Footwear
- ☐ Sturdy, comfortable boots
- ☐ Lightweight camp shoes

Bedding
- ☐ Sleeping bag
- ☐ Foam pad or air mattress
- ☐ Ground sheet (plastic or nylon)
- ☐ Dependable tent

Hauling
- ☐ Backpack and/or day pack

Cooking
- ☐ 1-quart container (plastic)
- ☐ 1-gallon water container for camp use (collapsible)
- ☐ Backpack stove and extra fuel
- ☐ Funnel
- ☐ Aluminum foil
- ☐ Cooking pots
- ☐ Bowls/plates
- ☐ Utensils (spoons, forks, small spatula, knife)
- ☐ Pot scrubber
- ☐ Matches in waterproof container

Food and Drink
- ☐ Cereal
- ☐ Bread
- ☐ Crackers
- ☐ Cheese
- ☐ Trail mix
- ☐ Margarine
- ☐ Powdered soups
- ☐ Salt/pepper
- ☐ Main-course meals
- ☐ Snacks
- ☐ Hot chocolate
- ☐ Tea
- ☐ Powdered milk
- ☐ Drink mixes

Photography
- ☐ Camera and memory stick
- ☐ Filters
- ☐ Lens brush/paper

Miscellaneous
- ☐ Sunglasses
- ☐ Map and compass
- ☐ Toilet paper
- ☐ Pocketknife
- ☐ Sunscreen

- ☐ Good insect repellent
- ☐ Lip balm
- ☐ Flashlight with good batteries and spare bulb
- ☐ Candle(s)
- ☐ First-aid kit
- ☐ Your FalconGuide
- ☐ Survival kit
- ☐ Small garden trowel or shovel
- ☐ Water filter or purification tablets
- ☐ Plastic bags (for trash)
- ☐ Soap
- ☐ Towel
- ☐ Toothbrush
- ☐ Fishing license
- ☐ Fishing rod, reel, lures, flies, etc.
- ☐ Binoculars
- ☐ Waterproof covering for pack
- ☐ Watch
- ☐ Sewing kit

Index

About the Author

Carrie L. Stambaugh is an Ashland, Kentucky, resident. Born in Cincinnati, Ohio, she has spent most of her adult life in Kentucky working as a journalist. Carrie is the editor of the *Greater Ashland Beacon*. She and her husband, Carl, have two golden retrievers, whom they enjoy taking with them on hikes and paddles. In addition to the Appalachian Trail, Carrie has logged thousands of miles hiking in all but a handful of states.

American Hiking
Society

Because you
hike.
We're with you
every step of the way

As a national voice for hikers, **American Hiking Society** works every day:

- Building and maintaining hiking trails
- Educating and supporting hikers by providing information and resources
- Supporting hiking and trail organizations nationwide
- Speaking for hikers in the halls of Congress and with federal land managers

Whether you're a casual hiker or a seasoned backpacker, become a member of American Hiking Society and join the national hiking community! You'll enjoy great member benefits and help preserve the nation's hiking trails, so tomorrow's hike is even better than today's. We invite you to join us now!

American
Hiking
Society

www.AmericanHiking.org • info@AmericanHiking.org